Penguin Education

Corporate Recovery

Penguin Modern Management Texts
General Editor: D. S. Pugh

Stuart Slatter

Corporate Recovery

*Successful Turnaround Strategies
and their Implementation*

PENGUIN BOOKS

Penguin Books Ltd, Harmondsworth, Middlesex, England
Penguin Books, 40 West 23rd Street, New York, New York 10010, U.S.A.
Penguin Books Australia Ltd, Ringwood, Victoria, Australia
Penguin Books Canada Ltd, 2801 John Street, Markham, Ontario, Canada L3R 1B4
Penguin Books (N.Z.) Ltd, 182–190 Wairau Road, Auckland 10, New Zealand

First published 1984

Made and printed in Singapore by Richard Clay (S.E. Asia) Pte Ltd

Set in Times Roman 9/11 (Linotron 202)

Contents

List of Figures

List of Tables

Acknowledgements

The research on which much of this book is based would never have been possible if it had not been for the many senior executives who gave so generously of their time. My thanks are due to them for providing the insights which have made the case-histories – some of which are included in Part Four of the book – such fascinating and instructive reading. Many of the same executives subsequently proof-read the draft case-histories and provided me with useful comments. I would also like to thank the various Masters degree students at the London Business School who have assisted me over recent years in collecting and analysing data about 'turnaround' firms.

Various colleagues at the London Business School have assisted in this project over the years and made useful comments about my findings and conclusions. In particular, Jeremy Smithers was helpful with the analysis of the L B S database, and Andrew Likierman and Olga Aikin have provided me with useful comments about parts of the manuscript. Derek Pugh provided encouragement from the outset, for which I am most grateful.

Special thanks are due to Ronald Cohen of M M G Ltd for providing me with some of his ideas about implementing divestment strategies, and to Gilbert Cottrell of Cape Town, who developed the acquisition framework shown as Figure 10.1. Last, but by no means least, my thanks are due to Hilda Silverman, who diligently and cheerfully typed the various drafts of this manuscript.

Part One

Factors Determining Decline and Recovery

1. The Scope and Nature of the Recovery Problem

Corporate recovery is about the management of firms in crisis, firms that will become insolvent unless appropriate management actions are taken to effect a turnaround in their financial performance. They are failing companies which, if not already on the brink of insolvency, will be within two or three years if specific turnaround strategies are not adopted. Firms in need of the management action outlined in this book go well beyond British Leyland and other much-publicized 'lame ducks' of British industry. Many of the traditional blue-chip firms of British industry – ICI, Courtaulds, Tube Investments, to name but three – are, at the time of writing, in the process of adopting turnaround strategies even though they are not about to become insolvent. Other firms in need of the turnaround approach are those that have just been acquired. Good post-acquisition management, which is a key factor for success in any acquisition, requires much of the same approach outlined in this book. Turnaround management therefore is not a freak occurrence, it is part of everyday business.

The management approach to turnaround situations is described in this book from the perspective of the chief executive or general manager. It assumes basic business knowledge about how a firm operates and about the functional disciplines of accounting, finance, marketing, production and personnel. We focus on the appropriate strategies necessary to restore the firm to financial health and the specific problems encountered in implementing these strategies. Typically, there is considerable time pressure to achieve results, so that the mode of operation in a recovery situation is often quite different from that described in the standard management textbooks.

1. What is a Turnaround Situation?

There is no hard-and-fast definition of what consitutes a turnaround situation. We use the term here to refer to those firms or operating units (the latter will be included under the generic term 'firm' or 'company' from now on) whose financial performance indicates that the firm will fail in the foreseeable future unless short-term corrective action is taken. The profit performance of such firms as measured by return on capital employed is likely to be considerably below what one would expect for the type of business in which it is engaged. Our definition includes firms that do not have a current cash crisis, and is therefore a wider definition than that used by some writers who equate turnaround situations with the existence of a cash crisis.[1]* Certainly whenever there is a cash crisis there is a turnaround situation but, under the definition used in this book, a turnaround situation may exist without a cash crisis. A broad definition of what constitutes a turnaround situation recognizes that firms often exhibit symptoms of failure long before any crisis begins. Such firms are often stagnant businesses with underutilized assets and ineffective management. Many such firms have survived over the years *in spite of* their poor management. If a stagnant business is not turned around, a crisis situation will eventually ensue because the management of such a firm is unlikely to be taking the necessary steps to adapt to the changing product-market environment in which the firm is operating. Stagnant businesses are often in stable and mature industries with a competitive advantage that exists for largely historical reasons (e.g. an advantage due to location). They are often businesses which are family-controlled or controlled by the board of directors. By adopting turnaround strategies early enough, recovery can take place without the traumas usually associated with a crisis situation.

Profitability alone is not a reliable measure of the existence of a turnaround situation. A growth-oriented firm that has grown too fast may continue to be quite profitable while at the same time being in a severe cash-flow crisis. This was the position of the Lex Service Group in 1973/74, which for a while was technically insolvent, although a receiver was never appointed. Alternatively, the fact that a firm reports a loss in a single year does not of itself indicate a turnaround situation. There may, for example, have been an extraordinary write-off of assets during the financial year, while the rest of the business remained reasonably healthy. On the other hand, a large loss in just one year in one operating unit can place the whole firm in jeopardy. Burmah Oil's loss on tanker chartering, coupled with the decline in the Stock Market valuation of its B.P. shares in 1974, is a classic

---

* Superior figures in the text refer the reader to the Notes, which are to be found at the end of each chapter.

example of a company which had been showing reasonable profits suddenly finding itself in a turnaround situation. Total debt to shareholders' funds increased from 43% to 190% in one year. The profit picture of the typical turnaround situation, however, is several years of successively lower profits culminating in a loss situation and a cashflow crisis.

If no corrective management action is taken in a turnaround situation, the firm becomes insolvent, since external events can only postpone insolvency, not avert it. Where specific corrective action is taken by management, the outcome can be either successful or unsuccessful. Where recovery is accomplished, the firm is described as a successful turnaround. Attempts at recovery may, however, be unsuccessful, in which case the firm becomes insolvent and falls into receivership or liquidation.

2. Sustainable Recovery

The aim of this book is to describe the corrective actions management needs to make to achieve recovery in a turnaround situation. However, just as it is difficult to give a precise definition of a turnaround situation, so it is difficult to define what we mean by corporate recovery. There is no absolute measure, but it is worth distinguishing between firms which survive but never make an adequate return on capital employed, or survive only in the short term and then become insolvent, and those which achieve what we call *sustainable* recovery. Sustainable recovery involves achieving a viable and defensible business strategy, supported by an adequate organization and control structure. It means that the firm has fully recovered, is making 'good' profits and is unlikely to face another crisis in the foreseeable future. The corrective action described in this book is aimed at assisting management to achieve sustainable recovery, although it is important to realize at the outset that many turnaround situations can never achieve such a position.

Sustainable recovery requires the firm to develop sustainable competitive advantage. This is an important concept and is the basis of developing a viable and defensible business strategy. We know from basic economics that the firm can only make above-average profits (economic rents, in economists' jargon) if the market in which it operates is imperfect. The process by which firms develop and exploit these market imperfections is the basis of competitive business strategy. There are three main sources of competitive advantage for the firm to exploit – economic factors, organizational factors and political/legal factors:

(*a*) *Economic factors*: provide the firm with three sources of sustainable competitive advantage: (a) absolute cost advantage over competitors because the firm has control of or access to cheaper sources of raw material, cheaper labour, or proprietary production know-how; (b) relative cost advantages due to the presence of economies of scale; and (c) product differentiation advantages (e.g. brand name, control or access to distribution channels and superior product technology).

(*b*) *Organizational factors*: relate to the quality and expertise of management, which in turn affects the quality of strategy implementation. Good implementation can be a major source of competitive advantage if the firm's 'economic' strategy is sound, but good implementation of a poor strategy is wasteful and ineffective.

(*c*) *Political and legal factors*: may also give the firm a competitive advantage, e.g. when government purchasing departments favour domestic (rather than foreign) manufacturers.

The mere existence of any of these factors does not imply competitive advantage, since competitive advantage is a relative concept. Thus for example, a firm may have a good brand name and proprietary technology but be at a competitive disadvantage because, although competitors may lack proprietary technology, competitors have an even stronger brand name and can take advantage of economies of scale due to their larger size.

Firms that are unable to develop any competitive advantage may recover, but their profits will be unexciting and they will be highly susceptible to further crisis in the future. Other firms in a turnaround situation may be at such a significant competitive disadvantage that insolvency will occur despite the best efforts of the most able management. Although this book is concerned with recovery, not insolvency, it is worth taking a few moments to see how some of the management principles described herein are applicable to insolvency situations.

3. Insolvency

Until the end of the nineteenth century, a firm was either solvent or insolvent. If the firm was insolvent, its assets were taken over and distributed among the creditors: there was no in-between situation. However, the Companies Act of 1893, later replaced by the Companies Acts 1948 and 1981, allowed for the appointment of a receiver and manager to salvage as much of the firm as possible. A receiver is usually the agent for a debenture holder, someone who has a secured loan against the company. Unlike a liquidator (whose objective is to wind up the company and terminate its existence), the basic role of the receiver is to realize the assets of the company for his client (although he has a certain duty to protect the interests of other secured or preferential creditors). Once the receiver has collected the money owing to his client, the receiver may leave and normal business will be resumed; alternatively, the liquidator (often the firm's own auditors) steps in and distributes any assets that are left, first to the creditors and then to the shareholders.

The job of the receiver is to sell the assets of the firm, but typically the individual appointed (usually a chartered accountant specializing in this work) is both 'receiver and manager', in which case he can continue to run the business as well as sell the assets. Most receivers go to considerable lengths to try to rehabilitate the ailing firm, and will try to salvage as much of the firm (and as many jobs) as possible, although their objective is typically narrower than that of management in a still solvent firm.

Management involved in taking corrective action in turnaround situations has a lot to learn by watching the receiver at work. The receiver uses two basic strategies: gaining control and divesting assets – both of which are key strategies in effecting corporate recovery. The receiver moves quickly to implement these strategies, typically giving orders through the existing management. Control for the receiver involves protecting assets and is often achieved by temporarily freezing the situation: all deliveries in and out are stopped, the physical assets are secured by changing all the locks, the chequebooks are collected and the banks told to stop payment of cheques. The receiver can then set to work to assess the firm's financial position while at the same time placing high priority on the collection of cash from debtors. The receiver's next step is to begin divestment of the saleable assets with the aim of repaying his client's debenture. Since assets are usually worth more as a going concern, the receiver will continue to run the business in the short term until a purchaser can be found. While many firms have been sold largely intact after receivership – although usually with considerably fewer employees – a purchaser cannot always be found. Looking at recent insolvencies, the truck manufacturers Foden (discussed in Chapter 19), the engineering group Fairbairn Lawson, clothing manufacturer Cope Sportswear and the larger part of the insolvent toy companies Dunbee Combex Marx and Lesney Products have all been successfully divested, although Bamford's, the agriculture equipment manufacturer, were less lucky.[2] At Bamford's, where the recovery attempt (discussed in Chapter 18) failed, the liquidator first kept on 300 of the 600 employees, then cut the number to 200; finally when the business did not look saleable, he reduced the firm to a spare parts manufacturing operation.

The relatively high frequency with which firms (or at least their component parts) survive after insolvency tends to indicate that if appropriate corrective action had been taken early enough, insolvency could have been avoided. Unfortunately, the appropriate action is often unpalatable to managers because it involves divestment and other changes in strategy and operations.

4. Size of the Recovery Problem in the U.K.

The 1980–82 recession increased the number of turnaround situations to a new record, although there are no firm statistics on the subject since there is no single definition of what constitutes a turnaround situation. The need to formulate and implement turnaround strategies is always present and has been growing over the last twenty years: historically, about 20% of quoted companies, and probably a greater percentage of smaller independent companies, have been in need of such strategies each decade. The need is always greatest in periods of recession and slow economic growth. Government statistics on business failure give some indication of how the need has increased (see Table 1.1), but a better indication of the need for recovery is provided by analysis that predicts company failure. Work undertaken by Perform-

Table 1.1: *Business Failures in England and Wales 1971–82*

1971	3,506	1977	5,831
1972	3,063	1978	5,086
1973	2,575	1979	4,537
1974	3,720	1980	6,890
1975	5,398	1981	8,607
1976	5,939	1982	12,067

Source: CSO.

ance Analysis Services Ltd estimates that among the 850 largest U.K. *manufacturing* concerns, about 15–20% run the risk of insolvency at any one time.*

To put turnarounds in perspective, in 1978 the author undertook a study of publicly quoted firms in the United Kingdom over a fifteen-year period (1961–76). For the purpose of that study, a turnaround situation was defined as a firm whose 'real' profit before tax (measured in 1970 prices) had declined for three or more successive years; and a successful turnaround was defined as a firm whose real profits before tax increased in four out of the following six years.[3] Using this definition, 20% of the approximately 2,100 firms that were publicly quoted firms for part or all of the period 1961–76 were classified as in need of turnaround.

For the reader of this book, however, the interesting question is what happened to the firms that were identified as experiencing three or more years of real profit decline. Of the 437 firms so identified, only 102 continued to show a fourth year of profit decline, and only 18 showed five or more years of consecutive decline. On average, about one in four of the firms managed successful recovery (see Table 1.2). The remaining firms either became insolvent or, more commonly, were acquired. Even a successful turnaround does not guarantee a firm's independence, however. About a quarter of all those firms identified as successful turnarounds over the period were themselves acquired by 1976. It is interesting to note that most acquisitions of firms that had experienced one or more loss-making years took place between one and three years *after* the last reported loss. This may indicate that many of the firms were able to adopt recovery strategies adequate for

Table 1.2: *Chance of Successful Recovery*

No. of years of declining earnings (in 1970 prices)	No. of firms needing recovery	No. of firms successfully recovered	Recovery success (%)
3	335	81	24
4	84	23	27
5	13	2	15
6	5	1	20
TOTAL 437		107	AVERAGE 24

Source: The Author.

* The risk of failure is analysed using the Z-score model discussed in Chapter 2.

survival, but were unable to achieve sustainable recovery, as described earlier in this chapter.

By way of comparison, a U.S. study by Bibeault found that 27% of U.S. quoted companies were in need of a turnaround during a ten-year period.[4] The need for a turnaround was defined as the existence of a loss situation or a severe decline in profit of 80% or more in a single year. One-third of these firms were, according to the author, successful turnarounds.

5. Corporate Recovery and the Business Environment

The subject of corporate recovery has become a major topic of media discussion as U.K. industrial output has declined and unemployment has risen to levels which were unthinkable only five or ten years ago. What has happened? Much of British industry makes standard products little differentiated from those of overseas manufacturers. When they first came on the market they may have been unique but, as the technology became available worldwide, the products took on the characteristics of commodity products. Couple this with a slowdown in the growth of world economic output and the result is severe price competition. The problem is exacerbated by the presence of excess capacity in many industries, such as steel, consumer durables, automobiles, textiles, tyres, chemicals, diesel engines, etc.; it was further exacerbated in the U.K. in 1979/80 by the high value of sterling due to the government's economic policies. In such an environment, the key to success is to have a cost structure which is as low as or lower than one's major competitors – competitors who may be based in Japan, Taiwan, Malaysia and other newly industrialized countries. The problem is not unique to Britain – it is a phenomenon common to the Western World.

A partial explanation for this state of affairs is the change in the global competitive environment that has resulted from the economic take-off of Japan and the newly industrialized countries.[5] The problem originated in the late 1960s when some of the less developed countries began to shift from protection and import substitution to export-oriented policies. At about the same time (although it is practically impossible to prove a causal relationship), the growth rates of the *developed* countries started to slow down, while growth in the developing countries continued unabated.

Fast economic growth together with government policies in the newly industrialized countries have caused price levels for manufactured goods to decline, relative to the price of raw material commodities. Manufacturing industry in countries like Britain has therefore lost out. At the macro-level, the effect of these events has been to increase the ratio of manufacturing to total net output in the developing countries and to reduce the average ratio of industrial to total employment in the industrialized world.

To cope with this situation one either needs a large home market to provide a volume base for one's industry, or one needs to adopt a strategy based on product technology (as in Germany). In the long run, neither one of these approaches may alone be adequate when one sees the two major world manufacturers, the U.S.A. and Japan, attempting to adopt both approaches. British manufacturing industry, with but a few exceptions, has adopted neither approach. In many instances, it is now too late to do anything about it and may well have been wishful thinking in the first place. Suitable recovery strategies are no longer available at either the government or firm level.

The impact of the changing world environment on company profits has been dramatic. The pre-tax return on trading assets of U.K. companies (excluding North Sea activities) declined from 12.5% in 1967 to 8.7% in 1970 and to 4.7% in 1978.[6] However, these figures include the retailing and wholesaling trades, which are largely immune to international competition and are better able to cope with inflation (through frequent price adjustments) than is manufacturing industry. Within the manufacturing sector, some industries have fared better than others. Some, such as textiles, shipbuilding, vehicles, household goods and engineering, appear to have been losing money in real terms since the late 1970s – a pattern reflected in the stock market performance of these sectors. Figure 1.1 provides an example of the Stock Market performances of the packaging and paper sector, as compared to the *Financial Times* 'All Share Index' for the period 1962–79. Figure 1.1 also shows the Stock Market performance of Inveresk, a recovery situation described in Chapter 18.

The worst-performing sectors are all characterized by intense price competition in both their home and export markets. They have lost substantial market share to foreign competition – and the trend is continuing. In some sectors U.K. firms no longer provide an effective presence in the market. Not surprisingly, it is in those sectors adversely affected by foreign price competition that the corporate recovery problem is most common. A selection of industries and markets

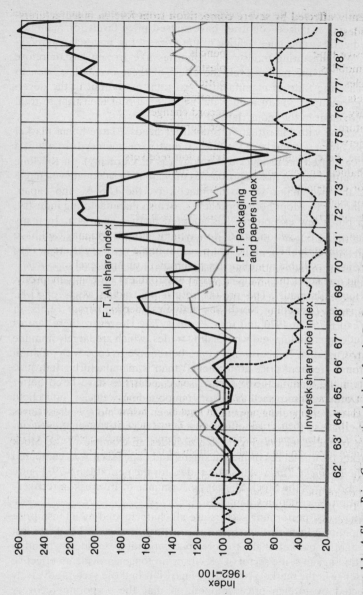

Figure 1.1: *A Share Price Comparative Analysis for the Packaging and Paper Industry 1962–80*

Source: London Business School Share Price Data Bank (courtesy of Mr P. Zinkin)

currently affected by severe competition from foreign manufacturers includes:

adhesive tape	pencils
automobiles	plastics
bicycles	pottery
carpets	printing
cutlery	record changers
furniture	refrigerators
leatherware	steel
marine diesel engines	television receivers
mechanical engineering	textile fibres
motor components	toys
motor cycles	tyres
paper and packaging	washing machines

While the problem is perhaps most acute in these and similar sectors, the reader should be aware before proceeding any further that, for many firms in these industries, sustainable recovery will be *impossible* to achieve. We will show in Chapter 5 that, of the ten firms studied that became insolvent despite *serious* attempts at turnaround, all ten were characterized by severe price competition from overseas.

Notes

1. D. Bibeault, *Corporate Turnaround*, McGraw-Hill, 1981.
2. 'Life After Bankruptcy', *Financial Times*, 5 February 1981.
3. This is a similar definition to that used by D. Schendel, G. R. Patton and J. Riggs in their article 'Corporate Turnaround Strategies', *Journal of General Management*, except that they normalized income by way of GDP inflator/deflation to exclude the effects of the business cycle.
4. D. Bibeault, op. cit.
5. M. Beenstock, 'The Causes of Slower Growth in the World Economy', London Business School Note, 1980.
6. 'The 1970s: Few Winners in the Table of Honours', *Financial Times*, 22 December 1979.

2. The Causes and Symptoms of Decline

Before we can start to talk sensibly about turnaround strategies, we need to have a good understanding of just how and why firms find themselves in a crisis situation. This is an enormously large topic, since each major cause of decline is a potential book in itself. A number of interesting books have already been written on this topic, most notably *Corporate Collapse* by John Argenti[1] and *Corporate Bankruptcy in America* by Edward Altman.[2] The aim of this chapter therefore is only to summarize the causes and symptoms of corporate decline.

When analysing a firm's decline, the reader should be careful to distinguish between causes and symptoms of failure. Symptoms are merely 'tell-tale' signs – danger signals, if you like – which a perceptive analyst outside the firm can discern. Symptoms give clues as to what *might* be wrong with the firm, but they do *not* provide a guideline for management action. What is important – if we are to help the sick firm to recover – is to find out the basic causes of the firm's problems. The medical analogy is apt: pain and fever are symptoms of an illness, not its cause, and the doctor who treats merely the symptoms may well find himself with a dead patient. So it is with a firm in crisis. This chapter discusses causes and symptoms separately, so that the reader is aware of the very important difference between the two.

Developing a suitable system to classify the factors causing decline is not as easy as it may seem at first glance. One can, if one wants to, trace virtually all the reasons for declining performance back to 'bad management', arguing that it was either poor decisions or inaction on the part of management that were the cause of all the firm's problems. Even where the cause of decline is primarily due to environmental factors beyond management control, one can argue that management should have forecast such events and planned accordingly. This approach is not very useful, however; it merely locates the blame for a firm's decline without providing those charged with the recovery task with any useful analytical information.

As soon as one looks deeper into the problem, however, one is confronted by a classic 'chicken and egg' situation. Which is the true causal factor and which the effect? For example, one might identify intense price competition in the marketplace as a causal factor of decline . . . but is this the real cause or is it the firm's inferior cost position relative to that of its competitors that is the cause? If *this* is the cause, is it due to lack of market share, or to the firm's conservative financial policy of not investing in modern plant and equipment, or to both? If financial policy is to blame, what causes management to adopt such a policy? . . . and so here we are, back once again with management! In practice, a chain of interrelated causal factors and multiple causes can be identified in most situations. Which causal factors are identified, therefore, requires a considerable amount of subjective judgement, and this is reflected in the writings of various authors and researchers.

In a study of forty U.K. turnaround situations, I have identified eleven frequently occurring factors which are the principal causes of corporate decline. The factors I have identified are very similar to the factors identified by Argenti, which he developed by summarizing the literature and talking to receivers and others involved in failing company situations. The difference is largely one of classification. The causes of decline I have identified are compared to those identified by Argenti in the U.K. and by Schendel and Patton in the U.S. in Table 2.1. My eleven factors are, I should stress, the *principal*, not the *only*, causes of decline. Unlike Schendel et al., I have omitted strikes as a principal cause of decline – which may come as a surprise to some readers. It was certainly a contributory cause of decline at Foden's and at E.C. Cases (the Welsh fence manufacturer), for example, but in each situation other, more important causal factors were at work. None of the lists of causal factors of decline explicitly mentions the organization structure, and yet this is clearly a contributory cause of high overheads, low labour productivity and lack of control. Great care should therefore be exercised in using any checklist of causal factors.

1. Poor Management

The personal characteristics of the chief executive and the key management personnel play a major role in causing decline. Sheer incompetence and/or lack of interest in the business are common characteristics of a firm in decline. There are many books and articles on the characteristics and skills required of good managers, and I do not intend to summarize them here. What is worth emphasizing,

Table 2.1: *Causes of Corporate Decline*

Slatter	Argenti[1]	Schendel, Patton & Riggs[2]	Sigoloff[3]
Lack of financial control	Accounting information		Lack of control
Inadequate management	Management	Management problems	Peter Principle Management without guts Interpersonal conflict at decision-making level
Competition	Firm unresponsive to change	Increased competitive pressure Lower revenues*	Change in technology Firm hostage to current product-markets
High cost structure relative to competitors		Higher costs	Development of locational disadvantages
Changes in market demand		Demand declines	Change in marketplace
Adverse movement in commodity markets (including interest rates)	Normal business hazards		Increasing cost of debt
Operational marketing problems		Marketing problems	Poor distribution
Big projects	Big project		Dependence on single customer
Acquisitions			
Financial policy	Gearing		Limited financial resources

Table 2.1 (continued)

Slatter	Argenti[1]	Schendel, Patton & Riggs[2]	Sigoloff[3]
Overtrading	Overtrading		Sales growth faster than working capital
		Strikes	

1. J. Argenti, *Corporate Collapse: The Causes and Symptoms*, McGraw-Hill, 1976, Chapter 7.
2. D. Schendel, G. R. Patton and J. Riggs, 'Corporate Turnaround Strategies: A Study of Profit Decline and Recovery', *Journal of General Management*, 1976.
3. From lecture given by Mr Sanford Sigoloff at Graduate School of Management, UCLA, 27 May 1981.
* Lower revenues include lower prices, excess industry capacity and product obsolescence.

however, are the major management defects in the composition and methods of operation of the management team. There are five principal factors to consider:

(a) *One-man rule*: The presence of a dominant and autocratic chief executive characterizes many failing firms. Typically, such a chief executive makes all the major decisions in the firm and will not tolerate dissent. He is the typical Zeus-like character described by Charles Handy in his book *Understanding Organizations*.[3] One-man rule, although always risky, is not necessarily bad per se. Many of the most successful firms have been built up largely on the efforts of an autocratic chief executive (e.g. Trust House Forte under Sir Charles Forte, Warburgs under Sigmund Warburg, Grand Metropolitan under Sir Maxwell Joseph, G.E.C. under Lord Weinstock). As long as such companies remain financially successful, everyone points to the vision and leadership of the chief executive as a key factor for success; however, as soon as trouble occurs, that same individual is blamed for the trouble. This is just as it should be, since the causes of early success are often the causes of later failure; but it nevertheless highlights the fine line separating the positive and negative effects of one-man rule. The main difference between the successful and the unsuccessful autocrat appears to lie in their differing attitudes towards change and new ideas. The successful autocrat is usually willing to adapt to changing business conditions and to be receptive to new ideas from subordinates and outsiders, while the unsuccessful autocrat is not.

(b) *Combined chairman and chief executive*: In those firms where the position of both chairman and chief executive is held by the same individual, there is no effective watchdog over the activities of the chief executive. The separation of positions, while providing some safeguard to shareholders, will not of itself ensure that the chief executive's actions are monitored effectively. Much depends on the personalities of the individuals involved. This is particularly true where the chairman is non-executive and all the 'real' power lies with the chief executive. Who runs Lonrho, for example? Is it the chairman, Duncan Sandys, or Tiny Rowland?* I know of another public company – which shall remain nameless – where the chief executive will not allow the non-executive chairman to talk to the other directors, all of whom are executive directors, unless he himself is present!

(c) *Ineffective boards of directors*: Many readers might consider this to be a symptom rather than a cause of decline, but an ineffective board of directors means that planning, resource allocation and control decisions – key decisions affecting the 'guts' of the business – are poorly made.

An ineffective board of directors can arise for a number of reasons, the most important of which are:

- non-executive directors who do not participate. One highly successful unit trust manager once told my class at the London Business School that he would not invest in any company which had, as directors, peers of the realm, members of parliament or retired generals, because in his experience they were ineffective as board members. (As an aside, he went further and said he would like to see photographs of directors in the annual reports – because he does not trust anybody who wears a beard!)
- executive directors who participate only when the topic of discussion directly affects their area of responsibility or expertise
- an unbalanced board in which board members are all engineers, all accountants, or whatever. Failing firms – particularly smaller firms – are often characterized by unbalanced skills at board level. Argenti has pointed out the need for adequate financial representation at board level and the need for a balanced top management team. In the U.K. the issue of having a balanced board and a balanced top management team is often one and the same issue, since most boards are heavily oriented towards executive directors.

* Tiny Rowland is, of course, a major shareholder, which adds to his effective power.

When this is not the case, both the board and the management team need to be balanced

- lack of communication among board members with consequent lack of consensus agreement on the direction the company is going. U.K. research has shown that those companies in which there is a high degree of consensus among board members concerning company objectives out-perform those companies where consensus does not exist.[4]

(d) *Management neglect of core business*: When firms reach a certain stage of development, they typically start to diversify.[5] This pattern has been observed and recorded in the U.K. by Channon.[6] Diversification means further growth, something most managements find exciting and challenging. But herein lies the danger. The development of new business takes more and more of top management's most scarce resource, time, with the result that their core businesses are neglected. The consequences of this can be quite disastrous, since the core businesses are likely to be mature businesses that are generating a substantial portion of the cash flow needed to fund the acquisition and new venture programmes. A good example of this was the U.S. multinational, United Brands Inc., whose diversification in the late 1960s and early 1970s led to neglect of its two core businesses, Fyffes bananas and Morrell meat. The diversification programme, which took the company into such ventures as Baskin-Robbins Ice Cream (later sold to J. Lyons), became a substitute for the original business, not a supplement. Eventually, problems emerged in the core business and the company experienced heavy losses, with the unhappy result that the company chairman, Eli Black, took his own life by jumping off the top of the Pan Am Building in New York City.

(e) *Lack of management depth*: My research has shown that lack of adequate management skills at the level below that of chief executive is a contributory factor causing decline. It is, however, nowhere near as important a factor as the quality of the chief executive; as the case histories at the end of this book will show, turnarounds can often be accomplished successfully without changing any management other than the chief executive. Lack of management depth tends to be found most often in those firms where decline has been relatively slow, because in these situations the better managers have usually left long before the ultimate crisis occurs. Where the crisis is caused by one or more relatively sudden events (as was the case with Burmah Oil and

Ultra Electronics, for example), the quality of management is generally acceptable.

2. Inadequate Financial Control

Apart from poor management, lack of adequate financial control is the most common characteristic of declining firms. It is a major cause of decline because weak control usually means that management is unable to pinpoint the products and customers on which it is losing money; and, sometimes more important in a crisis situation, which products or businesses are using cash and which are generating cash.

Lack of financial control may mean any or all of the following are absent or inadequate:

- cash-flow forecasts
- costing systems
- budgetary control.

There are still many firms – mainly smaller firms – in which all three are totally absent. The only financial information that exists is financial accounting information: statutory accounts prepared by outside auditors at year end. In this situation, management may not realize until some months after the financial year end that they lost money in the previous year. Financial accounting does not provide adequate control information – it is aggregate data and is received too late to be of use. From the point of view of control, what is important is management accounting information on a frequent basis. In hospitals, the patient's pulse and temperature are measured every few hours as an indicator of more fundamental problems. With firms, similar constant vigilance is required, so that swift corrective action can be taken if unforeseen problems develop.

In larger firms, the problem is more typically one of inadequate systems rather than no systems at all. Budgets, costing systems and cash-flow forecasts are not new ideas for most managers these days, but the mere existence of these systems does not guarantee that they are implemented effectively. There are four common problems.

(a) *Many management accounting systems have been poorly designed*: They are too complex, they produce too much poorly presented information and, more important, produce the wrong information required by general management. How many boards of directors and top management groups receive a package of monthly information which has taken many man-hours of overhead to produce, but which is totally useless? In my experience, the number is legion – and is found even among the fifty largest companies in the U.K. The blame for this must lie with top management. They have to ask themselves the basic question: 'What information do we need to run our business effectively, and *when* do we need it?' These are not easy questions to answer, therefore many managements delegate this non-delegatable task to accountants and systems specialists, who proceed to design systems based on what they *think* is required.

(*b*) *Management accounting information is poorly used*: Is the information provided used as a guide to management action? In large part, the answer to this question depends on whether management is 'numbers-oriented'. There are many chief executive officers who just do not understand how to use accounting information; they do not understand the language of business. They are like businessmen trying to do business in a foreign country without being able to speak the language.

(*c*) *The organizational structure hinders effective control*: One of the functions of a well-designed organization structure is to aid management control. I have noticed two aspects of this problem in my work. First, over-centralization seems to make control more difficult. In the RFD Group, for example (see page 295), centralization was a causal factor in the decline, as it meant that it was more difficult for management to find out what was really going on. Second, the hierarchical level at which control is placed in the organization structure is often too high. 3M (UK) Ltd have, for example, found that by locating budget responsibility lower down the organization, control and productivity have been improved.[7]

(*d*) *Methods of overhead allocation distort the costs*: Most firms adopt a product-line costing system in which overheads are allocated to individual product lines on the basis of labour content, machine hours or total variable costs. Such a system assumes that the cost of serving one customer is the same as serving the next customer. This is not the case, however, unless the firm is competing in a single homogeneous market segment, which is rare. Most firms market their products or services to a range of customers in different market segments, with the result that the actual overheads associated with one transaction may be quite different from those associated with another transaction for the same product.

3. Competition

Both price competition and product competition are common causes of corporate decline. In practice they often occur together, although I will discuss them separately.

3.1 Product Competition

The product life-cycle concept has long been recognized as a useful tool for business analysis, although its general validity has been rightfully questioned.[8] The idea of the life cycle is that after an initial start-up period, successful products go through a growth phase, a maturity phase and, eventually, a decline phase as new and improved products are brought on to the market. The length of the life cycle varies enormously from one industry and product to another, from a few months in high fashion clothing, for example, to many years in, say, English reproduction furniture. The basic idea, however, is that products eventually become obsolete as new technology is developed or improved, or substitute products are introduced and consumer preferences change.

The reasons why firms do not develop new products to replace obsolete products are many. They include:

- lack of success with new product introductions. The failure rate of new products is very high[9]
- belief that the old product is still the best on the market
- inadequate financial resources and technical know-how to develop new products
- lack of ideas for new products.

A firm that fails to respond to changing market needs or that responds too late to changing needs is likely to find itself heading towards extinction. Responding to market needs does not necessarily imply following the market trends. The firm may not have the resources to develop any competitive advantage as technology or consumer needs change; however, if it wants to survive as an organization, it must respond by diversifying, entering joint ventures, or following some other strategy.

3.2 Price Competition

Severe price competition is probably the most common cause of decline in manufacturing industry in Britain and other Western countries. In studies of turnaround situations it does not show up as the single most important factor because, in many cases, firms are unable to recover from the effects of such competition and so die, or are able to change their product market focus before price competition causes a severe crisis. In either case, the turnaround situation is absent.

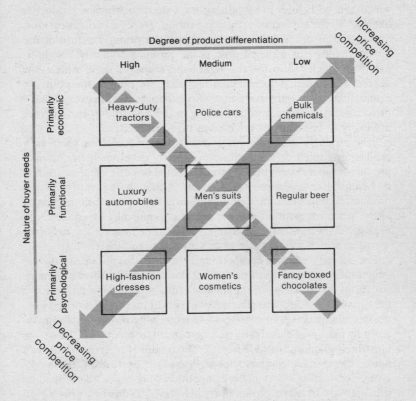

Figure 2.1: *The Effect of Product Characteristics on Price Competition*

Source: Adapted from C. W. Hofer, 'Conceptual Constructs for Formulating Corporate and Business Strategies', Intercollegiate Case Clearing House, Boston, No. 9-378-754, 1977, p. 20. Reprinted by permission.

However, as was pointed out in Chapter 1, the decline in many sections of British industry is directly attributable to price competition from overseas competitors. Motor cycles, cars, cutlery, ball bearings, machine tools, textiles, paper, carpets, radio, television and household appliances are all examples of whole sectors of the economy where individual companies have declined due to foreign price competition.

The existence of price competition in a market is largely a function of the nature of the product and the structural characteristics of the industry. Hofer has produced a useful matrix, shown in Figure 2.1, which can be helpful in visualizing the extent to which a product is likely to be the subject of price competition. He uses two dimensions, the degree of product differentiation and the primary nature of the buyers' needs (for what purpose is the product primarily bought?). Products which fall in the top right-hand corner – those with a low degree of product differentiation and that are bought for primarily economic reasons – are true commodity products and are exceptionally price sensitive. Those products falling in the bottom left-hand corner are likely to be relatively price-insensitive products.

Few products are truly price insensitive because, as soon as a product is copied or a substitute product is developed, the original product, even if differentiated by brand name or design features, starts to behave like a commodity product. Although the nature of the product is important in determining whether price competition is likely, price competition will not occur automatically or uniformly in a given market. There are likely to be some market or customer segments which will be more price sensitive than others.

The severity of price competition in a market will depend on the structural characteristics of the market. Porter has identified five major structural determinants of the intensity of competition in an industry: the threat of new entrants, the threat of substitute products or services, the bargaining power of suppliers, the bargaining power of customers, and the nature of the rivalry among current competitors. These are illustrated graphically in Figure 2.2. The reader is referred to Porter's book, *Competitive Strategy*, for a discussion as to how these five groups of factors affect price competition and hence the individual firm's ability to make profits in its industry.[10] Industries with a high degree of price competition are generally less profitable industries since above-average levels of profitability (economic rents) are harder to generate, while some industries are clearly more profitable than others. What is of greater interest when studying the causes of decline is the way in which the degree of price competition changes over time.

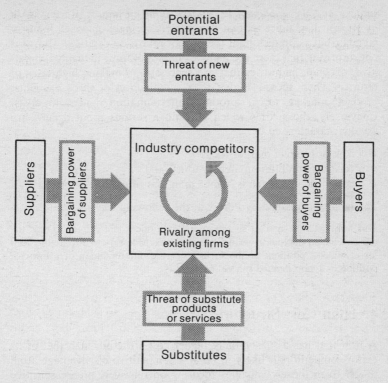

Figure 2.2 *Forces Driving Industry Competition*

Source: Michael Porter, *Competitive Strategy*, New York Free Press, 1980. p. 4. Reprinted by permission.

Typically, price competition increases as an industry matures, with the result that the key factors for success change. When the industry growth rate starts to slow down, price competition begins to become more important and margins decline. The result is an industry shake-out in which those competitors with higher cost structures may find themselves unable to compete.

While an industry as a whole may be subject to increased price competition, not all firms within that industry will necessarily suffer the same fate. A firm's success, as measured by its profitability, is *not only a function of the industry (and other external) variables over which the firm has no control, but is also a function of the firm's strategy and the quality of its strategy implementation.* Recent work by Rumelt has indicated that firm effects strongly outweigh industry membership as predictors of the rate of return on capital.[11] Thus it is not surprising that there are many examples of firms in highly competitive, declining industries that are successful in making high rates of return.[12] Their success is due to a combination of three elements: product market focus, product differentiation and low costs. Conversely, those firms which get into a serious profit decline are usually characterized by:

- a lack of product market focus
- a relatively undifferentiated product, and
- a cost structure which is higher than that of major competitors.

The issue is explained by Porter in the following way:

This firm lacks the market share, capital investment and resolve to play the low-cost game, the industry-wide differentiation necessary to obviate the need for a low-cost position, or the focus to create differentiation or a low-cost position in a more limited sphere.[13]

4. High Cost Structure

A firm that has a substantially higher cost structure than that of its major competitors is likely to be at a competitive disadvantage at all times. Even those companies focusing on relatively price-insensitive product-market segments will probably have lower profit margins than their direct competitors, with the result that they will generate less profit and less additional borrowing power. With less funds available than competitors, they will not be able to invest so much on new product development and marketing, and will, therefore, be less capable of building and defending their market position. However, the more common problem encountered in turnaround situations is the inability of firms of compete on price because their cost structure is too high.

There are six major sources of cost disadvantage which can lead to a firm having to charge higher prices than its competitors: (1) relative cost disadvantages due to the firm's inability to take advantage of economies of scale and its lack of experience as compared to competitors; (2) absolute cost disadvantages which result from competitors controlling strategic variables not available to the firm itself; (3) cost disadvantages due to diversification; (4) cost disadvantages due to management style and organization structure; (5) operating inefficiencies due to lack of investment and poor management; and (6) unfavourable government policies.

Each type of cost disadvantage will be explained briefly.

4.1 Relative Cost Disadvantages

There are two types of relative cost disadvantage: those due to scale effects and those due to learning-curve and experience-curve effects. Scale effects refer to the way in which the unit costs of a product decline as the absolute volume per period increases, whereas learning- and experience-curve effects depend on cumulative volume.

(*a*) *Scale economies*: The presence of economies of scale, in whatever function of a business, give a cost advantage to the larger firm. Economies of scale arise from specialization of labour, the indivisibility of technology, spreading fixed costs over a larger volume and the application of the concept of mass reserves. They can be present in nearly all functions of the business, and are often more important in purchasing, marketing and distribution than in manufacturing. It is very important for management to analyse each element of the firm's cost structure separately to determine the particular relationships between unit costs and scale. Where significant scale economies exist, it is the smaller firm which is always at a cost disadvantage.

(*b*) *Learning- and experience-curve effects*: These effects are independent of scale; thus it is possible for a smaller firm that has been in an industry a long time to have lower costs than a new entrant who lacks experience and is likely to incur heavy start-up costs. In practice, however, scale economies and experience-curve effects are often found side by side, since it is usually difficult for a small firm to keep its experience proprietary. Learning-curve effects apply only to labour costs, while experience-curve effects may apply to nearly all cost components.

4.2 Absolute Cost Disadvantages

Absolute cost disadvantages are independent of size or cumulative output. There are a number of sources of such disadvantages:

- Ownership or control of raw material supply by competitors. Where this occurs, the disadvantaged firm is forced to buy its raw materials from a competitor who is more vertically integrated. This has been the cause of many independent retail petrol stations going out of business in the U.K., since they are forced to buy their supplies from the big oil companies who are also retailers themselves. Esso and Shell in particular have at times raised the wholesale price of petrol without passing on the increase in their own petrol stations. Since petrol is a fairly price-sensitive product, the independent petrol stations have been unable to pass on the cost increase and many have gone out of business.

- Access to cheaper labour. The location of manufacturing facilities can lead to significant cost disadvantages due to differences in wage rates, and differences in productivity which are independent of capital investment and training efforts. Cheaper labour is obviously an important strategic factor in industries where the manufacturing process is labour intensive, but it is a mistake to think it is important only in such industries. Access to cheaper labour is important in all industries where price competition occurs and the profit margin is low. For example, in an industry where wages costs represent only 20% of the manufacturer's selling price and the typical after-tax profit margin is only 2%, a firm whose wage rates are 10% higher because of its location (say, in the London area as opposed to South Wales) may make no profit at all.
- Proprietary production know-how. A firm relying on widely available production technology may find itself at a competitive disadvantage against a firm that has developed proprietary production processes. Many Japanese companies, Hitachi for example, place considerable weight on this aspect of their competitive advantage.
- Favourable site location. A new competitor in a market may find itself at a cost disadvantage as compared to established competitors who managed to obtain property at lower prices.

4.3 Cost Disadvantages Due to Diversification Strategy

Diversified firms may find themselves at a cost disadvantage in a particular product-market area because of high allocated corporate overheads. The mix of businesses that a diversified firm chooses to be in directly affects its overhead structure. Let us assume firm X competes in three different business areas, A, B and C; its main competitor, Y, in business area A is another diversified company operating in business areas A, D and E. Firm X may find itself at a cost disadvantage if its businesses B and C have a higher overhead cost structure than businesses D and E. This situation is a direct result of the diversification strategies adopted by the two companies. A similar situation will occur if firm Y regards its business area A as a 'loss leader' business which is subsidized by profits from its other business areas, or if it regards business A as merely a vehicle for disposing of by-products from businesses D or E.

4.4 Cost Disadvantage Due to Management Style and Organization Structure

The issue of management style is important because it directly affects the overhead structure. The chief executive who relies heavily on staff personnel will incur heavier overheads and thus be at some cost disadvantage, as compared to the chief executive who decentralizes responsibility down to the line managers. Organization structures with large head-office 'bureaucracies' are increasingly being recognized as inefficient and cost ineffective. For example, the new chairman of Britain's largest manufacturing company, ICI, has gone on record as saying that ICI is overmanaged and overmanned at the centre.[14] This is a common problem with large, complex organizations and inevitably leads to higher costs.[15] Managerial style and organizational structure also have an indirect effect on labour productivity. A hierarchical organization with poor communications typically leads to lower productivity at the plant operating level.

4.5 Operating Inefficiencies

Operating inefficiencies are due largely to poor management; they may be found in all functions of the firm. With the high propensity of bad management in turnaround situations, it is not surprising that operating inefficiency is a major cause of corporate decline. Operating inefficiencies affect all elements of the cost structure. Some of the areas in which inefficiencies may, directly or indirectly, cause higher costs are:

- low labour productivity
- poor production planning
- lack of adequate maintenance
- plant layout
- allocation of salesforce time
- allocation of advertising and promotional expenditure
- distribution and after-sales service
- terms of trade that 'encourage' a large volume of small orders
- office procedures.

4.6 Unfavourable Government Policies

Government policies with regard to subsidies, taxes, exchange rates, pollution-control requirements and the like may put some companies at a severe cost disadvantage. Governmental factors have become increasingly important in those industries where the firm needs to compete on a global basis to remain competitive. Subsidies by foreign governments have put U.K. companies at a cost disadvantage in the paper and carpet industries, for example. Relatively inefficient French and German paper mills managed to penetrate the U.K. paper market in the late 1970s as the result of large government subsidies. In a similar way, U.S. carpet companies have penetrated the U.K. market for carpets made from synthetic fibres as a result of low energy prices in the U.S.A., and a number of U.K. carpet manufacturers have gone out of business as a direct result.

It is not always foreign governments that cause U.K. companies to find themselves at a cost disadvantage. The British government's economic policies had the effect of raising the exchange rate of sterling and making British exports less competitive overseas during 1980. The U.K. government's fuel-oil tax is another example of government actions affecting costs. This tax has put energy-intensive businesses like petrochemicals and fibres at a substantial cost disadvantage, as compared to competitors from continental Europe.

5. Changes in Market Demand

A reduction in the demand for a product or service, or a change in the pattern of demand, to which the firm does not respond can be important causal factors in a firm's decline. A drop in demand for a product is either a secular decline (part of a long-term trend), or a cyclical decline whereby demand is tied to the familiar business cycle and will eventually recover. A third type of decline, seasonal decline, is not a significant causal factor in decline, except when a company is in a weak financial condition, and then it may be the trigger for change or receivership.

5.1 Secular Decline in Demand

Just as the products of an individual firm may become obsolete because new, improved products are introduced, so the demand for industries and product classes within industries may decline over time. Secular trends can sometimes be reversed as new uses are found for old products, for example, but this is rare. One of the starkest examples of a secular decline, and a very rapid one at that, was the drop in demand for electrical central-heating equipment after the OPEC oil crisis of 1973/74 which led to the insolvency of Dimplex (see page 401). Secular decline is brought about by the same environmental factors – technological change, economic conditions, changing social and cultural norms, political events – which prompt demand for new products. The marketing concept was really born out of concern for the consequences of secular market decline.

5.2 Cyclical Market Decline

The world economy and the economies of all individual countries have experienced regular economic cycles of boom and recession for over a hundred years, and maybe considerably longer. The timing of these cycles is exceptionally regular. The average time from the peak of one cycle to the peak of the next (as measured by industrial output indicators) was about $4\frac{1}{2}$ years. Furthermore, the individual cycles tend to be asymmetrical: the downturn phase takes longer than the upturn phase. From 1950 to 1980 the average length of the downturn phase was about 33 months as compared to 21 months for the upturn phase. Small wonder that economic news is normally gloomy! While the timing of these cycles is fairly regular, their amplitude (i.e. the depth of the recession or the height of the boom) is exceptionally difficult to forecast.

Each industry is affected in a somewhat different way by the business cycle. Some industries lead the cycle and others lag behind. Demand fluctuations in some industries are much smaller than that of the economy as a whole, while others are much greater. Some, like the food and tobacco industry, are affected much less than those industries manufacturing capital goods and deferrable items of consumer expenditure, such as furniture. In the furniture industry, for example, demand increases about 18% when disposable income increases by 10% and declines by about the same amount when disposable income decreases.

The effect of these cyclical swings in demand can be very serious for companies that already exhibit a number·of the other causal factors of decline at the start of a recessionary period. Recession alone rarely, if ever, puts a company into a turnaround situation; but recession coupled with factors such as lack of financial control, a weak competitive position and a financial policy of high gearing (or just a weak balance sheet for historical reasons) can spell disaster. Recession tends to expose a company's competitive weaknesses, although the source of these weaknesses is often the result of management decisions or acts of omission during the previous boom phase. Management is usually too busy just meeting demand in a boom period to worry about whether it is losing market share (and hence eroding its relative cost position *vis-à-vis* competitors); decisions to build extra capacity are usually taken at this time with insufficient attention given to the state of market demand when the new capacity comes on stream. The Norcros kitchen furniture subsidiary, Hygena, was a case in point: a capacity expansion decision was made late in the 1972/73 boom but, by the time the additional capacity was ready, furniture demand had dropped drastically. Subsequently, Norcros incurred large write-offs as capacity was reduced in the late 1970s.

Very often the effect of severe recession is a two-stage process. The first recession weakens the company financially, but it survives. In the intervening boom the company's position improves but it does not fully recover before the next recession comes along. Many furniture manufacturers have exhibited this process over the last ten years. Historically, managers in the industry – most of them are owner managers – have operated on the basis of breaking even during recessionary periods and making good profits with which to repay their bank borrowings in boom times. This approach worked quite well for many years, and at the end of 1973 the industry was relatively healthy after the 1972/73 boom (which was the biggest boom since the Second World War). The recession that lasted from 1974 to 1976 took its toll of some companies, but most survived, thanks to extensive bank borrowings. However, the subsequent boom, which peaked in 1978/79, was not strong enough for companies to repay their loans and to finance working capital requirements. The result was that many companies entered the 1980 recession in a relatively weak financial position. The sudden drop in demand at the beginning of 1980 sent many companies into immediate receivership or liquidation. In the year ending October 1980, approximately 15% of all U.K. furniture companies ceased to exist.

5.3 Changing Pattern of Demand

Demand for a particular product may not decline but the way in which it is distributed and purchased may change. If this is the case – and management does not or cannot respond – it will soon find itself in difficulty. The history of the soft drinks company, Tizer, provides a good example of what I mean by a changing pattern of demand and how it differs from the idea of product obsolescence. During the 1960s, Tizer continued to sell its product in returnable bottles via the small corner shop, while the market trends were towards non-returnable bottles and cans sold via the grocery multiples. Tizer's management failed to respond to these two discernible trends. There were two problems – first, Tizer's product packaging was obsolete and, second, Tizer's distribution strategy did not take account of the changing pattern of demand.

6. Adverse Movements in Commodity Prices

One of the so-called business hazards which can be a major causal factor of decline is adverse movements in commodity prices. During the 1970s, a number of firms have been adversely affected by movement in commodity markets – Burmah Oil in shipping, Barker & Dobson in sugar, Fairey in foreign exchange – to name just a few. If one classifies interest rates and property price fluctuation as commodities – as I have chosen to do – we quickly see such fluctuations as a major cause of decline of many property companies and in other companies which became involved in property development (e.g. the retail furniture group, Maple Macowards; the hotel group, Norfolk Capital), and in those financial institutions that lent heavily to the property sector (e.g. Keyser Ullmann and Wm. Brandt's). As interest rates rose to record levels, property incomes lagged behind, causing property developers to default in large numbers.

7. Lack of Marketing Effort

The vast majority of firms that are in a period of profit decline are characterized by management and employee complacency at all levels in the organization. This complacency is often most clearly visible to outsiders in the firm's approach to marketing. Lack of marketing effort may take many forms but, typically, one finds:

- a poorly motivated salesforce with a non-aggressive sales manager
- ineffective and wasted advertising
- efforts not targeted on key customers and key products

- poor after-sales service
- lack of market research/knowledge of the customers' buying habits
- outdated promotional material or a lack of promotional material
- weak or non-existent new-product development function.

In those firms where lack of marketing effort has been identified as a major factor causing decline, the basic problem is usually a management problem. The marketing director and/or the sales manager are incompetent, and are unable to provide the direction and leadership required to compete effectively in the marketplace. Lack of marketing effort alone may cause sales and profit to erode, as it had done at Thomas Cook (the travel agent and tour operator) under nationalization. But lack of marketing effort is often found in conjunction with more fundamental marketing problems of a strategic nature such as severe price and product competition. Managements (and their professional advisers) often fail to distinguish between marketing problems of an operational nature and those of a more serious strategic nature.

8. Big Projects

The 'big project' that goes wrong because costs are underestimated and/or revenues are overestimated is a well-known cause of failure. The definition of what is a big project is, of course, arbitrary, but I have chosen to include under this heading all 'one-off' capital and revenue projects which commonly cause decline with the exception of acquisitions. Acquiring poor firms and poor post-acquisition management are sufficiently important causes of decline to warrant separate attention later. Diversification as a cause of decline is not synonymous with acquisition because diversification may be implemented internally as well as by acquisition. Diversification will, therefore, be treated under both the 'big project' heading and acquisition.

Perhaps the best rule of thumb relating to big projects is that put foward by Sir Kenneth Cork, the well-known receiver: no firm should enter into a contract which, if it went wrong, would by itself cause the firm to become insolvent.

There are five ways in which the 'big project' can go wrong.

8.1 Underestimating Capital Requirements

This may arise because of

- poor cost estimates at the project planning stage
- poor project control during the implementation of the capital expenditure
- late design changes
- a variety of external factors which delay the project and increase capital costs, but over which the firm may have little control (e.g. strikes by contractors, bad weather, technical difficulties with new machinery during installation, late delivery of equipment and materials, etc.).

The various causes of delay feed on one another, leading to what has been described as a 'cycle of mutual demoralization'. Materials are delivered late, which leaves men with nothing to do; they blame the management and vent their feelings by walking out; process plant equipment manufacturers are told of the delays and decide it does not matter if they complete their orders late; the client company reckons the project is now running so far behind that it might just as well make a few late design changes.[16]

8.2 Start-up Difficulties

Even after completion, capital projects may experience a variety of start-up difficulties which elevate operating expenses above the forecast level. Technical difficulties with plant and equipment, particularly new state-of-the-art equipment, can lead to high wastage, significant downtime and even loss of customer confidence if order backlogs develop. Sometimes the problem is organizational rather than technical, and is symptomatic of poor project planning. Thus, the RFD Group's decision to shift their Ulster factory to Newcastle took no account of the fact that the skilled workforce would not move. The new plant was never started up and was eventually sold (see page 299). Perhaps the most common organizational problem leading to higher operating costs than expected is the lack of adequately trained employees. Many firms are surprised, when they open up a new plant, to see how long it takes for the new plant to operate at a similar level of productivity to their existing plants. The same applies to an even greater degree for service operations. Successful firms in service industries tend to grow only as fast as they can recruit and train personnel because they know that, if they expand too fast, poor service levels can cause the whole business to start to decline. It is not uncommon to hear the consumer say: 'They were all right until they grew too big.'

8.3 Capacity Expansion

Capacity tends to be increased either to meet growing demand, or as a prelude to increasing market share, or both. The errors that companies make in this area relate to timing, and the feasibility of filling the extra capacity. The timing issue is related to the question of demand cyclicality and forecasting. In a cyclical industry, a firm may be burdened with the additional overheads associated with new capacity just at the same time as demand turns down, as was the case in part with Hygena. More often than not, the error lies in believing the feasibility of filling the extra capacity at a profit. The root cause in such situations is poor strategic judgement. Foden's (see page 394) is a classic example in which capacity expansion was a direct cause of decline. Very often the strategic error and timing error go together. Thus, in Hygena's case it was not only a timing issue but also a mistaken belief on the part of Hygena's (and presumably Norcros's) management in the strength of Hygena's competitive position in the market. Hygena believed they were at the top end of the kitchen furniture market, whereas in fact this was not so – a fact the German manufacturers made plain from the mid 1970s onwards.

8.4 Market Entry Costs

Market entry refers to the introduction of new products into new and existing markets, or even the introduction of a firm's existing products into new markets. There are different risks associated with each type of market entry. When new products are being introduced, product development costs may be higher than anticipated; when new markets are being entered, market development costs may be higher. Where the firm is diversifying (i.e. introducing totally new products into totally new markets), the firm faces both technological and marketing risks.

Nearly all firms experience marketing failures from time to time – even firms normally regarded as highly successful – and it can be argued that, without taking the risks associated with new products and new markets, few firms would be successful. For example, Mothercare (the maternity and babywear retailer) opened up thirty-five new stores in Germany in the early 1970s. The result was a disaster and all but one store were eventually closed; however, Mothercare was growing profitably in the U.K. at this time and therefore did not experience a profit decline.

There are also many examples of growth firms in high growth industries falling into a crisis situation as the result of marketing and/or product development costs that are higher than anticipated. E.M.I.'s brain scanner is a classic example of a good product which required much greater resources than management had originally anticipated. The large amount of cash required to market the scanner was the key causal factor in the demise of E.M.I. High market entry costs are typically a principal cause of failure of high-technology companies.

Some quantification of the typical risks associated with market entry is provided by Biggadike's empirical analysis of the top 200 companies in the *Fortune* '500' in the United States.[17] He found that the average corporate venture suffers severe losses through the first four years of operation and needs eight years to reach profitability.

8.5 Major Contracts

Poor cost-estimating and pricing decisions on major contracts are a common cause of decline and even failure, particularly in the construction and capital goods industries. This is most prevalent where orders are won through a process of competitive tendering. Research has shown that errors are more likely to be found in the cost-estimating process than in the pricing decision.[18]

9. Acquisitions

Acquisitions have played an increasingly important role in the corporate strategy of large and medium-size firms during the past twenty years. As the use of acquisitions has increased, so has the incidence of acquisitions being a direct cause of corporate decline. Acquisitions are used primarily by firms either to implement growth strategies in industries in which they already compete or to implement diversification strategies into both related and unrelated industrial sectors. They have also been used as an opportunistic method of growth by financial conglomerates, such as the failed Slater Walker empire and the more successful Hanson Trust.

Empirical evidence suggests that the incidence of failure varies according to the type of acquisition. For example, Kitching in a study of ninety European acquisitions[19] (and in a similar U.S. study[20]) found that acquisitions in related business areas were viewed by management as being more successful than those in unrelated areas. However, as I will show in the next section, related diversification is not always preferable to unrelated diversification.

While the incidence may vary by type of acquisition, my own research suggests that there are three aspects of acquisitions that may cause firms to enter into a crisis situation:

- the acquisition of 'losers' – firms with weak competitive positions in their own markets
- paying an unjustifiably high purchase price for the acquired firm
- poor post-acquisition management.

9.1 The Acquisition of Losers

I use the term 'losers' to refer to firms with weak competitive positions in their own markets. They need not necessarily be losing money at the time of acquisition, but often do so soon afterwards. Losers are typically firms that lack the key factors for success in their market place: they have no competitive advantage that can become the basis of a defensible business strategy. They often have obsolete products or suffer from severe competitive pressures due to their inferior cost positions. To the extent that market share is an indicator of competitive advantage, Kitching's work also supports this view. He found that acquisitions were more successful when the acquired firm had a high market share. 'Losers' themselves typically exhibit many of the factors causing decline that are discussed in this chapter.

Conventional wisdom, coupled with Kitching's empirical work on types of acquisition, has led many corporate managers to believe that related diversification is safer than unrelated diversification. This is not *always* so. I will use the matrix in Figure 2.3 to indicate why. The matrix relates the type of diversification to the existence of competitive advantage in the acquired firm. Acquired firms which I have referred to as prime acquisition candidates are those that are in related businesses and that have competitive advantage. These are the best acquisition candidates, provided the purchase price is not too high (see next section) – but they are very often the firms least likely to be for sale. Under conventional wisdom, firms falling into the top right-hand corner of the matrix would seem to be the next most attractive acquisition candidates, since they are in related businesses. However, for such acquisitions to be successful they require the successful transfer of resources and skills from the parent company to the acquired

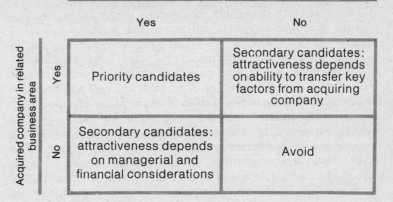

Figure 2.3: *Diversification Type and Competitive Advantage*

company. In practice, this transfer is very difficult to achieve, and often proves elusive for firms even in the same industry. Staveley Industries' strategy of acquiring failing companies in the machine-tool industry during the 1960s is a good example of this. Examples can be found among large, relatively well-managed firms. Cadbury-Schweppes, for example, was unsuccessful with acquisitions it made in the food industry in Europe in the late 1960s. Rather than buying a weak firm in a closely related industry, it may be preferable to buy a firm in the lower left-hand quadrant of the matrix, i.e. a firm in an unrelated business, but one which possesses the key factors for success. The latter are unlikely to cause corporate decline unless either of the two causal factors indicated below are present.

The worst of all possible worlds is the acquisition of unrelated firms with no competitive advantage in their marketplace. Such acquisitions are to be avoided at all costs but, unfortunately, they are very common. Typically, when a firm with a weak competitive position is acquired, the new subsidiary becomes a cash drain on the parent company. With a weak competitive position, it is unlikely to be generating a large cash flow from operations even if profitable, and may require large cash in-flows to keep pace with increased working capital requirements due to inflation, and to replace old and inefficient machinery. Having just purchased the company, management throws 'good money after bad' in the hope of justifying their acquisition decision. The sunk cost argument escapes them.

9.2 Paying Too Much for the Acquisition

Academic research shows that the financial benefits of acquisitions typically accrue to the seller and not to the purchaser.[21,22] Many acquirers pay a considerable amount of goodwill (the amount paid in excess of net asset value) for firms they acquire. If the acquisition is of a public company, large premiums in excess of the market capitalization at the time of the bid are often paid. The only way firms can justify paying large premiums is either if they have some unique ability to operate the acquired firm, if the acquisition will mesh with their existing businesses, or if they can see that the industry they are entering is in disequilibrium and there is therefore an opportunity to make above-average returns in the future.[23] No wonder the more successful acquisition-oriented firms like Hanson Trust rarely pay much goodwill for the firms they acquire. Paying too much for an acquisition rarely leads to a crisis by itself but, when coupled with the acquisition of a 'loser' or with poor post-acquisition management, paying a high price can be disastrous.

9.3 Poor Post-Acquisition Management

Poor post-acquisition management has been identified as the single most common cause of failure when making acquisitions. What happens after the acquisition depends primarily on the acquisition objective. Was the firm bought as an independent operating unit, or with the intention of integrating it into an existing operating unit? Acquisitions tend to be most successful when they are integrated into existing operations. It is when they continue as an independent operating unit that post-acquisition problems tend to emerge. The problems are of two types: either the new owner leaves the acquired firm alone and fails to exercise adequate managerial and financial control over its activities; or he becomes involved in managing the business, but in so doing he meets significant organizational resistance to change. Resistance is to be expected in the post-acquisition phase since the organizational culture of the acquiring firm is likely to be quite different from that of the acquired firm. Typically, an aggressive, power- or task-oriented organization moves into a static organization, or a task-oriented organization acquires a power-oriented (often family) firm.[24] The result is a clash of organizational cultures which, if not well managed, can lead to inefficiency and eventual loss. Management of the new subsidiary spends its time fighting its new owners, rather than running its business.

10. Financial Policy

There are at least three types of financial policy that are direct causes of failure:

- a high debt/equity ratio (high gearing)
- a conservative financial policy
- the use of inappropriate financing sources.

10.1 High Debt/Equity Ratio

The use of a moderate amount of debt financing (both short-term and long-term) is generally regarded as sound business practice, providing the firm can earn a rate of return on the incremental investment (made possible by the borrowing) greater than the interest payable on the debt. For many firms, a high debt/equity ratio is the result rather than the cause of corporate decline. In these situations, bank borrowings escalate as losses mount due to price competition, inefficient manufacturing, etc. Where gearing is a causal factor of decline, the aggressive use of debt financing is a conscious, voluntary management action. Property companies and the rapidly growing acquisitive conglomerates of the late 1960s were firms that used such a strategy.

Appropriate gearing ratios depend to a large extent on the characteristics of the industry or industries in which the firm competes. In cyclical industries with a high fixed-cost structure, high gearing ratios are likely to be riskier than in industries with only one or neither of these characteristics. What is appropriate will also depend on the debt structure (short-term versus long-term) and on the timing of the principal repayments. For example, a firm with bunched maturity dates may be able to support considerably less debt than a firm in which maturity dates are spread out.

10.2 Conservative Financial Policies

Where a firm's financial policy is characterized by lack of re-investment in plant and equipment, a high dividend payout ratio, high liquidity and low gearing, the financial policy is usually regarded as 'conservative'. In many cases this amounts to a liquidation policy; it should therefore hardly be surprising to see the firm move into decline. Tizer Ltd, an example I used earlier in this chapter, was such a firm during the 1960s, but the phenomenon was common to much of British industry, particularly before the era of high inflation. The old Norton-

Villiers-Triumph, the now defunct motor-bicycle manufacturer, and British Leyland are both regarded as having not re-invested and paid dividends out of capital during the 1950s and 1960s. Whereas a highly aggressive financial policy can lead to the development of a rapid crisis situation (as at Burmah Oil, for example), a conservative financial policy has the dubious merit of prolonging the decline phase of the firm. Evered Holdings is a good example of a firm that has been in decline for almost ten years but has so far averted insolvency as the result of conservative financial policies (and strong financial control).

10.3 Inappropriate Financing Sources

The failure to match borrowings and lendings was a major cause of the secondary banking crisis in the 1970s. Banks borrowed short-term money and invested in long-term projects which were illiquid in the short term. The decline of U.D.T., for example, was in large part due to this factor.

11. Overtrading

Overtrading is the process by which a firm's sales grow at a faster rate than the firm is able to finance from internally generated cash flow and bank borrowings. The failure of Brentford Nylons was due very largely to this factor. Overtrading can occur solely as a result of poor financial control, in which case the lack of adequate control is more accurately the cause of the decline. Very often, however, there is another factor at work: the firm is going after sales growth, regardless of whether or not it is profitable. Margins are reduced to increase volume and unprofitable customers are added just to increase sales volume. Overtrading is a characteristic of growth firms.

Frequency of Causal Factors

Lists of causes are useful, but managers need more than just a check-list. They need to know the *principal* causes of declining performance. How often do they occur and under what circumstances? Are the causes of decline the same in service businesses as in manufacturing businesses? Are they the same in large companies as in small? Are they different for businesses with low market share and high market share? Do they differ by industry? By the stage of evolution of the industry?

Do diversified firms decline in a way that is different from single business firms? The number of situational settings that could be analysed is enormous and yet, to date, almost nobody has studied these empirical situations. The first study to analyse the frequency with which different factors cause decline (and recovery) was the work by Schendel, Patton and Riggs in the United States,[25] but this was based solely on publicly available information. My own studies, in both the U.K. and U.S., which are based on both published data and interviews with management, attempt to go a little further than Schendel, Patton and Riggs's work, but one must be careful in drawing definitive conclusions from such

Table 2.2: *Frequency (in %) of Causal Factors of Decline in Forty U.K. Recovery Situations*

Causal factor	Total sample	Successfully recovered	Failed to recover
(Sample size)	(40)	(30)	(10)
Lack of financial control	75	73	80
Inadequate management:			
chief executive	73	67	90
other	12	7	30
Competition:			
price competition	40	20	100
product competition	18	17	20
High cost structure:			
operating inefficiency	35	36	40
high overheads	30	20	50
scale effects	28	17	70
Changes in market demand:			
cyclical	33	40	30
secular	18	17	20
pattern of demand	7	6	10
Adverse movements in commodity market	30	30	30
Lack of marketing effort	22	17	40
Financial policy	20	20	20
Big projects:			
capital	17	20	10
revenue	15	20	10
Acquisitions	15	13	20
Overtrading	—	—	—

Source: The Author.

studies, since the results are heavily dependent on the classification of causal factors, the size of the sample and the characteristics of the sample companies.

Table 2.2 shows the frequency of causal factors leading to decline in my sample of forty U.K. public companies operating in both the manufacturing and service sectors. Each of the firms in the sample experienced at least three successive years of declining profits in real terms. Care should be used in interpreting the data, however, since there are noticeable differences in the frequency of causal factors in the firms that eventually recovered and those that became insolvent despite recovery efforts. The significance of this finding is discussed in Chapter 5. One factor, overtrading, did not appear in the U.K. sample at all, although it was more significant in a U.S. sample which contained more growth businesses. Lack of financial control and inadequate top management at the level of the chief executive are clearly the major causes of decline and occur almost twice as frequently as any other single factor. Lack of financial control and poor top management, however, are more likely to be a cause of decline in manufacturing businesses than in service businesses, although they were prime causal factors in one-half of my limited sample of firms in service industries. There are two other factors that clearly distinguish the decline phase in manufacturing from service businesses: first, price competition and high manufacturing costs are very important causal factors of decline in manufacturing industries, but not in service industries; and second, the business cycle and adverse movements in commodity markets tend to play a larger role in the decline of firms in service industries. They are contributory factors in manufacturing industry, as was explained earlier in this chapter, but service industries appear particularly vulnerable to them.

The sample of forty firms contained firms that were in a crisis, defined here in terms of a cash-flow crisis, and other firms which were not in imminent danger of receivership but whose performance had clearly deteriorated or stagnated. Inadequate top management, lack of financial control and various operating inefficiencies explained the decline of most firms falling in the non-crisis category. The causes of failure in firms in crisis included these same groups of factors but, *in addition*, there were three other groups of causal factors that were usually present:

- changes in market demand, particularly those due to the business cycle

- commodity market fluctuations (as defined earlier)
- big projects, of both a capital and a revenue nature.

From my analysis, it appears that a crisis situation is likely to occur most frequently when a firm, already weakened by poor management, lack of control and inefficiency, is subjected to adverse movements in market demand and commodity prices, price competition and to 'one-off' problems resulting from the so-called big project. The number of factors causing decline in crisis and non-crisis situations lends further evidence to support this view. My research showed that there are twice as many causal factors of decline in crisis situations than in non-crisis situations.

Symptoms of Decline

For the outsider such as the banker or investor, the symptoms of decline are often easier to detect than the causes of decline, although it is not always clear what is a cause and what is a symptom. The most commonly used symptoms indicating that a firm is in need of a turn-around are financial indicators, although many experienced bankers, receivers and consultants have a number of non-financial factors which they also take into account.

I will next discuss briefly a few of the major symptoms of decline, although I expect most readers will be able to add to my list some symptoms which they have found to be good indicators of impending failure. Almost anything that a firm does wrong (and *all* firms make mistakes) is potentially an indicator that all is not well. However, the major symptoms (not causes, remember!) which I have observed are as follows:

(*a*) *Decreasing profitability*: Where the profitability trend is lower in absolute terms, the firm is clearly in decline, but it is usually more meaningful to adjust for inflation and show profits in real terms. Profits before tax and trading profits (before interest, tax and extraordinary items) are usually better indicators of the true health of the business than after-tax profits. Other measures of decreasing profitability are lower profitability as a percentage of sales and a declining rate of return on investment.

(*b*) *Decreasing sales volume at constant prices*: Again, analysis of sales trends is more meaningful after adjusting for inflation. Sales figures should also be analysed in accordance with the accepted industry criteria. For example, a retail operation should usually be judged on sales per square foot.

(c) *Increase in debt*: An increase in the firm's gearing, its debt-to-equity ratio, is a widely accepted indicator of impending trouble.

(d) *Decrease in liquidity*: Firms fail because they run out of cash. Measures of liquidity such as the current ratio (current assets/current liabilities) and the acid test (current assets less inventories/current liabilities) are common indicators of liquidity. However, as we shall see in the next section, these ratios are not good predictors of failure by themselves. Debtor days, creditor days and inventory turnover are other commonly used indicators of liquidity.

(e) *Restricted dividend policy*: A reduction in dividends may be necessary for a firm to conserve cash or to satisfy debt covenants. Reducing or eliminating dividends usually indicates a serious situation.

(f) *Accounting practices*: The use of generally *unacceptable* accounting practices[26] and undue delays in publishing annual financial statements are often symptoms of decline. A change of auditors – particularly from a reputable firm to one less well known – may also indicate trouble.

(g) *Top management fear*: A common characteristic of firms that are out of control is fear on the part of top management. As a crisis situation develops, fear increases to the point at which management may become totally incapacitated. It is not unusual for receivers to find mail unopened and problem letters stuffed in desk drawers.

(h) *Rapid management turnover*: A rapid succession of senior managers, and particularly of new chief financial officers, may indicate a high degree of disagreement at the top management level.

(i) *Declining market share*: Market share analysis forces a firm to compare its performance with that of its major competitors. A declining share indicates a firm is losing out to competitors, a conclusion which might not be obvious from sales analysis if there is inflation and real growth in the industry.

(*j*) *Lack of planning/strategic thinking*: Strategic planning is now a widely accepted tool to assist management in thinking about the direction of their business. The mere existence of a strategic planning system is not enough to assure a firm's health, and the total absence of formal strategic thinking *may* have no adverse effect on a firm; however, most firms in need of turnaround are characterized by a noticeable lack of strategic thinking.

This is by no means an exhaustive list of symptoms. As with causes of failure, no single symptom will indicate the need for a turnaround; rather, a combination of adverse symptoms is required. The financial indicators are the ones on which most external observers rely. Many businessmen use financial 'rules of thumb' as to what the appropriate financial ratios should be in a particular situation, although these can be misleading. One guide as to the appropriate 'rule of thumb' to use is to compare the firm in question with the financial ratios of its major competitors (obtainable from Inter Company Comparisons Ltd and available in most business libraries).

Predicting Company Failure

A number of attempts have been made to predict company failure based on financial ratios, although it is recognized that, at best, financial ratios can only be used as a warning system. The first attempt (1966) to predict bankruptcy was made by Beaver, who considered the firm to be a reservoir of liquid assets, supplied by cash inflows and drained by cash outflows. The solvency of the firm was defined in terms of the probability that the reservoir will serve as a cushion against variations in the cash flows. The main assumptions underlying this model were that the probability of failure was smaller if the reservoir and the cash flow from operations were both large, and that the probability of failure was higher if the debt and working capital were large. Beaver used a paired sample: seventy-nine failed firms and seventy-nine non-failed firms of the same asset size in the same industry, and calculated six ratios for each firm for a one-year period.[27] He found that not all ratios predicted equally well and that cash flow to total debt was the best predictor; it worked quite well even five years before failure. This ratio has also been found to be the best predictor in the U.K.[28] Of the other ratios used, Beaver found that liquidity ratios (e.g. current assets to current liabilities) were not good predictors of insolvency; and that net income to total debt, and total debt to total assets, were better predictors. The concept of the firm as a reservoir of liquid assets was also used by Wilcox to derive the probability of failure of firms, using what is known as 'the gambler's ruin' approach.[29]

Perhaps better known than the work of Beaver and Wilcox is that of Altman, who used five financial ratios and a statistical technique known as linear discriminant analysis to classify firms as solvent or insolvent.[30] Altman calculated an index, which he called a Z-score, which was calculated as follows

$$Z = 1.2\,x_1 + 1.4\,x_2 + 3.3\,x_3 + 0.6\,x_4 + 1.0\,x_5$$

where
Z = index
x_1 = working capital/total assets
x_2 = retained earnings/total assets
x_3 = earnings before interest and tax/total assets
x_4 = market value of equity and preferred stock/total liabilities
x_5 = sales/total assets

The Z values were used to classify firms as either bankrupt or non-bankrupt. Where the Z-score was below 1.81, the firm was considered to be failing; where it was above 2.99 it was healthy. Altman's results were 95%* accurate one year prior to bankruptcy, and 72% accurate two years prior to bankruptcy. The Z-score has been found not to be a good predictor for longer than two years before bankruptcy – which, it could be claimed, is not much use since most investors and banks know (or should know) from more conventional analysis that a firm is headed for insolvency two years before it actually happens.

Altman's work has been applied to U.K. financial data by Argenti[31] and Taffler.[32] Taffler's study concluded that financial gearing and profitability measures were the most significant ratios in predicting failure, and that liquidity ratios are of less importance in predicting a firm's chance of failure than the more fundamental aspects of its structure, such as its earnings ability and the size of its liabilities. Both Argenti and Taffler recognized that the Z-scores used by Altman as cut-offs will be different in the U.K., will differ by industry and will change over time as economic conditions change. Great care must therefore be exercised before relying on the Z-score, or indeed any predictive tool.

A form of linear discriminant analysis has also been used on U.K. data for the period 1972–8 at the London Business School, with the

---

* Subsequent work on later financial data indicated the accuracy of classification one year prior to bankruptcy was only 82%.

result that cash flow to total debt (Beaver's best predictor) and the number of negative cash-flow periods in the last seven years proved to be the most reliable predictors of 'problem' firms.[33]

Summary

This chapter – the longest in the book – has distinguished between the causes and symptoms of failure. Eleven causal factors of decline were identified, although many of the causal factors are interrelated. The factors were: lack of financial control; inadequate management; price and product competition; high cost structure; changes in market demand; adverse movements in commodity markets; lack of marketing effort; big projects; acquisitions; financial policy; and overtrading.

A twelfth factor – organizational structure – was not explicitly stated but was regarded as a factor contributing to high cost structures and lack of control. It is rare that any one factor by itself will precipitate the need for recovery action. The need for recovery is usually brought about by a combination of factors, although lack of financial control and poor management stand out as the most frequent causes of decline. Finally, various symptoms of decline were identified and the methods used for predicting company failure were briefly reviewed.

Notes

1. J. Argenti, *Corporate Collapse: The Causes and Symptoms*, McGraw-Hill, 1976.
2. E. Altman, *Corporate Bankruptcy in America*, Heath, Lexington, Mass., 1971.
3. Charles Handy, *Understanding Organizations*, Penguin Books, 1976.
4. P. Grinyer and D. Norburn, 'Strategic Planning in 21 U.K. Companies', *Long Range Planning*, Vol. 1, No. 4, August 1974, pp. 80–88.
5. B. Scott, 'Stages of Corporate Development', Intercollegiate Case Clearing House, Harvard Business School, Boston 9-371-294, BP 998, 1971.
6. D. Channon, *The Strategy and Structure of British Enterprise*, Macmillan & Co., London, 1973.
7. 'How to Spend a Penny and More Than Save It', *Financial Times*, 29 August 1980.
8. R. Polli and V. Cook, 'The Validity of the Product Life Cycle', *Journal of Business*, Vol. 42, No. 4, October 1969.
9. *Management of New Products*, Booz Allen & Hamilton Inc., New York, 1965.

10. Michael Porter, *Competitive Strategy: Techniques for Analysing Industries and Competitors*, New York Free Press, 1980.
11. R. P. Rumelt, 'How Important is Industry in Explaining Firm Profitability?', UCLA Working Paper, June 1981.
12. W. K. Hall, 'Survival Strategies in a Hostile Environment', *Harvard Business Review*, September–October 1980, pp. 75–85.
13. M. Porter, op. cit., p. 41.
14. 'An Altogether Unusual Chairman', *Financial Times*, 1 April 1982.
15. Charles Handy, 'This is the Age of Apollo', *Across the Board*, May 1980.
16. 'A Bad Record to Live Down', *Financial Times*, 28 February 1980.
17. Ralph Biggadike, 'The Risky Business of Diversification', *Harvard Business Review*, May–June 1979, pp. 103–7.
18. K. Simmonds and S. St P. Slatter, 'The Number of Estimators: A Critical Decision for Marketing under Competitive Bidding', *Journal of Marketing Research*, May 1978, pp. 203–13.
19. J. Kitching, 'Winning and Losing in European Acquisitions', *Harvard Business Review*, March–April 1974.
20. 'Why Mergers Miscarry', *Harvard Business Review*, November–December 1967.
21. G. Mandelker, 'Risk and Return: The Case of Merging Firms', *Journal of Financial Economics*, No. 1, December 1974, pp. 303–5.
22. J. R. Franks, J. E. Broyles and M. J. Hecht, 'An Industry Study of the Profitability of Mergers in the U.K.', *Journal of Finance*, No. 32, December 1977, pp. 1513–25.
23. M. Porter, op. cit., Chapter 16.
24. Charles Handy, *Understanding Organizations*, Penguin Books, 1976.
25. D. Schendel, G. R. Patton and J. Riggs, 'Corporate Turnaround Strategies: A Study of Profit Decline and Recovery', *Journal of General Management*, Vol. 3, No. 3, Spring 1976.
26. See J. Argenti, op. cit., pp. 141–2.
27. W. H. Beaver, 'Financial Ratios as Predictors of Failure', *Journal of Accounting Research*, Vol. 5, pp. 71–111.
28. 'Diagnosis of Financial Health by Cash Flow Analysis', confidential student project, London Business School, 1980.
29. J. W. Wilcox, 'The Gambler's Ruin Approach to Business Risk', *Sloan Management Review*, 1971.
30. E. I. Altman, 'Financial Ratios, Discriminant Analysis and the Prediction of Corporate Bankruptcy', *Journal of Finance*, Vol. 23, No. 4, September 1968, pp. 589–609.
31. J. Argenti, op. cit., Chapter 5.
32. R. J. Taffler and H. J. Tisshaw, 'Going, Going, Gone: Four Factors which Predict', *Accountancy*, Vol. 88, No. 1003, March 1977, pp. 50–52, 54.
33. 'Diagnosis of Financial Health by Cash Flow Analysis', op. cit.

3. Characteristics of Crisis Situations

1. Introduction

If no attempt is made to reverse the causes of decline identified in the previous chapter, a crisis situation will develop. The word 'crisis' has been defined in the management literature as a situation that 'threatens the high-priority goals of the organization [i.e. its survival], restricts the amount of time available for response and surprises decision-makers by its occurrence, thereby engendering high levels of stress'.[1]

Crises originate as threatening events in a firm's environment and from defects within the organization. The purpose of this chapter is to explore further the defects within the organization that give rise to crisis, but also and more importantly, to discuss the way in which crises affect the behaviour of the firm and the individuals in it. Only once we understand the characteristics of crisis situations can we begin to understand the strategies and tactics necessary to end the crisis and effect a successful turnaround.

The forces causing decline are present, to some degree, in all firms. Why is it, therefore, that some firms are able to cope successfully with the problems they face while others end up in a turnaround situation? Some writers on organizational design have identified a variety of factors that facilitate organizational adaptation to changing circumstances and increase the ability of the organization to cope with crisis. By studying these factors we can gain an appreciation of the firm's susceptibility to crisis, and a better understanding of what happens in a crisis situation.

Crisis induces stress, which has a negative impact on managerial behaviour, and this in turn has a deteriorating effect on the whole organization. Crisis tends to accentuate the internal factors causing decline, reinforcing and accelerating the downward trend. If no action is taken to effect a turnaround, the end result is insolvency and failure. The need for a turnaround is usually present in the period of managerial complacency which tends to precede the onset of crisis. With a little luck, something will trigger a turnaround before a severe crisis develops, as happened at Muirhead in the early 1970s;[2] but managerial behaviour will not usually allow this to happen, and outside intervention is necessary to trigger the change process.

2. Susceptibility to Crisis

The causal factors of decline that were identified and discussed in the last chapter interact with one another to cause a crisis to develop. An interesting model of corporate crisis has been proposed by Smart, Thompson and Vertinsky to identify those corporate characteristics which increase or decrease the vulnerability and susceptibility of organizations to crisis.[3] Theirs is a theoretical model rather than one based on empirical observation, but it is interesting because it attempts to relate three groups of causal variables to market performance and susceptibility to crisis. The three groups of variables are:

- competitive and environmental variables (product-market decisions, business cycles, etc.)
- managerial characteristics, such as individual capabilities and management styles
- organizational attributes, such as resources and structures.

For those who like diagrams, the model is illustrated in Figure 3.1.

The causal variables affect crisis susceptibility in the following ways:

(a) The external environment is an important determinant of susceptibility to crisis. A firm competing in a business where there are sharp and unpredictable fluctuations in the environment will have difficulty in maintaining market alignment and will therefore be more susceptible to crisis than a firm in a stable market environment.

(b) Managerial characteristics, such as individual capabilities, personal biases and management styles (together with the organizational attributes discussed below), determine the quality of decision-making in a firm, which in turn affects its susceptibility to crisis. Where decision-making quality is low, the firm is more susceptible to crises: it is less able to cope with a crisis induced by the outside environment and is more likely to generate a crisis internally as the result of operating inefficiencies, conservative financial policies, etc.

(c) Organizational characteristics affect the quality of decision-making but, in addition, they have a more direct effect on crisis susceptibility. The existence of organizational slack – a concept which describes built-

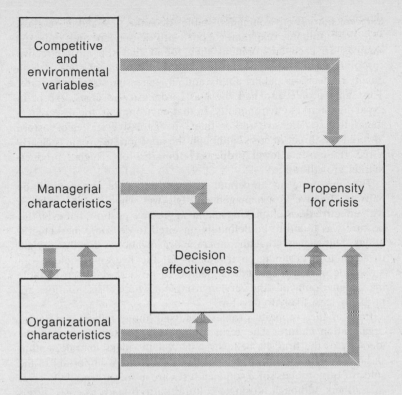

Figure 3.1: *A Simple Model of Crisis Susceptibility*

Source: Adapted from a conceptual model of corporate crisis developed by C. F. Smart, W. A. Thompson and I. Vertinsky, *Journal of Business Administration*, Vol. 9, No. 2, Spring 1978, p. 59. Reprinted by permission.

in inefficiencies or reserves – can increase a firm's resilence to crisis by spreading risk. Organizational characteristics are also important determinants of the firm's ability to implement its decisions: for example, effective implementation requires an organization that is neither overly rigid nor too unpredictable. The size and complexity of an organization also increases the chance of implementation failures.

The many interrelationships that exist between the three groups of variables have been developed into a simulation model by Smart *et al.*, to determine the most appropriate corporate profile for five different market environments: stable, declining, expanding, cyclical and discontinuous (expanding, but with a sudden and dramatic slump).[4] In each environment they found that the most effective corporate profile combined a democratic management style, a high quality of decision-making ability and an aggressive strategic posture. This same profile also had the least propensity to crisis, except in expanding market environments. In that environment, the researchers found that a defensive rather than an aggressive strategic posture lowered the threat of crisis, although the appropriate profile is clearly a risk trade-off: a lower propensity for crisis or a higher product-market growth rate.

The only time an autocratic management style appeared to be halfway effective as a management style was when it was combined with effective decision-making and an aggressive posture, but even this posture was found to be definitely unsuited to *declining* market situations. This suggests that an autocratic organization is usually too rigid to adapt to a declining environment. Of the five environments, an autocratic management style appeared to be best suited to a stable market environment – the very environment where crisis situations are probably least likely to develop.

Each of the corporate profiles discussed above reflects a different organization culture. The term 'organization culture' describes the ideology of the firm: its beliefs, goals, values, ideas, morale, enthusiasm, etc. The concept of an organization culture is important to the study of turnarounds since some cultures are more susceptible to crisis than others, although no single cultural pattern leads to crisis. Firms exhibiting power cultures (the one-man-bands of the previous chapter) and bureaucratic-type role cultures (firms governed by rules and procedures) appear to be most susceptible to crisis. In the power culture, the susceptibility to crisis depends on the quality of the key decision-maker(s), whereas in a role culture, the firm is 'slow to perceive the need for change and slow to change, even if the need is seen'.[5]

The reader should be careful, however, not to fall into the trap of believing that a firm's susceptibility to crisis is easy to diagnose. The processes which produce crisis are substantially the same as those that produce success.[6] There is a fine line between success and failure, and success itself can easily lead to crisis. When firms are successful, they tend to crystallize their successful activities as standardized programmes; but this makes them less sensitive to their environment because they respond to their environment in a standardized way and do not perceive many of the small differences among environmental events. Successful firms are usually able to buffer themselves from their environments (by building up inventories and through vertical integration, for example) and are able to build up slack resources, both of which allow firms to become less sensitive to their environments. By loosening connections with its environment, the firm is in greater control of its destiny (which is important if it is to be successful), but at the same time is increasing the risk of developing erroneous perceptions about its environment.[7]

3. The Impact of Crisis on Managerial Behaviour

How do managers, both individually and as a group, respond to crises, once they have started to develop? As one would expect, response to crisis situations varies with the people concerned and the type of crisis. For some individuals, crises may actually improve the quality of their decision-making, but these individuals are more likely to be turn-around experts who thrive on crisis situations, rather than the existing management of a firm headed towards insolvency. Where poor management is a major causal factor of decline, case-studies clearly show that the capacity of managers to cope with a growing crisis is severely impaired. Management develops what has been referred to by one writer as 'the paranoid reaction characteristic of crisis behaviour'.[8]

I have already defined a crisis situation as one characterized by surprise, short decision time and a high threat to important values. The effect of these three characteristics is to increase the stress on both the organization and the individuals in it. It is generally recognized by students of organizational behaviour that some degree of stress is a necessary prerequisite for problem-solving, for without it there is no motivation to act. However, beyond a certain point stress becomes anxiety-producing rather than motivational and may even lead some individuals to believe that 'the worst would be better than this'.[9] Experimental findings tend to indicate the existence of a curvilinear relationship (an inverted U) between stress and the performance of individuals and groups.[10]

A useful way of showing how crisis situations affect managerial behaviour and decision-making performance is shown in Figure 3.2. While really only a series of hypotheses (since not all the cause and effect relationships have been proven), it appears to be a reasonable

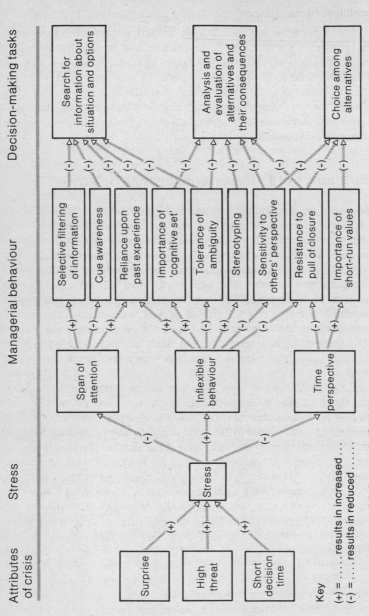

Figure 3.2: *Managerial Behaviour in Crisis*

Source: Adapted from Ole R. Holsti, 'Limitations of Cognitive Abilities in the Face of Crisis', *Journal of Business Administration*, Vol. 9, No. 2, Spring 1978. Reprinted by permission.

representation of the principal effects of a crisis situation. The basic idea is that crisis causes stress, which, in turn, affects managerial behaviour (cognitive performance), which in its turn affects the quality of decision-making. Holsti has identified the major effects of crisis-induced stress as being a reduction in management's span of attention, an increase in their managerial inflexibility and a reduction in their time perspective.[11] I will next examine each of these three effects.

3.1 Reduction in Management's Span of Attention

The beginning of a crisis usually results in a faster pace of activity as individuals begin to realize something has to be done about the threatening situation. In many firms, particularly larger ones, the effect of the faster pace is to increase the volume of communications, resulting in information overload.* The typical managerial response to this phenomenon may take any or all of the following forms:

- the search for information within the communication system becomes less thorough, and management becomes more selective in what it hears and believes
- danger signals are ignored because unpleasant information and information which does not support existing beliefs tend to be rejected
- management responds to information in terms of their own personal predispositions and past experiences
- decision-making becomes increasingly less integrated, which means that less strategic (integrated) decisions are made. Instead, decisions are made on a more simplistic, one-off basis.

3.2 An Increase in Managerial Inflexibility

Intense and protracted stress tends to make individuals extremely inflexible, and to reduce their ability to cope with complex problems. The typical behaviour patterns that have been recognized are:

- tolerance for ambiguity is reduced[12]
- the decision-maker develops a single or dominant view of the world through which he or she interprets information. The view is likely to be a learned response transferred from a previous situation

---

* Information overload could, of course, already be present before a crisis is reached, and may itself be a contributory cause of the crisis in some firms.

- the dominant view is maintained in the face of information which clearly calls for a reappraisal
- the decision-maker's view of the world may be characterized by stereotypes rather than an appreciation of the subtleties of the situation[13]
- the personality characteristics of the decision-maker become emphasized. For example, the anxious become more anxious, the repressors become more repressive, etc.[14]
- there is a trend towards increased autocratic behaviour unless democratic values are unusually well established.[15]

The effect of this behaviour is to reduce the identification of alternative actions and to limit the evaluation of whatever alternatives are identified, consequently reducing the quality of decision-making.

3.3 A Reduction in Management's Time Perspective

Severe stress usually focuses attention on the present and immediate future rather than on longer-range considerations, something which makes sense in a severe financial crisis. However, perceived time pressure may adversely affect decision-making. A moderate level of time pressure can enhance an individual's level of creativity and performance, but beyond a certain level it can be particularly harmful. Complex tasks for which there are no established decision rules or standard operating procedures tend to suffer most from time pressure.[16] Managers tend, in these situations, to adopt a single approach that they have used before and to continue applying it, irrespective of whether it is appropriate.[17] Furthermore, when decision time is short, managers' ability to estimate the consequences of a particular decision is likely to be impaired.

4. The Impact of Crisis on the Organizations

The development of a severe crisis situation does not occur overnight. The typical firm goes through stages of crisis development, although in some firms, particularly where crisis results from rapid growth, some of the stages may be very short. There are four stages of crisis development. Figure 3.3 depicts each of the four stages and the dominant organizational characteristics at each stage.

At the initial stage – the hidden crisis stage – the management group and the organization are unaware of the existence of a crisis. Often,

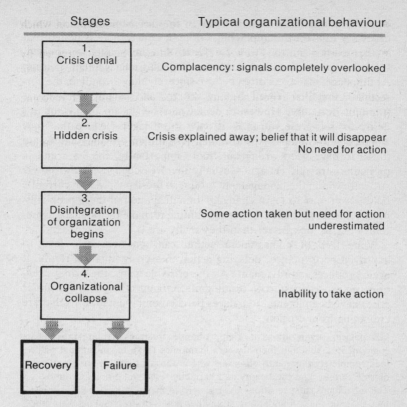

Figure 3.3: *Four Stages of Crisis Development*

this is due to lack of adequate control systems – not just financial control systems, but more informal systems that monitor and interpret unexpected environmental events. Typically, the firm will be complacent and may even be arrogant about its capabilities and market position. Once the signs of crisis become visible within the firm (second stage), management begins to look for reasons to 'explain the crisis away'. Two arguments are often put forward. First, the signs of crisis are attributed to the firm's efforts to change (e.g. new products, new capital investment, etc.) and it is only a matter of time before performance will improve. The second argument is that poor performance results from short-term environmental pressures beyond the control of the firm (e.g. exchange-rate fluctuations, economic recession, etc.).

Both these arguments support the view that no management action is necessary to avert the impending crisis; in effect, there is denial that a crisis exists at all, or at least a denial that any change is required. Optimism about the future is still the prevailing management rhetoric. At this stage, managers often believe sincerely they are still on the correct path, that their overall strategy is correct and that any problems are transient in nature. However, denial may be due to management's desire for self-preservation. Not only do managers believe that they will be blamed and perhaps lose their jobs if their previous actions are found to have been wrong but, more importantly, change – and in particular strategic change – usually involves changes in the power structure within the management group, so those people who currently hold power tend to resist change.[18] In anticipation of these problems, management may start creative accounting to make the financial symptoms of crisis look better than they really are.[19]

While lack of management action can, on occasions, lead to improved performance, delaying action in a crisis situation rarely, if ever, produces improvement. As the crisis deepens, the firm's structure and processes start to disintegrate. Organizations that encounter crises have been likened to palaces perched on mountain-tops that are crumbling from erosion:

Like palaces, organizations are rigid, cohesive structures that integrate elegant components. Although their flawless harmonies make organizational palaces look completely rational to observers who are inside them, observers standing outside can see that the beauty and harmony rest upon eroding grounds . . . The inhabitants' first reactions to crises are to maintain their palaces intact – they shore up shaky foundations, strengthen points of stress and patch up cracks – and their palaces remain sitting beautifully on eroding mountain-tops.[20]

This is the third stage of crisis development: management now recognizes that a crisis exists and takes some actions, but the need is underestimated. Inflexibility and many of the other behavioural characteristics discussed in the previous section begin to affect management. Decision-making groups tend to become smaller at this time as autocracy increases and the perceived need for secrecy and improved co-ordination grows. With less consultation and increasing time pressure, there is a greater tendency to rely more heavily on those who support the prevailing wisdom in the firm. The dissident director or manager with an alternative point of view is increasingly ostracized from the decision-making group.

The actions taken in the third stage do little more, however, than temporarily slow down the process of decay. The palaces start falling apart. But in spite of this, management still continues to send out optimistic press reports stating how 'everything will be O.K. tomorrow'. The classic hockeystick forecast (a short period of continuing decline followed by a sudden and prolonged up-turn in performance) is the order of the day. The organizational cracks eventually cause collapse (fourth stage). It becomes evident to everyone that top management have been making faulty predictions, and severe doubts arise as to whether management is capable of coping with the crisis. If management were any good, surely they would have taken appropriate action in the first or second stage? The processes of disintegration at work in the fourth stage include the following:

- There is a decrease in decision-making behaviour and more general discussion of the need to make decisions.
- Commitment to organizational goals declines and individual managers become more self-oriented.
- The budget cuts and reorganization of the third stage cause power struggles that undermine co-operation and cause top management to centralize control even further.
- Expectation of failure grows, thus making failure more likely.[21]
- The most able people leave, so the average level of competence falls.

These processes reinforce one another. Top management becomes incapacitated and morale declines to an all-time low, causing an even further decline in efficiency.[22] The organization has collapsed. The result is almost certain to be insolvency unless an appropriate recovery strategy can be adopted.

5. Crisis and Change

Once a crisis has become severe and both management as individuals and the organization as a whole have begun to exhibit some of the negative behavioural characteristics discussed in this chapter, dramatic action is necessary if recovery is to be achieved. If the onset of crisis is caught early enough – preferably at the first stage, but no later than the second – a serious crisis can be averted and less dramatic action *may* be enough for recovery to proceed. However, the same order of strategic change, in terms of product-market reorientation, financial policy, control systems, etc., may be necessary at an early stage as at the late stage, since the causes of failure will be the same. What will be different at the early stage will be the amount of organizational change necessary.

The earlier the developing crisis is tackled, the less organizational change will be necessary and the more chance there is of saving the firm and instituting a successful turnaround. Ideally, a firm will embark on a turnaround strategy before a real crisis develops (i.e. at the 'hidden crisis' stage). However, a crisis is frequently necessary before change can be achieved, since it is only then that the necessary organizational *un*learning can take place, and the old management be removed.

Sometimes the disintegration that precedes the start of a turnaround can actually facilitate a turnaround. This arises because organizations have to unlearn what they know before they can start to be 're-programmed'.[23] For example,[24] they have to:

- lose confidence in their old leaders before they will listen to new leaders
- abandon their old objectives before they will adopt new ones
- reject their perceptual filters before they will notice events they had previously overlooked
- see that their old methods do not work before they will invest in and adopt new methods.

The problem of organizational unlearning is important because it relates to managerial judgement, and judgement is a key ingredient in the decision-making process. In making a judgemental decision, a manager draws on his own personal pattern of beliefs and personal biases that he has developed from experience over the years. Some of these beliefs are extremely personal and may be Freudian in nature; others result from the fact the manager has operated in a given business system, such as an industry where there are well-established industry practices. Grinyer and Spender call an industry's pattern of managerial beliefs a 'recipe', although they recognize that within one industry a number of different recipes may co-exist. In their study of recipes in the Newton Chambers Group,[25] Grinyer and Spender found that the firm's commitment to a particular recipe had been reinforced by its past success, and that management adhered to the old recipe even after it had become obsolete. As financial performance declined, Newton Chambers' management adopted tighter financial controls and a policy of more aggressive implementation, which produced only a temporary recovery as slack was absorbed but failed to stop the decline. Only the adoption of a revised recipe brought in by new senior executives led to an eventual turnaround after a long period of severe crisis. Figure 3.4. illustrates the turnaround process as seen by Grinyer and Spender.[26]

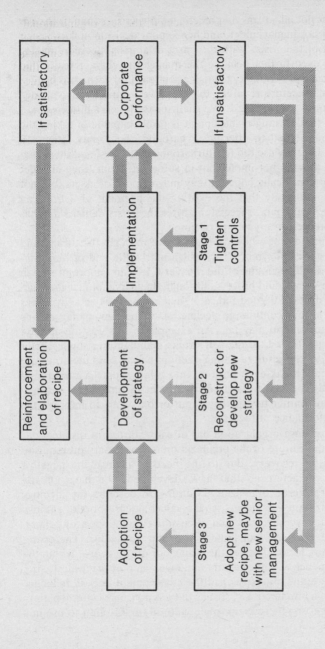

Figure 3.4: *A Model of the Turnaround Process*
Source: P. H. Grinyer and J. C. Spender, 'Recipes, Crises and Adaptation in Mature Businesses', *International Studies of Management and Organisation*, Vol. IX, No. 3, p. 122. Reprinted by permission.

Most – but not all – firms that meet a serious crisis situation already suffer from poor management, and hence poor decision-making, prior to the onset of the crisis. With the onset of a crisis, decision-making deteriorates even further because the managerial characteristics that increase a firm's susceptibility to crisis are intensified once crisis begins. Management therefore is rarely able to serve as an effective change agent to initiate a turnaround. We shall see in the case-histories later in the book that existing management is rarely capable of taking the drastic action needed to effect a turnaround. They may attempt a turnaround, but they use too few turnaround strategies, and those that they do use they do not implement in sufficient depth (they may cut costs, but not drastically enough; they may dispose of assets, but not enough). It is unlikely that the existing management of a firm can implement a turnaround successfully after the crisis denial stage has been in existence for any period of time.

The appointment of a new chief executive to begin the turnaround is, in some senses, a symbolic act which marks the end of the disintegration and the beginning of the recovery. It is an important step in initiating the turnaround process, although the arrival of new management is not of itself a good indicator that recovery is actually under way. The firm may continue to decline, since the new management's attempt at turnaround may fail. An example of this was the attempt to turn around Tizer Ltd, the soft drinks manufacturer, under Peter Quinn in 1970. The result of Quinn's actions was to send the firm from an approximate break-even position into a large loss. A turnaround can only really be said to begin at that point in time when management's actions (either new management or old) start to improve the financial performance of the firm.

For a firm whose organization has already started to disintegrate, a change in the culture of the organization is a necessary prerequisite for a successful recovery, due to the need to change the negative behavioural characteristics that have developed. We have already referred to the term 'organization culture' to describe the ideology of the organization – its beliefs, goals, values, ideas, morale, enthusiasm – although we have confined discussion to one aspect of culture: the effect of crisis on individual and group behaviour. There are, however, many factors besides the behaviour of the people within the firm that influence culture. History and ownership of the firm, its size, the technology, the objectives and the environment may all influence the culture of a firm in crisis.[27] Just as there is no single cultural pattern that leads to crisis, there is no single cultural prescription to use in a turnaround. Any cultural pattern may work. Handy's suggestion that a power culture is most appropriate for crisis situations, however, stands up well in practice, as we shall see when discussing the profile of the successful turnaround manager. This may seem contradictory to what has been said before about power cultures being most susceptible to crisis, but in fact it is not. The success of a power culture depends totally on the quality of the individuals within the organization and the extent to which they like to operate within that culture.

6. Intervention from the Outside

The trigger for change during a severe crisis is more likely to be an intervention from an outside source, most commonly banks or lending institutions, than management itself. To initiate change, the banks often have to precipitate a crisis or make the existing crisis more severe by refusing to extend overdraft facilities. The sequence of events over time is as follows:

Bank expresses concern → Bank expresses deep concern → Bank refuses to extend overdraft → Bank appoints a receiver

If possible, banks prefer not to have to appoint a receiver, although the trend in recent years has been for banks to put a firm into receivership rather more quickly, since early receivership is more likely to mean that the bank's loan is repaid. However, there is a certain stigma attached to a bank calling in receivers, and for most bankers there is a trade-off between their public image and the risk of loss.

As a firm's financial crisis becomes more severe, but before receivership, the bank may find it possible to initiate management changes at board level. Sometimes they may be able to make an extension of borrowing facilities contingent on a new chief executive being appointed; at other times, the most they can achieve is the appointment of a new chief accountant. It is not unknown for banks to lend a firm in distress an accountant on a temporary basis or to insist that a firm receives 'intensive care' from turnaround consultants or an independent firm of accountants. However, the clearing banks' record in initiating management change in the United Kingdom is not particularly good; that of the merchant banks appears to be better.

Another group of outsiders who increasingly are taking a role in instituting management changes are the institutional investors. Traditionally, institutions such as insurance companies and pension funds have avoided taking an active management role, as have the banks; but in recent years they have started to take a bigger 'behind-the-scenes role' (often in conjunction with the merchant banks) in obtaining management changes. The group that is potentially most influential in obtaining change are non-executive directors, if they exist. In theory they should have the best information, but very often they are powerless. Typically, they are appointed because they are friendly with existing management, not because they are independent outsiders who will audit management's performance. Non-executive directors can resign in protest against management's actions or inactions. . . . but they rarely do. The type of impact that turnaround manager Angus Murray had as a non-executive director at Newman Industries is very rare. In that situation, he agitated relentlessly against the way the group was being run by chairman Alan Bartlett, he refused to resign under pressure from the board, and eventually, with the assistance of one of the institutions, he managed to remove Bartlett.[28]

Change of ownership, usually by acquisition, is clearly the easiest way to initiate change. The old management can be replaced immediately; and the new parent company can, if it wishes, transfer resources in the form of cash and management skills to the ailing firm. These acts will not of themselves put an end to the crisis, but they do put an end to the threat of insolvency and give the necessary impetus for change.

Notes

1. Charles F. Hermann, 'Some Consequences of Crisis which Limit the Viability of Organizations', *Administrative Science Quarterly*, 1963, No. 8, pp. 61–82.
2. See case-history: Muirhead, p. 321.
3. C. F. Smart, W. A. Thompson and I. Vertinsky, 'Diagnosing Corporate Effectiveness and Susceptibility to Crises', *Journal of Business Administration*, Vol. 9, No. 2, Spring 1978.
4. Ibid.
5. Charles Handy, *Understanding Organizations*, Penguin Books, 1976, Chapter 7.
6. Bo L. T. Hedberg, Paul C. Nystrom and William H. Starbuck, 'Camping on Seesaws: Prescriptions for a Self-designing Organisation', *Administrative Science Quarterly*, 1976, No. 21, pp. 41–65.

7. William H. Starbuck, Arent Greve and Bo L. T. Hedberg, 'Responding to Crisis', *Journal of Business Administration*, Vol. 9, No. 2, Spring 1978.

8. Richard E. Neustadt, *Alliance Politics*, Columbia University Press, New York, 1970, p. 116.

9. See, for example, Kurt Back, 'Decisions under Uncertainty: Rational, Irrational and Non-rational', *American Behavioral Scientist*, No. 4, February 1961, pp. 14–19.

10. See, for example, Robert E. Murphy, 'Effects of Threat of Shock, Distraction and Task Design on Performance', *Journal of Experimental Psychology*, 1959, No. 58, pp. 134–41.

11. Ole R. Holsti, 'Limitations of Cognitive Abilities in the Face of Crisis', *Journal of Business Administration*, Vol. 9, No. 2, Spring 1978.

12. C. D. Smock, 'The Influence of Psychological Stress or the Intolerance of Ambiguity', *Journal of Abnormal and Social Psychology*, Vol. 50, 1955, pp. 177–82.

13. Ralph K. White and Ronald Lippit, *Autocracy and Democracy: An Experimental Inquiry*, Harper Bros, New York, 1960.

14. Thomas W. Milburn, 'The Management of Crisis', in Charles F. Hermann (ed.), *International Crises. Insights from Behavioural Research*, The Free Press, New York, 1972, pp. 259–80.

15. J. A. Litterer, *The Analysis of Organisations*, Wiley, New York, 1973.

16. J. Bruner, J. Goodnow and G. Austin, *A Study of Thinking*, John Wiley & Sons, New York, 1956.

17. John Steinbruner, *The Cybernetic Theory of Decision*, Princeton University Press, Princeton, New Jersey, 1974.

18. Richard Normann, 'Organisational Innovativeness: Product Variation and Reorientation', *Administrative Science Quarterly*, 1971, No. 16, pp. 203–15.

19. John Argenti, op. cit.

20. William H. Starbuck, op. cit.

21. Albert S. King, 'Expectation Effects in Organisational Change', *Administrative Science Quarterly*, 1974, No. 19, pp. 221–30.

22. Irving Janis. *Victims of Group Think*, Houghton Mifflin, Boston, 1972.

23. Bo L. T. Hedberg, 'How Organisations Learn and Unlearn', in Paul Nystrom and William Starbuck (eds.), *Handbook of Organisational Design*, Oxford University Press, 1981.

24. Richard M. Cyert and James G. March, *A Behavioural Theory of the Firm*, Prentice Hall, 1963.

25. Peter Grinyer and J. C. Spender, *Turnaround: Managerial Recipes for Strategic Success*, Associated Business Publications, 1979.

26. Peter Grinyer and J. C. Spender, 'Recipes, Crises and Adaptation in Mature Businesses', *International Studies of Management and Organisation*, 1979, Vol. IX, No. 3, pp. 113–33.

27. Charles Handy, op. cit.

28. 'Meet the Acceptable Face of Capitalism', *Sunday Times*, 2 March 1980.

4. Elements of a Successful Recovery Strategy

A successful recovery strategy consists of a number of generic turn-around strategies used in combination. I have identified ten major generic strategies which firms commonly use. This chapter discusses each of the ten strategies separately, while the following chapter discusses how these generic strategies are combined to formulate an appropriate recovery strategy in a given situation.

The ten generic strategies are:

- change of management
- strong central financial control
- organizational change and decentralization
- product-market reorientation
- improved marketing
- growth via acquisitions
- asset reduction
- cost reduction
- investment
- debt restructuring and other financial strategies.

1. Change of Management

1.1. New Chief Executive

Most, but not all, turnaround situations require new chief executives, since inadequate top management is the single most important factor leading to decline and stagnation. A change in top management may occur even if the need for turnaround was brought about by factors beyond the control of management. In such situations the chief executive becomes the scapegoat for the firm's problems, but his removal is tangible evidence to bankers, investors and employees that something positive is being done to improve the firm's performance.

The appointment of a new chief executive always has symbolic importance in that it is punishing the former chief executive whose strategies have threatened the very survival of the firm and with it the livelihood of the employees and others who are dependent on the firm. More importantly, however, a new chief executive is required to provide new perceptions of reality, develop new strategies and revitalize the organization.

Just as important as the decision to replace the chief executive, and therefore strategic in nature, is the decision as to the type of person required to be the new chief executive of a firm in need of turnaround. If the wrong man (or woman) is chosen, then the strategies and methods of implementation he (or she) decides upon to effect a turnaround may well be wrong, and the result will be insolvency. There are two schools of thought as to the appropriate type of person: one school believes that all the firm needs is an individual with good general management skills and no specific industry experience; the other school favours individuals who have had general management experience in the same or a very similar industry to that of the firm needing turnaround. Neither view is invariably correct – the answer depends on the characteristics of the turnaround firm. Is it a single business entity with a single general manager, or a diversified firm with requirements for general managers at both the corporate (or group) level and the subsidiary or operating unit level?

One useful concept to help us analyse the management problem is the concept of industry 'receipes'. In Chapter 3 we saw that when a recipe to which a firm is committed becomes obsolete, an adjustment in the firm's pattern of beliefs is required to reorient the firm. There are two ways of achieving this: by major innovation or by imitation of an already successful recipe. Grinyer and Spender suggest that imitation is both quicker (an important factor in turnarounds) and safer than innovation, and that the quickest way of imitating is the 'introduction of a tried, tested and currently successful recipe brought in by a chief executive with a track record of recent successes within the industry'.[1] One of the principal advantages of bringing in such an individual is that the period of learning that would otherwise be necessary before a new, viable product-market strategy can be formulated is done away with. Another advantage is that a new chief executive with an industry track-record is often in a better position to 'rally the management and shop-floor workforce previously demoralized by the persistent failure of the old methods of operating'.[2] There are dangers, however, in using the imitative approach. If the best recipe available within the industry is no longer suited to the environmental forces affecting the industry, then an imitative approach is no good.

The appointment of chief executives with appropriate industry experience should not be regarded as a cure-all. Many of the generic turnaround strategies discussed in this chapter can be implemented without a deep knowledge of the industry (e.g. financial control systems, debt restructuring and organizational change). Furthermore – and this is a key issue – an executive with industry experience who has been 'successful' in the industry but does not have experience in managing a turnaround situation may not be as good as an experienced turnaround man with no relevant industry experience.

A new chief executive's lack of industry experience tends to be *less important* in those situations where the turnaround firm is a diversified group consisting of a number of different businesses. There are at the very least two levels of turnaround management in these firms: the corporate (or group) management, headed by the group chief executive; and the management of the individual business units, each headed by a general manager or managing director. If a turnaround is needed at the business unit level, the issue as to whether industry experience is necessary for the general manager is similar to that of the single business firm discussed above. At the corporate level the issue is somewhat different. Just how important any specific industry experience is at this level depends on the nature and extent of the diversification. Is it related diversification with a common technology or customer base; or is it unrelated diversification of a conglomerate nature? The more related the business, the more some specific industry experience is likely to be valuable; but even where diversification is related, the job of the group chief executive is quite different from that of the chief executive of a single business firm, or of a business unit of a diversified firm. The group chief executive in the diversified firm manages a portfolio of businesses in the same way as an investment manager manages a portfolio of shares. He can buy and sell businesses, invest cash in growth businesses and receive dividends from stable and mature businesses. But there is one very important difference between the group chief executive and an investment manager: the chief executive *controls* his businesses, whereas the investment manager does not. Control is exercised in two ways: through financial control and through selection of the chief executives of the operating units or divisions. Viewing a diversified firm as a 'controlled portfolio' has become a widely adopted 'recipe' among those concerned with managing firms of this type during the 1970s.

In a turnaround situation, however, this recipe may well not work. The typical response of the group chief executive and his corporate team is to tighten financial control over the operating subsidiaries and to put heavy pressure on the subsidiary chief executives to achieve sales and profit targets. When a subsidiary's performance fails to improve, the subsidiary chief executive is replaced. This pattern was found to have occurred in the Newton Chambers engineering group prior to its acquisition by Central and Sheerwood. In one subsidiary, the chief executives were found to have lasted, on average, only eighteen months throughout the 1960s.[3] A similar rapid turnover of management also occurred at Redman Heenan International (see Chapter 12), and there are many other examples. Part of the problem arises because the group chief executive does not have sufficient in-depth understanding of the diverse businesses under his control. Thus, when it comes to replacing the subsidiary chief executive, nobody can judge whether a candidate has the necessary experience-based beliefs and abilities to be successful at running that particular business. What happens too often is that the group chief executive hires people with general management ability like himself, or with a track record in the type of business he believes the subsidiary to be in, rather than an individual with the necessary recipe for success. Where the group chief executive recruits individuals like himself, these individuals often have a good understanding of the financially oriented corporate recipe for managing a diversified firm, but they do not have the relevant experience to make the product-market decisions necessary for success. Basing their proposals on their study of changing group recipes at Central and Sheerwood, Grinyer and Spender propose the use of divisional chairmen, positioned between the group chief executive and the operating chief executives.[4] These divisional chairmen are not just mini-group chief executives who know the corporate recipe but, much more importantly, they know and understand the recipes needed by the operating units in their division. They act as communicators between corporate management and operating management. They must be powerful enough to support the operating unit at the corporate level and interpret financial data in operationally meaningful terms; at the same time they must be sensitive to corporate needs by implementing their requirements at the operating company level.

Not every good manager is good in a turnaround situation. It may be, for example, that an executive with industry experience who is used to operating in a large firm with detailed plans, rules and procedures cannot operate in the fast-paced turnaround environment; or a good executive may have been in one firm so long that he believes there is only one 'right way of doing things', in which case he may be too inflexible because the turnaround firm does not have the resources to work his way. Problems of this type are common when turnaround managers are recruited from large, bureaucratic firms in stable industries. The key word here is 'bureaucratic', because some large firms have a record of producing competent turnaround managers. The best example in the United Kingdom is G.E.C.; it is well known for its sound management methods and has produced many turnaround managers from its executive ranks (for instance, Dr Adolf Frankel at Staveley Industries and Brian Gould at Redman Heenan International).

The turnaround man needs to have special characteristics and skills that may be different from those required in a healthy firm. A turnaround situation requires a chief executive with: considerable leadership and motivational skills; flexibility; the ability and courage to make rapid decisions based on a minimum of analysis; the ability to work long hours under stress; and, most importantly, the ability to implement the turnaround strategies in the shortest possible time.

The characteristics required of the group chief executive in a diversified firm have been identified as: a broad field of vision; a questioning attitude towards the recipes adopted; a wide exposure to senior managers in industries with different recipes; and breadth of experience among key executives.[5]

Some of the decisions that the turnaround manager has to make are likely to be unpopular within the firm. There may be considerable resistance to change at all levels in the organization, and this makes the job of implementing unpopular decisions very difficult. For this reason, the type of person who has tended to be most successful as a turnaround manager is often a tough, no-nonsense manager who knows very clearly what he wants to do and will not allow anybody or anything to get in his way. These managers are not out to win popularity contests and, as a student once said, 'Many of these individuals will be the first to go when the revolution arrives!' They operate in a power culture: they are the centre of the firm, they make all the key decisions, and everyone knows it.

There are, however, two stereotypes that fit this profile of a turnaround manager: there are those who are openly tough, who are often abrasive, are disliked by many people but are respected because of what they can achieve; and then there are those who have the same toughness but who are naturally polite, courteous and even genteel. A student of mine once wrote, after interviewing a (successful) turnaround manager, who is regarded in the City as ruthless and lacking in integrity: 'He has the air of a country vicar, and appears quite unlike the stereotype hatchet man.'

We will see in Chapter 5 that the firm goes through a number of phases on its way to recovery. Many turnaround managers are, unfortunately, only good at operating in the early phases of recovery, not in the later ones when the emphasis is on building the organization for the long term. There appear to be three reasons for this. First, a number of successful turnaround managers have admitted to me that they become bored as soon as the excitement of the crisis situation has died down: they get a real sense of achievement out of dealing with crisis but do not get the same feeling from building up an organization, which is altogether a slower process. In short, they lose interest after about two years and begin to look for another turnaround situation. The second reason relates to the experience of the turnaround manager: he may be good as a hatchet-man, but is not familiar with the industry recipes necessary to obtain growth in existing and new product-market areas. The third reason why a single turnaround manager may not be good at running the firm during both phases of recovery relates to the way the organization responds to the actions taken during the survival phase. The issue is sometimes put more bluntly: is the hatchet-man, who has implemented cost reduction and asset reduction strategies, etc., the right person to build the organization for the long term? Will the lower levels of management and the employees ever trust a hatchet-man? Some people believe not, but there are many examples of managers who have undertaken both roles successfully in the same firm. The answer really lies in that difficult-to-define concept we call 'leadership'. The manager who is *only* effective as a hatchet-man is unlikely to be a real leader. His principal method of motivation will be fear – which may produce short-term results but is unlikely to be successful in the longer term.

1.2. Other Management

Views vary enormously among turnaround experts as to the need for major management changes at the level below that of the chief executive. At one extreme there is the following conclusion drawn from a Swedish study on responding to crisis:

Indiscriminate replacement of entire groups of top managers is evidently essential to bring organizations out of crises. The veteran top managers ought to be replaced even if they are all competent people who are trying their best and even if the newcomers have no more ability, and less direct expertise, than the veterans.[6]

One of the reasons for this belief is that, despite the efforts of the new chief executive, management may continue to adhere to the firm's traditional methods of operating, either because they refuse to change (because they believe the old ways are best) or because they are intellectually unable to adjust to the management approach adopted by the new chief executive. Some turnaround managers seek to re-educate their new colleagues, who they believe are 'not all bad', but this usually takes more time and energy than is available in a turnaround situation, where immediate results are usually required. Consequently, it is very common to hear turnaround managers criticize themselves for 'keeping a few managers too long'.

At the opposite extreme is the view that only the chief executive needs replacing, and that the new chief executive should work with existing management *as far as possible*. As usual with issues of this type, the best answer (there is no single correct answer) is likely to fall somewhere between the two views, depending on the characteristics of the turnaround situation. It is in fact rare that there are no other management changes. As we have seen, a lack of adequate control systems is the most common cause of failure, that usually points to the need to appoint a new finance director or controller, even if there are no other management changes. So important is the finance function in a turnaround situation that one well-known American turnaround expert, Sandy Sigoloff,[7] believes that the new chief executive officer should also be chief financial officer in the early days of the turnaround.

The need to replace management will depend to a large extent on the causes and speed of decline that preceded the turnaround. Where decline has been due to failure in a firm's peripheral activities or to poor financial strategy, few operating managers have usually been involved with the decline phase. For these reasons, no major managerial changes were made at Burmah Oil below the level of the chief executive. Also, where the decline has been brought on by too-rapid growth, the management problem is often only one of lack of control, and few changes are required outside the financial function. On the other hand, where decline is slow (perhaps lasting many years), there is a greater likelihood that any good managers the firm had will have left before a turnaround is initiated.

However, the speed and cause of decline are not the only factors influencing the need to change management. Both the management style of the new chief executive and the business culture in which he is operating will determine whether there is to be a major clear-out of the old management or only selected replacement. Some chief executives actually enjoy the power they derive from firing people; in some business cultures, such as that in the United States, there are likely to be more management changes than in others. A study of turnarounds of Californian growth firms indicated that there were major management changes at all management levels, despite the fact that all the firms were characterized by a very rapid decline phase.[8]

2. Strong Central Financial Control

The introduction of strong, central financial control at the beginning of a turnaround is virtually a law of turnaround situations. In Chapter 6 we will review the major controls that are necessary in a typical situation but, basically, financial control means cash flow forecasts, budgets, detailed knowledge of the manufacturing and overhead costs, and control over capital expenditure. Control needs to be centralized under the new chief executive (working with his financial director) because, in a turnaround, strict financial controls need to be imposed on the organization. The prevailing management culture of most turnaround situations is not geared towards strong financial control, with the result that, if less autocratic methods are used, the implementation process will take too long. For example, we know that when one firm is acquired by another, and the acquirer wishes to implement his own financial control systems in the acquired firm but does not want to upset the management, the implementation process can take three and even up to five years on occasions. In a turnaround, some form of effective system has to be operational within a matter of weeks, even if it is not an 'ideal' system. Consequently the use of a participative management approach in introducing and using new and improved control systems is not recommended in turnaround situations. One cannot, of course, expect the imposition of tight controls from above to be welcomed by lower- and middle-management levels; there will be resistance to change, but this is a management challenge that has to be faced. One way of helping to overcome this resistance is to couple tight central financial control with an organizational strategy of decentralizing decision-making responsibility.

3. Organizational Change and Decentralization

Organizational change should *not* be contemplated as a short-term turnaround strategy except under special conditions. It is often said that organizational change is riskier than strategic change,[9] but this is never so true as in a turnaround situation, where it can direct attention away from the economic problems facing the business. The reasons for this are as follows:

(a) The appropriate organization structure for a firm is determined at least in part by the firm's product-market strategy. Until such a strategy has been formulated, major organizational change is usually premature, even though analysis of the firm may indicate the existence of organizational problems such as lack of co-ordination, poor communications, too wide a span of control, etc. Organizational prob-lems are often *symptoms* of strategic problems, with the result that reorganization has little or no effect on the firm's performance except to cause confusion and mask the real problems facing the firm. I often refer to organization change as the 'aspirin effect': it attacks the symp-toms and not the causes.

(b) A new chief executive knows neither the strengths and weaknesses of the individuals in the firm nor how the 'informal organization struc-ture' works in the early days of a turnaround. It is totally inappropriate to design an organization based solely on what arrangement of boxes would, in theory, optimize co-ordination, communication and motiv-ation, for example. One cannot draw boxes and put people in them; one needs to balance the need for a logical structure against the personal and professional characteristics of the available management. Furthermore, one needs to know how the organization actually works in practice. Formal reporting relationships often bear no relation to reality, and it is more important to understand who lunches with whom or who plays golf with whom, to understand how decisions are actually made. The new turnaround manager, however perceptive, cannot have the in-depth understanding needed to make the correct decisions within days or even weeks of his arrival.

(c) Changing the organization is not merely a question of drawing up a new organization chart, writing new job-descriptions where appro-priate, and informing everyone of the changes. If this is all that is done, it is quite likely that the organization will either be totally confused or will continue to operate in exactly the same way it did before the changes were announced. Organizational change requires a consider-able amount of learning on the part of the firm. This takes considerable management time and effort, something which is likely to be scarce in the early stages of a turnaround.

There are at least four situations, however, under which a change in the organization structure may be useful and necessary. First, restruc-turing the organization may be necessary to facilitate the divestiture of part of the business. For example, we can see in retrospect that this was done at Colston Ltd, where the firm was divisionalized, allowing the loss-making Domestic Appliance Division to be sold off, thereby saving the group from almost certain receivership. Second, change can assist the chief executive to gain management control over the firm. One common organizational change that may take place almost as soon as a new turnaround manager is appointed is a *widening* of the span of management control at the top of the firm. Whether this occurs depends on the management style of the turnaround manager, but if he exhibits the typical characteristics discussed in section 1.1 of this chapter, he will want to operate in a power culture and gain management control rapidly. This approach can work well in a turnaround crisis. Organizational changes of this type are often found to be necessary when the turnaround firm is owner-managed, family-dominated, or where some manager has been running part of the firm as a private fiefdom. In these situations it may be impossible for the banks or minority shareholders to force out the chief executive or a particular family member completely. In fact, it may even be part of the negotiations with the bank (or whoever else is triggering the turnaround mechanism) that a turnaround manager will only be allowed in on the condition that Mr X remains in his job. Another situation in which a particular director – whom I will refer to as Henry – could not be fired was in the turnaround of a photographic equipment company, where Henry was the Agency Director who had close personal contacts with the overseas principals. The turnaround was an acquisition situation and all the agency agreements had become void, with the obvious danger that Henry, if fired, might be able to persuade the principals to sign new agency agreements with him personally or help them to set up their own U.K. distribution company. Although totally unco-operative with the turnaround team, Henry could not be fired; instead, he was removed from day-to-day operations such as purchasing and pricing, and given a staff position as Director of Agency Relations! The solution adopted in most situations is to push the former management 'upstairs' or 'sideways' so that the turnaround manager can take over effective day-to-day management of the firm, the division or the department.

The third situation in which structural change in the organization may be useful is found in *large* firms. Turning around a firm the size of British Leyland, for example, is altogether a different situation from turning around a manufacturing firm with annual sales revenues of, say, £50 million and 4,000 employees. In the large firm, a quick turnaround is almost impossible to achieve unless the cause of decline is a one-off event that has not adversely affected the core business (e.g. Burmah Oil). Where the turnaround is of a firm with a dominant core business which is in trouble, the appointment of an experienced chief executive and a new finance director is unlikely to have the same impact as in a smaller firm. The larger the firm, the more time the chief executive needs to spend building up his management team. There is a limit to what one man can do; he can formulate the strategy, but he needs competent management to implement it down the line. Thus, as soon as a firm gets too big for the chief executive to play a meaningful role in the day-to-day implementation of strategy, the turnaround process slows down and becomes more dependent on organizational development. Team-building, in particular, becomes important; but where management talent is short, there is much more likelihood of the organization structure being altered to fit the skills of the available management talent.

All three situations that have been outlined so far as exceptions to the rule of minimizing organizational change in the early days of a turnaround involve structural changes only at the highest management level. None of these exceptions involves changing the organization at middle-management levels and below. The impact of the fourth exception – organizational change to facilitate decentralization of decision-making – may, however, make its way right down the organization to the factory floor, depending on management's inclination. Many successful turnarounds are characterized by decentralization of decision-making to the general managers of operating units, while at the same time maintaining strong central financial control. Examples in this book include Staveley Industries (page 271), Redman Heenan International (page 279), the RFD Group (page 295) and Ferranti (page 359).

Decentralization may occur without any change in the organization structure, but two changes are often necessary. First, divisionalization may have to precede or accompany decentralization if the organizational structure of the firm is highly centralized to begin with (which, as we saw in Chapter 2, is a common characteristic of declining firms). Divisionalization (or breaking up the firm into operating units, each under the profit and loss responsibility of a general manager) is usually both necessary and possible in anything but a very small firm with only a few hundred employees. Most firms that have grown beyond the entrepreneurial stage are somewhat diversified and present opportunities for divisionalization. The optimum size for an operating unit will depend in part on the industry (the minimum efficient plant size, for example); but an increasing number of professional managers have come to believe that an operation utilizing more than 1,000 people is unwieldy from an organizational point of view. At that point or thereabouts, the chief executive loses touch with the workforce.

The second instance in which the process of decentralization usually demands organizational change occurs when decentralization is carried down the firm below the level of the subsidiary general manager. More often than not, decentralization by a group chief executive in a turnaround situation stops at the next level down in the hierarchy. A number of manufacturing firms, however, have claimed to be successful in improving productivity by flattening their pyramidal organization structure and giving more real responsibility to their supervisory and first-line management personnel. The result is greater job satisfaction for first-line management, more efficiency on the production line, and fewer layers of middle management. Information flows are improved both up and down the organization because lines of communication are shorter; but for decentralization of this nature to work effectively, management must adopt a policy of frequent and open communication with the shop floor. This issue is discussed further in Chapter 6.

Coupled with the move towards decentralization, one often finds a reduction in the size of head-office staff. Staff functions such as personnel, training, corporate marketing, planning and public relations are just a few of the non-productive head-office functions that are commonly cut back or eliminated altogether as part of a recovery strategy. In the large, diversified firm these functions are often second-guessing divisional management and rarely, if ever, assisting them to make better decisions. The head office 'specialists' are rarely cost-effective and are not needed if competent management is hired to run the divisional business units. Most of the work undertaken at head office is better carried out at the divisional level. It is no accident that the most successful diversified firms operate with very small numbers of people at head office.[10] The only head-office function of any size in a turnaround situation should be finance – which would consist of a treasury function, dealing with the firm's financial requirements (managing cash and dealing with the banks), and a financial control function, responsible for monitoring the business units and consolidating group financial results.

4. New Product-market Focus

Where one of the major causes of the firm's decline is lack of competitiveness in one or more of its product-market segments, it is imperative that the firm refocus its overall product-market strategy if sustainable recovery is to take place. Refocusing may also be necessary where the cause of decline is rapid growth. When profits decline as sales continue to grow, there is usually a need to refocus the firm's product-market strategy, since much of the marginal business the firm has obtained is likely to be unprofitable. Refocusing may involve:

- addition or deletion of product lines
- addition or deletion of customers (by customer type and/or by geographical area)
- changes in the sales mix by focusing marketing efforts on specific products and/or specific customers
- complete withdrawal from a market segment
- entry into a new product-market segment.

The decision to change product-market strategy is made by evaluating the appropriateness of both the firm's current strategy and all the strategic options open to the firm. The evaluation process is basically a question of finding the best match between the resources of the firm and the opportunities available to it – put another way, relating what the firm is *able to do* with respect to its resources with what is *possible* in the external environment. In practice, two types of product-market strategy are observable: those aimed at survival and short-term profits, and those aimed at long-term, sustainable recovery.

(a) Product-market strategies for short-term profitability: Where survival is a key issue, the short-time horizon means that product-market decisions are often of a surgical nature. The firm pulls out of complete business areas, either by closure or divestiture, and cuts out product lines and/or customers which are unprofitable or where the return on capital employed is too low. The emphasis is on cutting back the business to its profitable core. This is easy where the core is strong and only the firm's peripheral activities are weak. It is more difficult to achieve where the core itself is non-viable, in which case the chances of a successful turnaround are slim and the firm is likely to fail eventually.

Slightly less drastic are strategies which involve a shift in the sales mix by concentrating marketing efforts on selected product or customer groups where the short-term profit potential is greater. This does not necessarily mean focusing on those products or customers that show the highest percentage gross-profit margin – as we shall see in Chapter 10.

(*b*) *Product-market strategies for sustainable recovery*: Growth-oriented strategies are only possible once survival is assured or in turnarounds of stagnant firms where there is no financial crisis. The time horizon required to implement growth strategies is usually considerably longer than that required to drop products and customers. The major growth strategies which involve a change in product-market focus are new product development strategies (introducing new products to the firm's existing customer base), market development strategies (introducing existing products to new customers) and diversification (entering totally new areas of business). These strategies rarely work in a crisis situation. They divert management's attention from the problem at hand and often result in considerable extra revenue expenditure.

In his book, *Competitive Strategy*,[11] Michael Porter identifies three generic product-market strategies which can be used successfully to protect a firm against the forces that drive competition in an industry. These benchmark strategies are a cost leadership strategy (as adopted, for example, by the Japanese in the industries where they compete on a global basis), a product differentiation strategy and, lastly, a focused strategy. The latter involves the firm in selecting a narrow product-market segment in which it competes on the basis of cost leadership and/or product differentiation. It involves focusing the firm's limited resources on one or a few product-market segments, and either immediate or phased withdrawal from other segments. This is the only strategy that is available to the turnaround firm in the short term, since it is unlikely to have the large financial resources required for industry leadership based on either cost or product differentiation factors. If the turnaround firm is in an industry where a cost leadership strategy is the only one open to it (due to the commodity nature of the product), then the situation is clearly not recoverable. Where strategies based primarily on product differentiation are possible, the adoption of a more aggressive marketing strategy (see page 93) may help the turnaround firm improve its short-term market position, providing the product is not obsolete and aggressive selling rather than aggressive advertising is the key factor for industry success. If a considerable amount of new product development is required or large amounts of advertising money are required, a product differentiation strategy is possible only *after* survival has been assured.

The adoption of a focused strategy may of itself lead to a sustainable recovery, particularly if the chosen product-market segment is too small to be of interest to the industry leaders, or if the turnaround firm is better able to service customers' needs because the industry leaders are too diversified, too large or too bureaucratic. At other times, a focused strategy will provide the turnaround firm with 'breathing space' at a time when it lacks competitive advantage *vis-à-vis* the industry leaders. There are two dangers, however, in adopting a focused strategy. First, the adoption of a focused strategy may cause the firm's unit cost structure to deteriorate as volume – and hence economies of scale – is reduced. Both variable and fixed unit costs may increase. For example, variable costs may increase as purchasing power declines, and unit overhead costs may increase as fixed costs fail to decline in proportion to the reduction in sales volume. Second, the firm may find that a focused strategy is not a defensible strategy in the long term. This is often the case in those situations where focusing means adopting a segment-retreat strategy: a strategy under which the firm pulls out of the high-volume, price-sensitive segments of the market and concentrates on the least price-sensitive segments, where having lower unit costs than one's competitors is not so critical for success. The British motorcycle industry provides a good example.

As Japanese competitors – Honda, Yamaha and Kawasaki – attacked the high-volume, price-sensitive, small bike segment (below 125 c.c. engine capacity) of the motorcycle market in the 1960s, the British manufacturers phased out of that segment and concentrated on bikes with larger engine capacities. The Japanese, however, then attacked the 250 c.c.–500 c.c. segments, causing the less efficient and less marketing-oriented U.K. manufacturers to retreat to the large bike (over 500 c.c.) segment only. By the mid 1970s, the British were left as competitors only in the superbike segment (over 750 c.c.), but that area proved indefensible. The Japanese were by now many times the size of their U.K. competitors and over the years had been working hard to build up product differentiation advantages in the form of good brand-names, superior product quality and good distribution networks.

There are many other examples of U.K. firms – firms which are not referred to in this book as classic turnaround situations – that are in the process of adopting a focused strategy to improve profitability. Most of these are to be found in the declining industries referred to in Chapter 1. In the textile industry, for example, Courtaulds, ICI and Carrington-Viyella, all historically regarded as blue-chip British firms, have explicitly adopted focused strategies during 1980/82. Thus ICI pulled out of the low-value high-volume polyester filament business and concentrated its efforts on nylon.[12] Carrington-Viyella is focusing its efforts away from the high-volume low-value knitted goods and garments towards more specialized products.[13] British Leyland, on the other hand – a firm which is clearly out of focus at the present time, in that it is attempting to compete in both the low-volume specialist car market (e.g. Jaguar) and the high-volume mass market (e.g. Austin-Morris) – has decided *not* to adopt a focused strategy for recovery. The reasons for this are essentially political and are discussed in Chapter 11.

Clearly, the adoption of a focused strategy will not guarantee recovery. The viability of a focused strategy depends on the characteristics of the industry and the firm, and it may provide nothing more than a breathing-space while the firm works on developing a growth strategy aimed at sustainable recovery. Some firms adopt a focused strategy and fail because their strategy implementation is too slow. By the time they have actually focused their resources, any competitive advantage they might formerly have had in the segment they are focusing on has been eroded, or their resources have been so depleted that focusing means no additional resources are available for implementing the focused strategy (e.g. Alfred Herbert, see page 264). In Part Four we will see a variety of examples where focusing has been both an *adequate* product-market strategy for sustainable recovery (as at Redman Fisher Engineering) and an *inadequate* strategy (as at Inveresk).

5. Improved Marketing

Turnaround firms characterized by poor management rarely – if ever – have a well-executed marketing plan. The generic strategy referred to here as 'improved marketing' describes how the firm maximizes its profit potential within the product-market segments in which it has chosen to compete by adjusting the key elements of the marketing mix: product line, selling, pricing, distribution channels, advertising and promotion, service, etc. The most commonly used elements of the marketing mix in turnaround situations are selling and pricing.

We saw in the last chapter that turnaround firms usually contain a considerable degree of organizational slack. This is nowhere more evident than within the salesforce. Salesforce management is often weak, providing neither leadership nor control. Sales targets and call patterns are non-existent, salesmen are unmotivated and left on their own to roam aimlessly over their assigned territories. By installing new and more aggressive sales management capable of motivating the salesforce, a sudden increase in sales volume can often be achieved. Some changes in the salesforce may be required if the firm is to operate at maximum efficiency; but it is quite likely that at least one-half of the existing salesforce will be capable of considerably improved results, given the right motivation and direction. The adoption of a more aggressive selling effort depends on the turnaround firm's ability to supply the customer and its ability to finance the increased level of inventories and debtors that may be necessary as volume increases. There are examples of turnaround situations, as at the RFD Group, for example (see p. 295), in which the order backlog was so large that all selling effort had to be stopped at the start of the turnaround!

Pricing strategy is usually a critical area for immediate top-management attention. Pricing is critical because profits are *always* extremely sensitive to price: a given percentage increase in price will always have a bigger impact on profits than the same percentage increase in sales volume. Pricing decisions are also critical because, besides affecting short-term profitability, they may also affect the firm's market share and hence its long-term profit prospects. Two pricing strategies are commonly adopted: raising prices and lowering prices.

Many successful turnarounds have been characterized by immediate price increases but, for this to work, the product range must be sufficiently price insensitive, so that any fall in profits due to lower volume will be more than offset by increased profit margins due to higher prices. The danger with this approach is that the firm may be adopting a market share harvesting strategy (a strategy of losing market share to maximize short-term profitability), unless the firm was previously underpricing or is able to offset any loss in volume by improving its sales effort.

A harvesting strategy may be adopted in a turnaround situation due to the necessity of increasing short-term profits and providing the firm with a breathing-space while it implements more fundamental changes in the character of its business. Sometimes, however, a harvesting strategy will be the strategy of choice: for example, competitors in the British lead-pencil industry currently appear to be adopting a harvesting strategy by maintaining price levels in the face of low-priced foreign imports. They are relying on their brand-names and distribution strengths to permit them to charge relatively high prices because it is preferable (on discounted cash-flow criteria) for them to have a declining market share at high prices than to maintain their market share at lower price levels. A similar situation obtains in the pharmaceutical industry whenever products come off patent and generic equivalents are introduced on to the market.[14] The lesson to be learnt about a harvesting strategy is that, however attractive it may appear in the short term, it is a liquidation strategy and will not assist in achieving sustainable recovery.

Raising prices is not open to all firms, particularly those competing in price-sensitive markets. There is, however, one situation where prices have to be raised immediately, irrespective of the effect on sales volume. This occurs when the turnaround firm's selling price does not cover variable costs. Lowering prices in a turnaround situation is rare and dangerous – although it is difficult to generalize. The price elasticity of demand and the cost-price structure of individual product lines must be taken into account in assessing the situation. Where variable costs are a high percentage of the selling price, it is unlikely that volume can be increased sufficiently to offset the loss in gross-profit margins brought about by lowering prices. In such a situation, lowering prices is likely to *increase* the losses of the turnaround firm. Furthermore, lowering prices can lead to a price war with competitors who are more likely to have the financial resources to withstand and win such a war than the turnaround firm. The exception to the 'rule' about not lowering prices occurs when there is a need to give competitive discounts to the channels of distribution. When Hestair Ltd, a conglomerate that was successful in the early to mid 1970s, bought the photographic distribution company Johnsons of Hendon in 1972, Johnsons' discount on volume orders to photographic retailers was $2\frac{1}{2}\%$ less than that of its major competitors, with the result that major chains like Dixons would not buy from the company. By offering slightly larger volume discounts for larger quantity orders, sales and profits increased rapidly in the space of six months.

Lowering prices is all too often a tempting strategy for firms that see their sales declining and their competitive position eroding. Unfortunately, few turnaround firms have a strong enough cost position *vis-à-vis* competitors to adopt such a strategy. Furthermore, many industry situations are in fact characterized by a kinked demand curve, implying that if the turnaround firm lowers price most of its competitors will follow suit, so no further sales volume will be obtained. In some sectors of the retail trade where firms operate on negative working capital (i.e. they receive cash for sales before paying their suppliers), lowering prices to increase volume could work as a short-term turnaround strategy because increasing volume generates cash flow. This is, however, a risky strategy to adopt if the firm is starting from a weak competitive basis or has weak control systems – both of which are common characteristics of retail turnaround situations.

6. Growth via Acquisition

A somewhat surprising but quite common recovery strategy is growth via acquisition. This does not necessarily mean diversification into new product-market areas totally unrelated or only marginally related to the firm's existing business. It may mean the acquisition of firms in the same or related industries. Acquisitions are most commonly used to turn around stagnant firms: firms not in a financial crisis but whose financial performance is poor. The objective of growing by acquisition rather than by organic growth is related to the faster speed at which turnaround can be achieved by following the acquisition route. It is a strategy available to few firms in a crisis situation because they lack the financial resources to make an acquisition although, once survival is assured, acquisition may be part of the strategy to achieve sustainable recovery.

The acquisition of related businesses permits the organization to acquire firms that complement existing operations. The acquired firm may, for example, permit the acquirer to implement a product-market reorientation. Thus, Burton Group's acquisition of the Dorothy Perkins chain has helped Burtons to achieve its product-market strategy of shifting emphasis away from men's towards ladies' retailing. At other times, acquisition may improve the turnaround firm's competitive advantage or reduce its competitive disadvantage by providing, for example, access to new distribution channels, access to new technology or the opportunity to gain economies of scale by combining operations.

Unrelated acquisitions, or diversification, provide the means for entering product-market areas where the profit and growth opportunities are better for the turnaround firm. Many turnaround firms are in highly competitive or declining industries where the long-term choice for management is either survival by diversification or allowing the firm to die. There have been a number of studies to show that diversification as a business strategy does not pay off for the shareholders[15] and that the financial benefits accruing at acquisition go to the acquiree shareholders, not to the acquirer.[16] None of these studies, however, has looked explicitly at turnaround firms, and intuitively it seems reasonable that the results might be different for such firms.

The dangers of growth by acquisition are essentially the same for turnaround firms as for healthy firms making acquisitions: the acquisition price is too high, post-acquisition management is poor, the acquired firm's financial or market position is weaker than anticipated, etc. The danger of making a single, poor acquisition, however, is usually greater for a turnaround firm, where gearing is usually high and the financial resources available in an emergency rather thin. On the other hand, the danger of poor post-acquisition management may be reduced by management's familiarity with the turnaround process. But the opposite may also happen. If management has once been successful in pulling a firm out of a crisis by introducing tight management control, cost reduction and asset reduction strategies, etc., it may take on a false sense of belief in its own abilities to turn around acquired firms. The furniture manufacturer, PMA Holdings, provides a good example of a firm that was headed for a turnaround success, due in large part to growth through acquisitions, when it foolishly acquired the upholstered furniture manufacturer, Harris Lebus, when the latter was close to receivership. As an independent entity, Harris Lebus was in a non-recoverable situation. The acquisition, coupled with the cyclical drop in demand due to the 1980/81 recession, sent PMA itself into receivership in 1981.

7. Asset Reduction

An asset-reduction strategy is often an integral part of product-market reorientation. As the firm cuts out product lines, customers or whole areas of business, assets are liquidated or divested. In a severe financial crisis, however, the adoption of an asset-reduction strategy may be the only viable option left open to the firm if it is to survive. It has to divest itself of whatever assets it can realize quickly, so future product-market strategy may take second priority. It is not uncommon to find a firm having to sell the profitable part of its business in an attempt to survive. Toy manufacturer Airfix, for example, was forced to sell its profitable bathroom accessory subsidiary, Crayonne, in an attempt to save the parent company – although in the end this action proved insufficient and Airfix went into receivership in early 1981.

Since many turnarounds are characterized by a severe cash crisis, the generation of positive cash flow is an essential prerequisite of successful recovery. Actions to improve profitability may increase cash flow, but a specific asset-reduction strategy is likely to have a more rapid and dramatic impact on the firm's cash-flow position. Asset reduction can be accomplished within a non-diversified firm by reducing working capital and disposing of fixed assets; in a diversified firm there is the additional option of divesting or liquidating one or more subsidiary companies. A reduction of working capital requirements involves reducing debtors' days and cutting inventory levels. Rarely is it possible to extend creditor days since, in severe financial crises, creditors are usually already overextended and may only be supplying on a C.O.D. basis. Reducing fixed assets will involve selling surplus plant and machinery (which is often worth very little second-hand) and selling property, directly if it is surplus to requirements, or by arranging a sale and leaseback if it is still required.

Divestment of subsidiaries or business units is one of the most common recovery strategies employed by all but the small business sector. Divestment may be used as a strategy both to generate cash flow and also as a means of halting cash outflow resulting from severe operating losses. Divestment is always preferred to liquidation, even if the latter would, in the end, provide the greater monetary value. The reason for this is the longer time horizon that is required to liquidate a business than to divest it, and the large up-front cash outflows that may be involved in a liquidation. Redundancy payments and losses incurred during the statutory ninety-day notice period may mean that a firm will prefer to sell a subsidiary for a nominal sum of £1 (and pay the purchaser!) rather than liquidate the business.

Divestment, although a seemingly simple strategy, is not always easy to implement, due to the existence of high exit barriers – the impediments a firm encounters in attempting to leave an industry. Five principal sources of exit barriers have been identified:[17]

- specialized assets – both fixed assets and current assets – for which there is no ready purchaser
- fixed costs of exit arising from redundancy costs, contract cancellations, divestment costs, etc.
- interrelatedness with other product-market segments (as, for example, in a vertically integrated business)
- managerial or emotional barriers resulting from management's attachment and commitment to a business
- government and social barriers, due to concern for jobs and the welfare of the local community.

Some or all of these barriers may be present in a particular situation, although the emotional barriers to exit are usually removed by bringing in new top management.

8. Cost-reduction Strategies

Cost-reduction strategies are aimed at increasing the firm's profit margin (as a percentage of sales) and thus, indirectly, at generating increased cash flow. They may or may not be implemented in conjunction with a strategy of product-market reorientation. Cost reduction can be strategic, or operational, or both. Where it is strategic, its objective is to improve the firm's cost position relative to that of competitors. Where it is operational, the objective is to improve efficiency and bring overheads in line with volume.

The options open to a firm to increase profit margins are basically oriented at pricing and volume decisions (discussed earlier under the heading of 'Improved Marketing') or cost reduction. In a loss-making situation, profit margins are even more sensitive to a reduction in costs than an increase in price, although cost-reduction strategies usually take longer to show through in the form of increased profit margins than do price increases. Obviously, the cost-price structure varies with the nature of the business and, in some high-margin industries, costs are a relatively unimportant element in the profit equation. However, in most turnaround situations that are characterized by loss-making operations, the adoption of a cost-reduction strategy is necessary. This is not surprising when one considers that most turnaround situations are also characterized by poor management control.

9. Investment

Investment as a generic turnaround strategy is most common in situations where the turnaround firm has been acquired by a firm with adequate financial resources. Firms which remain independent during the recovery phase are rarely able to invest much in the business until any liquidity crisis has passed.

Investment strategies in turnaround situations are either aimed at reducing costs through the replacement of worn-out or obsolete plant and equipment, or at promoting growth, either organically or via acquisition. Under the framework adopted in this book for discussing recovery strategies, investment strategies are usually undertaken in conjunction with a cost-reduction strategy, a product-market reorientation strategy, or with growth strategies involving either aggressive marketing or acquisitions. The best-known example of an investment strategy being used to reduce unit costs and to promote organic growth is the U.K. government's multi-billion-pound investment in British Leyland.

Typically, management thinks of investment in terms of increases in fixed assets and working capital, but certain revenue expenditures also rank as investment strategies. To highlight this fact, firms like Texas Instruments distinguish between operating expenses and strategic expenses. Strategic expenses are project-oriented and discretionary. They can be postponed without limiting current performance.[18] A firm that has declined for product-market reasons is likely to need to invest in new product development and marketing if sustainable recovery is to be achieved. Such expenditures must also be regarded as investment strategies.

10. Debt Restructuring and other Financial Strategies

The turnaround firm that has reached a cash crisis is usually over-geared and must reduce its debt/equity ratio to acceptable industry levels before the firm can be said to have recovered financially. Cash-flow generation strategies, in particular asset reduction strategies, are most commonly used to reduce borrowings; but there are two financial strategies which are also commonly used: debt restructuring and raising additional finance.

Debt restructuring involves an agreement between the ailing firm and its creditors, usually the banks, to reschedule and sometimes convert interest and principal payments into other negotiable financial instruments. This may involve converting short-term debt into long-term debt, converting loans into convertible preferred shares or even equity, converting unpaid interest into loans, and forgoing interest due. The restructuring possibilities are many. Debt restructuring often involves the banks taking what the Americans call 'a hair cut' – accepting a lower amount than is due to them in full settlement of outstanding debts. This element was present in the rescue package developed for Sterling Credit, the instalment-credit, financial-services and insurance brokerage group, when Bankers Trust agreed to accept £750,000 in lieu of group debts of £1 million. As part of the same rescue package, the Midland Bank translated £750,000 of the group's overdraft into 'subordinated convertible unsecured loan at $4\frac{1}{2}\%$ over bank rate' interest on which is payable only if profits before tax exceed £400,000 per year.[19]

Historically, raising additional finance in the form of both new loans and new equity has been more common than debt restructuring in the U.K. Debt restructuring is a particularly common feature of U.S. turnarounds and reflects the differing banking practices in the two countries, although there are now signs that debt restructuring is becoming more popular in the U.K. The ability of the turnaround firm to raise additional capital from banks and investors is largely a function of their assessment of the new management and the firm's recovery prospects. There are situations in which raising additional finance is so critical that the firm is sure to go into receivership unless this can be accomplished. Sometimes the banks are persuaded that their own interests are better served by providing additional borrowing facilities and that their only chance of recovering outstanding loans is to lend yet more money! The provision of new equity from existing share-holders via a rights issue or from outside investors is common in the turnaround of firms where the chief cause of crisis has been rapid growth. We shall see in Chapter 11 that the provision of additional finance is a common characteristic of turnarounds in which the government has become involved.

A recent example in which major debt restructuring occurred and additional finance was also raised is provided by Massey Ferguson, the Canadian-based agricultural-equipment manufacturer. Massey Ferguson had over 200 bank and insurance company creditors from whom it had borrowed about C$1.5 billion without giving any security. The following financial package was agreed to by the lenders to avoid the firm going into receivership:[20]

- Massey Ferguson's principal banker, The Canadian Imperial Bank of Commerce (C.I.B.C.), agreed to convert C$100 million of debt into convertible preferred shares and to subscribe to an additional C$50 million of the same class of shares.
- The banks and insurance companies other than C.I.B.C. agreed to 'forgive' interest of C$200 million and to receive common shares of Massey Ferguson in exchange.
- The British Export Credit Guarantee Department, which was unable to forgive interest on its C$87 million of lending to Massey Ferguson, agreed to guarantee a further issue of C$90 million of convertible preferred shares.
- A further C$200 million was provided by the private placement of convertible preferred shares in Canada, supported by a guarantee from the Canadian and Ontario governments.

Notes

1. P. Grinyer and J. C. Spender, 'Recipes, Crises and Adaptation in Mature Businesses', *International Studies of Management and Organization*, 1979, Vol. IX, No. 3, pp. 113–33.
2. Ibid.
3. P. Grinyer and J. C. Spender, *Turnaround: The Fall and Rise of the Newton Chambers Group*. Associated Business Press, 1979.
4. Ibid.
5. Ibid.
6. William H. Starbuch, Arent Greve and Bo L. T. Hedberg, 'Responding to Crisis', *Journal of Business Administration*, Vol. 9, No. 2, Spring 1978.
7. Formerly Chairman and Chief Executive of Republic Corp., Dalyn Corp., Vice-Chairman of Kaufman & Broad, Inc., and currently Chairman and Chief Executive of Wickes Group Inc.
8. Stuart St P. Slatter, 'Turnaround Strategies in Californian Growth Firms', Working Paper, 1981.
9. H. Uyterhoeven, J. Ackerman and J. Rosenblum, *Strategy and Organization*, Irwin, 1973.
10. Stuart St P. Slatter, 'Patterns of Diversification Behaviour', London Business School Working Paper, 1980.
11. Michael Porter, *Competitive Strategy: Techniques for Analyzing Industries and Competitors*, New York Free Press, 1980.
12. 'ICI Sparks Off a European Shake-Out', *Financial Times*, 25 March 1981.
13. 'Hopes of Survival Rest on Early Benefits from Rationalisation', *Financial Times*, 26 February 1981.
14. Stuart St P. Slatter, *Competition and Marketing Strategies in the Pharmaceutical Industry*, Croom Helm, 1977.
15. M. Salter and W. Weinhold, *Diversification through Acquisition*, New York Free Press, 1979.
16. J. R. Franks, J. E. Broyles and M. J. Hecht, 'An Industry Study of the Profitability of Mergers in the U.K.', *Journal of Finance*, No. 32, December 1977, pp. 1513–25.
17. Michael Porter, 'Please Note Location of Nearest Exit: Exit Barriers and Planning', *California Management Review*, Vol. XIX, Winter 1976.
18. See Texas Instruments Inc., case-study in *Cases in Strategic Management*, by J. Stopford, D. Channon and J. Constable, Wiley, 1980.
19. 'Sterling Credit Unveils the Details of its Rescue Package', *Financial Times*, 21 October 1980.
20. 'The Company that had to Survive', *Financial Times*, 19 January 1981.

5. Formulating Recovery Strategies

The management actions needed to effect a turnaround involve deciding upon the appropriate set of turnaround strategies and implementing these strategies in as short a time span as possible. In the last chapter we discussed ten major generic strategies commonly used by organizations in turnaround situations. The ways in which these strategies are combined to provide a firm with an overall recovery strategy can vary enormously.

This chapter identifies and discusses the six factors that determine which combination of generic strategies is required to effect corporate recovery. Four types of recovery situations are then discussed, ranging from irrecoverable turnaround situations, in which there is little or no hope of survival, however good the management, to those in which sustainable recovery is possible. The turnaround manager may find most interesting the section describing the characteristics of successful turnaround strategies which emerged from my study of forty U.K. public companies. Since timing is an important ingredient in implementing any strategy, four phases of recovery have been identified, to help the manager focus on the typical sequence with which different strategies are used in a recovery situation.

1. Factors Determining Recovery Strategy

Six sets of factors determine which generic strategies are used in a turnaround situation. They are:

- the causes of decline
- the severity of the crisis
- the attitudes of the stakeholders involved in the turnaround process
- the firm's historical strategy
- the characteristics of the industry in which the firm competes
- the firm's cost-price structure.

Each is discussed in turn below.

1.1 The Causes of Decline

The principal causes of decline have a direct effect on deciding which generic strategies are required to effect successful recovery. Two U.S. authors, Hofer and Schendel, divide causes of decline into problems of ineffective strategy and problems of inefficient implementation;[1] they recommend that the appropriate management actions should be the formulation of a new strategy and improvements in implementation. However, this is of little help to the practising manager. The opposite approach, that of looking at individual causes and individual generic strategies, is little better and can be quite misleading. Clearly, poor management requires new management, inadequate financial control requires improved financial control, a high cost position requires a cost-reduction strategy, etc.; but *more* than this is required for the formulation of a successful recovery strategy.

Many causes of decline require the use of multiple generic strategies. For example, where price competition is a major cause of decline, it may be that the firm has to adopt a combination of cost reduction, asset reduction, product-market reorientation and improved marketing, investment and growth through acquisition, just to correct this one problem. Figure 5.1 shows the principal generic strategies connected with each of the major causes of decline. The reader should be aware, however, that this is an oversimplified picture since, as we saw in Chapter 2, turnaround crises are brought about by a combination of causes. My research shows that *the average number of generic strategies employed in successful turnarounds is considerably greater than the average number of factors causing decline*. Of course, this does not mean that the turnaround manager should necessarily go in with guns blazing on all fronts. Decline may be due to one factor – such as a single bad acquisition or heavy costs associated with a new product launch – and the appropriate recovery strategy is merely to divest the subsidiary in question or drop the new product. But (as we saw in Chapter 2) the causes of decline are usually multiple, which suggests that successful recovery requires management to use a number of different generic strategies simultaneously.

1.2 The Severity of the Crisis

The severity of the crisis facing the turnaround firm is a function of the causes of failure and the crisis stage (i.e. the degree to which the firm has progressed towards insolvency). The fact that a firm has been losing money for years means that it is clearly in a turnaround situ-

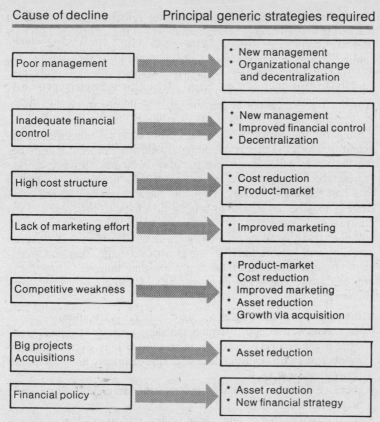

Cause of decline   Principal generic strategies required

| Poor management |
| Inadequate financial control |
| High cost structure |
| Lack of marketing effort |
| Competitive weakness |
| Big projects Acquisitions |
| Financial policy |

* New management
* Organizational change and decentralization

* New management
* Improved financial control
* Decentralization

* Cost reduction
* Product-market

* Improved marketing

* Product-market
* Cost reduction
* Improved marketing
* Asset reduction
* Growth via acquisition

* Asset reduction

* Asset reduction
* New financial strategy

Figure 5.1: *Influence of Causes of Decline on Generic Strategies*

ation, but does not mean that there need be a crisis. Whether a cash crisis develops is a function of the firm's balance sheet. The balance sheet will usually deteriorate when a firm is losing money, but the situation can continue for a number of years if management has adopted conservative gearing policies in the past and has maintained reasonable financial control, and the losses are not becoming progressively worse.

In a severe cash crisis, cash-generation strategies – asset-reduction and financial strategies involving debt restructuring (and possibly obtaining additional capital) – must take priority over all other strategies. These strategies must be supported by very tight financial control procedures involving daily – if not hourly! – cash management.

Cost-reduction strategies, product-market refocusing and improved marketing may all help generate cash flow, but the additional cash flow they are likely to contribute in the short term is likely to be *small* compared with that of the asset-reduction and financial strategies. In situations where no further capital is available, the firm's cash-flow limitations will usually mean that investment strategies and most growth strategies cannot be implemented until after survival has been assured and the balance sheet has recovered.

Similarly, the severity of the firm's profit crisis (as measured by the extent to which the firm is operating at below breakeven) determines the extent to which revenue-generating strategies (product-market reorientation and improved marketing) will be necessary in addition to a cost-reduction strategy. Even the most dramatic cost-reduction strategy may be *inadequate* to bring a firm back to breakeven,[2] as is illustrated in Figure 5.2.

Where there is no crisis, management usually has more financial flexibility and is more likely to use growth via acquisition and invest-ment strategies, although there is always some limit as to how fast a firm can grow. The major characteristics of non-crisis recovery situ-ations are:

• the same generic strategies are used as in crisis situations
• management uses approximately the same number of generic strat-egies in the recovery process as in crisis situations, even though the number of factors causing decline is approximately one-half that of crisis situations
• there is heavy emphasis on growth strategies, particularly acquisitions
• organizational change appears to be less important than in a crisis situation.

1.3 The Attitude of Stakeholders

Stakeholders are the various groups of people and organizations who influence the firm or are influenced by it. Typically, the firm's stake-holders include management, employees, shareholders, customers, suppliers, banks, government, the local community, competitors, trade unions, etc. In a turnaround situation, the relative power of the various stakeholders may be important in determining the recovery strategy.

If the shareholders act through their representation on the board of directors to change management before the firm reaches a crisis, recovery may be initiated relatively simply. In the absence of a crisis,

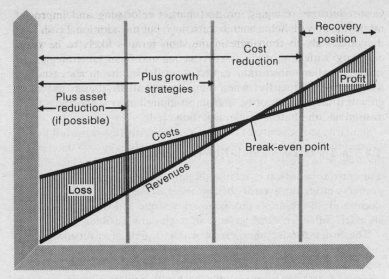

Figure 5.2: *Influence of Firm's Breakeven on Profit Recovery Strategy*

new management usually has fewer constraints determining the recovery strategy, although it is to be hoped that management action will take place under the watchful eye of the board and the principal shareholders. Few turnaround managers have this freedom unless the ailing firm has just been acquired – in which case the acquisition objectives of the acquirer determine the recovery strategy.

Once a crisis occurs, it is more likely to be the firm's creditors, usually the banks, that initiate the turnaround process. Bank influence varies enormously from one situation to the next, but in some instances the bank can be virtually running the firm and, in the process, be deciding which generic strategies should receive most management attention. Typically, an asset-reduction strategy designed to repay or reduce the bank's outstanding loans takes precedence (as it does, for example, when a receiver is appointed).

Where the government is involved in providing assistance, certain generic strategies are sometimes stipulated as part of the rescue terms: for example, Burmah Oil was forced to follow a divestment programme, and Ferranti was not allowed to close its transformer plant. (The issue of government influence on recovery strategies is further discussed in Chapter 11.) Powerful trade unions may act as a constraint on both cost-reduction and asset-reduction strategies if there is the likelihood of loss of jobs and changes in job practice. Strikes and sit-ins by the workforce were a common feature during the 1970s; they sometimes resulted in firms being unable to adopt the required recovery strategy.

Thus, stakeholders act in two ways to influence the recovery strategy: in a direct way when they stipulate what strategy should be followed or given priority, and in an indirect way when they act as constraints on strategy implementation.

1.4 The Turnaround Firm's Historical Strategy

The firm's historical strategy directly influences the appropriate recovery strategy, even if the historical strategy was *not* a cause of decline. Both the firm's product-market scope and the deployment of its assets influence which generic strategies are feasible.

The firm's product-market scope (or degree of diversification) is important since, in a diversified firm, we need to look at strategy at two and possibly more levels. A simple diversified firm will consist of a series of strategic business units, each with a relatively homogeneous product line sold to a relatively homogeneous group of customers. These units report directly to the corporate management that presides over a portfolio of business units. In a more complicated structure, the firm may be divisionalized, with each division consisting of a number of subsidiaries and each subsidiary consisting of a number of strategic business units. For our purpose, however, we need only consider the simple situation I have described, since conceptually we need only think of recovery strategies at the corporate level and the business unit level. At the corporate level, the mix of generic strategies available to management is limited to:

- new management
- strong central financial control
- decentralization (and divisionalization, if necessary)
- asset reduction via divestment
- growth via acquisition
- investment.

Other strategies such as cost reduction,* improved marketing effort and product-market reorientation are not feasible. They are strategies available only at the business unit level. Similarly, whereas divestment

---

* If there is a large head-office staff, cost reduction may also be appropriate at the corporate level.

and acquisition are not really feasible options at the business unit level, at the corporate level they are. It is extremely unlikely that all the business units or divisions within a diversified firm will be in need of turnaround. Thus, at the divisional level and below, the implementation of turnaround strategies will be selective. In a non-diversified firm, the strategies open to management are similar to those in an operating unit of a diversified firm.

1.5 Industry Characteristics

The characteristics of an industry in which the firm competes always influences strategy formulation, whether the firm is in a turnaround situation or not. Some key industry characteristics and the turnaround strategies they affect are now briefly discussed, although lack of space does not permit a full explanation of all the many industry characteristics that might be present in a specific situation.

(*a*) *Nature of the product*: The nature of the product and the nature of the customers' buying behaviour influence the implementation of the following strategies:

- Product-market focusing, which is often necessary in a turnaround situation, becomes increasingly difficult as the product becomes less differentiated and more price-sensitive.
- A strategy of increasing prices is not usually feasible for a firm with commodity-type products, although some groups of customers will be less price-sensitive than others and on some occasions may even 'subsidize' inefficient producers to maintain the flexibility of dual sourcing.
- The lead time required to increase the sales of consumer products is usually considerably shorter than that required to increase the sales of industrial products. Consumers switch suppliers more quickly than industrial users.

(*b*) *Market segmentation*: A market that is highly segmented due to varying customer preferences is more likely to allow the turnaround firm the opportunity to develop a focused and defensible product-market strategy.

(*c*) *Relative size and strength of competitors*: The firm is more likely to develop a successful recovery strategy in a fragmented industry than in an industry dominated by a few powerful competitors, or in an industry characterized by global competition based on technological and cost leadership strategies. In either of the latter situations, any move by the turnaround firm to take market share away from the leaders will be very costly and have a low chance of success.

(*d*) *Exit barriers*: The height of the exit barriers will determine the ease of implementing an asset-reduction strategy. Specialized assets for which there is no ready buyer pose the principal exit barrier, once new management has been installed and has eliminated the psychological resistance to exit inherent in the old management team.

(*e*) *Rate of technological change*: A slower rate of technological change favours the turnaround firm in terms of feasibility of implementing viable product-market and investment strategies. The greater the rate of change, the more financial resources are required to bring the firm back to a competitive position.

(*f*) *Threat of retaliation*: Where competitors are sleepy and poorly managed, there is less likelihood of retaliation to the turnaround firm changing its product-market emphasis or improving its marketing effort.

(*g*) *Bargaining power of customers*: Where powerful customers are absent, the turnaround firm has more chance of increasing prices (and vice versa).

(*h*) *Bargaining power of suppliers*: Where powerful suppliers are present, the turnaround firm has less bargaining power and less chance of achieving substantial price reduction in raw material and component costs (and vice versa).

(*i*) *Capital intensity*: The return on capital employed of capital-intensive industries is usually lower than less capital-intensive industries,[3] making some investment strategies relatively unattractive.

(*j*) *Industry growth rate*: The importance of industry growth rate is based on the premise that cash usage is proportional to market growth rate, that the feasibility of increasing market share varies according to the stage of growth, and that management should focus on different functional strategies at various stages of growth. The reader is referred to standard books on marketing and strategic planning for a more detailed explanation of these concepts,[4] since we are only interested here in how the stages of industry growth affect recovery strategies.

The lack of financial resources, poor management and lack of financial control which usually characterize turnaround situations may change substantially the traditional pattern of strategic responses expected at different stages of the life cycle. This is particularly true in the growth phase of the market when sales growth and investment strategies would normally be appropriate. Instead asset-reduction, cost-reduction and product-market refocusing strategies may be necessary to ensure survival. The generic turnaround strategies appropriate to the different phases of industry growth are shown in Figure 5.3.

Many of the industry characteristics that influence the formulation of recovery strategies are the same as those identified by Porter as factors influencing industry profitability.[5] This should not be surprising, since a firm's profit potential, and hence its recovery potential, in part is a function of the industry it is in. The chance of corporate

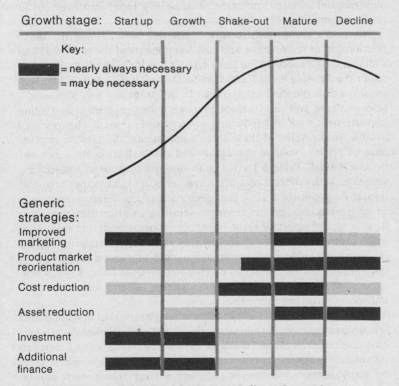

Figure 5.3: *Generic Turnaround Strategies at Different Stages of Product-market Evolution*

recovery in an industry with low profit potential must be lower than in an industry with higher profit potential, because it is easier to attract additional finance for investment and easier to follow an asset-reduction strategy of divestment because there are other firms willing to enter the industry.

1.6. The Firm's Cost-Price Structure

The strategies required to obtain short-term profit improvement are dependent to a large degree on the firm's cost-price structure at the time of crisis. This in turn is determined in part by industry characteristics and in part by the causes of decline. The cost-price structure is extremely important in determining whether management should focus short-term attention on a cost-reduction strategy, a marketing improvement strategy, or both, to achieve a rapid improvement in profit margins.

The firm's cost-price structure is derived by analysing the inter-relationship of the revenue and cost components of the profit and loss statement, and applying the same type of sensitivity analysis discussed under the heading 'Cost Reduction Strategies' in Chapter 4. Management controls the three components of the profit and loss statement – price, volume and costs – through its ability to implement marketing improvement and cost-reduction strategies. For small changes, say 5–10%, in the value of these three components, the relative importance of pricing, volume generating and cost-reduction strategies can be ascertained. Table 5.1 gives two examples of firms in loss-making situations with different cost-price structures, and shows the individual impact on profits of a 10% change in each of the three components. In both situations, profits are more sensitive to price than costs, but what is really important is the impact of reducing costs and increasing prices, compared to the impact of increasing sales volume. In situation B, increasing volume has considerably more impact on profits than it does in situation A, due to the much lower variable costs. Thus, where the contribution margin is small, increasing sales volume has little impact on profit improvement.

Sensitivity analysis of this type determines which are the most profit-sensitive components in the cost-price structure but takes no account of which components are the most feasible to change. The actions to influence components vary enormously in the ease with which they can be implemented and the time horizons over which they can be changed, and thus managerial judgement and common sense are required to determine the relative importance of the strategic alterna-tives.[6] Thus, as desirable as further price increases might be, the price elasticity of demand for the firm's product may effectively close this option. Similarly, once costs have been reduced to a certain point, additional cost reductions may not be easily obtainable, in which case management must turn to increases in sales volume to obtain additional profit.

Table 5.1: *Effect of Cost-price Structure on Short-term Recovery Strategy*

	Situation A	*Situation B*
Sales	£1,000,000	£1,000,000
Variable costs	(900,000)	(500,000)
CONTRIBUTION	100,000	500,000
Fixed costs	(200,000)	(600,000)
PROFIT/(Loss)	(£ 100,000)	(£ 100,000)

Profit/Loss after ± 10% change in components

± 10% change *in components*	*PROFIT/(Loss)*	*PROFIT/(Loss)*
Price*	Breakeven	Breakeven
Variable costs	(10,000)	(50,000)
Volume	(90,000)	(50,000)

* Assumes no loss in sales volume.

2. Effect of External Events on Recovery

External events over which the firm has no control play an important role in contributing to recovery in about one-third of all successful turnarounds. Unsuccessful recovery situations are less often helped by external factors. Just as cyclical down-swings in demand and adverse commodity price fluctuations are causes of decline, so can cyclical up-swings and favourable commodity-price changes influence recovery. Timing is, therefore, a crucial aspect that can either help or work against the successful implementation of a recovery strategy. Imple-menting a recovery strategy at a time of economic boom is much easier than during a recession.

The importance of the business cycle varies from industry to industry, but few firms can ignore it completely. In a highly cyclical industry, attempting to start a turnaround at the peak of the cycle or just after the peak is a virtual non-starter. Boom times tend to make a firm's competitive position look stronger than it really is; and it is only when recession hits that the weaknesses become obvious. The experienced turnaround manager will pick the timing of his entry into a new situation carefully to coincide with an up-swing in demand. It is not unknown for turnaround managers to be replaced when their strategies, although adequate and well implemented, do not achieve immediate profit improvement in the cyclical down-swing phase of a recession. A new manager is appointed at the bottom of the recession, he continues the same strategies started by his predecessor – but he is the hero of the hour as he takes advantage of the up-swing in demand while his predecessor is regarded as worse than useless!

There are some industries in which the impact of the business cycle, coupled with the inherent structural characteristics of the industry, means that periods of profit are followed by periods of loss, often for the whole industry. Firms in this type of situation are often competing in commodity or commodity-type industries, and may be referred to as cyclical recovery situations. An example of a firm whose profitability is cyclical is the whisky-distilling group, Tomatin, where loss-making periods are almost exclusively due to changes in world demand. The meat industry provides a good example: a firm like Thomas Borthwick goes from one crisis to the next, due to the difficulty of balancing demand and supply in a world market where weather conditions and disposable consumer income fluctuate widely.

The upswing in demand that helps recovery may sometimes be secular rather than cyclical in nature. For example, where the customer finds a new use for an old product, a virtually non-recoverable situation can quickly become viable. Thus, when the Economic Forestry Group acquired the sole remaining manufacturer of wooden spills (originally used for lighting pipes from open fires), the business was inactive but it is now a successful small business.

An increase in the price of 'commodities' can be a key factor in helping many businesses recover. At times of high interest rates even the most inefficient bank can make high profits; at times of rising property prices, over-geared property companies can recover a sound financial position. A good example of a firm recovering due to an increase in commodity prices was the Cornish tin mining company, St Piran. Long before the controversial Mr Jim Raper acquired control over St Piran in 1973, management had made a decision to increase output. The additional output came on stream just at the same time as the price of tin increased sharply. The effect was to increase St Piran's after-tax profits from £192,000 in 1976 to £1.8 million in 1978.

3. Types of Recovery Situation

Not all crisis turnaround situations are recoverable. As with all strategy formulation problems, the issue is fundamentally one of matching the firm's resources against the environment in which the firm is operating, in order to determine a viable future direction for the firm. The formulation of a recovery strategy is unique, however, in that its emphasis is largely oriented to overcoming constraints, both internal and external. It is aimed at eliminating the financial crisis, reversing the causes of decline, overcoming the resistance of stakeholders, overcoming the constraints of the firm's historical strategy and, in many situations, overcoming an unattractive set of industry characteristics. It should not be surprising, therefore, that many turnaround situations are not viable independent businesses. The number of turnaround firms that survive as independent entities is evidence of this (see Chapter 1).

The chances of recovery vary according to the combined effect of the six groups of factors influencing the development of a sound recovery strategy. There is a range of likely outcomes, from complete and sustainable recovery, through mere survival to short-term survival and, at the opposite end, failed recovery. Each of the six groups could, if desired, be analysed and weighted to show their effect on recovery, and a recovery index formulated, but this would be too subjective to be of use to anybody but the researcher and the ivory-tower planner. The range of outcomes is shown in Figure 5.4 and provides a useful classification of recovery types. Figure 5.5 shows a graphic representation of typical profit trajectories for the four types of recovery situation.

3.1 Non-Recoverable Turnarounds

Non-recoverable situations are of two types: 'no-hopers' and short-term survivors.

(*a*) *The no-hopers*: These are firms characterized by a serious attempt at turnaround, although they soon become insolvent or are acquired

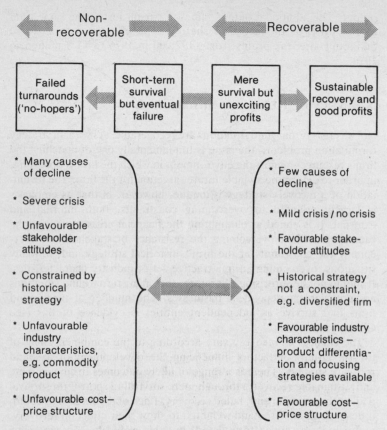

Figure 5.4: *Factors Determining the Feasibility of Recovery*

because, despite management efforts, they cannot exist as viable, independent businesses even in the short term. They are firms that will inevitably fail and, from an economic point of view, are not worth the effort of turning around. They are characterized by some or all of the following factors:

- decline in their *core* business area as the result of severe price competition from lower-cost producers who possess significant cost advantages due to scale and experience-curve effects
- indivisible assets – they are single-plant, and often single-product firms that cannot divest assets to generate cash flow.

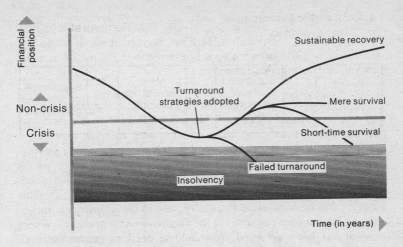

Figure 5.5: *Types of Recovery Situation*

- high fixed cost as a percentage of value added
- very fast decline in market demand.

Examples of such firms in this category are the failed turnarounds of the truck manufacturer Foden, the domestic appliance division of Colston, and the heating-equipment supplier Dimplex. Case-histories on Foden and Dimplex are contained in Chapter 19 of this book. The overriding characteristic of 'no-hopers' is that they are *all* faced with severe price competition from overseas competitors who have lower cost structures.

(*b*) *Short-term survivors*: These are firms that, if analysed over a five- or even ten-year horizon, look as if they have recovered. They may well have succeeded in improving real profits for four successive years or more (the definition of success used in Chapter 1), yet eventually they go into insolvency because they are unable to develop any sustainable competitive advantage. Two examples of firms exhibiting these characteristics were Bamfords (the agricultural equipment supplier), that went into receivership, and Inveresk (the paper manufacturer and distributor), that was eventually sold to Georgia-Pacific, a U.S. paper group. Case-histories on these two firms are to be found in Chapter 18.

3.2 Recoverable Turnarounds

Recovery implies survival, but there are degrees of survival and it is useful to distinguish between what is referred to in Figure 5.4 as 'mere survival' and sustainable recovery.

(*a*) *Mere survival*: Even if survival were possible, sustainable recovery may not be possible. There is a big difference in both the strategies and the management time and effort required to bring a firm to a survival situation and those required to achieve sustainable recovery. Sustainable recovery usually requires a shift in product-market emphasis and growth-oriented strategies such as new product development and/or growth via acquisition. In many situations, sustainable recovery will be impossible to achieve, due to the industry characteristics and the limited resources of the firm *vis-à-vis* competitors. Where survival has been achieved, stakeholders need to reappraise their investment and decide whether they will sell the firm 'while the going is good' or stay with the firm for the long term, with the aim of achieving sustainable recovery and a better return on their investment. The danger of sticking with a firm that achieves the 'mere survival' mode and no more is that the firm is more susceptible to crisis than the firm in a sustainable recovery mode, even if it is adequately managed. Examples of firms falling into thus category are provided by the case-histories on Evered & Company Holdings (a Midlands light engineering group) and Barker and Dobson (the confectionery and retail group), which have been included in Chapter 17.

(*b*) *Sustainable recovery*: Achieving sustainable recovery means successfully implementing a recovery strategy that permits the firm to make above-average profits in the long term. It is the ideal situation to aim for, but the dice are often loaded against this happening. Where the causes of the firm's decline are due to poor management, lack of control, general operating inefficiency or product-market weaknesses in a subsidiary, sustainable recovery is usually feasible; but if the causes of decline are related to the firm having a weak product-market position in its core business area, sustainable recovery may be impossible. A firm may have more chance of recovery as a subsidiary of a larger firm if the acquirer is prepared to invest large sums of money and time into turning the firm around. But even then recovery is not assured, as many acquisition-minded firms have subsequently found out. Sustainable recovery is usually easiest to achieve in a non-crisis recovery situation since, by implementing a recovery strategy before the onset of a crisis, the firm has greater financial resources available to it and a stronger competitive market position on which to build for the future.

Examples of firms that have achieved sustainable recovery are included as case-histories in Chapters 12 to 16. Problems of classification do arise, particularly between what is sustainable recovery and what is mere survival or even short-term recovery. While the classification of recovery types is presented here as a useful conceptual framework, few firms stay in a static position for very long, due to the changing nature of both internal resources and the external environment. All firms are susceptible to crisis (see Chapter 3), with the result that there is a natural tendency for firms to slip back towards less recoverable positions. Considerable managerial effort – and perhaps some luck – is required to keep a firm in the sustainable recovery box for a long period of time, due to rapid technological change and the increased competition which comes from slower growth in the world economy.

Any classification of firms is likely to be arbitrary, and the problem is well illustrated by comparing Inveresk and Redman Heenan International. Inveresk is described in Chapter 18 as a short-term survivor, yet it appeared to have achieved sustainable recovery by the mid 1970s, when it was largely unaffected by the 1974/75 recession. Redman Heenan, on the other hand, is described in Chapter 12 as a successful recovery situation, despite having reverted to a loss situation in 1980. Redman Heenan is classified as successful on the basis of the nature of the management actions and the results achieved in the five years after the 1973 crisis and, most important, on the basis of the underlying competitive strength of its major product-market areas. By contrast, Inveresk's competitive position was always weak, due to the dynamics of the pulp and paper industry.

4. Characteristics of Successful Recovery Strategies

There are substantial differences in the recovery strategies adopted by firms that are successful and those that are unsuccessful in achieving corporate recovery. My own study of forty U.K. public companies in the 1970s, thirty of which were successful recovery situations and ten of which were failures (in that they finally became insolvent despite serious attempts at recovery), indicates that:

- asset reduction and new management are the most commonly used generic strategies, closely followed by improved financial control and cost-reduction strategies. A new chief executive is usually necessary to effect a turnaround
- nearly all successful recovery situations are characterized by the use of cash-generation strategies (i.e. asset-reduction and new financing strategies), whereas only about one-half of failed recovery situations use these strategies
- divestment is the single most common cash-generation strategy, and is used by about one-half of all successful recovery situations
- successful recovery situations use more cash-generating strategies because they are often able to obtain additional bank borrowings or new equity, options that are not generally available to unsuccessful firms
- successful recovery strategies are more often characterized by improved financial control systems than are failed recovery situations. Failed recovery situations often take steps to improve control systems, but fail to *use* the resulting data to implement tight financial control
- cost-reduction strategies are frequently used as part of a successful recovery strategy, but are used even more frequently by firms that fail to recover
- improved marketing effort is common to both successful and unsuccessful recovery strategies, but successful firms tend to couple this with more fundamental product-market reorientation and growth through acquisition
- the most successful recovery strategies include significant organizational change in terms of both organizational structure and processes. Decentralization and improved communication between management and the workforce characterize successful recovery situations and are noticeably absent from failed recovery situations. Failed recovery situations make little or no effort at organizational change
- manufacturing and non-manufacturing businesses use essentially the same turnaround strategies, although organizational change appears to be less important in non-manufacturing businesses
- firms employing successful recovery strategies use almost twice as many generic turnaround strategies as firms employing unsuccessful strategies.

Table 5.2 compares the usage of the ten generic strategies in successful and unsuccessful recovery situations.

Table 5.2: *Comparison of Successful and Unsuccessful Recovery Strategies*

	Firms using generic turnaround strategy (%)	
	Successful recovery situations[1]	Failed recovery situations
Asset reduction	93	50
Change of management	87	60
Financial control	70	50
Cost reduction	63	90
Debt restructuring/financial	53	20
Improved marketing	50	50
Organizational changes	47	20
Product-market changes	40	30
Growth via acquisition	30	10
Investment	30	10

1. Includes non-crisis situations in both manufacturing and non-manufacturing industries.

Source: The Author.

The recovery strategies employed by U.K. companies in trouble do not appear to be significantly different from those used in other countries, although in any U.K. sample there is more likely to be a preponderance of firms in declining industries. However, my study of twenty Californian growth firms, all of which were in growth situations, tends to indicate a similar pattern of generic strategy usage to that in the U.K.[7] My California results, however, differ from those of Schendel and Patton, who found a much higher incidence of new product development, major plant expenditure and diversification, and a much lower incidence of new control systems in their sample of fifty-four successful U.S. recovery situations.[8]

Besides differences in the strategies employed, one big difference between recovery situations that are successful and those that fail is in the *quality* of implementation. Thus, a failed turnaround situation in which the chief executive is not changed may adopt a cost-reduction or asset-reduction strategy but does not follow through ruthlessly enough in its implementation. Good examples of the need for *more*, rather than less, action is provided by situations in which recovery is a two-stage process marked by the replacement of the 'new' chief executive. Both the Harris-Queensway (the carpet and furniture retailer) and R.F.D. case-histories provide examples of situations in which the first turnaround manager chose many of the correct turn-around strategies, but was replaced by someone who not only implemented more generic strategies but also implemented more vigorously those strategies begun by the first turnaround manager. Thus, successful recovery situations are characterized by *vigorous* implementation.

5. Phases of Corporate Recovery

Just as there are a number of stages leading to a crisis (as discussed in Chapter 3), so there are a number of typical stages that a firm goes through in achieving recovery. If it is assumed that the recovery phase begins when a new chief executive is appointed, there are four stages until recovery is achieved and 'normal' management strategies and procedures can become the order of the day. These are: the analysis phase; the emergency phase; the strategic change phase; and the growth phase

(*a*) *The analysis phase*: The analysis needed to begin implementing a recovery strategy may take any time from two to three days for a small firm, to six months for a large firm. Analysis involves problem identification, deciding the appropriate mix of turnaround strategies needed for short-term survival, and developing a detailed action plan. The action plan may include the need for additional analysis prior to taking decisions about the strategic change and growth phases of the recovery. The actual time available for analysis is obviously determined by the severity of the crisis and the size and complexity of the business.

(*b*) *The emergency phase*: This may begin as early as the first day the new chief executive arrives – at least as far as the implementation of new financial control systems are concerned. The emergency phase consists of those actions necessary to ensure survival and therefore tends to focus on those generic strategies that can most easily be implemented in the short term. Thus, one finds cash generation, cost reduction, increased prices and increased selling effort as the principal generic strategies used in this phase of recovery. The emphasis is on cash-flow and tight central financial control. Organizational change to facilitate control and management, particularly divisionalization and decentralization, may take place. Not all these strategies will be appropriate in a given situation; even where they are appropriate, the speed with which results can be achieved varies. For example, it is usually quicker to reduce debtor levels than to reduce inventories or divest a subsidiary; and raising prices has a quicker impact on profits than does an increased selling effort. The emergency phase is often characterized by surgery: divesting subsidiaries, closing plants, making employees redundant, firing incompetent managers, reducing surplus inventories, selling obsolete inventories, cutting out unprofitable product lines, etc. – all actions designed primarily to improve the cash outflow and stop the losses.

It is in the emergency phase also that the firm may seek additional financing to implement its recovery strategy. The experienced turn-around manager will also write off whatever assets he can and make reserves for future losses arising from plant closure and redundancies. He may often over-reserve, thereby keeping something 'up his sleeve' to 'write back' at a later date. In taking large write-offs at the beginning, the new chief executive is able to blame the problem on his predecessor, whereas if he 'under-reserves' he will have to write off a further amount at a later date – which will reflect poorly on him! The emergency phase will, typically, last from six to twelve months, but longer if appropriate recovery strategies are not adopted or are not well implemented.

(c) *The strategic change phase*: Whereas the emergency phase tends to emphasize operational factors, the strategic change phase emphasizes product-market reorientation. By good implementation of an appropriate recovery strategy in the emergency phase, the firm has assured short-term survival and can begin to think in the longer term. Efforts can and should begin in the emergency phase to focus strategy on those product-market segments where the firm has most competitive advantage (usually, but not always, those segments where it is profitable). However, product-market change usually takes time to implement and may require some investment, which may not be possible in the early phase of recovery. It is at this strategic change phase that management and/or shareholders may realize that the long-term viability of the firm looks doubtful, or that the investment of money and time required to achieve sustainable recovery is not worth the risks involved. They may, therefore, decide to look for a suitable purchaser for the business.

Assuming product-market reorientation appears viable, the strategic change phase is also characterized by:

- an increased emphasis on profits in addition to the early emphasis on cash flow. Return on capital employed is still unlikely to be satisfactory at this phase, although losses have been eliminated
- continued improvements in operational efficiency
- organization building – which may be important, bearing in mind that the organization may have been traumatized in the emergency phase.

One U.S. writer refers to this phase as one of stabilization, because the organization needs time to settle down and prepare for a phase of renewed growth.[9] New management will probably have brought with it a new organizational culture which will take time to become institutionalized. Stabilization is important, yes; but – alone – it is insufficient to give the firm a sound base for the future. That can only be accomplished by refocusing the firm's product-market position or sharpening its existing competitive advantages.

(d) *The growth phase*: Before this can begin, the firm's balance sheet must have improved; once it has the firm can start to grow, either organically through new product development and market developments, or via acquisition or both.

There is likely to be considerable overlap between the four phases of recovery. Not all turnaround firms go through each phase of recovery in sequence, since conditions may demand that a firm go through two phases at once as, for example, where the firm is in a severe survival crisis and strategies have to be implemented with little or no prior evaluation. The length of each phase is also likely to vary, due to the ease with which recovery can be achieved. Firms in growth industries, for example, are likely to be able to reach the growth phase much more quickly than firms in declining industries, since they are in a better position to raise additional finance.

Summary

This chapter has been concerned primarily with the combination of generic strategies that form an appropriate recovery strategy in a turnaround situation. Six groups of factors influence the choice of generic turnaround strategies, and there are significant differences between the strategies adopted in successful and unsuccessful recovery situations. In particular, successful firms use more generic strategies and do a better job of implementation. However, some situations are irrecoverable from the outset, and any attempt at recovery is largely a waste of effort. External events, notably the business cycle, play an important contributory role in aiding recovery. The typical firm places emphasis on different turnaround strategies at different times during corporate recovery, and a four-phase recovery cycle has been identified.

Notes

1. C. Hofer and D. Schendel, *Strategy Formulation, Analytical Concepts*, West Publishing Co., 1978.
2. See for example Hedlom case-study in H. Uyterhoeven, R. Ackerman and J. Rosenblum, *Strategy and Organisation*, Irwin, 1973, p. 716.
3. S. Schoeffler, 'Capital Intensive Technology v. ROI: A Strategic Assessment', *Management Review*, September 1978.
4. See for example P. Kotler, *Marketing Management* (4th edn), Prentice-Hall, 1980; and note (1) above.
5. M. Porter, *Competitive Strategy: Techniques for Analyzing Industries and Competitors*, New York Free Press, 1980.
6. S. St P. Slatter, 'Executive Diagnosis through Component Analysis', *Management Decision*, Vol. 11, Winter 1973, pp. 252–259.
7. S. St P. Slatter, 'Turnaround Strategies in Growth Firms', unpublished Working Paper, 1981.
8. D. Schendel, G. R. Patton and J. Riggs, 'Corporate Turnaround Strategies: A Study of Profit Decline and Recovery', *Journal of General Management*, Vol. 3, No. 3, Spring 1976.
9. D. Bibeault, *Corporate Turnaround*, McGraw-Hill, 1981.

Part Two

Implementing Corporate Recovery

In this part of the book we discuss the implementation of the turn-around strategies discussed in the previous chapters. In a crisis situation, implementation often begins on Day One of the recovery phase. Detailed implementation or action plans necessary to effect successful recovery will, of course, vary from one situation to the next; no two situations will be exactly the same. What follows in Chapters 6 to 10 is intended therefore only as a guide to managerial action. However, the nature of the change that is usually necessary in a crisis situation – the simultaneous implementation of a number of different turn-around strategies as quickly as possible – demands careful thought and attention to the problems of implementation. Too often, the correct strategies are poorly implemented.

6. *Implementation: The Early Days*

We have seen that the successful turnaround usually starts with the appointment of a new chief executive (whom I will refer to as the turnaround manager) and it is his actions in the early weeks with which we are concerned in this chapter. What he does at this time is usually critical to the success of the turnaround. The specific actions will depend on the cause and severity of the financial crisis facing the firm, but the turnaround manager should have a general plan of attack *before* entering the firm. Speed of action is essential, and the turnaround manager needs a proven framework within which to act. His previous management experience will influence what actions he takes,[1] but my own study and experience of successful turnaround situations indicates that the successful turnaround manager needs to undertake the following eight actions immediately on entering a turnaround situation, irrespective of the nature of the situation: gain management control; establish and communicate credibility with the firm's shareholders, banks, suppliers, unions, customers and employees; assess the existing management and replace if necessary; evaluate the business; develop action plans; implement organizational change if appropriate; motivate management and employees; and install or improve budgeting systems. The actions are discussed in approximately the order in which they are implemented but, as with strategy, the turnaround manager will have to be prepared to act on several fronts at once.

1. Gain Management Control

The most important first step for a turnaround manager is to gain control – not just financial control but also management control in the widest sense. It is a wise move to bring in a new financial director or controller on Day One of the turnaround. This is easier to accomplish if the company being turned around is a subsidiary or division of a larger company and a good management accountant can be seconded from head office, perhaps on a temporary basis, while a more permanent financial manager is recruited. If the company is independent, a new finance director may have to be recruited from outside. In either case, the turnaround manager should take immediate steps as soon as he knows of his own appointment to locate and recruit a good management accountant who can work rapidly under pressure.

The steps necessary to gain control are as follows, although much depends on the availability and reliability of existing data:

The legal formalities: If the turnaround manager is to be a member of the firm's board of directors, as is likely to be the case, the legal formalities of confirming his appointment as chief executive at a board meeting should take place immediately. Ideally, this will have been done before his arrival although, if necessary, it can be undertaken at short notice on his arrival. This action merely ensures that the turnaround manager does not act *ultra vires*.

Development of cash-flow forecast: In cash crisis situations, gaining immediate control over the firm's cash flow is the number-one priority. If the crisis is very severe and insolvency is imminent, it is not unknown for turnaround managers to telephone their bank(s) two or three times per day to determine the value of cheques that have been cleared, and thus credited to their account. In this way they know what funds are available to meet their liabilities. (Of course, such action is unlikely to give the bank(s) much confidence, but I will discuss dealing with the bank(s) later in the chapter.) One hopes that daily management of the cash-flow situation can be left to the new finance director, although the turnaround manager is generally going to require routine cash-flow information on a weekly basis for many months after the turnaround has begun. The information he requires is basically quite simple:

- opening bank balance(s)
- receipts from debtors
- amounts paid to creditors (including wages/salaries, etc.)
- capital items (receipts/payments)
- tax and dividend payments
- closing balance.

Establishing the current cash position is obviously a Day One activity for the turnaround manager, but he must then develop a cash-flow forecast for the next six or twelve months. Such a forecast may already exist, in which case the new chief executive (and the finance director) must 'go through it with a fine tooth comb' to determine the reasonableness of the assumptions underlying the forecast. If no such forecast exists, then a 'quick and dirty' cash-flow forecast must be prepared immediately – certainly by the end of the first week of the turnaround. Although management will want to prepare detailed budgets as soon as possible (see page 150), management should *not* wait for this to be achieved before preparing a cash-flow forecast.

What new management needs to know immediately is what its cash-flow position will look like over the next few months, assuming current operations continue unchanged. This is sometimes referred to as a momentum analysis. In particular, management will want to know when the next peak demand for cash is due. Are there loan principal repayments due? When do tax payments become due? Is there a seasonal inventory building period? In putting together such a forecast, new management should build on the knowledge and experience of the old management team if at all possible, but this may not always be easy to achieve. New management may find tremendous resistance from members of the old management team to the idea of putting together a 'rough set of numbers'. The new managers should not be deterred.

Good management will be aware of the obvious shortcomings of 'quick and dirty' forecasts. These early forecasts, however, are likely to play an important role in determining the severity of asset- and cost-reduction strategies required and in negotiating with the banks. Experience shows that this early forecast should be realistic, not optimistic. Besides being consistent with a 'no surprises' management philosophy, a good forecast may be of use in convincing the organization and unions of the severity of the crisis facing the company.

Implement centralized cash control: The immediate implementation of centralized cash control has proven to be a most successful means of gaining control in a turnaround situation. This action only applies to turnaround firms consisting of a number of operating subsidiaries or in those situations where the turnaround firm has just been acquired by another trading entity. Independent companies operating a single business already have central cash control by virtue of their structure.

What does central cash control involve? The basic idea is that all cash balances and bank loan facilities of the subsidiary companies are managed from the centre. A common approach is for the centre (group head-office) to have one central account against which all transactions are made. The individual operating companies may still carry on as though they have their own account with the local branch, but any cash balances are credited to the parent company on a daily basis and any negative balances are debited in the same way. The effect of this on the subsidiary company balance sheet is that cash balances and borrowings appear as zero, and the operating manager is held responsible only for working capital (defined as debtors plus inventories less creditors) and fixed assets (including any goodwill) that are employed in the business. Thus the subsidiary or divisional manager is held responsible for how the capital is employed but not how it is financed, even though the statutory financial accounts of the subsidiary may continue to show bank borrowings and the borrowing may be secured against specific assets in the subsidiary. In fact, the subsidiary manager should be expressly forbidden to borrow money from anybody but head office.

Expenditure controls: Immediate controls over both capital and revenue expenditure should be implemented. The most obvious and most direct control is to capture the chequebook and require all cheques to be signed by the turnaround manager or the new financial director if one has already been recruited. Typical controls over capital expenditure include:

- all capital expenditure shall require the approval of the chief executive (typically all small amounts of capital expenditure – often up to £1,000 – are treated as revenue expense items, and are therefore included in the profit and loss budget)
- all non-profit-earning capital expenditure or capital expenditure which is not absolutely essential to continue operations shall be delayed (e.g. the purchase of new cars).

Typical controls over revenue expenditure which can be implemented immediately include:

- all temporary employment shall halt
- recruitment of all indirect staff shall require the express approval of the chief executive
- recruitment of all direct labour shall require chief executive approval if redundancies are likely, and at all times if the firm is relatively small
- all pay increases shall be temporarily frozen

- offers outstanding to new recruits shall be reviewed and rescinded if necessary
- all foreign travel shall require top management approval
- any price increases from suppliers shall be summarily rejected (see Chapter 9 for further discussion)
- all contracts (e.g. waste disposal, office cleaning contracts, etc.) requiring renewal shall need chief executive approval.

These 'Day One' expenditure controls may actually have more impact on employee attitudes than on cash flow and profit, but the aim is to get the management team at all levels in the firm sharing the values and standards of the turnaround manager. Further specific controls will be added at a later date but, by instituting these controls, the turnaround manager can avoid unnecessary future commitments.

Inventory controls: Every firm needs an inventory control (or stock control) system. If the firm does not have one already in existence, then it is imperative that a simple system be introduced rapidly. Where there are a large number of inventory items, as with a wholesaler, priority should be given to gaining control in accordance with the pareto principle, i.e. control over the 20% of the items which account for 80% of the value of the inventory. Again, speed is essential and, in the absence of any reliable system, a simple card system is likely to be more appropriate than a more sophisticated computer-based system.

Whether there is a system already in existence or not, the new chief executive will want to hold a full 'stock-take' soon after his arrival, to establish the current inventory position and to identify old or obsolete inventory with a view to disposal and/or write-off. This will help in controlling purchasing, since by comparing sales or material usage in the most recent accounting period with actual inventory levels, new management can identify surplus inventory and potential shortfalls in supply. These findings may in turn affect short-term production decisions.

Debtor control: An ageing analysis of debtors and a review of the firm's credit policy are two crucial steps that need to be undertaken within the first few days of the turnaround manager beginning his job. The typical ageing analysis will show debts outstanding by the number of days since the date of invoice:

	Amount outstanding (£)	%
under 30 days		
30–60 days		
60–90 days		
over 90 days		
Total debtors		100%

A reduction in outstanding debtor days may provide management with one of the quickest methods of improving short-term cash flow. How this is carried out is discussed in Chapter 7, although basically it is a question of enforcing already established credit terms by calling or visiting customers or stopping further sales until outstanding debts are paid. A review of the firm's credit policy may sometimes indicate a need for immediate change, as occurred for example at M.F.I., where it was necessary to stop extending credit to mail-order customers (see page 312); but management should be extremely careful about imposing an immediate change in credit terms in all but exceptional circumstances. The impact on customer goodwill can be enormous, and the turnaround firm is in no position to lose this unless it is part of a strategy of withdrawing from a product-market segment.

Improved security: Where a firm has had lax management control systems, the firm may be losing considerable quantities of raw materials or finished goods or both (depending on the nature of the products) as a result of theft. In the case of the soft drinks manufacturer Tizer, it was estimated that approximately 10% of the firm's total output was being pilfered by staff in 1970/71,[2] the year before the firm was acquired by Armour Trust. This occurred primarily because there were no controls over how many cases the low-paid van-driver salesman (who sold goods primarily for cash) took out of the depot or how many they brought back at the end of the day. Perhaps even more amazing, however, was the revelation that, at one depot, the workforce turned down the concentrate drip-tap during bottling, so there was sufficient concentrate available at the end of the day for the workforce to have their own production run!

Reliable inventory control and cost control systems will help reduce theft – though even then there will be crooks who beat the system –

but there are a few simple controls that are suitable for immediate implementation, for example:

- restricting access to sites or areas to specific individuals
- spot checks on inventories (used effectively in retailing, for example)
- changing locks with limited key distribution
- spot checks on delivery vehicles leaving the plant
- close inspection of all goods inward to see that the quantity agrees with the delivery note and that the delivery note agrees with the suppliers' invoice
- control over returns, replacements, samples, etc.

Each business demands different controls to ensure losses are minimized, and management must be careful that these controls are not so elaborate that the cost of implementing them exceeds the expected benefits. Nevertheless, management needs to be alert to how the firm could be swindled.

2. Establish and Communicate Credibility with Stakeholders

Public relations is a most important part of the turnaround manager's job. In a crisis situation there is rarely time to develop a detailed public-relations plan, and the turnaround manager must operate largely from instinct. Initially, the new chief executive needs to obtain the stakeholders' co-operation, and the key to doing this is establishing credibility. Several factors contribute to the turnaround manager's ability to achieve credibility: his personality, negotiating skills, persuasiveness, understanding of the firm's problems and previous track record. Establishing credibility is often conditional on previous management being completely removed from the firm. This means that it is sometimes necessary to change auditors and professional advisers who have become tarred with the same brush as the previous management.

Each of the major stakeholder groups with whom new management needs to communicate in the early days of the turnaround is discussed below:

Banks: Usually the most influential stakeholder group in a crisis turnaround, due to their ability to appoint a receiver, the banks must be visited and kept informed at all times. The turnaround manager should never postpone seeing the banks until his recovery plan is ready. He must see them immediately, inform them of his plan of attack and let them know how long he will need to put together a recovery plan. In a serious financial crisis, the initial meeting with the bank often focuses on persuading the bank to delay appointing a receiver until the turnaround manager has had time to assess the situation and present a detailed recovery plan. By the time the recovery plan is ready – which may take anywhere from two weeks to three months, depending on the size of the firm and the urgency of the situation – the turnaround manager hopes he will be able to show some positive improvements in cash flow, and this will help convince the bank that the firm should not be put into receivership. It is at this point that the turnaround manager may attempt to restructure the firm's debt and/or obtain additional financing.

Suppliers: The turnaround manager may need to buy time from the firm's trade creditors to avoid them applying for a creditor winding-up order, and/or to ensure continuity of supplies during recovery. Trade creditors are usually unsecured creditors and rank *after* secured creditors, government taxes, winding-up costs and employee salaries in any winding-up.[3] The suppliers' greatest leverage comes from threatening to stop supplies, but in situations where there are no alternative sources of supply, cutting off supplies may mean that management has no alternative but to ask the bank or the court to appoint a receiver. More common than cutting off supplies completely is the practice of supplying the turnaround firm on a C.O.D. or cash-with-order basis. Whatever the specific situation, it is important that the turnaround manager should visit the firm's key suppliers and explain the situation to them. Most suppliers are quite understanding and realize (with some persuasion, perhaps) that they have more chance of being paid if they co-operate with new management rather than push the firm into receivership or liquidation, when there will be prior claims by other creditors on the disposable assets.

Unions: The new turnaround manager should meet with key union officials at the local and regional level (and maybe even at the national level, in the case of a very large firm) to seek their co-operation for the turnaround effort. He should also hold a similar meeting with the shop stewards inside the firm. The turnaround manager must be totally honest – *no* promises should be made. The urgency of the situation needs to be outlined to the union leaders. They may welcome the new chief executive and even have specific ideas as to what type of recovery strategy is required. Listening to what they have to say is important even if the turnaround manager disagrees with their views, otherwise the new relationship will get off to a bad start. Regional and, sometimes, local officials are often more understanding of the nature of the crisis than the firm's own shop stewards, whose own jobs may be at stake in the recovery process. Winning the confidence and support of regional officials can be most important in promoting a co-operative industrial-relations climate during recovery. Before meeting with the union officials, the turnaround manager needs to be fully briefed by the existing personnel/industrial-relations staff to identify union attitudes and union leaders known to be 'friendly' to the firm. In other words, the turnaround manager needs to do his homework about the individuals with whom he will be talking. He should be aware that the union leaders themselves have probably done their own homework on the new chief executive. It is not uncommon for unions to seek 'references' on the new chief executive from the employees of firms where the turnaround manager has worked previously. The real crunch on the union front comes if the recovery strategy involves redundancies. This issue is discussed separately in Chapter 9, but the turnaround manager should be aware that the unions usually ask if there will be redundancies or demand a pledge that there will be no redundancies at this first meeting. The turnaround manager must never give any promises at this point.

Customers: Turnaround managers often fail to keep their customers informed of developments and thereby risk losing sales to competitors, who may take advantage of the turnaround firm's crisis by spreading rumours, perhaps that the firm is insolvent and about to go out of business or that a given product line is to be axed or a plant to be closed. If the initiative for the turnaround is acquisition by another firm, then an announcement should be sent to customers emphasizing the new owner's commitment to the industry, and appropriate advertisements or news releases should be made to the trade press. These communications should be supported by the salesforce at their next visit to the customer. Where there is only a change of management, advertisements may be inappropriate, but personal calls by the turnaround manager to the largest customers, a news release, perhaps in the form of a profile of the new chief executive with appropriate quotations, and direct communications via the salesforce will be important.

Employees: Communicating with employees is always a key ingredient of any general management job. It is particularly vital in a turnaround situation and is discussed under motivation in a later section (see page 148).

Public relations in its widest sense is a key aspect of the turnaround manager's job. While much of this activity of necessity take place on a face-to-face basis, the press can play an important role. Favourable press comment can help build credibility and unfavourable reports can just as quickly destroy it with most stakeholder groups. Local newspapers and trade newspapers in particular can be extremely helpful to the turnaround manager, and the cost will be no greater than providing the editor or writer with a free lunch!

3. Assess Existing Management and Replace if Necessary

There is a lot of truth in the old saying that a manager is only as good as the people working for him. No manager can do everything himself – if he tries to, he will usually fail. Recovery must take place through the management structure. Therefore, one of the first things the turnaround manager needs to do is to evaluate the quality of the management team to determine if new management is required. This is particularly true when attempting a turnaround with a large firm or with a smaller diversified firm. Typically, the turnaround manager will spend about two hours with each of his immediate subordinates at some time during the first two or three days on the job, and a shorter period of time (say half an hour to an hour) with other managers further down the line. How many it will be necessary to talk to depends on the size of the firm. In these initial meetings, the turnaround manager will be trying to diagnose the firm's problems and to understand how the organization works, and in the process will be evaluating the managers. Do they know what they are talking about? Do they talk sense? Where do they contradict one another? Do they appear capable of doing their job? The turnaround manager's assessment is unlikely to be completely accurate, and he is likely to stereotype individuals, based on his previous management experience. He will make some mistakes. Some managers will be replaced who should not have been, and others will be kept when they should have been replaced. In talking to turnaround managers, one finds that they usually talk about having kept some people too long, of having given them the benefit of the doubt when they should have been axed early on. Rarely does one find regret at having replaced a manager, although this is hardly surprising since one does not know how well they would have performed had they stayed.

Besides holding a face-to-face meeting with managers, another common method of assessment is to set managers specific projects and deadlines to assist in problem diagnosis. Those who are able to sell themselves in the face-to-face meeting may show up as lightweights – and vice versa – after having to 'perform'. Where the turnaround manager does not have industry experience, he may find it exceptionally difficult to evaluate the quality of the technical personnel. In these situations, some turnaround managers find it useful to bring in an outside 'expert' to assist in the evaluation process.

The time required to assess management will vary according to the size of the firm and the philosophy of the turnaround manager. Typically, decisions are made quickly; it seems that making snap judgements about people is a characteristic of many turnaround managers. The turnaround manager will not always be able to make all the changes he wants to, due to such factors as equity ownership, family relationships, the existence of specialized know-how or contracts, and the impossibility of finding suitable replacements in the short term. However, once the decision has been made to replace a particular manager, there are a series of decisions to be made:

- how is the manager to be removed? Is he to be made redundant? Can he be persuaded to resign?
- what compensation should he receive?
- how long should he stay on site after being informed that his services are no longer required?
- how are new managers going to be recruited? By whom and when?

The method of implementing management changes is important since it reflects on the leadership style of the turnaround manager and, if not handled correctly, can have an adverse effect on the firm. Jim Slater was once quoted as saying: 'I believe in being firm in decision and considerate in execution.'[4] While such quotes are clearly public relations oriented, it is true that unless a turnaround manager handles management changes in a fair and reasonable manner, he may find it difficult in a later assignment to recruit good staff. Some of the issues raised above are discussed in Chapters 8 and 9; if in doubt, the turn-around manager should always take legal advice. The incumbent normally has considerable legal protection in the U.K.; but few turn-around managers are put off by this if they believe change is necess-ary. Sometimes they may use the organizational structure to shift individuals sideways as a halfway measure,[5] but most are prepared to risk having to negotiate a claim for unfair dismissal in the belief that a good manager can more than offset any claim, and that by the time any claim is paid the firm will be in a stronger financial position.

There is one cardinal rule in making management changes in a turnaround situation: do not remove the incumbent from his job if the job is critical to the day-to-day operation of the firm and there is no competent replacement. I know of one situation in which an over-zealous turnaround manager in a small Californian firm dismissed his production manager and then found that nobody else knew 'the secret' of making a certain product. The production manager had to be re-hired three months later, but this caused the turnaround manager other problems – the production manager had changed sex in the meantime!

There is a school of thought that says that pay in lieu of notice is preferable and that managers should clear their desks and vacate their office by the end of the day on which they are told they are no longer required. The rationale for this is that, once given notice, the manager will become 'disruptive' by demotivating his subordinates and others. Each situation must be assessed on its own merits. Where the job is not critical to daily operations and the attitude of the manager concerned is known to be potentially disruptive, this philosophy is probably to be preferred.

Recruiting capable new management is not always as easy as it sounds. The turnaround firm in crisis may find it difficult to attract good managers from more secure situations; furthermore, the time required first to find and then to bring on board a new senior manager may be quite protracted. Many senior managers are required in their contracts to give considerable notice of their intention to leave. For this reason, the turnaround manager very often has to make do with existing management in the emergency phase of the recovery process. One approach that has been used successfully in the emergency phase is that of bringing in consultants specializing in turnarounds. A vari-ation of the approach was used by Angus Murray at Redman Heenan

International when a 'commando force' of individuals known to Murray were hired on a temporary basis to assist in the turnaround effort.[6]

4. Evaluate the Business

The turnaround manager should already have started his diagnosis of the firm's problems *before* his first day on the job. He will have asked many questions before accepting the job, have analysed available financial data, have taken a tour of the main physical facilities, read market reports and other background data. From this data alone, the turnaround expert will have developed a feeling for the principal causes of decline and will have some idea about the type of recovery strategy required. The emphasis in diagnosing the firm's problems and developing an appropriate recovery strategy must be on speed. There is little time for detailed analysis, although in less serious crisis situations it is not unusual for firms to call in consultants to develop a recovery strategy. Because speed is essential, the turnaround manager tends to compare the turnaround firm with various 'rules of thumb' and other firms with which he has been involved over the years. Typical financial rules of thumb relate to such measures as expected pre-tax profit margin, asset turnover, stock turnover and debtor days. Thus one might expect to see the following financial performance in the 'average' firm, although comparison with similar firms in the same industry (using data in the U.K. generated by Inter Company Comparison Ltd, that is available in most business libraries) is more reliable.

Average firm	Gross profit margin %	Pre-tax profit margin %	Asset turn	Inventory turn	Debtor days
Manufacturer	30	10	2×	3×	45–75
Sub-contract manufacturer	25	5	4×	4×	60–90
Wholesaler	15–20	2–3	10×	8–12×	30–60
Contractor	10	5	5×		90–120

One common rule of thumb that is useful in understanding the rapid evaluation necessary in turnaround situations is the pareto on 80:20

concept; this states that the significant items (or factors) in any given group normally constitute a relatively small proportion of the total items (or factors) in the group. It is useful in assisting new management to focus on the key problems and key issues facing the firm. There are likely to be innumerable problems – 'a can of worms in every cupboard', perhaps – but only a few of the problems facing the firm will be critical to its survival. Identifying these issues or, as one turnaround manager puts it, 'finding the jugular vein', is the key to the successful recovery of the turnaround firm.

The appropriate analysis will vary, depending on the nature of the firm's business; in a diversified firm, the first three pieces of analysis listed below will need to be undertaken at both the corporate and subsidiary company levels. The following therefore provides only a guide as to the type of analysis that should be undertaken:

- analyse the profit and loss statement for the last 3/5 years:
  - express the gross profit and the individual cost components as a percentage of sales. Look for the trends
  - re-express the sales revenue and profit (or loss) before tax in real terms (i.e. in today's prices) by applying an inflator to previous years' figures
  - calculate the breakeven sales level
  - understand the cost–price structure of the business
- analyse the year-end balance sheets for the last 3/5 years and estimate the latest balance sheet position:
  - calculate inventory turnover, debtor days, creditor days, current and acid-test ratio
  - calculate long-term debt and total debt as a percentage of shareholders' funds
  - calculate the asset turnover for each year
  - calculate profit as a percentage of average capital employed
  - identify off-balance-sheet items, e.g. leased assets and factored receivables
- compare the firm's financial ratios with those of similar firms
- analyse historical cash flows to determine how the firm has arrived in a cash-flow crisis
- undertake sales analysis:
  - identify the major product lines using the pareto concept
  - go back at least three years and show historical sales trends by value and unit volume (if appropriate). Use moving annual totals if the business is seasonal
  - identify growing and declining products

- identify seasonal patterns
- analyse order books: how firm are the orders?
- undertake profit and contribution analysis for the major selling product lines, using best estimates if there is no realistic costing system (do not wait for accurate costs – there isn't time)
  - calculate the contribution (sales price less variable costs) for the major selling product lines
  - estimate the gross and net profit margins, using two or three different methods of allocating overheads
  - identify the product lines which contribute most of the profit (Note: these may not be the same product lines as account for most of the sales)
  - identify the product lines that do not provide a contribution and those that appear to provide a contribution but not a profit. This analysis can be refined later as existing systems are improved
- undertake customer sales analysis:
  - group customers (e.g. retail chains, independents, wholesalers) and rank customers within each group according to the previous year's sales
  - identify the largest customers (the 20% that account for 80% of the sales), and determine which ones are growing and which are declining
- undertake customer (market segment) profitability analysis:
  - determine gross sales derived from each customer group (gross sales rather than net sales are preferable, as the effect of discounts can then be separated out)
  - determine the gross profit margin for each group of customers and express as a percentage of gross sales.* This shows the effect of the differing sales mix by customer group
  - allocate marketing overheads to each customer group according to the actual or estimated costs incurred by selling to that customer group (see Exhibit 10.1 and discussion on page 227)
  - include a charge for interest on the working capital associated with the customer group, or at least on the outstanding debtors. In a low-margin business, it is not uncommon for the interest charge to eliminate the contribution
  - determine the true profitability of *individual* customers as far as possible since, although a customer group may show a profit or loss, this is an average figure and masks the winners and losers.

* Further analysis to break down the gross profit from each customer group by product line may be important in some situations.

No one customer grouping or market segmentation will be correct. Ideally, this analysis needs to be undertaken for a series of different customer groupings, so that the 'good' customers are separated from the 'bad'

- analyse back orders to determine the level of customer service provided (i.e. what percent of orders can be filled within a stipulated time period):
  - identify the 'problem' products
  - what are the causes of any problem?
- analyse complaints
- analyse key manufacturing data to determine plant utilization and efficiency:
  - determine capacity and capacity utilization
  - analyse time lost due to machine breakdowns, bottlenecks, etc.
- analyse personnel data:
  - identify number of employees by function and by location
  - identify those employed less than one year (they can easily be dismissed if necessary, see Chapter 8)
  - learn the background and qualifications of key managerial and technical personnel
- undertake competitive position analysis for each of the 'key' product lines, using the standard strategic concepts now available:[7]
  - concentrate on the big-volume product lines, the big-profit product lines and those losing money
  - determine the nature of the firm's competitive advantage or disadvantage in each case.

This is not an exhaustive checklist, merely my starting point for diagnosing problems and developing a data base for formulating a recovery strategy. By itself, the analysis rarely provides answers and the conclusions that one can draw from much of the quantitative analysis are more often symptoms than causes. Nevertheless, this analysis will focus the attention of the turnaround manager on the key problems and key issues; he should then be able to choose the appropriate set of turnaround strategies required in any given situation.

In diagnosing the firm's problems and deciding on the appropriate course of action, the turnaround manager must ask lots of questions and be a good listener. He must be sceptical of any numbers he is provided with and must dig hard to get the facts. Getting the facts – 'the unshakeable facts', as Harold Geneen, formerly chairman of ITT, used to say – is one of the hardest parts of the turnaround manager's job. Existing management may find it difficult to distinguish fact from fiction: what has been regarded for years as a truism is often a myth. Furthermore, self-protection and resistance to change means many managers will be 'covering up' . . . not necessarily lying, but distorting the facts.

5. Action Planning

Once the turnaround manager has decided on the appropriate recovery strategy, he must develop an action plan in conjunction with his management team. Action planning is designed to overcome four familiar implementation problems that are common to all business situations but more acute in a turnaround situation, due to the time pressures. These are:

- not having enough time to do everything and not being sure what to do first, thereby resulting in wasting time on less critical tasks
- becoming immersed in day-to-day problems and details, thereby losing sight of the few really important activities that affect results
- the chief executive not always being certain of what is expected of him and assuming that the banks, shareholders and board of directors know what he is doing
- the chief executive irritating and confusing the people who work for him; therefore he does not get the best out of them.

The answer to each of these problems lies in concentrating on a small number of issues that will produce the greatest cash flow and/or profit, then setting up good communications to ensure that everybody in the firm knows what these are. Action planning assists in this process by providing a framework for implementation. There are four steps in action planning:

(a) identify and list the tasks needed to implement the recovery strategy. Go through each functional area or department to determine which tasks need to be undertaken.

(b) assess the relative importance of the tasks, and rank in order of priority according to which has *greatest* impact on results.

(c) for each task, develop practical action steps. Do not jump straight to the obvious. There is usually more than one way of tackling a task.

(d) agree short-term actions with subordinates. Decide what is to be

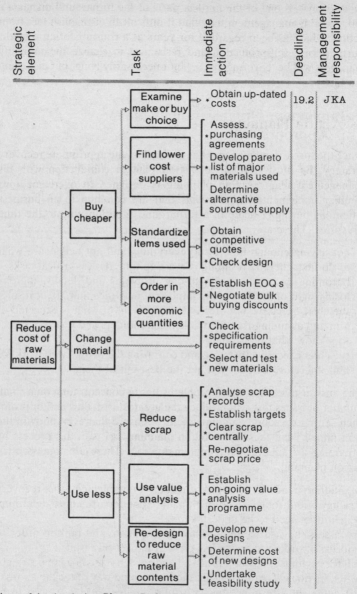

Figure 6.1: *An Action Plan to Reduce Cost of Raw Materials*

Source: Stuart St P. Slatter, 'Executive Diagnosis Through Component Analysis', *Management Decision*, Vol. 11, Winter 1973.

done, by whom and when. Assign specific management responsibility and set up review dates. Keep it short and simple, but put it on paper to make it formal.

Figure 6.1 provides an example of an action plan to implement part of a cost-reduction strategy.

6. Implement Organizational Change if Appropriate

In Chapter 4, we indicated that divisionalization and decentralization was an appropriate turnaround strategy, although organizational change below the top management level was usually inappropriate in the early days of the recovery period. Implementing divisionalization and decentralization, like any other organizational change, requires unlearning and learning. It requires new perspectives and new managerial behaviour, both of which may take time to occur. Organizational change is not simply a question of the chief executive sending out a memorandum, new job descriptions and a new organization chart, although he will probably do that. For organizational change to be effective, on-the-job training is necessary. This is all very well in theory, but there will be considerable pressure on the turnaround manager for results in the emergency phase of recovery, and little or no time for training and organization-building. Thus, organizational change in a turnaround often goes hand in hand with new top management; where existing management remains, they will have to sink or swim in the new, decentralized management culture. Some will adapt while others, who were perfectly competent in the old organizational structure, are like fish out of water in the new one. The risks connected with organizational change are clearly high, due to the time pressures in a turnaround, but my research tends to show that organizational change, and decentralization in particular, is a risk worth taking in spite of the fact that a second set of management changes may have to be made if the existing managers cannot adapt to the new structure.

In adopting a divisionalized, decentralized structure, it is important that a specific action plan be developed and that top management knows what it is doing before it acts. It must communicate clearly, not only with the managers directly concerned but with all the employees, as to the rationale and expected benefits from the change.

7. Motivate Management and Employees

Corporate recovery means change, and change within firms tends to be resisted since some individuals will invariably be affected in a way they do not like. The achievement of a sustained recovery requires that the organization be motivated towards this end: it is achievable through the leadership of the chief executive and the establishment of good communications and performance standards within the firm.

We all have a vague notion of what we mean by leadership, but it is a concept difficult to define accurately. In a turnaround situation it means: giving a sense of direction by setting priorities and short-term goals; establishing a sense of urgency; defining responsibilities; resolving conflict; conveying enthusiasm and dedication; and giving credit where it is due and rewarding it accordingly.

At the beginning of this chapter I discussed gaining control in financial, rather than organizational, terms. Organizational control, however, is an important concept and one which the turnaround manager is concerned about in the first few weeks on the job. The turnaround manager, as the new chief executive, clearly has a power base derived from his position in the firm, his ability to reward subordinates and his expertise, and this may be enough to gain control. There are well-known turnaround managers who operate on the basis of 'I am the new chief executive, therefore you will . . .'. One such manager (who shall be nameless) once reported to my class at London Business School that, on acquiring a firm in need of turnaround, he arrives by helicopter on Day One and looks for somebody to dismiss, usually the general manager. In this way he established his authority immediately! This particular individual has, by most standards, been very successful. However, my view and that of others in this field is that, while the turnaround manager needs to be autocratic in the early days of the turnaround, it is only the manager's personal leadership skills that will improve morale and motivate the organization to meet the longer-term goals.[8] Without such skills, short-term profit improvements can be achieved, but sometimes at the expense of organizational morale.

Communications is a line management function, so the chief executive must always be the chief communicator. In a turnaround, the chief executive usually has to have direct communication *further down* the organization than may be common in a healthy firm. The reason for this is that the management and organizational culture which the turnaround manager has inherited is usually not used to open communications. In fact, as we saw in Chapter 3, secrecy is a common characteristic in crisis situations. Thus, unless there is a large number of new managers down the organization – which is unlikely, at least in the emergency phase of recovery – the turnaround manager must take on more of this burden. The type of communication necessary depends on the size and diversity of the firm. In a large firm, in-house newspapers and audio-visual presentations may be necessary. Thus British Leyland used film to inform the workforce of Sir Michael Edwardes's recovery plan. But for management and the salesforce, the necessary communications can be achieved through short, regular meetings.

It is very easy in the heat of the emergency phase to forget about or to postpone communications, despite having good intentions. In particular it is easy either to think one's subordinates know what one wants, or to think that because you have told them once you really communicated with them. What you as a turnaround manager may think is communication overkill will rarely be so in practice. The type of turnaround strategies adopted in a recovery situation and the speed with which they have to be implemented are often so alien to the existing management that effective communication is more important than ever.

The establishment of performance standards plays a key role in changing the culture of an organization. Such standards start at the top with the turnaround manager. In his daily contact with managers and employees, the chief executive's actions and behaviour are constantly being watched and commented on by subordinates. Even seemingly trivial actions convey messages about the chief executive's values and expectations. However, for performance standards to be effective they must be measured. The effective implementation of a budgetary control system is a great help in this area, although many of the performance standards required in a recovery situation are qualitative by nature and require a performance appraisal system. The turnaround manager will be unlikely to give personnel systems top priority – at least in the emergency phase – with the result that performance measurement is either financial or highly subjective in the early days of recovery. In the longer term, formal appraisal systems are clearly part of sound management practice.

The turnaround manager needs to plug himself into the grapevine in the first few days in the firm if he is to be effective from an organizational standpoint. It may be the receptionist, the switchboard operator, the security guard or the ubiquitous tea-lady, but most organizations have a few people who know what is happening and/or are aware of rumours and simmering problem situations. The grapevine may not only be important in assisting the development of implementation tactics; it may also provide information eliminating waste and theft.

8. Installation or Improvement of Budgetary Systems

The turnaround manager cannot gain full control until he has a fully effective budgetary system in the firm. Few turnaround firms have such a system, so either a new system will have to be installed or improvements made to the existing system. The size of the firm and the current state of its financial control systems will determine the necessary actions to be taken. Discussion here will be confined to a few points of special relevance to the turnaround manager; the reader is referred to standard books on financial control for details of how to install a budgetary system.

(a) A satisfactory budgetary system may be in place already, but what is required is for management to use the budget as a daily management tool.

(b) If there is a budget in existence, new management will want to determine how realistic it is. If the firm is currently meeting budget, and future projections do not indicate any significant change, the budget may be realistic, although clearly this would not be true if the firm were in a deteriorating competitive position or a rapidly declining market.

(c) If there is no budget in existence, the turnaround manager will need to make some very rough projections of the current situation (referred to earlier as a momentum analysis) on arrival, so that he can produce the cash-flow forecast mentioned at the beginning of this chapter.

(d) Developing and installing a new financial control system will take from one to six months, depending on the size of the firm. Decentralization can assist in the installation of budgetary control systems by establishing manageable profit centres. Detailed budgets and revised cash-flow forecasts should be prepared as soon as the recovery plan has been formulated, otherwise the turnaround manager will not be able to determine whether his recovery plan is working.

(e) The sales budget will be the most difficult component to forecast, particularly if there is heavy reliance on market improvement or product-market reorientation strategies. The precise impact of increasing prices and increasing or retargeting selling effort is also difficult to forecast in the absence of reliable historical data on the shape of the sales response function.

(f) Computerized information systems may be required, but any consideration of such systems has typically to be postponed until after the emergency phase, particularly in a large firm.

(g) The budget system is one of the major motivational tools used by the turnaround manager in that it lays down clearly defined performance standards.

The typical turnaround firm does not require complicated bureaucratic systems – just the opposite: simplicity is the key if managers are to be totally familiar with their budgets and variances.

Summary

The eight actions outlined in this chapter are geared to implementing both the organizational and control strategies required in a turnaround and planning what other strategies are required to achieve corporate recovery. While the turnaround manager will primarily be concerned with these eight steps, he may be simultaneously beginning to implement the cost-reduction, asset-reduction and revenue-generating strategies discussed in the remainder of this book even *before* the evaluation and action planning phases have been completed. Some of the strategies required, particularly those relating to cost- and asset-reduction, are so obvious and the time pressure so great that 'ten minutes' of analysis may be sufficient before implementation begins. Even in the case of divesting a subsidiary, the decision may be taken with virtually no analysis. Ideally, one will want time to make some evaluation, but crisis turnarounds demand action, and analysis (and discussion) invariably has to be cut short in order to start the implementation phase.

Notes

1. See Chapter 4 for a discussion of the background of the turnaround manager.

2. Estimates given by A. Balcombe, Director of Armour Trust (who purchased Tizer in December 1971), during lecture at London Business School, February 1979.
3. Companies Acts, 1948 and 1981.
4. Slater Walker case-study published in J. Stopford, D. Channon and D. Norburn, *A Casebook: British Business Policy*, Macmillan, 1975.
5. See Chapter 4.
6. See Chapter 6.
7. See, for example, Michael Porter, *Competitive Strategy*, Free Press, 1980; and C. Hofer and D. Schendel, *Strategy Formulation: Analytical Techniques*, West Publishing, 1978.
8. C. Remick, 'Time for a Turnaround? Take Comfort, Take Stock, Take Action', *S.A.M. Advanced Management Journal*, Autumn 1980.

7. *Implementing Asset-reduction Strategies*

Most companies utilize asset-reduction strategies when in a recovery situation. These strategies comprise fixed-asset-reduction strategies and working-capital-reduction strategies. The approach used for implementing each of these strategies is quite different.

Reducing fixed assets usually means divestment (or disinvestment). Divestment may mean seeking a buyer for a semi-autonomous division or operating unit, or it may mean selling off less than a full operating unit such as a plant, a product line or specific assets such as land, machines, warehouses, office buildings and vehicles. While divestment is the obvious way of reducing fixed assets, sale and leaseback of property, plant and machinery is an alternative method of raising cash in the short term. The reduction of working capital is achieved primarily by reducing inventories and debtors and (where possible) extending creditors.

1. Divesting Operating Units

A small group of top management personnel is usually given responsibility for conducting a divestiture, once the strategic decision has been made. There are at least three reasons for this. First, companies tend to divest in secret, fearing that knowledge of the decision would depress morale and efficiency of the unit concerned. Second, the head of the operating unit being sold is almost never the right person to sell his company. Divestiture is an admission of failure and generally brings out differences of opinion between those responsible for the divestment situation and those who are not (i.e. top management). And third, few managers have anything to gain from helping with divestiture: it is an ungrateful task with 'no tomorrow'.

However, although top management has the responsibility for implementation, it rarely has the time to implement a proper divestment programme. This is generally true whenever divestment occurs, but is particularly true in a recovery situation. Top management has neither the time nor (very often) the inclination to make a thorough analysis of the unit involved and its industry. As we saw in Chapter 4, divestment decisions often have to be based on something less than an in-depth analysis of the situation. Furthermore, they do not have adequate time either to search for buyers or to negotiate with more than one or possibly two potential buyers at the same time.

In addition to a lack of top management time, divestitures in recovery situations are usually subject to very strong time pressures. The operating unit concerned may be incurring large operating losses that are a cash drain on the business, and/or the cash proceeds from its sale are urgently needed to help save the parent company. Other factors also contribute to the time pressure. Management will want to execute the divestiture rapidly so as not to leave the company 'on the market' for too long, as this may scare off potential buyers or force a reduction in the asking price. The longer the company is on the market, the greater the possibility of leaks. Premature leaks can lead to industrial action, key personnel leaving and general loss of employee motivation. The combination of lack of management time and the need for speedy action results in companies not realizing divestitures as effectively as they should.

Rigorous action planning is required to maximize the cash flow from divestiture. A critical error many companies make in divestiture is to focus on the value of the business to them instead of focusing on the value of the business to others. There are three questions management should ask:

- What are we selling?
- Who is potentially the best type of purchaser?
- What is it worth to him?

The following five-step approach to divestiture is a tried and tested approach to ensure that the firm is successful in its divestment programme.

1.1 Preparing A Prospectus

The first step in implementing the divestiture is to prepare a prospectus which describes the operating unit being sold in an *objective* manner. Table 7.1 outlines the major headings that might be included in a typical prospectus. However, rather than being purely descriptive, the prospectus should be analytical. It should answer questions such as:

Why have gross margins fallen or improved? Why have manufacturing costs increased? Has this been an industry trend or not?

Table 7.1: *Outline of a Prospectus for Divesting Operating Subsidiary*

Section heading	Content summary
Executive summary	One-page summary of prospectus highlights.
The product line	Description of what business the firm is in.
The market	Market size, growth rates, etc.
Competition	Identify competitors, market shares and competitive forces in the industry segments in which the firm competes.
Economics of the business	Cost-price structure.
Management and organization	Brief curriculum vitae of management team; details of organization structure, number of employees, pension funding, union agreements, etc.
Production	Description of plants and manufacturing process/equipment.
Balance sheet	Year-end balance sheets for last three years together with analysis, explanation and description of fixed assets.
Historical performance	Analysis of profit and loss statements for last five years, explaining performance.
Future performance	Projected financial statements for next five years together with details of new products, etc.

Let us take an example of a small food company, where our findings are as follows:

- the company's sales have failed to grow as fast as expected
- it has made operating losses for the past four years
- its products are relatively undifferentiated and have had to contend with severe price cutting by the industry leader
- its plant is far too large for its foreseeable needs and its rent cost inordinately high
- its national sales and merchandising network is too expensive for its present sales volume.

An analysis of the company's strengths against the background of its environment might yield the following conclusions:

Product line: its products are complementary to other food products

Brand-names: the company's main brand-names are associated with high quality at the top end of the market, and could possibly be transferred to complementary products

Production capacity: its sachet-filling capacity is in great demand in other segments of the food industry

Distribution network: its products are sold through both high-volume outlets and traditional retailers

Management: the managing director is leaving, but the manufacturing and marketing directors are very competent and would remain after a sale.

Each of the above conclusions is a potential selling point. The analysis has shown that the company is not 'all bad'; in fact, there are a number of valuable operating 'assets' for sale. Not surprisingly, the typical prospectus does not dwell on the weaknesses of the operating unit, on the basis that one does not usually sell anything by pointing out the weaknesses and that what may appear as a weakness to the seller may actually be a strength for a potential buyer.

A discussion of the assets for sale and what a potential purchaser would be buying from a financial point of view is necessary. To what extent is the latest balance sheet a fair representation of the value of the business that is for sale? Subsidiary balance sheets are often quite meaningless, and the balance sheet may need to be restructured following a sale. Has the business been financed by debt from the parent company? Has the parent given guarantees for bank indebtedness, or does the company have its own banking relationships? Would the current level of shareholders' funds support current indebtedness without new parent-company guarantees? Are the assets undervalued or overvalued? All these questions, and more, should be answered in the prospectus.

Some discussion as to what a prospective purchaser might do with the company from a financial point of view might be included as a selling point (e.g. selling off fixed assets, reducing working capital, etc.) The existence of tax loss carry-forwards that may be available to a potential purchaser may also be an important selling point, although the value of tax loss carry-forward is often put at no more than about 10% of its nominal value, and often less.

The one thing the prospectus does not usually include is the asking price. The aim of the prospectus is to provide a reasonably objective description of the company and to stress what is being sold in both operating and financial terms. The aim is to get prospective purchasers sufficiently interested to learn more and enter into negotiations. From the seller's point of view, he wants to get prospective purchasers committed to the idea of purchasing the company before discussing price. Psychologically, this gives him a negotiating advantage.

The preparation of a prospectus or selling document can substantially increase one's chance of a successful divestiture. It does, however, take time to prepare; but it means that one has something 'concrete' with which to approach a potential purchaser. The time taken to prepare a prospectus will obviously vary according to the size of the company, the complexity of the business and the extent to which the required data are readily accessible. However, a skilled individual should be able to prepare a 'professional' prospectus in ten to twenty man-days of work. In a recovery situation, top management will be very unlikely to have this time available, unless the parent company is fairly large and can put one executive in charge of divestitures. Planning staff, if they exist, should be able to prepare an adequate document. In small to medium-size companies, the chief executive may find it pays him to obtain outside assistance in this task. Consultants and firms specializing in divestment work, rather than traditional merchant banks, would be likely resources.

1.2 Identifying Prospective Purchasers

Having prepared the prospectus, the second step is to determine who is potentially the best type of purchaser. Using our food company example, we may come to the conclusion that the purchase of the company would make most sense for someone:

- selling a complementary line of products
- needing sachet-packing capacity for his own products
- seeking to introduce his existing product line in either high-volume or traditional outlets
- looking for an operating unit that has the management and space for future expansion.

Companies fitting this description are then identified by desk research, using Kompass, trade directories, etc., and a list of possible candidates is prepared. Their accounts are then studied to eliminate those incapable of making an acquisition of this size, and press clippings and similar information are collected to see if any of these companies has an explicit or implicit strategy that could be aided by the acquisition of the company to be divested. The possible candidates are then placed in order of priority interest as likely purchasers.

1.3 Valuing the Business

The final step before approaching potential purchasers is to calculate what the business might be worth to each of them. The types of question that might be asked include the following:

- What future profits can be derived over the next five years by each buyer?
- What is the impact of his financial position and what risks would he be running?
- What price would provide him with a return on investment equal to that of his current business?

Management will obviously look at different methods of valuing the business, such as net asset value, some multiple of historical earnings (if there have been earnings), net asset value adjusted for the fair market valuation of property, future discounted cash flow; and will probably arrive at high and low figures. However, the true value of the business is only what somebody is prepared to pay for it. For example, selling excess manufacturing capacity at a time when there is substantial industry over-capacity will mean that assets may be sold considerably below book value (a figure which itself is based on historical costs). The value of the business may even be zero, and a purchaser cannot be found at any price – in which case liquidation is the obvious alternative. However, liquidation may be an expensive business where redundancies, leases and other contracts are involved, with the result that it may be cheaper to pay management or an entrepreneur to take control of the business. Assuming the business has some potential to somebody, the final price likely to be obtained lies somewhere between the value to management divesting itself of the business and the value to the potential purchaser.

In recovery situations, management's time horizon will be an important element affecting the price. If the company is about to go into receivership or be forced into liquidation, management may well accept a lower price than it would otherwise in order to obtain a quick sale to improve its cash-flow position. If the parent company is in a desperate situation, it may well obtain a lower price than it would otherwise, because, if potential purchasers know (as they should) that the parent company has to divest itself of a particular operating unit very quickly, they are in a relatively strong negotiating position.

One planning step that should be undertaken concurrently with the three planning steps mentioned above is for management to think through all the practical implications of the divestiture. The types of questions that should be asked are as follows:

- Will sale to the parties envisaged be referred to the Monopolies Commission? How long would this delay the sale, and what would be the financial implications of the delay?
- Can trade-union support for a sale to the parties envisaged be expected? If not, what short-term industrial relations strategy should be adopted?
- What is the most tax-effective way of selling the company?

1.4 Approaching Potential Buyers

Now management is ready to approach potential buyers. The usual approach is to 'sound out' a few potential buyers at a time, say half-a-dozen – those at the top of the priority list – to see if they would be interested in acquiring a business in 'industry X with a turnover of approximately £Y million'. The 'sounding out' is done either by a short letter or telephone call to the chief executive of the prospective purchaser. At this stage it is not normal to divulge much information. Certainly, the prospectus is *not* sent out unless the chief executive contacted (or one of his subordinates, if he has referred the inquiry down to him) expresses an interest in learning more about the opportunity presented to them. Confidentiality is stressed in all communications, and it is usual practice to ask for the prospectus to be returned if the prospective purchaser is not interested in pursuing discussions.

In some situations, top management may prefer to have a third party contact prospective purchasers for them. This may arise because management lacks the time, or feel they do not have the skills to 'sell' a company, or want to maintain secrecy for as long as possible. If they make the initial contact themselves, their identity is immediately known to every prospective purchaser, whether or not he has any real interest in the purchase. By using a third party, confidentialities can be maintained for a longer period of time, since the third party can sound out the potential interest of prospective purchasers without divulging the name of the company for sale. This will not always be feasible, as in an industry or market segment where there are few competitors or where the product or service is unique, since in these situations it may be hard to give any facts at all without divulging the identity of the company. This third-party role is often played by merchant banks – although the experience of some companies is that merchant banks too often put up the 'For Sale' sign and hawk companies around indiscriminately. Certainly, the major merchant banks rarely develop a prospectus of the type discussed earlier and prepare a carefully screened list of likely purchasers.

1.5 Communicating with the Management of the Business Being Sold

Up to this point in the divestment process, top management may have been able to avoid informing the chief executive or general manager of the business being sold of their plans. Whether or not maintaining secrecy for so long is a good idea is debatable. The subsidiary chief executive may have to be brought in at the prospectus-writing stage if top management lacks adequate information about the business being sold. Furthermore, it could be a positive step, in that he may have good ideas as to prospective purchasers or ways in which the business can be best presented for selling purposes. Management's decision will usually depend on their assessment of the chief executive's likely reaction to the news of divestiture. If he is likely to be co-operative or they want to keep him, they will tell him early on. If he is likely to be strongly opposed to the sale, they will usually delay telling him – although they will have to inform him once interested buyers want to visit the company. It is quite rare that a business is sold over the head of its chief executive, with him knowing nothing of it until the deal is signed and sealed. In recovery situations, the reaction of chief executives to the news that they are to be divested is often favourable – perhaps more often than in 'normal' divestiture situations. This is particularly true in those situations where a new top management 'turnaround' team has arrived. The management style and new organizational culture may be anathema to the subsidiary management, and they will be happy to be sold – with luck, to an organization which will cause a minimum amount of upheaval.

Divestiture is facilitated if the general manager and his team co-operate. The subordinate managers will usually be influenced by the general manager's stance. Co-operation will mean, first, that prospective purchasers are not actively discouraged from buying the business when they visit the plant. This can happen; the general manager and/or his team may try to sabotage the sale *per se*, or they may be selective in their sabotage, only discouraging purchasers for whom they would not like to work. Sometimes sabotage of this nature can signal the fact that the general manager (and possibly his team) want to buy the business themselves at a knock-down price when no buyer can be found. To the seller, co-operation can mean not only making the finding of a buyer easier, but also the chance to obtain a better price for the business. A prospective buyer will consider the business to be worth more if it has a management team prepared to co-operate enthusiastically with a new owner (assuming, of course, they are a reasonably competent team).

2. Management Buy-outs

One likely purchaser that top management should not forget is the existing management of the company to be divested; this is one reason why subsidiary management should be informed at an early date. Although the managers are unlikely to have the funds available to pay the purchase price themselves, the idea of management buy-outs (or, as the Americans say, leveraged buy-outs) has become increasingly popular in recent years. The idea is not new but has gained increased popularity in the late 1970s, and some City institutions, notably Investors in Industry and Candover Investments, have been extremely active in providing finance for such ventures. There are many variations, depending on the financial creativity and negotiating ability of the parties involved, but the basic idea is as follows. Management finds one or more financial backers and together they form a new company to buy the company being sold. Since management is likely to have little in the way of cash available to invest in the new company, the equity base is kept relatively small to permit management to subscribe for a substantial share of the equity. The balance of the funds required to buy the company is provided by the financial backer(s) by way of term debt, preference shares or some form of convertible instrument. Some of the finance is typically provided by the clearing banks as an overdraft facility to fund working-capital requirements, in which case the backers' loans are subordinated to those of the clearing bank.

Management's share of the equity depends on (i) the amount of cash they are able to raise themselves; (ii) their management track record; (iii) the prospects for their company; and (iv) their negotiating ability. The financial backer, however, is likely to want a substantial proportion of the equity to provide him with enough capital gain for an above-average return on his total investment. It is difficult to generalize as to what percentage of the equity management might obtain; the range tends to vary from about 15% up to about 70%. Many management teams will aim for control (i.e. 51% of the shares). A few greedy ones will want 75.1% ownership, so that the financial backer cannot call an extraordinary general meeting; but this is unlikely unless management is able itself to put up about half of the total capital required.

Having established the new company, the idea is that the principal and interest on the loans are repaid out of internally generated cash flow. There are likely to be dividend restrictions on the common stock until all, or at least a significant portion, of the debt has been repaid. Thus, although the financial backer may not have majority ownership, he often has effective control through loan covenants and debenture agreements.

3. Divesting Specific Assets

The approach used for divesting operating units can be used for selling off assets surplus to the future requirements of the business and other assets such as product lines, franchise rights, etc. The approach taken really depends on the type and value of the asset. The larger the asset, the more time and effort management will want to take.

Surplus land and buildings are usually disposed of through estate agents specializing in commercial property, although a private sale to companies with adjoining premises might be tried, prior to using agents. The thing to remember, in a recovery situation, about disposing of property is that it may take a long time to find a buyer, particularly at times of economic recession, and this is just the time when a recovery situation is most likely to occur. If one can afford to wait long enough, land and buildings eventually sell at a reasonable price which may be not too far from book value (or even considerably in excess of it if revaluation has not occurred); surplus plant and equipment may be more difficult to sell at a reasonable price. The demand for second-hand machinery is not great and the scrap value is usually low, although this obviously depends on the type of machinery. There may be an overseas market, often in less developed countries, as there was, for example, for large cranes used on North Sea oil-rigs up until the end of 1979. Typically, in recovery situations the machinery is old and obsolete and was one of the factors contributing to the company's initial decline. There are companies specializing in the sale of plant and equipment, but the prices they offer are generally low – much lower than would be achieved by a private sale to a competitor.

The easiest assets to realize are usually surplus vehicles – trucks, vans and cars – for which there is an established market price unless the vehicles are specialist, custom-made vehicles.

4. Sale and Leaseback of Assets

Where the company's assets are not surplus to requirements, but where large amounts of capital are tied up in fixed assets, management may decide to realize cash for some of its assets through a sale and leaseback arrangement. This is easiest to implement for buildings, particularly good office buildings; but factories, plant and equipment can also be sold and leased back. There are many leasing companies, ranging from arms of commercial banks to the large insurance companies (which are most interested in property) and finance houses specializing in equipment leasing. Expert financial and legal advice is necessary before entering into such an agreement. (The financial implications of leasing can be quite complex, and it is not always intuitively obvious whether sale and leaseback makes sense from a financial point of view. There are, however, services available such as that provided by the London Business School for helping firms evaluate options.) Companies with severe liquidity problems will usually find it very difficult, if not impossible, to implement a sale and leaseback arrangement because their property is already likely to be mortgaged and the bank will have a charge of the remainder of its assets.

5. Reducing Working Capital

Actions to reduce working capital are typical of most recovery situations and can be implemented much more quickly than strategies to reduce fixed assets. We will start by discussing inventory reduction, then proceed to debtors and creditors.

5.1 Reducing Inventories

The method adopted for cutting back on inventories depends very much on the nature of the inventories. A different approach is required, depending on whether we are trying to reduce raw-material inventory, work-in-progress inventory or finished-goods inventory.

Raw-material inventory is typically the easiest and quickest to reduce. There are six major options which can be used in combination with one another. They are discussed briefly below:

(*a*) *Stop purchasing*: If the inventory is all current and likely to be used in production, a stop on purchasing is all that is required, assuming there are no supply contracts. If there are contracts, then management will have to attempt to renegotiate the contracts – something that may not be too difficult to do, bearing in mind that few suppliers will want to push hard for completion of the contract if there is a danger they will not be paid.

(*b*) *Cancel outstanding orders*: An even more immediate impact can be made by cancelling outstanding orders. If the goods are already in transit, the company can always refuse to accept delivery. Legally, they may be in breach of contract, but cancelling orders is common practice and usually of little consequence, unless the order is for custom-made components or parts which the supplier cannot easily sell elsewhere.

(*c*) *Return goods to suppliers*: If goods have been received but are not yet paid for, it may still be possible to return them without incurring a penalty. In many industries there is a noticeable increase in returns at times of economic depression. Sometimes the reason given for the return is the honest answer 'over-stocking' or 'over-ordering', but one also notices buyers becoming more quality-conscious and more strict about suppliers meeting delivery dates. (In the furniture industry, manufacturers often notice an increase in the number of items 'damaged in transit' during recessionary periods. The more cynical manufacturers believe that not all the damage is actually done in transit, and newly delivered goods may be purposely damaged by retailers to provide an excuse for return.) The number of so-called excuses for returning goods is large, and few suppliers take action against their customer, for fear of losing him permanently.

(*d*) *Order more frequently*: By purchasing in smaller quantities more frequently, management may be able to lower inventory levels. The financial attractiveness of this option depends on a trade-off between inventory carrying costs and purchasing costs, since the unit purchasing cost may be greater for smaller quantities. However, in recovery situations the immediate need to reduce working capital may be of paramount importance for survival, with the result that high unit purchasing costs will be accepted as a short-term price to pay for survival.

(*e*) *Change suppliers*: Many companies keep high raw-material inventory levels as a safety valve so that production will not be disrupted if a supplier is late delivering, has a strike or delivers faulty goods. This is hardly surprising in an age of general supply difficulties; yet in the short term it may be a luxury which the firm cannot afford, and in the long term it may be unnecessary. Management should look for alternative, more reliable suppliers so that they can hold lower safety stocks. However, there are risks involved in this action. Will the new supplier really supply on time? Will the quality of his product be consistent? The failing company needs only to have a disruption in its source of supply at a critical stage for it not to survive.

(*f*) *Sell surplus raw materials to third parties*: This is usually the option of last resort, since the selling price is likely to be substantially below the cost price. It is the action most often taken to eliminate obsolete inventory. There are companies that specialize in buying obsolete inventory, but they may offer as little as 10% of the original purchase price.

Reduction of work-in-progress inventories involves improved production scheduling or changes in manufacturing methods to reduce bottlenecks in the production flow. The results usually take longer to achieve than reducing either raw materials or finished goods, but this depends on the inefficiencies in the manufacturing system at the time.

Implementing a reduction in finished-goods inventory is accomplished by two actions: a reduction in output and by special marketing incentives to assist in the speedy sale of the goods. The first action is designed to realign production with expected sales level. It may involve redundancies and will certainly involve reducing raw-materials inventory levels as well. The introduction of special marketing incentives usually means lowering price by giving larger discounts. This is only justified if it is a short-term measure to alleviate a cash-flow crisis, even though it will hurt profitability in the short term. As a long-term strategy, lowering prices rarely works, as was discussed in Chapter 4.

5.2 Reducing Debtors

There are two aspects of debt control that typically need attention in a recovery situation: the enforcement of published terms, and an actual reduction in the number of debtors days outstanding. It is not uncommon to find poorly managed businesses in which the published terms of trade are not adhered to by customers; for example, where customers are granted a $2\frac{1}{2}\%$ cash discount for payment within thirty days of the date of invoice (or monthly statement), customers may still be deducting the cash discount even though they pay after the thirty-day limit has expired. Thus the first step should always be to ensure that current terms of trade are being strictly enforced. As we have already discussed, reducing the number of debtor days is often the quickest way of generating cash in a turnaround situation. There are a number of approaches that management can use:

(a) *Identify overdue accounts and place stop orders on them*: It is likely that some customers are considerably overdue in paying their accounts; no further goods should be dispatched or services provided until existing accounts have been paid. Customers should be informed of such action by management or the salesforce.

(b) *Contact customers*: This is the most obvious and direct approach. Telephone calls and personal calls to customers by management can have a direct impact on cash flow. Do not rely on the salesforce to do an effective job in this area in the short term if they have not been used to assist in debt collection in the past. Training salesmen to do this effectively takes time.

(c) *Tighten up on credit analysis*: It is very important to check the creditworthiness of one's major customers and one's overdue accounts at an early stage. The insolvency of a major customer could be the final nail in the coffin for the turnaround firm.

(d) *Factoring*: Most banks provide a factoring service for debtors. Terms and conditions vary, but essentially the firm will discount debtors, giving cash to the turnaround firm as soon as the invoices are sent out. The banks are then responsible for collecting the debts. In general, factoring is not as good an option as it sounds for the turnaround firm, since the banks can charge quite heavily for this service and, for a failing firm, may pick and choose the debts they will factor.

(e) *Change settlement terms*: Reducing credit terms and cash discounts can of course influence customer behaviour, but this can be a highly emotional area as far as customers are concerned. The turnaround firm needs every bit of support it can get from its customers in the emergency phase of recovery. It cannot afford to upset them; so it should be sure that any changes in settlement terms are not out of line with those of its competitors.

5.3 Extending Creditors

Few firms in a cash crisis have this option. Creditors have usually been extended as far as they will go – if not further – before recovery actions begin in a crisis situation. The extension of creditors is usually one of the first signs of financial weakness, and at least one of the major banks monitors creditor days as a key indicator of a firm's financial health. The issue with creditors is more typically that discussed in the previous chapter: trying to persuade them to continue supplying and to wait for payment.

8. *Implementing Cost-reduction Strategies*

We have seen that cost-reduction strategies are invariably a characteristic of successful turnaround situations. This chapter aims to provide some guidance in implementing such strategies and to highlight the practical problems and pitfalls managers are likely to encounter. Each of the major cost components – materials, direct labour and overheads – discussed in turn. Finally, some of the conditions for successful cost reduction are discussed.

It is not the aim of this book, however, to make the reader an expert in purchasing practice or in industrial engineering techniques. There are plenty of good books which adequately cover such topics in detail. Instead, we take the general management perspective: ensuring that all options are considered, the most feasible options are chosen, and sufficient attention is paid to the implementation process.

Cost-reduction strategies are likely to encounter considerable organizational resistance, particularly those strategies involving redundancies. Understanding the likely impact of cost-reduction strategies on morale (at all levels in the organization) and the effect this may have on organizational effectiveness is clearly something top management needs to give careful attention to before implementation begins.

1. Reducing Material Costs

The major options open to management to reduce material costs are to improve buying, use less materials and use different materials. These three broad options can then be broken down into more specific options, as was shown in Figure 6.1. All these options need to be explored if material costs are to be reduced by the greatest possible amount in the shortest possible time. It is not good enough to pick on just one dimension, say reducing wastage, and to think that with improvements in this area alone one is implementing a programme to reduce material costs. Yet in practice this is often what happens – particularly in those turnaround situations where management has not been changed.

I came across a good example of this in the upholstered furniture industry where a relatively large firm (which I will call firm X) initiated a series of profit improvement projects. (In effect, these were cost-reduction projects but it was politically more acceptable to refer to them as profit improvement projects!) Since material costs accounted for in excess of 60% of sales, one of the key areas was obviously a reduction in material costs. After a brainstorming session at which all the various options were discussed, the management team decided to look into ways of using less material, but decided against looking into improved buying practices. When asked why this was so, I was informed that 'there was no room for improvement in that area . . . the Assistant Managing Director was in charge of all purchasing and had been doing it for many years'! To have established a team to look into the company's buying practices was 'politically' unacceptable and would have been seen by the director concerned as a vote of 'no confidence' from his colleagues. Some time later, I was talking to one of their suppliers, who also supplied their major competitor. He indicated that there was no comparison between X and its major competitor in their purchasing at that time. Whereas the competitor was a hard negotiator on price, negotiated substantial discounts or refused to accept fabric that did not meet quality standards, firm X was just the opposite . . . Firm X was acquired a few months later to save it from receivership.

Although undue reliance on any one approach could be short-sighted, it is likely that one or two options will produce a quicker and/or larger pay-off in any given industry. Knowing which option is likely to provide the greater pay-off before one starts saves time and speeds up the recovery process.

1.1 Improved Buying Practices

There are three major ways of improving buying practice. They are: buying more cheaply; finding alternative sources of supply; and buying in economic order quantities.

The first and most obvious option for reducing material costs is to buy more cheaply, by trying to negotiate lower prices with existing suppliers. This option is perhaps the one most often ignored by managers of turnaround situations, because they believe the company is in no position to negotiate with suppliers, particularly if they have been purchasing reduced volume of late and have been slow in settling their accounts. But why not try? You know the old adage: 'If you don't try, you don't get.'

Admittedly, negotiating lower prices is likely to be easier for a new and more professional management team than for an existing management team. Suppliers rarely want to lose customers, and a new management team is in a much better position to convince the supplier that the future looks better than the past. They can present their plans for the future and try to convince the supplier that if he gives them a 'price break' now, this will help them buy more from that supplier in the future. New management may even have a successful track-record to back up such negotiating tactics. One example – which may seem unlikely to many readers – occurred when a new general manager, Roger Salway, arrived at Gilbern Motors (the now defunct Welsh car manufacturers) in 1974. At that time Gilbern was making two or three cars per week, and fighting for survival. Gilbern's raw-material costs as a percentage of sales were about 70%. A substantial portion of this cost consisted of the engine and chassis, which were bought from the Ford Motor Company. Manufacturing only two or three cars per week, Gilbern was hardly in a strong bargaining position *vis-à-vis* Ford; yet Ford reportedly gave Gilbern a 15% reduction in price, merely for the asking – far in excess of the Gilbern general manager's wildest dreams.[1]

The second option for lowering the cost of materials is to shop around for alternative suppliers. Dealing with new suppliers is always a risk, due to the unknowns involved (Is the quality of their product consistent? Do they deliver on time?), but in a turnaround situation the risk is likely to be greater still. A production stoppage or reduced level of output due to supplier problems can make all the difference between survival and receivership, or liquidation if the company is already in a severe cash crisis. Although it may be possible to find alternative suppliers who charge less than existing suppliers, the credit terms offered may be much stricter. Credit terms for new customers are often much harsher than for established customers, and if it is known by the new supplier that this new customer is in a turnaround situation, the wise supplier is likely to be cautious about extending credit. Existing suppliers tend to be more lenient, particularly if they have a long-established trading relationship with the company – although this will not always be true. Just as new management is more likely to be successful in obtaining lower prices from existing suppliers, they are also likely to be more successful in finding good alternative sources of supply. If they have industry experience, they will know which suppliers to go to, and may even go to suppliers with whom they have dealt before.

The third major option for improving buying practices is to buy more economically. This does not necessarily involve negotiating lower prices or changing suppliers, although it may be done in connection with these activities. Buying more economically means taking maximum advantage of suppliers' terms of trade, such as quantity discount schedules and minimum order sizes. This usually means purchasing in economic order quantities. It does not necessarily mean buying in larger quantities; it could mean smaller quantities. It is quite conceivable – particularly in times of high inflation – for it to be more economical for a company to place smaller orders and have to pay a higher price for its goods than to buy less frequently in larger quantities at lower prices. The decision as to which course one follows is a straight economic calculation based on a trade-off between purchasing costs and inventory-carrying costs. At what point are the combined costs minimized?

1.2 Better Utilization of Materials

In a company that has had poor management there is likely to be considerable scope for reducing unit material costs by improving material utilization. This may come about by reducing scrap, reducing the amount of material actually used in the production process, reducing the amount of material used in the product itself, or by actually changing the materials used in the product. The key skills required to reduce costs in this area are product and process engineering skills, although all functional managers are likely to become involved in the process. In turnaround situations, having a quick impact in this area may or may not be possible. The technical knowledge and experience of the manufacturing manager is crucial here. Has he (or she) specific industry experience manufacturing similar products? If the answer is yes, the manufacturing manager may be able to 'eyeball' the situation, based on his or her previous experience, and identify major cost-saving opportunities, even if good production control reports are unavailable. But after new management has made a series of initial changes (based on what seems obvious from their previous experience), dramatic changes in material utilization are unlikely to be achieved. The situation will then resemble what obtains when the turnaround is being attempted by existing management. Management may be unable to identify or unwilling to admit that large and immediate opportunities exist for improved material utilization. So what happens then?

One quite successful method companies have used to overcome this problem is to institute value-analysis programmes. Value analysis is the systematic examination of design and other factors affecting the cost of a product (or service) in order to devise means of achieving the specified purpose most economically at the required standard of quality and reliability.[2] Value analysis looks at what the product is intended to do and what each of its components is intended to do. Above all, it questions all the assumptions underlying the design of the product. An interdisciplinary approach, using a project team composed of people with different functional expertise, is often recommended as the best way to approach value analysis. But if this approach is to work, it is vital that top management should take an interest in and control the work and results of any value-analysis programme. Value analysis would normally start with the big products first (the 80:20 rule again!), since it is here that a small percentage change in raw-material costs will have the greatest impact on profit.

There is a danger in concentrating too much effort, however, on traditional value-analysis programmes. If we are not careful, we can become too product-engineering oriented while neglecting what may be a more important area – process engineering. Value analysis may help reduce scrap levels due to inefficient product design, but high levels of scrap could be due to inefficient manufacturing methods. Machinery which is poorly maintained or is inadequate for the job could be the prime cause of poor material usage. In this situation, the company's need is for production engineering rather than product engineering. However, since the most dramatic effect of implementing improved production engineering lies in the area of labour and over-head costs, further discussion of this topic is postponed until later in this chapter.

1.3 Using Different Materials

Value analysis may lead to the conclusion that material costs can be reduced by using a different material. The selection and testing of new materials, however, can be a long job and there are few examples of this happening in recovery situations. When using different materials, managers should be aware of the interdependency of material costs with direct-labour costs and overheads. Cheaper substitute materials may, for example, increase labour costs by increasing the length of the manufacturing process, and increase overheads by increasing the demands on the quality control section. Conversely, a more expensive material may actually reduce labour and/or overhead costs. Management must always think through the economic impact of all its decisions.

2. Reducing Unit Labour Costs

Just as there are a number of different alternatives for reducing the unit cost of raw materials and bought-in items, so there is more than one way of reducing labour costs. The two major alternatives for reducing unit labour costs are, first, an increased level of productivity and, second, a reduction in total labour costs. Management often uses the two approaches together, but in some situations only one or the other approach is feasible. We will start by looking at the major ways in which management can increase productivity in a recovery situation.

2.1 Increasing Productivity

Management often thinks of increasing the productivity of labour as a goal which can be achieved slowly over a number of years through a series of small, incremental steps. The use of learning curves and experience curves as tools of management, both of which relate labour costs to total output, have tended to reinforce this belief.[3] Our concern here, however, is on increasing productivity in the short term, in obtaining rapid and sustainable improvements which will help the company achieve improved cost performance. That short-term increases in productivity are possible was demonstrated nationally by the three-day work week during the power strike in 1974; but sustaining increases usually requires a long period of good management.

How can management, particularly new management, determine whether increased labour productivity is possible in the short term? And if it is, how can it be achieved?

The existing level of productivity and the industrial relations climate are the two factors that have most influence in determining whether or not increased productivity is possible. There are few recovery situations where increased productivity is not possible. Where the decline has been caused by poor management and lack of management control, it is extremely unlikely that productivity will be near or above the industry average, even after allowing for differences in the capital/labour ratio. While a comparison with industry productivity figures may give a rough guide, there is little substitute for a good production manager who has industry experience. Industry data will show the extent to which productivity is above or below the industry norm but will not give any clue at all to the feasibility of rapid improvement. The experienced production manager, on the other hand, will be able to make a rapid assessment of current practices and compare them to the norm in companies in which he has worked. He will be able to isolate rapidly those characteristics of the production system which seem to him to be costly and ineffective. The type of prior industry experience that the production manager has had, coupled with his own personal prejudices, determines what he considers to be the critical improvement areas. In some turnaround situations, particularly those in stagnant or declining industries where there has been very little innovation in the manufacturing process for a long time, a good production man from outside the industry may be what is required. But care should be taken, since each industry (and, very often, segments within the industry) has its own unique production requirements which can be learned only from experience within that industry.

What are the options open to management for improving productivity in the short term? The options are not mutually exclusive but we will discuss them under the following five headings:

- change of management style
- change of the organization structure
- introduction of incentive payments (productivity deals)
- change in production methods
- recruitment, selection and training of staff.

(*a*) *Change of management style*: The effect of different management styles on productivity is very difficult to quantify. We know that the Japanese style of management has been very effective. Even in the U.K., Japanese managers believe they can obtain levels of productivity out of a British workforce comparable to the levels they achieve in Japan. The Japanese zipper company, Y.K.K., is a good example here, and the decision by several other Japanese firms to locate plants in the U.K. explicitly took potential productivity levels in the U.K. into account. Although Y.K.K. and other Japanese examples are very different from the typical turnaround situation in that they start with a new labour force and a new plant, there are lessons to be learned. Japanese managers typically spend more time on the factory floor, often working alongside the labour force. The production managers are not absentees, spending their time in plush executive offices with a range of perks and status symbols! They learn and understand the detailed problems on the factory floor, they get to know the workforce – in short, they attempt to break down any barriers that exist between management and the workforce.

There is no one style of management that works best in all situations. Management must realize that their behaviour is constantly being observed, noted and discussed by both subordinates and staff. Even minor management actions transmit messages about the type of person the manager is and about his expectations. Many turnaround managers are characterized by power orientation, desire for action, and the use of a Machiavellian management approach.[4] If such an individual is chosen as a turnaround manager, he will quickly transmit his value system to the whole organization (provided it is not too large), or to that part for which he is responsible. The usual effect is to instil some degree of fear into the organization.

Fear may not be all bad. Some degree of fear can provoke an improvement in performance in the short term, and if it is later moulded into a positive, performance-oriented management style it can lead to a sustained improvement. However, as we shall see later in this chapter, direct hierarchical pressure may lead to hidden organizational costs within about six or twelve months. Any positive effect of instilling fear can be lost very quickly. The letter to the workforce from the new managing director, saying that the company is about to go into receivership or liquidation if there is not an immediate improvement in productivity, rarely has much effect after the first week. For a few days output may be increased, but unless the exhortation to work harder is accompanied by more permanent and substantial changes in organization design (structure, control systems, performance evaluation, etc.), little change can be expected.

(*b*) *Change of the organization structure*: A noticeable feature of some successful recovery situations in manufacturing industry is a flattening-out of the traditional pyramid structure. In much of British industry, the typical organizational structure at the plant level is to have a hierarchical pyramid structure with many levels of junior and middle management between the production manager and the non-supervisory staff on the factory floor. The engineering function is totally separate from production, only coming together at the level of the plant manager, and sometimes not even there but higher up the organisation still. In such an organization structure, budget responsibility does not usually start until junior- or middle-management levels, say at the departmental manager level, with the result that first-line supervisors and foremen are rarely held accountable for the performance of their operating units. If something goes wrong or if improvements in working methods are possible, the supervisory staff have neither the authority nor the inclination to improve the situation. This is a pity, since those supervisory staff nearest the workforce are often the best qualified to make suggestions for improvement.

A number of firms reported (during my research) that they had been able to harness the unused potential of their supervisory personnel to very great effect by eliminating the multiple layers of junior- and middle-management personnel. Such action naturally increases the span of control at more senior management levels, but successful turnaround managers appear to be able to cope with a wider than normal span of control, an apparent characteristic of managers who prefer to operate in a power culture.[5] Management responsibility is thereby forced down the line to the shop-floor level, with the result that job satisfaction and motivation are improved.

(c) *Productivity deals*: British management has rarely been successful in negotiating long-term productivity deals with its workforce, whether unionized or non-unionized. Short-term productivity increases have been rarer still. There are few examples of companies in turnaround situations having made productivity agreements which have later been judged as successful. More typical is the experience of British Leyland. In 1977, the BL workforce voted 2–1 in favour of an industrial relations reform package, including the introduction of an incentive scheme. However, management failed to reach union agreement on the introduction of incentives in spite of a warning by the chairman, Sir Michael Edwardes, that the introduction of an incentive scheme was 'crucial to the survival of the company'. Two years later, the scheme was still not agreed.

If the experience of productivity deals negotiated between unions and management as part of the annual wage negotiations has not been good, what other alternatives are there? One scheme now being tried by the Birds Eye division of Unilever is the use of productivity councils.[6] In 1979, they set up productivity councils at each of the division's six manufacturing sites, with each council made up of representatives from each of the recognized unions, together with management representatives. The councils differ from consultative councils and works and liaison committees in that they are intended to go beyond discussion and exchange of views and come up with suggestions for genuine productivity improvements. The main features of the scheme are as follows: first, the councils are largely trade-union controlled, and it is the unions who decide the strength and composition of management representation; second, it is largely left to the unions to come up with productivity improvements (thereafter to be sorted out and approved by management); third, all productivity discussions are kept entirely separate from the annual pay negotiations; finally, any savings or benefits accruing from changes agreed in the councils are split fifty-fifty between the unions and the company, but with the unions deciding how their share should be split among themselves.

The types of changes that have been made to date at Birds Eye include meal-break changes to help maintain production line speeds and working beyond normal time when workers on the next shift are late for work. Agreements involving the erosion of traditional union demarcation lines have been more difficult to achieve (particularly with the craft unions), although some simple work formerly reserved for craft union members can now be done by process workers from other unions in order to keep production lines going.

The productivity council idea is not so different from the Japanese idea of 'quality control circles'.[7] In both cases the underlying philosophy is the same: genuine productivity increases can only be achieved by involving the workforce on the factory floor. One of the difficulties of implementing any such idea in many turnaround situations is the lack of good control data by which productivity improvements can be measured. Jointly agreed work study standards are required; these take time to develop, particularly in situations where no standards have existed due to poor management and the workforce are likely to be suspicious of any measurement procedures.

The usefulness of productivity deals and productivity councils in turnaround situations depends on the time scale to which management is working. You may be able to get rapid results if the company is close to receivership and you can convince the workforce that this is so and that the company's survival (and their jobs) depends on the successful implementation of a productivity scheme. Normally, productivity gains due to incentive payments accrue only slowly. This is not to say that the turnaround manager should make no attempt at improving productivity using these methods – he should – but that immediate pay-offs are hard to achieve. An apparent exception to this was the productivity deal struck at Perkins Engines in 1980, which is reported to have achieved an increase in labour productivity of 13%.[8]

(d) *Change in production methods*: A skilled production manager with industry experience will often be able to walk into a plant and see that the way in which the production line is set up is inefficient. The work flow may be inefficient, there may be bottlenecks in the production process that can be avoided at little extra cost: all common production problems that can hinder productivity. With the right leadership (right management style), it may be possible to implement some of these changes quickly. The speed of change will depend on the nature of the problem, the technology involved and, most importantly, the ease with which the co-operation of the workforce can be obtained. In a smaller job shop operation, change will obviously be easier than in a large flow line or process machinery plant. Rapid change may be near impossible in a unionized plant containing a number of different unions all working on the same production line but with each union having clearly demarcated lines of responsibility.

Inefficient manufacturing plants are usually characterized by an above-average level of downtime, resulting from either poor production planning, machine breakdowns, or both. Inefficient production planning is a characteristic of many turnaround situations in manufacturing, yet it is not always easy to correct this immediately. Production planning in turnarounds is often harder than it might otherwise be, due to the unreliability of the sales forecasts and the pressure to keep inventories to a minimum due to the firm's cash shortage. Yet it is a high priority area for management attention if the desired customer service levels are to be achieved, inventory levels minimized and unit costs of production kept to a minimum.

(e) *Recruitment, selection and training of staff*: Although management may have put strict controls on all recruitment at the commencement of the recovery programme, some recruitment will probably be necessary to replace staff who have left or been dismissed due to incompetence. The need to fill vacant positions gives management an opportunity to change historical recruitment and selection procedures, and thereby upgrade personnel quality. In recovery situations where the company is being rescued from liquidation or redundancy, management will find that all the workforce has been made legally redundant and it is in a position of being able to rehire only those staff members who are likely to be most productive. Villiers Engine, for example, had this opportunity when the company was bought from the liquidator. Such opportunities can lead to an immediate and sustainable improvement in productivity.

Training *per se* can be an important method of increasing productivity but the results are usually achieved more slowly. If some training is already taking place at shop-floor and supervisory level, training is unlikely to be an immediate area of top management concern in the first few months of a recovery programme, unless there are major changes in operating methods or organizational structure or systems being implemented. Where such changes do occur, training should be a critically important part of the implementation programme. Short-term emphasis on training will be unlikely to produce substantial additional benefits if there are no changes in operating methods, since the staff will already be some way down the learning curve. Where training is non-existent or totally inadequate, then there may be some significant benefits which can be achieved in the short term, even if operating procedures are not being changed. Training can have an important motivating effect on personnel, a factor which could be more important in improving productivity than the fact that staff are able to perform the tasks demanded by the job more efficiently.

2.2 Reducing Total Labour Costs

Perhaps the most obvious way to reduce total labour costs is to reduce the size of the workforce through a forced redundancy programme. The implementation of such a programme requires careful planning if it is not to backfire on management, and therefore the next chapter is devoted solely to this important issue. There are, however, a number of alternatives to forced redundancy, and it is these alternatives that we will outline in this section.

The major alternatives to a forced redundancy programme for reducing total labour costs are as follows:

Alternatives:
easier to
implement

{
Natural wastage accompanied by a no-hiring policy
Encouragement of early retirement
Voluntary redundancies
Cut out or reduce overtime
Reschedule work and paid vacations
}

Alternatives:
more difficult
to implement
$\left\{\begin{array}{l}\text{Short-time working}\\\text{Work sharing for alternating periods of work}\\\text{Cutting wages, salaries and bonuses}\\\text{Postponement or freezing of pay increases}\\\text{Transferring staff to other group companies}\end{array}\right.$

We saw in Chapter 5 that fairly drastic management action is usually required if sustained recovery is to be achieved. Obviously each situation will be different, but we must bear this in mind when deciding how to reduce labour costs. Combining all the alternatives mentioned above may be insufficient to provide the necessary cost savings, and the only answer is forced redundancy. However, most of the alternatives listed above are complementary to forced redundancy and will be implemented either before or at the same time as any redundancy programme. Some of the alternatives are relatively more easy to implement than others, but there are potential pitfalls of which management should be aware in implementing most of the alternatives.

The easier alternatives: Allowing the size of the workforce to decline through natural wastage and to accompany this by a no-hiring policy is the route that most managers prefer to reduce total labour costs, if at all possible. The feasibility of this option depends on the employee turnover rate. If the turnover rate is high, quick cost savings may be achieved in a relatively painless way, although there may be substantial complications if redeployment of the remaining staff is difficult due to the lack of transferability of skills within the organization, or for reasons of union demarcation. In theory the idea is fine, but in practice it is more difficult (the wrong people tend to leave!), and management finds itself having to make exceptions to the no-hiring policy. The same problem may occur where voluntary redundancy and/or early retirement is offered to the workforce. Early retirement and voluntary redundancy programmes have other pitfalls associated with them. For example, it may not be possible for the firm to offer pension terms attractive enough to persuade employees that early retirement is a good idea. The existence of unfunded pension liability is nowadays a major problem for firms wanting to implement early retirement or any redundancy programme. Substantial cash payments to the pension fund may be necessary – payments which a firm in a recovery situation may be unable to afford.

Voluntary redundancy programmes can also backfire, as occurred with one public company (1980 sales in the range of £15–20 million).

The managing director decided one morning, without any careful planning, that he would seek to reduce the company payroll at all levels by asking for voluntary redundancy. He called a board meeting for that afternoon, received approval for the idea, and the announcement was made the same day. By that night he had the 'resignation' of nearly all his senior managers, including a number of the executive directors! Next morning, he quickly back-tracked, admitted the whole thing was an error of judgement, persuaded the managers to stay on and cancelled the offer of voluntary redundancy. Consequently there were no cost savings at all; the company was acquired soon thereafter to save it from receivership.

It is important that management understands that all the easier alternatives require the *co-operation* of the workforce, and that the full implications of such measures should be carefully thought through in advance. Even apparently simple measures such as cutting out unnecessary overtime, rescheduling work to reduce overtime, rearranging paid vacations during relatively slow business periods, all require co-operation. Essentially, these measures require increased productivity from the remaining workforce and should be implemented side by side with the actions discussed in the earlier section on increasing productivity. These two sets of actions may interact with each other: a decision to cut out overtime or institute a voluntary redundancy programme may by itself cause productivity to increase by taking up

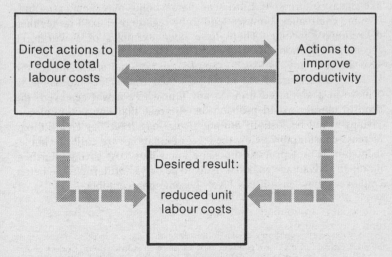

Figure 8.1: *Interactions Affecting Unit Labour Costs*

the slack in the organization; but at the same time an action to improve productivity (e.g. the introduction of an incentive pay deal) could result in less labour being required and hence total labour costs being reduced. Figure 8.1 illustrates the interaction.

The more difficult alternatives: Methods of reducing total labour costs that have been classified as 'more difficult' are those alternatives that are likely to have greater impact on employee morale or which are nearly impossible to implement. Short-time working has recently become a popular option in the U.K. under the auspices of government support. It has the benefit of saving redundancy payments, but is usually regarded as a temporary measure. In the longer term, say over the next twenty years, as the permanent level of unemployment in the U.K. economy increases, short-time working could become work sharing, whereby two individuals both work half time at one job. This is not unknown; there are a few examples in academic institutions in the U.S. where a husband and wife share one job. The idea of work sharing has been advocated as one way of dealing with the longer-term unemployment problems facing the U.K. but it is currently difficult for management to implement, because it is not widely accepted as a social practice.

A permanent cut in pay below the level already in existence is extremely difficult to implement, although at first glance it may seem like an easy alternative. Cutting an annual bonus may seem easier but, in some companies, bonuses tend to be regarded as fixed rather than discretionary income. There have been examples of a workforce accepting reductions in pay as evidence of their commitment to help save the company, but such examples are rare and are mainly in the U.S.A. Any enforced cut in wages would usually be impossible to achieve in a unionized firm. In any firm where it was achieved, the drop in morale would probably be so great that any potential cost savings would be lost. Instituting a total pay freeze or giving a pay increase considerably below the level of inflation* are easier to implement but do not provide the same immediate cost saving. Furthermore, any advantage gained is likely to be only short term as the better employees may leave if pay levels become unacceptable.

---

* Unit labour costs would only decline in this situation if the pay increase was less than the price increase of the firm's goods or services, since an individual firm's prices do not always increase with inflation.

3. Reducing Overhead Costs

Overhead costs are all those costs, including non-cash charges on the business such as depreciation, which are generally regarded as fixed costs in the short term. Some overhead costs such as energy costs are, in fact, semi-variable in that they change with production volume, but this distinction does not affect our discussion.

The way in which management approaches an overhead-cost reduction programme may be similar to programmes for reducing material costs and unit labour costs, since bought-in supplies and services, and people costs (salaries, etc.), typically make up a high proportion of the overhead cost structure. To the extent that this is so, we will not repeat what has already been said, nor preview the discussion of redundancy programmes in the next chapter. Rather, we will discuss the major issues management is likely to incur in each of the functional areas in deciding which overheads can be reduced and by how much. In each case, the starting point is to break down the cost components by department. The key questions are the same in all areas: is the particular cost really necessary, and do the benefits outweigh the costs?

3.1 Manufacturing Overheads

There are two basic approaches to reducing total manufacturing overheads and still staying in business: first, a reduction in the scale of operations by the complete elimination of a discrete part of the manufacturing process, as when a plant is closed, for example; and second, improving efficiency within the existing scale of operations. Unit overhead costs can, of course, be improved solely by increasing sales and hence increasing manufacturing volume.

We have seen that, from a strategic point of view, recovery is often achieved by plant closure since improving efficiency, however well executed, will be insufficient to provide the necessary revenue-cost savings. Plant closure may have the additional advantage of providing a saleable asset, something very important to a company in a recovery situation with a severe liquidity crisis. The next chapter provides a detailed framework for planning and executing a plant closure, although it emphasizes the redundancy problem rather than the manufacturing problems encountered when closing a plant (e.g. the problems of transferring production to another plant).

Eliminating a discrete part of the manufacturing process involves, first, being able to identify the step function within the manufacturing operations and, second, being able to show that elimination of the step function provides an incremental cash flow to the company. If additional capital investment is required, the incremental cash flow should have a positive net present value although, in a severe recovery situation, management may be willing to eliminate a step function in overheads as long as their action has an immediate positive impact on net cash flow. The step function within the manufacturing system need not be at the plant level – it could be within the plant. By rearranging plant layout, for example, it could be possible to free up part of the plant that would be shut down (or, perhaps, leased), thereby saving all overheads with the possible exception of rates, insurance and some building maintenance costs.

If plant closure is not a viable option, not even in part, then improving efficiency within the existing scale of operations may be all that is possible. In practice, management often undertakes both actions simultaneously; closing down some plants while improving the efficiency of others. Many of the commonest actions to reduce overheads of a continuing operation are similar to those already discussed under the headings of improving productivity and reducing total labour costs. The real difficulty that arises in recovery situations is assessing how much indirect labour is required on a departmental basis. Ideally, one would use work study measurement to ascertain the 'true' manpower requirements of the business, but in a recovery situation there may be insufficient time and money to undertake a detailed work study exercise. Furthermore, if work study is being introduced for the first time, it can lead to suspicion and rumours of mass redundancies long before management has the data on which to act. Consequently, one finds a lot of intuitive judgement or 'seat-of-the-pants' decision-making when it comes to reducing manufacturing overheads. Once again, this points to the need for experienced manufacturing personnel.

The critical areas of manufacturing overheads will vary from company to company; but there are two overhead-cost areas which are apt to have been neglected in typical turnaround companies: maintenance and quality control. Both of these are crucial functions in a manufacturing business, and it is quite possible that *greater* rather than fewer resources will have to be devoted to these areas if they have been neglected in the past. However, each area of manufacturing overhead needs to be studied separately and in depth if maximum savings are to be achieved. Many overhead costs can be reduced in recovery situations if there is a determination to examine each cost component logically.

Energy costs (for electricity, gas and oil) provide one example of an area in which management in general are paying more attention to costs nowadays. The cost savings achieved by some companies have been quite remarkable and are illustrative of the potential cost savings that are nearly always to be found in recovery situations. For example, 3M U.K. (the British subsidiary of Minnesota Mining and Manufacturing, best known for its 'Scotch' tape products) claims that without the energy conservation programme it began in 1975/76, its 'current annual fuel bill would almost double to about £2.5 million'.[9] It is claimed by 3M that in the early stages of their programme they were able to achieve significant energy conservation with little or no capital expenditure. Later measures required capital expenditure, but often the payback was under two months. Their overhead reduction programme in the energy area clearly goes beyond just insulating boilers, turning down thermostats, installing spray taps in washrooms and turning off lights, although these measures are a start in the right direction.

What is particularly interesting about 3M's experience is their management approach to reducing manufacturing overheads. It is a good illustration of what we have been talking about in this chapter: placing responsibility for cost improvements down the organization. The engineering organization in a 3M plant was typical of many British companies, with shift foremen reporting to a maintenance engineer, who in turn reported to the plant engineer, who was responsible for budgeting and forecasting engineering expenses on a plant-wide basis. At the operational level, mistakes during one shift were invariably blamed on the previous shift, so nobody was held responsible. The solution found by 3M was to push responsibility for budgeting and forecasting down to the level of the shift foreman, who is now responsible for forecasting labour and material requirements for his operational area for the budgeting period in the light of the planned production levels. In addition, 3M gave the shift foreman (now called an area foreman) responsibility along with the production foreman for the whole production process; the former controls all technical labour and materials and manages the planned maintenance programme, as well as the production process, to obtain maximum machine utilization. The manager of engineering services at 3M is quoted as saying: 'It is also vitally important that engineers and maintenance groups, when investigating situations which have caused breakdown or lack of production, do *not* blame others or equipment for the breakdown. Problems should be accepted, put right, then discussed with the persons concerned. This cools down the situation and when they are aware that it is now their fault, they take responsibility for the situation.'[10] This management philosophy appears to work much better than a hierarchical structure where all responsibility is at the top . . . there is too much passing the buck in those situations.

3.2 Marketing and Distribution Costs

Six major cost components may need to be examined: salesforce costs, advertising and promotion costs, sales office costs, marketing management costs, service costs and distribution costs (including both warehousing and transportation). It has already been pointed out that greater care should be taken in reducing overhead costs in these areas because they may be immediately obvious to customers. For example, a cut in service levels, even temporarily, can lead to a rapid loss of trade confidence in the company's future ability to supply and to a loss of sales at a critical time. From a recovery point of view, the good thing about cutting marketing costs is that the time required to implement cuts is usually very short, although the same is not true of distribution costs. The danger, however, is that the lead time to increase expenditure is often much longer: for example, it is much easier and quicker to cut the size of a salesforce than to build a new one or expand an existing one.

It is beyond the scope of this book to outline the various analytical tools available for determining optimal marketing expenditure. These are well documented in the marketing literature. It is important to remember, however, that the firm's product-market strategy needs to be developed before any really drastic cutbacks are made in the marketing area. Irreparable damage may be done by wielding axes without thinking of the strategic consequences.

The key question to ask in all cases when marketing-cost reductions are being contemplated is: are current operations cost effective? The severity of the turnaround crisis will influence the answer to this question, since a sizeable portion of marketing expenditure may not affect short-term sales volume. Advertising, promotion and some selling and service expenditure may be more of an investment for the future than a necessary expense to obtain sales in the short term. In some businesses (e.g. mail-order houses) the lag effect is minimal, but in other businesses (such as capital goods and industrial projects), the time between initial marketing expenditure and the collection of sales revenues is measured in years. Where the marketing time horizon is long, there will be a temptation to cut those costs not necessary for short-term survival. Management's time horizon for the turnaround will also influence the action taken. Does management want a quick recovery, with the idea of selling the business as soon as short-term profits pick up, or are they committed to the business over the long term? There are great dangers in taking the short-term approach, and most successful recovery situations point to a balance between the short-term demands of survival and the need for longer-term actions to achieve a sustainable recovery.

From the point of view of implementation, cutting out or reducing advertising and promotion costs are the easiest steps to take since they rarely involve loss of jobs. Furthermore, it is rare that an organization cannot be more effective in its advertising and promotional expenditure. Admittedly, we have to contend with Lord Leverhulme's famous dictum, 'Half of all advertising is wasted, but we don't know which half,' but some common-sense analysis of customer buying behaviour, together with some analysis of how the company is currently allocating its advertising expenditure, together with a comparison of competitors' advertising expenditure based on published data,[11] can often pinpoint potential areas for improvement. One of the most common areas for improvement in companies that have declined is to find that their advertising expenditure is spread too thinly over a large number of products; the advertising message is being drowned by competing messages from competitors' products. Unless the company can afford to spend sufficient funds to get above the market segment noise-level, it may be better to cut out advertising expenditure altogether for that product.

Reducing overheads associated with the sales function usually implies such actions as reducing the size of the salesforce or eliminating regional sales offices, since controls over items such as travel and entertainment expenses are rarely sufficient to make much of an impact on profitability. The main point to remember, if cuts are made here, is to ensure that the customers do not suffer while the selling effort is reorganized.

In those companies where distribution costs are significant, a substantial effort may be required to reduce both warehousing and transportation costs. The approach and problems are similar to those for reducing manufacturing overheads, except that changes to the distribution system may affect finished-goods inventory levels and hence cash-flow requirements. Inventory levels, which affect warehousing costs, also affect production costs. The point to remember is that manufacturing and distribution costs are interdependent and that the balancing of inventory-carrying costs against production costs is a key management decision. There may be some obvious room for improvement in a recovery situation where little analysis is required other than adopting a heuristic approach, but in most cases good cost data are required (and are often unavailable), and sufficient time must be allowed to undertake the detailed financial analysis. The reader is referred to a good operations management book for further details of the analysis required.[12]

Research and Development Costs: R. & D. costs present turnaround management with something of a dilemma. In the short term it is a luxury which management may not be able to afford, yet in the long term the company's survival may depend upon it. A very careful assessment of R. & D. expenditure is needed to determine:

(a) the current state of individual projects. At what stage of completion are the various projects? How long before the new product will be ready to market (or test market)? Timing and the commercial prospects for the project are all important;
(b) the technical feasibility or likely chance of success of each project;
(c) the expected cash outflows over the life of each project;
(d) the market prospects for each new project.

If the turnaround manager does not have the skills to assess the technical feasibility of the R. & D. projects, he has two options, assuming the projects are not of a high technology nature. First, he may try himself to assess the projects – not so much from a technical point of view as from a market demand and competitive point of view. Some simple questions, such as who else is doing research in this field, can often provide enough rationale to cut a project. My own experience in a recently acquired small chemical company where I knew nothing of the technical details was as follows:

Self: How long before this project is likely to be completed?
R. & D. Manager: About ten years.
Self: Who else is doing research in this area?
R. & D. Manager: British Petroleum and I.C.I.
       DECISION: CUT PROJECT

The company's ability to compete with the giants was clearly nil, a ten-year time horizon was well outside the bounds of the acquisition objectives. The decision was obvious.

Second, the turnaround manager can call in one or more outside experts to give opinions. A long and detailed study will not usually be necessary unless the company is at the frontier of technology. Some firms will obtain opinions at virtually no cost (except in management time) by courting technical consultants with the prospect of an assignment in the future!

Rapid assessment of R. & D. projects, particularly by management inexperienced in the industry or the technology, may of course lead to the wrong decision, although the impact of a bad decision in this area will not usually affect short-term recovery. Assessing R. & D. projects is somewhat similar to market research. It is more accurate in telling you that you will *not* succeed than in telling you that you will.

Other overhead costs: One will usually find a wide variety of costs under the heading of general and administrative overheads. Many of the overheads will be establishment charges, e.g. rates, insurance, cleaning charges, cafeteria charges; other categories will be for business services such as telecommunications, auditors, merchant bankers, lawyers, trade association dues, training-board levies, etc. Many bought-in services may not be strictly necessary, and many other costs are actually negotiable, although few companies take much effort to reduce them. Gardeners, chauffeurs, the company Rolls Royce, the company weekend retreat, the chairman's London office, the company flat are all examples of overheads not necessary for running the firm, and will be prime targets for quick and easy cost reduction (and possible asset realization).

As always, it is difficult to generalize when firms, even within the same industry, have different overhead structures; but two general overhead areas where costs have increased sharply in recent years are telecommunication costs and data processing costs. The starting point in both cases is to identify and analyse the costs of each activity. Analysis of the costs may involve collecting and collating data from several geographical and organizational locations in a form not previously kept. Useful data can often be generated within a month by keeping records of telephone, telex and copying-machine usage by department, for example. In the data processing area, costing procedures are usually sadly lacking and few companies are able to answer the questions in Figure 8.2 satisfactorily to demonstrate that their data processing overheads are under control.

One area of overheads in which additional costs may have to be incurred is plant and office security. Due to the lack of control systems in many recovery situations, theft can be quite significant. Tighter security is often necessary in conjunction with improved control systems.

Figure 8.2: *Questions To Ask About Computer Overheads*

- Is there a separate computer systems development budget?
- Is there an established software capital investment procedure in use? Are projects ranked?
- At what capacity is computer equipment being utilized?
- By how much are computer operating costs declining or increasing?
- Are there established procedures for requesting and continuing maintenance expenditure?
- Does every maintenance expenditure require a rigorous assessment of the costs versus the benefits of the expenditure?
- What would the day-to-day business impact be of reducing maintenance expenditures on existing computer systems by 20%?

Adapted from: W. D. King, 'The Six Phases of Cost Reduction', *Business Horizons*, August 1973.

4. Conditions for Successful Cost Reduction

Cost reduction involves change: change in established methods of operation, change in the organization structure, change in the organization culture and, more importantly, change in the attitude of management and staff. In a recovery situation where management has been lax, the change brought about by a cost-reduction exercise may be nothing short of traumatic for the organization. While most turnaround situations will be characterized by a fairly high degree of organizational slack – unused human resources – drastic cost-reduction programmes may cause organizational distress. The internal state of health of the organizational machine, as reflected by the loyalty, attitudes and motivation of staff, internal communications and industrial relations, may begin to suffer, with the result that the goal of a sustainable reduction in unit costs is not achieved. Likert and Seashore have pointed out that there are organizational costs associated with a cost-reduction exercise and that these may be high and hidden.[13] They point out that productivity increases and lower unit cost do not arise directly by implementing a cost-reduction programme, but through a set of intervening variables. The idea can be illustrated graphically as follows:

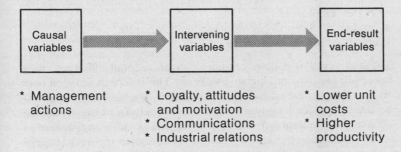

Causal variables	Intervening variables	End-result variables
* Management actions	* Loyalty, attitudes and motivation * Communications * Industrial relations	* Lower unit costs * Higher productivity

At the outset of a cost-reduction programme, management's actions may appear to be well accepted by the staff (perhaps only by the surviving staff if redundancies are taking place) and there may even be a sense among some employees that 'it's about time somebody did something about this [expletive deleted] place'. Within two to three months, there may be an immediate improvement in productivity and a reduction in costs. If there is less than enthusiasm for some of the changes management has instituted, the greater will be the direct hierarchical pressure necessary to ensure the changes are implemented. Where new management is involved, more direct pressure will usually have to be exerted in those situations where there is a high degree of loyalty to the old management, where the staff have been kept totally in the dark about the company's financial position, and where the new management's own style is very different from that of their predecessors.

The greater the degree of direct hierarchical pressure, the greater the hidden costs to the organization in terms of not being able to sustain the early cost improvements. In the initial months, there may be few noticeable effects unless the plant is highly unionized and management is trying to push through changes without union agreement. But after about six months, one often begins to see signs of hostility to the hierarchical pressure from lower levels of management and non-management staff. As the months progress and pressure is maintained for lower costs, distress increases and the intervening variables show signs of deterioration. Some or all of the following signs may occur:

- confidence and trust in management declines, leading to information flows becoming filtered and distorted
- absenteeism increases
- the employee turnover rate increases, particularly among the 'better' employees
- product quality and customer service deteriorate
- efforts to restrict production take place.

The end result is a deterioration in organizational efficiency, with lower productivity and higher unit costs. The resulting situation may be an improvement on the original situation, but the cost savings will be insufficient for long-run survival. If this pattern of organizational behaviour is widespread, it may provide one possible explanation as to why 'twiddling the knobs' is rarely an adequate recovery strategy and why more drastic action is required (see Chapter 5).

How can management overcome this problem? Clearly, the organization needs fine tuning. Some slack is required, if stress is not to turn into distress. Management needs to measure the intervening variables regularly, so that it can identify trouble-spots immediately and take corrective action as required; but tight control will not reach the cause of the problem. What is needed is a more participative or co-operative approach to cost reduction. Furthermore, in medium-size to large firms, top management has neither the time nor the detailed knowledge of operations to implement a cost-reduction programme by itself. The establishment of a series of departmental or interdepartmental teams to look at various cost categories with specific cost-improvement targets established by top management is the most useful approach. Each taskforce will need to agree target dates for completion of its task and will need to be monitored and possibly given assistance in analysing the activities of the business (particularly if the taskforce members have operated historically in an intuitive rather than an analytical mode).

One former consultant has given the following guidelines for the successful implementation of a cost-reduction programme:[14]

1. A significant improvement goal, such as 20%, will be established by top management in each area.
2. Every aspect of the way a given activity is now being performed will be challenged.

3. All improvement opportunities – not just some – are identified.
4. Any improvement will require significant change in the way an operation is run.
5. A systematic, aggressive follow-up will be needed to ensure that savings are realized.

A useful management tool for implementing a cost-reduction programme is zero-base budgeting. Since one of the first tasks to be undertaken in implementing any recovery strategy is establishing a budget for the next twelve months, the introduction of zero-base budgeting can be a useful additional tool. Whereas typical budgeting procedures look at actual, historical expense levels and then make allowances for changes in volume, sales mix, inflation, productivity and other planned management actions, zero-base budgeting does not take into account historical expenditure. It looks at each cost component and asks basic questions about the activity, such as:[15]

- Should the activity be performed at all?
- What should the quality level be? Are we doing too much?
- Should it be performed in this way?
- How much should it cost?

Notes

1. Source: Lecture by Roger Salway, former Director of Gilbern Motors, at the London Business School, February 1974.
2. Brian Day, 'How to Value Materials', *Management Today*, December 1976.
3. See, for example, Bruce Henderson, *Henderson on Corporate Strategy*, Abt Books, 1979.
4. See Chapter 4,
5. Charles Handy, *Understanding Organizations*, Penguin Books, Chapter 7.
6. 'Breaking the Ice at Birds Eye', *Financial Times*, 15 February 1980.
7. 'What Western Managers Can Learn from Japan's Quest for Quality', *Financial Times*, 11 March 1980.
8. 'A "Fair Day's Work" Paves the Way Ahead', *Financial Times*, 23 February 1981.
9. 'How to Spend a Penny and More Than Save It', *Financial Times*, 29 August 1980.
10. Ibid.
11. From data provided by Media Expenditure Analysis Ltd, for example.

12. See, for example, G. W. Plossl and O. W. Wight, *Production and Inventory Control*, Prentice-Hall, 1967.

13. R. Likert and S. Seashore, 'Making Cost Control Work', *Harvard Business Review*, November–December 1963.

14. William D. King, 'The Six Phases of Cost Reduction', *Business Horizons*, August 1973.

15. Robert N. Anthony and James S. Reece, *Management Accounting*, Irwin (5th edn), pp. 718–19.

9. Planning and Executing Redundancy Programmes

Management's major preoccupation in planning workforce reductions is usually centred around what the trade union reaction will be. Will there be a strike? Will there be a sit-in? If so, for how long? The likelihood of a redundancy programme causing a major industrial-relations problem can be avoided or substantally reduced by careful and detailed action planning.

Careful planning alone, however, is insufficient. The prevailing economic climate and political mood are important factors determining the acceptability of industrial action. As one executive member of the Confederation of Shipbuilding and Engineering Unions said in 1979 about Sir Michael Edwardes's plan for 25,000 redundancies at British Leyland; 'Public sympathy for B.L. workers is so low that a confrontation with management and the Government at this stage would be disastrous.'[1] In fact, the large number of redundancies and plant closures that have occurred during 1980 and 1981 could never have occurred so peacefully at any other time in the last twenty years.

Immediate action to reduce total labour costs is characteristic of very many recovery situations. We have already discussed the importance of installing strict controls over hiring and the use of overtime but these actions, important as they may be, are often insufficient and a more drastic programme – a forced redundancy programme – to reduce the size of the workforce may be necessary. This may cover labour engaged in the manufacturing process as well as employees involved in the typical overhead functions. It often arises as the result of plant closure.

Making employees redundant is a highly emotive issue and has ramifications throughout the whole environment in which the company operates. While often necessary for the survival of the company, a redundancy programme that is implemented poorly can be extremely risky, and may even put the very survival of the company in jeopardy. There are innumerable examples of strikes and sit-ins that have been caused by management trying to implement a redundancy programme. More seriously, some companies have gone into receivership when strikes occurred after redundancy programmes were announced. The factors surrounding each redundancy situation are likely to be different but, whatever the situation, the need for careful planning before the redundancy programme is announced clearly pays off. In one large U.K. company (1980 sales of £450 million, and itself a subsidiary of one of the U.K.'s largest companies), the top twenty executives spent an estimated 1,400 man-days in planning the implementation of a redundancy programme by which 750 people out of a workforce of 30,000 were made redundant. This was over and above the estimated 400 man-days spent on developing a cost-reduction strategy. The danger in this situation lay in the fact that management spent too much time on this issue, to the detriment of the rest of its business – although, in retrospect, most agreed that the time spent on detailed action planning was well spent.

Management will always have to develop an implementation plan suitable for its own situation and the remainder of this chapter presents a framework to assist management in preparing such a plan. The following seven aspects are considered:

- organization of the planning effort
- the legal position on redundancy and dismissal
- preparation of a short-term industrial-relations strategy
- preparation of contingency plans
- deciding the redundancy details
- preparation of a master statement
- developing a communications programme.

1. Organization of the Planning Effort

Planning the redundancy programme is usually undertaken by a small ad hoc management group, other managers being informed only on a 'need to know' basis. The number of people needing to know will depend on the size of the company and the type of cost-reduction strategies being implemented. If a plant is being closed or a cutback in the workforce involves rearranging the manufacturing process, it is likely that a larger number of people will have to be involved in the planning process, once the basic decision to proceed has been made. For example, transfer of work from one unit to another may involve engineering studies at the plant level and the purchase of new capital equipment for which there is a long lead time; in these circumstances it may be necessary to bring quite junior management levels into the planning process.

A typical planning team might consist of the senior manager with line responsibility for closing the plant (say, a divisional chief executive), together with senior managers from each of the major functional departments. It is likely that a major redundancy programme will affect all departments in some way. The manufacturing operation is nearly always affected directly. The marketing department will need to assist in the preparation of contingency plans for use in the event of industrial disruption; the finance department will require to undertake detailed calculations on the redundancy terms; and the personnel and industrial relations people obviously play a key role. The public relations manager will have to become involved at this stage, as may other specialist groups, such as the legal department and the property manager. In a large company, the membership of the ad hoc group will be different from that of the working party or management groups which originally made the strategic decision to follow a cost-reduction strategy. This is usually appropriate as preparation of action plans is operational rather than strategic, but there should be some overlap because the rationale behind the strategic decision should influence the way in which the redundancy programme is implemented.

2. The Legal Position on Redundancy and Dismissal

Before management begins to plan any reduction in the size of the workforce (including employees at the management level), they should be fully conversant with the complexities of the legal situation relating to dismissal. Unless the firm has its own industrial-relations experts who are fully conversant with the law – as will often be the case in large firms – it may be necessary to seek legal advice. This section is intended only as a summary of the major issues for management, *not as a legal text* on which dismissal decisions should be based.

An employee who is dismissed may have claims against the firm for any or all of the following: wrongful dismissal, redundancy and unfair dismissal. So that management may be aware of what they can and cannot do under the law, each will be considered in turn. The main statutes with which management should be familiar are the Employment Protection (Consolidation) Act of 1978 and the Transfer of

Undertakings (Protection of Employment) Regulation 1981. The latter is particularly important when redundancies involve reorganization and restructuring.

2.1 Wrongful Dismissal

This occurs when the employer dismisses an employee in breach of contract. An employer can always terminate a contract of employment but he must give proper notice, which is either that set out in the contract, or the minimum laid down by Section 49 of the 1978 Act, whichever is the greater. The minimum notice periods laid down in the Act depend on length of service, but there is no qualifying period of employment necessary (as there is with unfair dismissal). The minimum notice periods for persons employed for four weeks or more are:

Period of Continuous Employment	*Period of Notice*
4 weeks–2 years	1 week
2 years–12 years	1 week per year of service
Over 12 years	Not less than 12 weeks

The employer may always give wages in lieu of notice; he does not have to give reasons for the dismissal if full notice or wages in lieu of full notice are given. The employer can only dismiss the employee summarily or with lesser notice if the employee has broken his contract in a major way. Claims are limited to the amount the employee would have received had he been correctly dismissed, but the employee must take steps to mitigate his loss by seeking alternative employment, and this is taken into account in assessing damages.

2.2 Redundancy

An employee is redundant only if he is *not* replaced after dismissal. If two jobs are combined, a redundancy occurs, but if work is re-allocated among staff and the same number of staff are required, there is no redundancy. What constitutes a redundancy is defined in Section 81 of the 1978 Act: it involves chopping the position along with the occupant. When an employee is made redundant, the employer is obliged by law to compensate the employee. This payment is known as a redundancy payment. The law sets down a minimum sum that must be paid although, as we shall see later, many firms pay considerably in excess of the legal minimum amount. The amount of redundancy payment guaranteed by law depends on the age, current earnings and length of service of the employee, but there is a maximum weekly wage, currently £135 (gross), and compensation is awarded only for a maximum of twenty years' employment. The statutory payments based on age are as follows:

Age in years	Statutory redundancy payment
18–20	$\frac{1}{2}$ week's wage per year of employment
21–40	1 week's wage per year of employment
Over 40	$1\frac{1}{2}$ weeks' wage per year of employment

Thus, the maximum redundancy payment demanded by the law for any employee is £4,050 (£135 × $1\frac{1}{2}$ × 20). Employees must have two years' continuous service, working at least sixteen hours per week, or five years' service working eight hours per week, to qualify for redundancy payments.

The government will repay employers 41% of any statutory redundancy payment, but if the employer pays any amount in excess of the statutory sum, the entire amount is borne by the employer. If the employer becomes insolvent and is unable to pay the redundancy money, the government will pay up to eight weeks' wages out of its Redundancy Fund. When making ten or more employees redundant at one establishment, the employer must inform the Department of Employment according to specified notification procedures. Failure to comply with these regulations can lead to a 10% reduction in redundancy rebate or a fine.

2.3 Unfair Dismissal

All terminations of employment other than mutual terminations give rise under the law to a presumption of unfair dismissal. Thus, even in situations where the employer 'persuades' the employee to resign or agrees to a 'mutual' termination of the employment, it is nearly always assumed by an Industrial Tribunal that the employer has brought pressure to bear on the employee, and that termination is in fact unilateral by the employer. Every employee who has worked at least sixteen hours per week (or eight hours per week for five years) for 52 continuous weeks (or 104 weeks if the firm employs less than twenty people) has the legal right *not* to be unfairly dismissed by his employer.* What constitutes dismissal is defined by Section 55 of the 1978 Act, and the provisions relating to fairness of dismissal are

* There is no qualifying period if dismissal is due to sex, race or union membership.

covered under Section 57 of the same Act. The law clearly places the burden of proof that the dismissal was fair on the company – the company is virtually guilty until proven innocent. The company's justification must be twofold: first, there must be a substantial reason for the dismissal which a reasonable employer could use to dismiss; second, it must be fair to dismiss for this substantial reason. Many companies have gone to great lengths to establish procedures which meet the basic requirements of natural justice which are demanded by Industrial Tribunals when hearing the claims of former employees. Thus, it is important that the treatment received by any individual employee should be comparable to that received by other staff in similar situations. Most importantly, the procedures taken leading up to dismissal must be fair and be seen to be fair. Looking at the situation of an individual manager who is claiming unfair dismissal, an Industrial Tribunal might ask the following questions:

- Was the manager warned of his shortcomings?
- Was he given an adequate chance to improve his performance?
- Was he given a 'fair hearing' – a chance to explain his side of the situation?
- Was the dismissal decision unbiased?

The maximum amount a firm is likely to have to pay for unfair dismissal has been calculated in Figure 9.1. This table shows the basic compensation (which is calculated in the same way as the redundancy payment), together with the additional amounts for which an employer could be liable. In each case, the maximum weekly wage for calculation purposes is £135.

Trying to determine what constitutes or is likely to constitute unfair dismissal is a tricky issue for management. In the past, managers have often been under the mistaken impression that by getting a dismissed employee to sign an agreement accepting a sum of money as full and complete settlement of all claims, contractual, statutory or otherwise, that he might have against the company, they are safe from a future claim for unfair dismissal. This is not true. Such a settlement is not binding where rights to unfair dismissal are present: the employee cannot contract out of his statutory entitlement. However, this situation differs from that in which an employee is persuaded to terminate his contract of employment by a financial inducement. In that situation there is no dismissal, merely a mutual agreement to terminate the contract. There is clearly a fine line here as to what is and is not dismissal. Any agreement made with an employee which involves him or her giving up the right to claim unfair dismissal should be recorded by a Conciliation Officer (on his Form COT 3), otherwise it will be a legal nullity. The Conciliation Officer has no right to approve the agreement; his duty is merely to record it.

Figure 9.1: *Compensation for Unfair Dismissal*
(*Maximum Amounts Payable as of February 1982*)

	Basis of calculation[1]	Maximum amount payable[2]
Basic compensation	1½ (weeks) × £135 × 20 (years)	£4,050
Compensatory payment for loss of earnings	Lost earnings while out of work. Difference between new salary and old × number of years until retirement.	£7,000
Additional payments for refusal to reinstate[3]	26 (weeks) × £135	£3,510
Higher additional payment where refusal to reinstate based on discrimination[4]	52 (weeks) × £135	£7,020

NOTES
1. Actual weekly wage is used if wage less than £130 per week.
2. Claimant has duty to mitigate his loss, and compensation will be reduced accordingly.
3. Minimum amount is 13 weeks × weekly wage.
4. Minimum amount is 26 weeks × weekly wage.

2.4 The Need to Consult Unions

Under the Employment Protection Act 1975 (as amended by the 1978 Act), management has a duty to consult with trade union representatives on redundancy if a union is recognized for collective bargaining purposes. The statutory minimum consultation periods depend on the number of employees being made redundant. Where the number is in excess of one hundred, ninety days' consultation is required. Section 90 of the Act defines the nature of the consultation:

For the purpose of the consultation required by this section the employer shall disclose in writing to the trade union representatives

- the reasons for his redundancy proposals;
- the numbers and description of employees whom it is proposed to dismiss as redundant;
- the total number of employees of any such description employed by the employer of the establishment in question;
- the proposed method of selecting the employees who may be dismissed; and
- the proposed method of carrying out the dismissal with due regard to any procedure, including the period over which the dismissals are to take effect.

Paragraph (7) of the same section goes further to state that 'in the course of the consultation required . . . the employer shall consider any representations made . . . and reply to those representations and, if he rejects any of those representations, state his reasons'. If a union complaint is made that the firm has not complied with the law, the firm has to show in front of an Industrial Tribunal that there were special circumstances that made consultation impractical or that the firm had done what could be regarded as reasonably practical. If the firm cannot make such a case, the union may apply for a 'protective award' to compensate employees for the loss they have suffered through non-consultation.

It is possible that in the future there will be European legislation making consultation and disclosure of information mandatory. Currently, a European Commission proposal is calling for mandatory disclosure of a wide range of information on a regular basis in all companies with more than one hundred employees.[2] The proposal is in line with the voluntary guidelines on disclosure put out by O.E.C.D. (Organization for Economic Co-operation and Development) and by the I.L.O. (International Labour Organization), and is similar to industrial practice in West Germany, Holland and Belgium. The proposal, as far as it relates to redundancies and plant closure, is as follows: if a parent company considers making important changes affecting employees, such as closures or transfers, either regarding the parent company or any of its subsidiaries, it would be required to send detailed information on its plans to each of its E.E.C. subsidiaries forty days before implementing the decision. Subsidiary managements would be required to transmit this information without delay to employee representatives and to ask for their opinion within a period of not less than thirty days. Where there was no communication or consultation, employee representatives would be authorized to open consultation and, where appropriate, negotiation with the parent company management.

3. Preparation of a Short-term Industrial-relations Strategy

The principal industrial-relations objectives in the implementation of a redundancy programme are likely to be minimization of industrial disruption and maximum co-operation from both departing and remaining employees. The legal requirements relating to redundancy and the possible consequences of poor implementation of a redundancy programme make it imperative that management develop a short-term industrial-relations strategy to meet these objectives. The short-term strategy should obviously be consistent with the firm's longer-term industrial-relations strategy, but we will not concern ourselves with this issue here.

The nature and extent of consultation that will take place between management and unions is a critical decision-making area. Consultation means different things to different companies. At one end of the spectrum, it means involving the workforce in decision-making; at the other end, it means little more than informing the workforce about decisions that have already been made and that will not be changed. In practice (although this is changing), few companies involve the workforce in decision-making – many still do not involve their managers! – but even fewer involve them when plant closure and redundancy decisions have to be made. If management believes the rationale for its cost-reduction strategy is absolutely watertight and that its own previous decisions were all correct – in other words, that the present situation has absolutely nothing to do with them – they may be more willing to take a consultative approach. But consultation takes time – a long time, as witness the nationalized industries – and in many recovery situations urgent action precludes much consultation. Most managements prefer to get by with the minimum amount of consultation likely to be acceptable to the unions under the law. Their approach is to try to convince the unions that the decision is correct for the future well-being of the company and that it is useless to pursue alternative suggestions to the proposed redundancy programme.

In a receivership situation, gaining workforce acceptance is usually easier, although one receiver told me once how he had been known to allow handwritten memos and working papers to fall into union hands on purpose to 'help' the union understand the seriousness of the situation. Where the company is not in receivership, few unions are likely to accept closure without first challenging it. They will usually ask for additional information with which they hope to discredit the company's case and lead to the negotiation of an alternative decision. In the case of Bowater's newsprint mill at Ellesmere Port, which was reported to have lost about £7 million in 1980, a workers' action committee was formed when plans were announced to close the plant as of November 1980 and make 1,600 workers redundant. The committee waged a much-publicized campaign to try to make management change its mind, but eventually they capitulated and started talks on severance terms, even though they still continued to try to persuade the company to postpone the closure date.[3] This is not an atypical situation.

What is critical for management in such a situation is to have decided in advance which issues are negotiable and which are not. Few managements will want to encourage negotiation but, to meet with the legal requirements discussed above, a degree of consultation or negotiation will have to be permitted. Requests for additional information must be considered, bearing in mind the legal position, the damage that may be caused if a request is refused, and the danger of encouraging negotiation. In some cases, management will also consider the danger of exposing weaknesses that exist in the rationale for the redundancy programme, or exposing their past forecasting mistakes. Management must think about what additional information might be requested and be prepared with answers – answers that show their redundancy decision is firm and will not be changed by negotiation or industrial disruption. Common practice is for management to regard the redundancy decision itself as non-negotiable and to negotiate as and when necessary on such issues as the size of redundancy payments, retention payments, work arrangements during the period leading up to a closure, etc. The message management puts across in these situations usually goes as follows: 'The redundancy programme is necessary to improve the efficiency and profitability of the business . . . that the loss of jobs is deeply regretted but will help save the jobs of the remainder of the workforce . . . and that those who lose their jobs will receive generous severance terms and all assistance . . . etc., etc.'

How does management go about putting this message across, so as to meet its industrial-relations objectives? The approach depends on both the history and the current state of consultation within the company and, more specifically, on the quality of personal relationships and understanding that exists or can be established between management and senior trade-union officials. Where there has been a history of consultation and good industrial relations, the workforce and full-time union officials will already be aware of the company's financial situation, and thus the announcement of a closure or drastic cutback will not come as too great a shock. Where there is a low degree of awareness among employees as to the company's commercial and financial situation, the shock will be greater and the reaction more hostile. In some situations there will be time, prior to the announcement date, to 'condition' the workforce. This implies carrying out a communication programme to alert the workforce to the fact that measures must be taken to improve financial performance and that remedial actions to cut costs and improve performance are being studied. New management entering a potential recovery situation can take this approach only if time permits.

Management should always make use of the existing consultative machinery and use previously agreed procedures wherever possible; but in nearly all cases, these should be supplemented by unofficial contact with carefully selected, full-time union officials before the announcement of redundancies. This is very common practice prior to a plant closure or a major redundancy programme being announced. Management often finds union officials at district, regional or national level to be more understanding (in private) of the need for redundancies than are shop stewards who may themselves be affected by redundancy notices. Unofficial contact is designed to obtain the understanding of a few influential officials as to why redundancies are inevitable. In this way, management hopes to meet its legal obligation for consultation, obtain the co-operation of officials in persuading their plant representatives to accept redundancies, and avoid spreading the conflict to other plants or divisions within the company. Where plant closure is concerned, obtaining co-operation during the closure period is absolutely critical. Although there are clear advantages to be gained from pre-announcement contact, there are risks in this approach. The major risk is one of premature announcement. In its unofficial contact, the company can only *request* secrecy until announcement date – it cannot enforce it. Consequently, those officials selected must be favourably disposed towards the company, have good personal relationships with the personnel or industrial relations director or one of the senior directors, and be judged as persons who will maintain confidentiality despite strong loyalties to break it.

More extensive consultation than has been discussed here sometimes occurs, particularly in the nationalized industries. At both British Leyland and British Steel, for example, lengthy discussions with full-time union officials have taken place before redundancy plans have been announced. In October 1979, the Chairman of British Leyland, Sir Michael Edwardes, managed to persuade the executive of the Confederation of Shipbuilding and Engineering Unions (which represents seventeen unions within B.L.) to support his plan to close plants and shed 25,000 jobs, although the company's senior shop stewards voted almost unanimously to oppose the plan. A referendum was held, and 87% of employees were in favour of the plan.[4] B.L.'s use of referendums has certainly been useful in reducing the power of shop stewards who were unrepresentative of popular opinion. In B.L.'s case, a referendum may be the only method of consultation capable of resolving fundamental issues where plant loyalties and inter-union rivalries create large divisions within the workforce, but few managements and unions will want to copy B.L.

4. Preparation of Contingency Plans

Management should always be prepared for the likelihood of industrial disruption following the announcement of a redundancy programme. Trade-union reaction varies from company to company and, indeed, from plant to plant within the same firm. Reaction also changes with the industrial and political climate. In the mid-1970s, a shop stewards' committee faced with closure would call an immediate sit-in and try to form a workers' co-operative. Recently, the top priority has been the size of the redundancy payment, although sit-ins still occur from time to time.

In the ideal situation there will be no industrial disruption when the redundancy programme is announced, but management need to institute contingency plans for each of the following scenarios: a work-to-rule or go-slow, a short strike (say, of one to two weeks), a long strike and a sit-in. The effect of each scenario should be costed out in terms of lost contribution resulting from lost production and the extra redundancy payments that might have to be paid to buy acceptance of closure from the majority of the workforce. With a company already in a recovery situation, serious industrial disruption at a time of critical cash shortage can easily lead to total failure. Management must be aware of the cost consequences that will occur under each scenario and take steps to alleviate the consequences of industrial action. Detailed contingency plans for each scenario should be prepared. A typical plan might include the following elements:

- the possibility of obtaining supplies from alternative sources
- the possibility of stockpiling, prior to the announcement, in other depots/plants unaffected by redundancy plans
- the establishment of customer priority lists
- a special communications plan with customers during the interruption
- the establishment of a special management accounting information system so that management can *rapidly* assess the financial impact of the dispute
- a promotional plan to recapture lost business and restore trade confidence as soon as any industrial action has ended.

A sit-in is far and away the most difficult situation for management to handle, and the reason it happens in the first place is usually as the result of lack of consultation and lack of planning. To avoid the possibility of a sit-in, management have been known to take drastic pre-emptive action, as happened when Racal closed Decca's Battersea works in 1980. The union had been informed that the plant would close on Friday, 3 October 1980, but management became paranoid about the possibility of an occupation at Battersea. Security guards were posted outside the plant. On Monday, 15 September, employees arrived at work to discover the factory gates locked. They were informed that the factory was closed and that they should return on the following Friday to collect their pay and belongings. On the Friday, the workers returned to find their personal lockers in the street outside the locked factory gates. They were paid their money through a window!

5. Deciding the Redundancy Details

Management must have carefully worked through all the details of the redundancy programme prior to the announcement date, even if it plans to negotiate some of the details with workforce representatives after announcement. The major issues to be resolved ahead of time are: (i) the timing of the announcement; (ii) the procedure for selecting personnel to be made redundant; (iii) the size of the redundancy payments; (iv) the size of retention payments (if plant closure is involved); and (v) provisions for helping redundant staff find new jobs.

Timing of the announcement: By law, the company has to give notice of redundancy, or pay in lieu of notice. The period of notice depends on the size of the firm, but for a large company is ninety days. If a company is in a severe cash crisis, management may have little choice but to make the announcement as soon as possible so that the notice period can start running. Companies finding themselves in a less severe crisis may have more time and can plan the announcement date to gain maximum industrial-relations advantage: for example, it is usually unwise to announce redundancies in the middle of annual wage negotiations. Announcement dates should also be considerate of the many seemingly trivial things that, for the want of a little foresight, could be avoided. Announcing redundancies when the senior shop steward is on holiday, for example, is hardly likely to be treated very kindly! Fridays tend to be the preferred day for announcements because, first, the press and City have little time to digest what is happening and, second, the workforce has the weekend to 'put things in perspective'.

Procedure for selecting personnel to be made redundant: At the shop-floor level, length of service and job type are the most commonly used criteria for deciding who will be made redundant. The unions prefer to operate a seniority system of job security – last in, first out – believing this to be the most equitable solution. From a management point of view, however, job type must also be an important criterion, since increased efficiency is most likely to come by rearranging job tasks. Among management personnel, different criteria tend to be used, even where managers are union members. Performance appraisal, promotability, as well as type of job and ability to adapt to a new management style (after new management arrives), may all be taken into account. Unions tend to be more flexible at management level although, in my own experience, an official of A.S.T.M.S. (Association of Scientific, Technical and Managerial Staffs) asked if management could find Mr X a job, even though they knew he was quite ineffectual. In subsequent discussions, it came out that Mr X was one of the few A.S.T.M.S. employees on the site who actually attended union meetings! The easiest personnel for management to make redundant are those who have been in the company for only a short time, and it is quite common for new management to ask immediately for a list of those employees who have been in their jobs for less than twelve months. Although an employee has to be employed continuously for two years to be eligible for redundancy payments, management regards the twelve-months limit as more important, since after that period the employee can sue for unfair dismissal. There is no problem dismissing anyone with less than one year's continuous service, subject to the necessary notice being given.

Size of the redundancy payments: The minimum payments are, of course, established by law, but employees have come to expect substantially more than the minimum amount. The financial situation of the company (of the parent company, if we are dealing with a subsidiary), management's sense of social responsibility and union bargaining power will determine the size of the payments. As a rule of thumb, managers sometimes think of $2\frac{1}{2}$ × the statutory minimum as being the norm. These sums are far lower than the highly publicized redundancy payments of £20,000 offered to some British Steel workers – these are exceptions, not the rule. Redundancy payments are currently tax free in the hands of the recipient up to an amount of £25,000.

Size of retention payments: Where a plant is being closed, we have seen that a considerable length of time may elapse between the announcement and the date at which the redundancies take effect, and that some of these redundancies will be staged as the plant runs down. In these circumstances, it is common practice for management to make retention payments over and above the agreed redundancy amount to encourage staff not only to stay until the plant is finally closed but also to co-operate to make sure the plant is closed at an agreed time. It is not uncommon for workers to go slow in order to extend the life of a plant they know is going to be closed. For example, part of the huge loss on British Shipbuilders' order for twenty-four ships for Poland has been attributed to the fact that about half the ships were built in yards scheduled for closure and that workers had 'gone slow' to extend the life of the yards.[5]

Provisions for helping redundant staff find new jobs: One noticeable feature of many redundancy programmes is the effort management makes to help workers find alternative employment. Sometimes this is used as a low-cost bargaining tool with the unions or as a means to alleviate the stigma of redundancy tarnishing their image as a good employer; at other times it may be done out of a genuine sense of social responsibility. Whatever the reasons, more managements are taking specific steps to help their redundant employees. Usually this takes the form of giving preferential treatment to redundant employees if there are job openings elsewhere in other plants (or elsewhere in the group), establishing a local job centre with the help of the Department of Health and Social Security, and perhaps assistance in writing curricula vitae.

From time to time, however, one hears of more progressive schemes, such as that which occurred at Massey-Ferguson's combine-harvester plant in Kilmarnock, Scotland, which closed early in 1980 with the loss of 1,500 jobs. While management and workers disagreed about the need to close the plant – as they nearly always do – the two groups set up a joint committee to seek a new owner for the plant or, failing that, to find sub-contract work to keep part of the plant going. The unions agreed with Massey-Ferguson that (a) if the company was determined to leave, industrial action would not be taken to hinder the company because it would only damage the chances of finding new work for the plant; (b) preserving the jobs at Kilmarnock was more important than negotiating the size of redundancy payments; and (c) until new work or a new owner could be found, the plant needed Massey-Ferguson's management expertise.[6] For its part, Massey-Ferguson set up a new company and stated that it would be willing to be a partner in any new venture, contributing the machine tools and other fixed assets (which probably had low resale value) as its share of the equity, and would continue to put sub-contract work from its other U.K. factories into Kilmarnock to provide a base load. The attitude of the workforce was vitally important in persuading management to take such an initiative. The Managing Director of Massey-Ferguson U.K. put it this way: 'The most significant asset we have in trying to get new work is the commitment of the workforce and the workforce's representatives. That kind of determination deserves support, and it will get it from the company.' Of course, such attitudes do not occur by themselves – they reflect a history of good industrial relations. It is noteworthy that Massey-Ferguson management emphasized the success of its workforce in meeting production targets over recent years and its co-operation in cutting costs, rather than publicizing the losses of the Kilmarnock plant, to justify the decision to close the plant.

6. Preparation of a Master Statement

A number of larger companies have found it useful to develop a master statement setting out the rationale for their plant closure or redundancy programme. This statement, which usually takes the form of a report, is designed to serve as the basis for the development of the firm's communication programme with the various interest-groups affected by the cost-reduction programme.

A typical master statement for setting out the rationale behind a plant closure decision would include the following:

(*a*) *Historical perspective*: a review of the company's (or division's) sales and profit performance over the past five years. This might include analysis of the company's historical forecasts of demand as compared to actual sales volume, analysis of the firm's forecast and actual market share; reasons for deteriorating market performance, etc.

(*b*) *Financial performance over the last five years*: a highlight of the key financial data expressed both in current values and real terms (after taking out the effects of inflation). It might be useful here to make a comparison of the firm's financial performance against that of its major competitors.

(*c*) *Future performance*: predictions of future market demand and the firm's share of that demand, together with a momentum analysis* showing the firm's expected financial performance in profit and cash-flow terms.

(*d*) *Analysis of the cost-reduction opportunities*: identification and discussion of the various cost-reduction opportunities considered by the company and the detailed analysis showing why the chosen strategy is the preferred option. This would include detailed financial evaluation of the options, showing the cash-flow implications and effect on profitability.

Where firms are trying to become more efficient but are not actually in danger of failing, preparing the logic to justify drastic cost savings

---

* A momentum analysis is a projection of a company's future financial position, over a period of, say, three to five years, assuming no change in the company's strategy and mode of operations.

is more difficult to do. What happens in this situation is that companies look for reference points against which to compare their level of profits as forecast by the momentum analysis. Examples of reference points commonly used by firms are:

- their own historical level of profitability measured in terms of profit as a percentage of capital employed
- industry or sector average levels of profitability
- the average financial performance of the leading firms in the industry
- the performance of the market leader.

A master statement of the type described above is usually designed for the exclusive use of senior management, and is not for general distribution inside or outside the company. Besides providing the basis for the preparation of a detailed communication programme, a master statement ensures that senior management are all fully conversant with the same set of facts and logic on which the cost-reduction decision was based. This is most important once the public announcement has been made, since management must appear consistent and cohesive in any discussions they may have to enter into with unions and other interested parties. This is particularly true as far as the quantitative data is concerned – management must commit to memory a few key figures that support their argument. If the unions refuse to accept the cuts and hard negotiating takes place, there is absolutely no room for management to be quoting different sets of figures to union officials.

7. Developing a Communications Programme

The successful implementation of a redundancy programme requires a carefully thought-out and detailed communications programme to all persons affected by or interested in the redundancy issue. The main objectives of a communications programme are to establish an understanding throughout the company that the redundancies are necessary, to ensure that the redundancy programme is implemented with a minimum of disruption, and to create a favourable impression with various interest-groups outside the company (e.g. shareholders, customers, consumers, politicians, etc.). The development of a suitable communications programme is discussed under three headings: situational factors affecting communications programme, establishing a communications policy, and the action programme.

7.1 Situational Factors Affecting Communications Programme

The type of communications programme a company develops is very dependent on the company's culture and the history of industrial relations in the company. The types of questions that management need to answer include the following:

- What statements have been made to the workforce concerning the future of individual plants and/or the security of jobs?
- Is there a well-established system of communications between management and its workforce? What is management's credibility?
- Does the company have a good ongoing dialogue with senior trade union officials? Can it rely on senior union members for support in the communications programme?
- Are there strong leaders among that part of the workforce which is to be made redundant who may oppose the redundancy plans?
- Is management totally committed or will the doubts of some individuals about the correctness of the redundancies show through? If members of management are to be made redundant, will they have to participate in the communication process?

Answers to these and other such questions provide the background against which a communications programme should be established.

7.2 Establishing A Communications Policy

The firm's communications programme will be based on the Master Statement, the short-term industrial-relations strategy, the details of the redundancy programme, and the situational factors discussed above. The statements communicated to the various target audiences would normally include:

- the rationale underlying the cutback
- a statement concerning the company's market performance and its long-term plans for improvement
- company policy for dealing with the redundant employees
- the relationship between the redundancy programme and previous statements made to the workforce concerning their security of employment
- any proposed organizational changes associated with the redundancies.

Where the redundancy programme involves plant closure, there are additional issues to be covered. These may include plans for transferring production to other plants, the effect on the company's other plants, its distribution and marketing activities, and possibly a statement relating the current closure plans to the company's longer-term production strategy.

The rationale for the redundancy programme will, of course, have to be communicated very clearly, but whether the full rationale as developed in the Master Statement or only part is communicated is an issue for top management to decide. In some instances management will wish to avoid telling the whole truth to avoid what they think will be loss of credibility due to poor judgements in the past. At this point, the reader may ask quite legitimately: is this ethical? Shouldn't management be forced to disclose everything? I will leave the reader to decide the answer for himself. Sometimes a Master Statement will include details of future plant closures and redundancies three or five years hence. Such long-term plans are, by their nature, uncertain; they can change within a few months. In these circumstances, the justification for management saying nothing would appear to be greater.

If management adopts as its industrial-relations stance that the decision itself is non-negotiable, the communications programme must emphasize that the board's decision is final and that no other options will be considered. In these circumstances, no mention should be made of the various cost-reduction alternatives outlined in the Master Statement. Instead, the attention of unions and employees should be directed away from the other alternatives and towards severance terms and any benefits, such as job opportunities, elsewhere in the company. Attempted pacification can sometimes verge on the ludicrous: for example, in February 1980, Thames Board, the cardboard manufacturing subsidiary of Unilever, announced that it was to close one of its two board mills at Purfleet, Essex, in August, with the loss of 800 jobs. At the same time, however, the company said they would probably be creating about 600 jobs during 1980 at Workington in Cumbria – fine, but not much consolation for the Purfleet workforce.

Generally, companies prefer to adopt a low profile in the public arena when it comes to redundancies; for the larger companies, however, this is not always possible. Consequently, press conferences at the national level are usually avoided, since they have the opposite effect: they tend to generate news and raise the profile. The timing of the announcement can help maintain a low profile. This is another reason why Friday noon is often regarded as the best time for announcement: many journalists are just about to pack up for the weekend, and by Monday the news will be stale!

7.3 The Action Programme

The first step in developing a communication action programme to implement the communications policy is to define the target audiences. With whom does management have to communicate? Although the overall communications strategy will be the same for all audiences, the approach used and the message sent may need to be adapted for different audiences. For most companies, the target audiences will be the same and will consist essentially of the same groups that should be contacted at the beginning of a turnaround (see Chapter 6). Some of the target audiences are only indirectly affected by the redundancy programme, but they need to be kept informed of the facts from a public-relations point of view and may even become involved in subsequent discussions.

Having identified with whom they have to communicate, management then has to decide *what* they are going to communicate to each target audience, *how* they are going to communicate it, *who* is going to communicate it and *when*. The main target audiences and a typical way of dealing with each group are listed below:

- *Top management*: Although all members of the top management group are likely to know about the redundancy programme at an early stage of planning, it is vital that all directors and senior managers fully understand and support the programme. It is expected that all members of this group will be fully conversant with any Master Statement that has been prepared, and will be briefed by the chief executive.

- *Key management*: Those involved with announcing the programme need to be thoroughly briefed two or three days before the announcement date. The briefing needs to be detailed, perhaps taking the form of a well-prepared slide presentation, giving detailed information as to why the redundancies are necessary, but giving no discussion of the alternatives as included in the Master Statement. The key management briefing should cover the briefing details for announcement day, so that all managers are thoroughly conversant with the action plan. The meeting should probably be held off-site.

- *Other management*: In large companies, there may be other middle and junior managers who are not key management as defined above but whom top management would like to brief separately from the general staff. Typically, these managers would receive a presentation similar to the key management group's, early on the morning of the announcement or late the previous day (possibly at a meeting held off-site).

- *The staff*: Some managements hold separate meetings for the redundant staff and the surviving staff, but this approach is rarely used for a plant closure or a large-scale across-the-board redundancy. Separate meetings are more applicable if a clearly defined department or product line is being closed down. In large, multi-site companies it is usually necessary to have a number of separate meetings for all staff at the same time, including meetings at all sites *unaffected* by the redundancy programme. In those site locations where redundancy is to occur, all employees are usually handed an envelope with a letter from the chief executive at the end of the meeting telling them whether they personally are affected by the redundancy. The letter is often accompanied by a statement, usually signed by the company secretary, giving formal notice of the redundancy decision. In some cases, this approach is supplemented by a personal letter from the company chairman posted to the homes of all employees; and this is followed by individual interviews for all those facing redundancy. At each meeting, the communication message must be adapted to the situation at hand. Some site locations, for example, might actually gain jobs and such benefits should be stressed during briefing sessions at those sites. Management should be prepared to spend considerable time briefing employees at sites unaffected by the redundancy programme. This is critically important, since the announcement of cutbacks at one plant may lead to suspicion and a feeling of job insecurity at other plants. Field sales and distribution staff should not be forgotten – they are the critical interface with the customer – and they should be thoroughly briefed (see Customers, below).

- *Union officials*: We have already discussed the desirability of briefing key union officials prior to announcement day. Typically, the most senior union officials involved would be given a fairly detailed briefing by the personnel director or another director who has good relations with these officials, at a personal meeting.

Smaller firms will probably deal only with local district officials one or two days in advance of the announcement. Internal union representatives will usually be given a less detailed (more selective) presentation on the day of the announcement – one or two hours before the official announcement. This may take the form of a slide presentation similar to that given to management, but suitably amended.

- *Public officials*: If the company is a major employer in its local community, or is located in an area where there is already a high level of unemployment, or is a large, nationally known company, it may be useful to meet with a few selected public officials. One or two officials of substantial political stature or influence may be seen one or two days ahead of the announcement (e.g. the local member of parliament), but each situation is different and will depend on previous contacts with the public officials concerned. In addition, some companies send advance copies of their press release together with an accompanying letter to local councillors, the Secretary of State for Employment, their sponsoring ministry, the Confederation of British Industry and any other public organizations with which they have contact from time to time. Such announcements are sent out only as a 'courtesy' measure and are dispatched either on announcement day or, at best, the day before announcement.

- *The media*: If the company's communications policy is to adopt a low profile, the company will issue a press release designed to create support for the redundancy decision and to minimize adverse press reaction. The 'best' situation the company is likely to achieve is to gain a favourable reaction from the 'quality' press (say, *The Times*, the *Guardian*) and no adverse reaction from the popular press (the *Sun*, the *Mirror*, etc.). Management should be well prepared for questions from the press and 'questions and answers' should be prepared ahead of time and distributed to all senior management. There should be only one contact for media inquiries, who will be responsible for liaising with senior members of management where their specialist input is required. Where the redundancy programme affects a number of locations, the main press release may have to be supplemented by appropriate local information. To maintain a low public profile, management may want to avoid national television and radio interviews, although such interviews will usually be preferable to an offhand, 'no comment' reaction which may be interpreted as anti-media and lead the public to believe that management has something to hide.

- *Customers*: The reaction of customers to a redundancy programme, and more particularly to a plant closure, may be apprehension about future service levels, so the communication action programme should emphasize that the customer will not be directly affected by the redundancies or facility closure. The principal methods adopted by management are letters to customers and press releases to the trade press. The preparation of model answers to questions that might be posed by customers can be useful additional material for the sales and distribution departments. Very large, important customers may need to be visited individually soon after the announcement or, indeed, telephoned on announcement day to give them necessary reassurances.

- *Other interested audiences*: There may be other target audiences that should be contacted on announcement day. If the firm is a public company, for example, press releases should be sent to the stock exchange, to stockbroker analysts and other financial institutions. If the firm is in a recovery situation, its bankers will probably know in advance of its redundancy or closure plans. Trade associations may be notified and sometimes suppliers, too. Exactly who is notified outside those directly involved with the programme will vary from one situation to the next. As a guideline, any person or group that could have an adverse effect on the outcome of the redundancy programme, due to their influential position, should be notified.

Figure 9.2 shows the general outline of a typical communication action programme. In practice, however, the communication action programme will need to be much more detailed. An important preliminary step is the preparation of the communication material and its approval by top management. For the key management group on downwards, detailed briefing documents, slide presentations, general notices, press releases, questions and answers, and letters need to be prepared for each of the target audiences well ahead of time. The communication material must be consistent with the Master Statement and the industrial-relations strategy, so it is recommended that drafts of all material (and drafts of any necessary local variations, e.g. local press releases) be reviewed and approved at top management level.

Figure 9.2: *Summary of Typical Communication Action Programme*

Target audience (to whom)	Message to be communicated (what)	Method of communication (how)	Responsibility (who)	Timing (when)
Top management	Master Statement rationale	group meeting	Chairman/Chief Executive	2–4 weeks before announcement
Key management involved in communication	detailed	group meeting with slide presentation, general notice	Chief Executive	2–3 days before announcement
Other middle and junior management	detailed	group meeting with slide presentation, general notice	Chief Executive	late on day prior to announcement
All other employees	selective	group meetings, personal letter, general notice	Chief Executive	announcement day
Senior union officials	detailed	personal contact	Personnel Director	2–3 days before announcement
Local full-time union officials	detailed	personal contact	Chief Executive and Personnel Director	1 day before announcement
Internal trade union officials	selective	group meeting with slide presentation	Chief Executive/other Directors	announcement day
Public officials	detailed or selective	personal meetings, letters, questions and answers	Chairman, Chief Executive (depending on political stature)	1–2 days before announcement
Customers	selective	letters, trade press, questions and answers	Sales Director	announcement day
Media	selective	press release, questions and answers sheets	Public Relations Manager	announcement day
Investment community	selective	copy of press release	Public Relations Manager or Finance Director	announcement day
Trade association	selective	copy of press release	Sales Director or company contact	announcement day

Summary

This chapter has developed an action framework for implementing a forced redundancy programme. The decision to implement such a programme is often relatively easy to make on analytical grounds, but its implementation can be much more complex and time-consuming. The important point is for management to take time to plan the execution *in detail*. A seven-step planning approach has been suggested in this chapter.

Where a redundancy programme is being carried out by a new chief executive or a new management team, every effort should be made to make the redundancy programme a model of good communications with management, supervisors, unions and plant operatives. We have seen that good communications is a key factor for turnaround success, so management should make every effort to boost the morale of the survivors by showing them that new management intends to operate in a more open and communicative style than the previous management.

Notes

1. 'Referendum Management – the Workers Must Decide', *Financial Times*, 22 October 1979.
2. 'Multinationals and Disclosure of Information', European Communities Commission Background Report 13EC/B52/80.
3. 'Severance Talks Mark Collapse of Bowater Workers' Campaign', *Financial Times*, 22 October 1980.
4. 'Referendum Management – the Workers Must Decide', *Financial Times*, 22 October 1979.
5. '£40 Million Lost in Polish Ship Deal', *Financial Times*, 28 February 1980.
6. 'Harmony amid the Wreckage', *Financial Times*, 26 November 1979.

10. Implementing Revenue-generating Strategies

Three revenue-generating strategies were identified as commonly used in turnaround situations: marketing improvement strategies, product-market reorientation and growth by acquisition. Any in-depth discussion on implementing product-market changes and implementing an acquisition programme would require a book on each, so this chapter does little more than provide a broad overview of the key implementation steps and a discussion of the specific issues that may arise in a turnaround situation.

I will discuss the three strategies in the order in which they are used in the recovery phase of a turnaround.

1. Marketing Improvement Strategy

A market-improvement strategy can be implemented relatively quickly; it therefore lends itself to the emergency phase of recovery. The major actions involve

- changing prices
- achieving product–customer focus
- improving selling efforts
- product line rationalization
- reducing or focusing advertising and promotion efforts.

A word of caution is needed before we start to discuss the implementation of these actions. Whereas the implementation of cost-reduction and asset-reduction strategies can be achieved without making a major impact on customers, great care should be taken when implementing marketing changes. It is one thing to upset the organization, quite another to upset one's customers! The turnaround firm is more often than not in a position of weakness in the marketplace, therefore the turnaround manager must think very carefully about the consequences of any actions that are likely to have a negative impact on customers.

1.1 Changing Price

In Chapter 4 we saw that increasing price is a common and effective turnaround strategy in many instances. It can be implemented more quickly than any other strategy available to the turnaround manager. Price increase can be achieved by raising list price, or by reducing discounts, or both. Price decreases, on the other hand, are usually implemented by offering large discounts or holding prices while cost inflation continues.

(a) *Raising list price*: This is the quickest and safest method of increasing price, since changing discounts is more complex, has greater impact on distributors, and requires more detailed cost and market information than is often available at the start of the recovery phase. There are three questions to consider:

(i) On which products should the price be raised? The same percentage price increase on all product lines is unlikely to be appropriate unless the product range is very narrow. Management therefore needs to assess the price elasticity of demand for the firm's major product lines, paying careful attention to the firm's competitive position *vis-à-vis* competitors. Competitors' prices should be quickly collected (if not already known) and managerial judgements will have to be made about product comparability and price elasticity. It is unlikely that management will be able to determine how much volume will be lost for a given price increase with any degree of accuracy – since neither historical information nor the time required to undertake a market study is likely to be available. In the final analysis, the decision will rest on the argument: if I raise price $x\%$ I can afford to lose up to $y\%$ in volume for the net profit effect to be beneficial. Does it seem reasonable to think I will lose less volume than $y\%$? Some of the factors to take into account when assessing price elasticity include:
- Products that already have high margins can often stand a further price increase more easily than low-margin products, since their competitive position is likely to be stronger.
- Infrequently purchased consumer goods tend to be less price-sensitive, since the user often cannot remember how much he or she paid on a previous occasion.
- If there are few sources of supply for a product or few comparable products on the market, price increases are usually easier to implement.
  High switching costs and fragmented buyers also lead to price inelasticity.

(ii) How much should the price be raised? Again, this is dependent on the shape of the price-demand curve; but for nearly all products there is a price premium, above which demand falls off very strongly. In the case of the British motorcycle industry, one of the strategic options considered by the Boston Consulting Group was a strategy involving a 10–15% price premium over Japanese competitors. The potential premium that can be charged over the mean market price must depend on the nature of the product and competition, but 10–15% would appear to be at the high end of the spectrum. Consumers are often relatively price insensitive within a certain price range. Thus, they may decide they want to spend about £50 on buying a camera, in which case raising the price from £47.75 to £52.95 may have almost no impact on sales volume. Unless the firm has a tremendous order backlog and wants to discourage more orders, there is probably a limit to the extent to which price can be increased at one time without losing customer goodwill. Customers have grown used to frequent price increases in the 1970s, due to higher levels of inflation, but if prices are raised substantially in excess of inflation, customer resistance and loss of goodwill may ensue. As a general guide, raising prices more than 50% faster than the rate of inflation at any one time should be avoided.

What is the best timing for raising prices? Most firms' terms of trade explicitly state that prices can be raised at any time, and legally management can raise prices on any orders which have not yet been dispatched to the customer. Adopting this tactic, however, can aggravate customers unnecessarily and it is usually preferable to make price increases effective only on new orders taken from a specific date, even though the full impact of the price increase will be delayed. If the firm has excess inventories and desperately needs cash, it may wish to give customers advance warning of the price increase, in the hope of liquidating excess inventory, but the benefit of increased profits, and hence increased cash flow, in the future must be balanced against the short-term need for cash.

(iii) What should be done about contracts? Today's turnaround firm may have escalation clauses built into its contracts, having learned from the lessons of others who did not take this precaution in the 1974/75 recession. However, even if escalation clauses are included, previous management may have totally miscalculated its costs of performing the contract, and the increased costs that may be recuperated under the escalation clause will be narrowly defined. In these circumstances, new management should always attempt to renegotiate the terms of the contract. Management may have more leverage than it thinks, since the customer will not want the firm to fail before its contract is completed.

Another timing issue relates to the length of time elapsed since prices were last increased. If the last price increase was more than six months ago, there is no problem; prices should probably be increased automatically, to take account of inflation. If less than six months have passed, it is harder to justify another price increase, particularly if inflation is relatively low, compared with historical levels. Adverse movements in exchange rates and other external 'shocks' may warrant more frequent price adjustments.

(*b*) *Changing discounts*: There are two types of discounts with which the firm is concerned: volume (or quantity) discounts and settlement discounts. Changes in a firm's discount structure tend to lead to more customer reaction than change in list price. Such discounts tend to be customer-oriented, whereas list price tends to be product-line oriented. As a method of implementing an overall price increase, cutting discounts should therefore be avoided, particularly in the emergency phase of a turnaround when it is more important than ever not to upset the firm's customers. Cutting discounts should be used only as a discretionary tactic to discourage certain classes of unprofitable customers. How we determine who these customers are will be discussed later in this chapter, but typically we are talking about large customers who demand extra large discounts or small customers whose volume is insufficient to cover the costs of doing business with them. Legally, the firm has to offer the same terms to all customers, but clearly some discount schedules will appeal to some customer groups more than others.

In my experience, it is sometimes more important for the turnaround firm to have a competitive discount structure than for it to have a competitive list price, although this will depend on the nature of the product and the channels of distribution. Where the firm sells direct to the customer, the customer is interested in the net price paid, rather than whether the list price is high and the discount large. Where the firm sells through a distribution channel, the situation is different. In this case the discount structure influences the distributors' incentive to push the firm's products. A discount structure uncompetitive by only 2½% of the end-user selling price on a highly differentiated product can make a big difference in the distribution channel's interest in selling the product. Thus, just as reducing discounts can lead to a loss of sales volume, so increasing discounts can lead to substantially increased volume. Whether this strategy is appropriate depends on the cost-price structure discussed in Chapter 5.

Very often the greatest pressure against raising prices comes not from the customers but from the firm's own sales department. The sales manager and the salesforce are usually the last people to want a price increase since they may well believe that any price increase makes their job more difficult. (When one finds a sales department readily agreeing to a price increase, one can be practically sure that the suggested price increase is too low!) Resistance from the salesforce will probably be greater in those situations where a large portion of their remuneration is based on sales performance. Where the turn-around management team is new to the industry, it is imperative for management to listen to and evaluate the sales department's views, prior to making changes; but once a decision has been made, it must then communicate and sell the need for price changes to the salesforce. A sales meeting will almost always be necessary prior to raising price. By correct presentation of the price increase to the customer and by harder selling, the salesforce plays a key role in assuring that volume does not drop when prices increase.

The firm's own prices and those of competitors should be constantly monitored and a formal pricing review undertaken at least once every six months. Thus, although the turnaround manager may have increased prices within a month of arrival largely on the basis of his 'gut feel' for price elasticities, he will almost certainly have a chance to correct any mistakes and refine the pricing strategy within six months.

1.2 Achieving Product-Customer Focus

One of the keys to implementing a successful recovery strategy within a given business area or product-market segment is concentrating efforts on a small number of products and a small number of customers. The choice of products and customers made in the emergency phase of recovery may not be appropriate for the subsequent growth phase, at which time a more fundamental shift in the firm's product-market strategy may be appropriate; but in the short term, the firm's choice of business is constrained by its history and lack of financial resources. Thus it can only improve its performance in the short term by focusing on particular products and particular customers. How does the firm go about doing this? Criteria for selecting the specific products chosen for emphasis include:

- sales volume: generally the bigger selling products are more attractive due to the greater opportunity they provide for leverage
- growth rate: declining products are generally unattractive as their competitive position is usually weak – although this is not always so and a declining product with strong brand loyalty can often be milked for cash
- gross margin or contribution: products with a higher gross margin are more attractive, all other things being equal
- speed of buyer response: consumer goods are usually more susceptible to a rapid sales increase through increased marketing effort than are industrial goods
- seasonality: this determines at what time of the year certain products can be emphasized
- length of manufacturing cycle: the shorter the cycle the quicker sales action translates into profit and cash flow.

The criteria are *not* mutually exclusive and trade-offs may have to be made, e.g. products sold primarily for consumer use may have to be emphasized over industrial-use products, in spite of their having a lower gross margin, due to the consumers' faster response to marketing effort.

Selecting customers is much the same process, and many of the same criteria apply. The key difference with customers, however, is the need to determine customer profitability – something which is usually missing in most control systems and almost never found in a turn-around situation. The need arises because the firm's largest customers are not necessarily the most profitable, as was the case at Harris Lebus Ltd which was losing money on its largest customers, the multiple furniture retailers, before it was acquired by P.M.A. Holdings. The objective of customer profitability analysis is to determine the contribution provided by each customer after deducting variable marketing costs associated with that customer (e.g. discounts, distribution costs, selling, after-sales and servicing costs) and interest charges on the working capital tied up in debtors and inventories for that customer. Table 10.1 shows a typical customer profit and loss statement. Ideally, customer profitability analysis is undertaken on a customer-by-customer basis. If there are few customers this may be possible, but where there are many customers this will not be possible until the firm's information systems have been improved, and even then it may be impracticable. More commonly, the firm's customers are segmented into groups, based on the nature of their business, size or location. The danger of grouping customers together is that the resulting 'contri-

bution before unallocated overheads' is an average marginal contribution figure and may hide unprofitable accounts. Such an analysis
involves a number of assumptions with regard to allocating marketing
overheads and the appropriate grouping of customers; but whatever
assumptions are used (and several alternatives should be used, particularly in regard to customer segmentation), startling results may emerge
at three levels:

(i) The different sales mix of different customers turns up substantial
differences in gross profit margins. (Thus, for example, in the brewing
industry small independent grocers provide a gross profit margin
about twice as high as supermarket chains, due to the inclusion of high-
margin bottled beer in their sales mix, whereas the supermarkets buy
mainly canned beer.)

Table 10.1: *Typical Customer Profitability Analysis*

	Customer Group A £	Customer Group A %	Customer Group B £	Customer Group B %	Customer Group C £	Customer Group C %
Gross sales		100		100		100
less: cost of goods sold	—		—		—	
Gross profit						
less: allocated marketing overheads:						
discounts[1]						
selling[2]						
distribution[3]						
order processing[4]						
advertising[5]						
service/warranty[6]	—		—		—	
Contribution before unallocated overheads						
less: interest on working capital employed	—		—		—	
Net contribution	—		—		—	

NOTES:
Possible basis of allocating marketing overheads:
1. actual discounts received
2. time spent with each customer group
3. size and frequency of drops
4. number of orders during period
5. by gross sales of products advertised
6. time spent with each customer group

(ii) A different picture may emerge when marketing overheads are allocated to customers. Discounts may be the only true variable cost if distribution is in-house, but most marketing overheads can be cut back relatively quickly (as compared to production overheads), so it is not unreasonable to show them as variable, even in the short term. Typically one will find that whereas discount costs may be high for large customers, distribution costs may be relatively low, although this is not the case in the furniture industry, for example, where the multiples receive volume discounts but require relatively small drop shipments to individual stores.

(iii) Finally, the concept of a notional interest charge to customers can often demonstrate that the firm loses or makes money on customers, depending on how quickly the customer pays and what he requires the firm to hold by way of inventories. Thus the higher the level of service required by the customer and the greater the safety stock levels required, the less profitable that customer is. Again, it is often the largest customers in many businesses that are the slowest payers and that demand the holding of inventory by the manufacturer.

The reader should now be able to appreciate that it is not *always* wise to focus on the largest customer. If volume is required and the large customers are profitable, the greatest profit leverage is obtained by concentrating on those customers – but this is not always the case. In the emergency phase of recovery, accurate information is unfortunately not always available for undertaking anything but an extremely crude customer profitability analysis. In particular, gross profit margin by customer or customer group may be missing.

Having chosen the products and customers on which to concentrate short-term marketing efforts, the turnaround firm must then shift its marketing resources to these customers. The primary means of implementing this is by targeting selling and promotional efforts, topics which are covered later in this chapter.

1.3 Improved Selling Effort

Before discussing ways of improving the cost effectiveness of the salesforce, let me reiterate that increasing sales volume is often the wrong strategy to adopt in a turnaround situation. What may be needed is for the salesforce to refocus its efforts on the most profitable product–customer segments, rather than to go out seeking more volume from the historical product–customer base. In some situations, as occurred at the R.F.D. group (see page 295), the strategy may even be to *reduce* selling effort. Whichever is the appropriate strategy, many of the tactics required to improve the cost effectiveness of the selling effort are common to all situations; the difference lies only in the instructions to the salesforce and not in the tactics necessary to achieve a competent salesforce. In Chapter 8 I talked about ways of reducing selling expenses; in this section I shall concentrate on how the firm can get more productivity out of its salesmen. There are a number of components.

(*a*) *Sales management*: Sales management – which usually consists of the general sales manager or sales director and regional sales managers – plays a pivotal role in implementing an improved selling effort. It is extremely difficult to implement the necessary changes without a capable and co-operative sales management. Not surprisingly therefore, new sales management is often required in a turnaround situation. After the finance director, the sales manager is usually the most frequently replaced individual in the management team. It is well known that a good salesman does not necessarily make a good sales manager, and this is particularly true in those turnaround situations where the emphasis is on focusing for profit rather than increasing sales volume. There will be situations, however, where the skills needed of the sales manager lie not in planning, organizing and controlling the sales force, but actually in getting out into the field as a key account salesman. This exception withstanding, there are several basic elements of the sales manager's job which are particularly vital in a turnaround situation. These are:

- planning and controlling the selling effort so that the salesmen's time is correctly allocated to key products and key customers
- motivating and training the salesforce
- monitoring sales performance
- evaluating and replacing salesmen where necessary
- communicating new management's marketing plan and philosophy to the salesforce.

A sales manager who has not been used to operating in this mode is unlikely to be the appropriate person to fill the position in a turnaround situation.

(*b*) *Targeting the sales effort*: In Chapter 4, we saw that it is important for the turnaround firm to concentrate its efforts on selected product lines and selected customers if it is to achieve a sales increase. This is achieved by planning and controlling the use of the salesman's time. Two steps are involved:

(i) Categorizing customers by sales potential into A/B/C customers and those not worth calling on. 'A' customers are currently large customers or customers who should be large customers, and warrant frequent calling, say once every two weeks. 'B' customers are important and profitable customers, but do not warrant the personal attention of 'A' customers. Unlike the 'A' customers, their loss would not be catastrophic. 'C' customers have still less potential, but can be profitable customers if the overheads associated with servicing them are kept in line. Thus, whereas 'A' customer may receive weekly calls, the 'B' customer would receive monthly and the 'C' quarterly calls. Typically, this process involves the elimination of small and unprofitable accounts; these are either ignored, are passed over to wholesalers for servicing or are positively discouraged from ordering by the discount structure, minimum order sizes, or surcharges.

(ii) Selecting specific product lines for promotional effort. Most often, a salesman has limited time with any one customer and cannot effectively sell more than three products in one visit. Sales managers generally like their salesmen to emphasize one major product and two minor ones during a single visit. Which products are being promoted at any one time will depend on the product-market strategy (see Chapter 4) and the season. The salesforce will usually emphasize different product lines each journey cycle.

(c) *Salesforce motivation and training*: The implementation of a targeting effort requires a considerable change in the behaviour pattern of the salesforce. To achieve the desired end, sales management must motivate and control the activities of the sales force.

The personal leadership skills of the sales management team can play an important role in improving salesforce motivation; but just as important are compensation and training. A tough approach which says 'Increase sales or else . . .' is unlikely to work. The need for a reasonable incentive plan for the salesforce should be obvious, but it is surprising how few U.K. firms in a turnaround situation have an adequate salesforce incentive scheme. Certainly not all sales situations lend themselves to incentive pay schemes, but where a quick increase in sales volume is necessary as part of a recovery strategy, additional salesforce incentives can and do work wonders. I stress 'additional' here because, unlike the U.S.A., cutting basic pay and increasing the incentive element will not usually work in the U.K. environment. Some managers worry about the salesforce earning 'too much'. This is a short-sighted view and certainly does not worry firms like I.B.M., whose salesmen can earn more than many of their senior managers. A good salesman always pays for himself, providing he sells the right products to the right customer at the right price.

The incentive scheme should clearly be designed in such a way as to promote the type of sales behaviour required by management. I was once involved in a situation where the salesmen regarded themselves as 'ambassadors', not as salesmen, and I was told so by one of the veterans. 'We do not take order,' he said, 'the retailers always phone them in to the office.' In this particular situation in the photographic industry, twenty-three salesmen brought in only a hundred out of the firm's 1,500 orders per week. This problem was tackled in three ways: by providing special financial incentives for every order actually taken by the salesmen over a certain value, by training courses stressing the need to 'close the sale', and by management communicating their disapproval of the 'ambassadorial' role.

Salesforce training can also play a big role in motivating salesmen, but can demotivate if not done well. I can remember announcing to the same salesforce, whose average length of service was almost twenty years, that they were all going on a training programme, for many the first in their working lives. The initial shock and outrage were calmed two minutes later by the introduction of the individual who was to run the training session. What a pro! Five minutes later, after a string of the dirtiest jokes, nearly all the salesmen wanted to go for training. A few of them were beyond training, but the exercise was a much-needed morale-booster at a time of uncertainty.

(*d*) *Monitoring sales performance*: Simple sales control systems should be instituted at the same time as the firm's other control systems. The sales manager should be responsible for the following:

- analysis of actual product-line sales against budget on a monthly basis, although in the depth of a crisis weekly analysis will be necessary. If volume and price variances can be separated, so much the better; but this assumes a reliable standard costing system, which is absent in the majority of turnaround situations
- monitoring sales to the few key accounts, any one of which, if lost, would severely effect the firm's profit position
- implementing simple salesforce controls such as the achievement of sales targets by territory, weekly call/order reports showing daily calls and orders, the following week's call schedule, etc.
- analysis of sales trends (using moving annual totals if the firm is in a seasonal business)
- monitoring the sales impact of special promotions.

Old behaviour patterns die hard and not all can be changed by motivating salesmen to seek new targets. Changing call patterns requires very close control, since salesmen typically like to call on friendly customers (where they receive tea or coffee!), on customers who are close to home, or on customers with whom they have a good personal relationship, irrespective of whether they are ideal customers from the firm's point of view.

(*e*) *Communicating with the salesforce*: We have already discussed (in Chapter 6) the need to communicate both within the firm and outside it. The salesforce are of course key players in this process, and it is most important that they have a positive attitude to the changes that are occurring inside the firm. This can be helped by open communication and dialogue between the salesforce and management. Management must give a clear indication to the salesforce that it knows what it is doing, but words alone are rarely enough in a turnaround situation: some tangible evidence of future benefits for the salesforce needs to be forthcoming as well – hence the need for salesforce motivation and training.

(*f*) *Evaluating and replacing salesmen where necessary*: Different sales territories nearly always have different sales potential, even though salesforce boundaries may originally have been drawn with equalization of sales potential in mind. We have already discussed cutting salesforce size as a means of cost reduction, particularly when 90% of the sales volume is brought in by, say, 50% of the salesforce. When this situation occurs, sales territories are redrawn, and the worst performers are made redundant. However, this is not always the situation. The number and location of sales territories may be more or less correct, but the performance of several salesmen may be unacceptable. For some, this may be obvious in the first month of the recovery; for others, it becomes obvious when they fail to adapt to the new sales management style. The idea of being told whom to call on, how often, and what to say is too much for the 'old guard'; they are not motivated by the new incentives and hate the idea of control.

Replacing salesmen can be a time-consuming activity, particularly if a large number need replacing: the process may take two to three years if the salesforce is relatively large. Recruiting and training new salesmen is, of course, a lengthy and expensive process; in the U.K. the problem is compounded by the legal difficulty of removing the old salesmen. If you are replacing them you are not making them redundant, hence the firm has to show cause for dismissal, which means warning letters and often an out-of-court settlement for unfair dismissal as was discussed in Chapter 9.

1.4 Product-line Rationalization

Most turnaround situations are characterized by product-line prolif-
eration *within* the product-market segment in which the firm competes.
This is manifested in a wide range of models, sizes or colours and, in
the worst situation, in all three. The product line has proliferated as
the result of lack of control. Detailed sales and cost figures are required
to undertake product-line rationalization, and criteria must be established for screening products; but the following guidelines can be kept
in mind:

- custom-made products or frequent product modification to suit the
  needs of individual customers is rarely profitable unless the business
  is set up specifically for the task
- if sales are declining and the product is losing money, cut it out or
  raise prices (which may have the same effect)
- eliminate immediately any products not covering variable cost
- eliminate all products which are not growing or are growing only
  very slowly and whose total sales are below a certain annual rate
- eliminate low-profit-margin product lines requiring high capital
  investment to stay profitable.

The difficult decision in product-line rationalization is deciding what
to do with those products which provide a healthy contribution but do
not provide a profit after allocating overheads. There is no problem
if overheads can be reduced by *more than* the amount of the contribution when the product is eliminated, but this is often not the case
within a product-market segment where many fixed costs are shared
jointly by a number of products. The answer to this dilemma is either:
(i) to ensure that the contribution lost by cutting out one product is
recouped by persuading the customer to switch to a standard product
instead; or (ii) to recoup the lost contribution by way of increased sales
and profit from the reduced product line. (The rationale for this is that
a narrower product line enables the firm to concentrate its efforts and
lower its unit costs.[1]) In practice, firms have found both these options
to work effectively.

As soon as the turnaround manager raises the issue of product-line
rationalization, he can expect to hear the old guard (and the sales
department, in particular) cry out in horror. Their argument usually
goes that the firm's sales of its major selling products are dependent
on also selling products *a* . . . *b* . . . *c* . . . *x*, *y*, *z*! Rarely, if ever, is
this a valid argument for a firm in a turnaround situation. The counter-
argument hinges on the fact that there are few examples of firms having

been adversely affected by not offering a full line. One may also be able to disprove the critics by demonstrating that the key customers who purchase the major selling products do not buy the products destined for the chop. Carrying a full line may be a valid strategy for a healthy market leader; it almost never is for a firm losing money.

Cutting out a product line usually means stopping production or not stocking a product line. This implies liquidation of inventories and a reduction in debtors, possibly even the sale of machinery. Thus some cash flow may be generated in the process, although write-downs may have to be taken on inventory and sale of plant.

2. Implementing Product-market Change

Product-market refocusing involves developing and investing in some business areas and neglecting or divesting others. This has already been discussed in Chapter 4.

It is beyond the scope of this book to elaborate on how the reader should undertake the strategic analysis necessary to determine the product-market strategy appropriate for his firm. The basic concept of strategy requires matching the firm's internal resources against the threats and opportunities in its environment, while simultaneously taking account of the values and attitudes of management. The last ten years, however, have seen the development of a large number of new concepts and tools to aid strategic analysis, with the result that there are now a series of management guidelines to help determine whether or not a strategy is likely to lead to sustainable profits. The concept I prefer most is that of sustainable competitive advantage, which was discussed briefly in Chapter 1. Basically, the firm needs to go through the following four steps:

(i) divide the firm into strategic business units (S.B.U.s) or product-market segments;
(ii) analyse the growth and profit potential of each S.B.U., using a framework similar to that of Porter;[2]
(iii) determine which viable and defensible strategies are open to the firm in each product-market segment; and
(iv) determine what strategy the firm should adopt in each product-market segment, given the firm's limited financial and human resources.

In large firms it will not be possible to evaluate all business units at the same time, although it is important, before any detailed strategic analysis is undertaken, to make a rough categorization of firms into 'winners', 'losers', and 'satisfactory but unexciting'. An experienced turnaround manager can accomplish this through an analysis of available financial data and by a one-day meeting with the managers responsible for that unit. Recovery effort can then be focused on the 'winners' and 'losers', while detailed investigation of the remaining business units is postponed to a later date.

The losers will be subject to any or all of the generic turnaround strategies already discussed, but most commonly to divestment or closure. The winners will be the recipients of any investment money available and of close management attention. In focusing attention on the winners – the businesses that will pull the firm through its crisis and provide a sound base for future growth – management needs to

- develop a detailed marketing and operational plan for the business
- transfer the firm's best managers to the business or recruit new management from outside who already have the recipe for success in that business
- assign profit centre responsibility
- make sure that investment is concentrated on the 'winners' and not dissipated on replacing worn-out plant and financing inflation in the unexciting businesses. It is through the resource-allocation process that strategic change is implemented
- develop an ongoing profit-improvement plan for the business to ensure maximum efficiency
- begin to develop new products
- improve the control systems to meet the expected growth
- develop a sound management team using organizational development techniques
- start training programmes
- quantify targets and set deadlines
- communicate the firm's objective to all concerned.

In short, the implementation of product-market change is accomplished through the installation of sound management practices. In the early days, however, significant organizational change may be necessary to ensure that refocusing actually occurs. Top management will need to devote a lot of time to ensuring that change occurs. I find that special control systems are required, along the lines of those developed for monitoring the action plans discussed in Chapter 6.

3. Growth through Acquisition

Acquisitions are used to implement growth strategies. This may involve acquiring firms in areas of business closely related to that of the turnaround firm; or it may involve diversification into unrelated areas. Except in the case of non-crisis turnarounds, acquisitions cannot usually be attempted until well into the recovery phase. The divestment programme must usually be well advanced and the balance sheet have largely recovered before acquisition can be considered.

The successful implementation of an acquisition programme consists of three planning steps and three implementation steps. These steps are outlined in Figure 10.1 and are discussed briefly below.

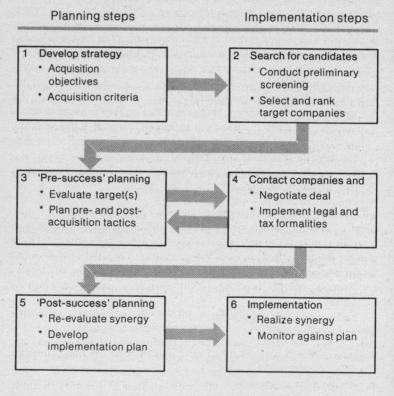

Figure 10.1: *Steps in the Acquisition Process*

3.1 Determine the Acquisition Objectives and Acquisition Criteria

The acquisition objectives depend on the overall product-market strategy chosen by the turnaround firm. Without a well-conceived strategy, no firm should make acquisitions. Is the firm looking for an acquisition to complement its existing business or to provide it with some business strength which it is lacking, or is it looking to diversify because there are no growth prospects in its existing businesses? Is it looking for an acquisition to help solve a management succession problem? Is it looking to spread the geographical deployment of the firm's assets? Acquisition objectives tend to fall into five categories:

(i) economic objectives: those aimed at developing a viable strategic position in one or more attractive economic sectors;

(ii) financial objectives: where the aim is to buy cheap assets, utilize cash generated from a divestment programme for which there is no use in the firm, or maybe asset strip. Conglomerate strategies are basically of this nature. Management's viewpoint is essentially short-term rather than long-term;

(iii) risk-reducing objectives: where the principal aim is to reduce the firm's vulnerability to dependence on a single product, a single market or a single technology;

(iv) organizational objectives: the purpose of the acquisition is to acquire management and/or an organization structure;

(v) socio-political or legal objectives: in which the aim is to enable the firm to achieve another part of its overall corporate strategy. Such objectives are rare for firms in a recovery mode.

Once the firm's acquisition objectives have been defined to the point of knowing which sectors are attractive and why, the firm is in a position to develop an appropriate set of acquisition criteria. These criteria should reflect not only the acquisition objectives but also the resources the firm is able to bring to the acquisition and the key factors for success in the product-market segments which the firm is evaluating.

The resources the firm is able to bring to the acquisition are usually defined in terms of:

- financial resources, which effectively determine the maximum size of the acquisition
- management and technical skills, which the firm believes are transferable to an acquired firm

- operating dimension, such as manufacturing capacity, access to distribution channels, supplier relationships, etc.

Where the firm's objective is to diversify into unrelated business areas, a set of diversification criteria need to be established against which the firm can screen industries prior to the establishment of acquisition criteria. The diversification criteria are a set of factors (suitably weighted by management, if desired) which describe the ideal business sector for expansion, with the aim of narrowing down the prospective sectors. In any business screening process, the criteria are likely to be both contradictory and subjective – thus few if any sectors will meet all the criteria. The criteria used by the Imperial Group which led to the eventual acquisition of the Howard Johnson restaurant and motel chain is illustrative of the type of diversification criteria a firm might use, although each situation will be different. Imperial's main criteria are reported to have included the following factors:[3]

- long-term growth prospects
- avoidance of commodity sectors characterized by low margins and high cyclicality
- avoidance of small fragmented sectors
- exclusion of capital-intensive heavy industries
- degree of sector competitiveness
- a sector with a relatively simple distribution process
- sectors consistent with the 'Imperial' image, not highly unionized and with little likelihood of government intervention.

After an initial screening involving considerable market and competitor analysis, Imperial were left with fifty-two possible sectors of the U.S. economy and they put these into three groups in order of priority. The top-priority group consisted of sixteen sectors, and it is from these sectors that possible acquisition candidates were selected.

Imperial's acquisition criteria were:[4]

- size of company – single large firm with national coverage
- existence of a high level of management competence
- key management willing to stay
- good and consistent earnings track record
- strongly branded goods or services
- company to have strength in adding value
- a corporate philosophy consistent with that of the Imperial Group (meaning a high level of corporate and individual integrity)
- profit record.

It is useful to compare Imperial's criteria with those of I.T.T. in Europe at the same time. I.T.T.'s criteria related to:

- size
- profit record
- management
- compatibility with I.T.T.'s existing skills
- market share
- growth potential
- balance sheet
- self supporting with regard to future cash requirements
- no minority shareholders.

For further discussion of diversification objectives and acquisition criteria, the reader is referred to Salter and Weinhold's *Diversification Through Acquisition*.[5]

3.2 Search for Candidates

Management's action plan for undertaking the search process depends on how narrowly it has defined the target sectors and management's familiarity with the industrial sectors at which it is looking. The search process can be very time-consuming, since making successful acquisitions is like launching new products: the success ratio is low and one generally needs to analyse many companies to find a single good candidate. Initially, desk research provides a list of firms competing in the target sectors; basic information can be collected from such sources as the trade press, trade association, the financial press, annual reports and company literature, stockbrokers' reports, Dun & Bradstreet reports, consultants' surveys, etc. Managements experienced in making acquisitions typically collect some of this data when analysing target sectors, since there is little point in undertaking a detailed analysis of an industry sector in the previous step if there are unlikely to be potential acquisition candidates available for sale. Thus a simultaneous study of market segments and target companies is often a useful approach to adopt.

In screening candidates, management should make sure it considers not only independent firms but also divisions of firms – on which it is often difficult to obtain much 'hard' data. As the portfolio concept of strategy has become popular at the corporate or group level, divestment of subsidiaries that no longer fit into the corporate portfolio has become increasingly common. The screening process is not very scientific although some managers like to develop an index against which they can assess how well each candidate scores against the acquisition criteria. This can be useful in helping to rank target companies, but is invariably subjective.

3.3 Pre-Success Planning

This is an important and usually neglected planning stage. It involves evaluating the target acquisition candidates in some depth. Ideally, one will want to gain access to the target company. For some acquiring firms, such access is often a prerequisite to the completion of negotiations. Where this is impossible, a considerable amount of data can be acquired about a company from the outside just by talking to suppliers, customers, competitors, bankers, analysts, ex-employees, etc. Some consultants are very good at doing a 'quick and dirty' analysis of an acquisition candidate without letting anyone know what they are really doing. Market surveys often have the analysis of one particular firm as their real objective! Pre-success planning, however, not only involves analysing the acquisition candidate as it stands today; it also and most importantly involves determining (in broad outline) what one can do with the candidate *after* it has been acquired. What scope is there to reduce costs, close facilities, add new product lines to the distribution system, etc.? These are strategic issues which clearly affect the value of the company to the acquiring firm. This requires some creative thinking and entrepreneurial flair on the part of the acquiring firm.

3.4 Contact Acquisition Candidates, Negotiate and Finalize the Deal

The priority acquisition candidates may be either contacted directly by the acquiring firm or may be contacted by intermediaries, such as merchant banks or consultants. The intermediary route can be useful to 'sound out' the candidate and get their management interested in the 'logic' of the deal, before announcing the identity of the acquirer. In practice, however, I believe the use of intermediaries to be more useful when divesting than when acquiring. Initial rejection by the candidate is to be expected, since most company chairmen know that if they begin by appearing to be a willing seller, the final acquisition price is likely to be lower. The acquiring firm should search for common ground with the acquisition candidate if at all possible, and should match their reasons for buying with the target company's reasons for selling. The acquirer has a big 'selling job' to do, since most boards of directors are very concerned with the type of firm to whom they are selling; most of all, they are concerned with their own job security, thus any 'guarantees' as to what will happen to them and their jobs after the acquisition become important elements in the negotiating process. Hence the seller must become involved in building up the rationale for the deal.

3.5 Post-Success Planning

After an acquisition has been successfully negotiated, it is necessary to develop a detailed post-acquisition plan for the business. Data and access which were previously unavailable should now be freely available, although the acquiring firm may meet some initial resistance from the organization in providing data. If this does occur, it is a good indicator of the difficulties the acquirer may face in implementing his post-acquisition plan. The plan should encompass both a strategic and an operational review of the business that has been acquired, and should develop specific strategies and tactics for achieving the acquisition objectives originally set by the acquirer.

3.6 Implement Post-Acquisition Change

Managing post-acquisition change is critical to making successful acquisitions. If the acquired firm is in a turnaround situation itself, turnaround strategies need to be implemented immediately. If the firm is in a sound financial position, more time can be taken; however, the best time for change is immediately after the acquisition since employees of the acquired firm are usually expecting change at this point in time. Of course, change should not be made for the sake of change, but at the very least the new owners should aim to achieve managerial and financial control. Many of the problems encountered in implementing post-acquisition change are similar to those encountered in implementing turnaround strategies; there are a few useful articles written specifically on this topic.[6]

Notes

1. P. Kotler, 'Phasing Out Weak Products', *Harvard Business Review*, Vol. 43, No. 2, March-April 1965, p. 107.

2. Michael Porter, *Competitive Strategy: Techniques for Analysing Industries and Competitors*, New York Free Press, 1980.
3. 'The Long Search that Led to Howard Johnson's Door', *Financial Times*, 17 December 1979.
4. Ibid.
5. M. S. Salter and W. A. Weinhold, *Diversification through Acquisition*, New York Free Press, 1979.
6. See, for example, C. M. Leighton and G. R. Tod, 'After the Acquisition: Continuing Challenge', *Harvard Business Review*, March–April 1969; and F. W. Searby, 'Control Post Merger Change', *Harvard Business Review*, September–October 1969.

Part Three

The Role of the State

11. State Involvement in Corporate Recovery

This chapter warrants a book in itself, since state involvement in rescuing ailing firms became increasingly common in the 1970s, both in Britain and in other industrialized countries. In Britain, state involvement has meant action by both the government and the Bank of England.

With the advent of the Industrial Reorganization Corporation (I.R.C.) under the Labour Government in the mid 1960s, the U.K. government began to take a more active role in rescuing sick companies in the industrial sector, although that was not the real intention of the I.R.C., which was established to help increase the efficiency of British industry by promoting mergers within industries. The intention was, by combining a number of smaller companies together, that the combined group would be able to achieve economies of scale and compete more effectively with foreign competition. Thus, Ransome Hoffman Pollard (R.H.P.) was formed in the ball-bearing business, British Motor Corporation was put together in the motor industry, and attempts were made to rationalize the machine-tool industry. The activities of the I.R.C. – although not always successful – certainly helped prevent or postpone business failures in many situations. What the I.R.C. seemed to fail to realize was that the merger or acquisition of firms rarely brings increased efficiencies unless accompanied by sound post-merger management. In fact, inefficiencies may actually increase as overheads rise and divisive splits develop within the new top management team as each manager retains loyalties to his former business. The I.R.C. lacked any means of ensuring that the planned merger benefits were actually realized.

The 1970s saw a new era in state intervention under both Conservative and Labour governments, to rescue failing firms, and new attitudes on the part of management in seeking state assistance in crisis situations. Many firms approached government, often in a last-ditch effort to prevent receivership or liquidation; but government action also became more direct. Thus, for example, when Fairey went into receivership in 1977 (due to horrendous losses in its Belgian aircraft manufacturing operation), the government stepped in and purchased Fairey from the receiver, even though there were many private-sector firms (Trafalgar House, for example) that were willing to take on the turnaround of Fairey.[1]

This chapter looks at the role the state has played in facilitating turnaround situations in the industrial sector from the early 1970s to the present day. The emphasis is on the *managerial implications* of state involvement, rather than on analysis of the policy issues involved. The problem of managing the nationalized industries* is beyond the scope of this book, and has been excluded. The problems facing the nationalized industries are unique, even though many of them (British Steel, for example) require the implementation of the strategies described in Chapter 4. The principal topics discussed in this chapter are: the kind of situation in which state rescue attempts are likely, the state's method of intervention, its effect on recovery strategy and strategy implementation, and its method of exit from recovery situations. Two of the more interesting cases of state involvement in the 1970s, Ferranti and Burmah Oil, are described in Chapter 16 and show that the framework for managing crisis situations presented in this book is equally applicable to those situations where the state becomes involved.

1. Types of Recovery Situations Involving the State

State involvement in rescuing sick firms stems largely from fear – fear of unemployment, fear of adverse balance-of-payments effects, fear of strategic dependency on foreign sources of supply, as well as fear of a collapse in confidence concerning the financial system, a key aspect of the country's economic infrastructure, and fear of losing national pride. Fear is often political as well as economic, since constituency parties and pressure groups can play an important role in influencing government actions. Thus, not surprisingly, state-sponsored rescue efforts rarely have the creation of economic wealth as a prime goal,

---

* My definition of nationalized industries includes those industries whose chairmen are members of the Nationalized Industries Chairmen's Group. They are: coal, gas, electricity, hydroelectricity, rail, post, telecommunications, water, atomic energy, National Bus Company, London Transport, British Airways, British Airports Authority, Civil Aviation Authority, British Transport Docks Board and Scottish Transport Group.

although efforts at rescuing Sinclair Radionics and other high-technology companies prove the exceptions.

Five business situations appear to attract state intervention: (i) crises of confidence in the financial system; (ii) large uncompetitive firms; (iii) smaller uncompetitive firms; (iv) defence contractors; and (v) high-technology firms.

1.1 Crises of Confidence in the Financial System

There were at least two examples during the 1970s of situations in which the state, under the aegis of the Bank of England, intervened to halt crises of confidence. The first was the secondary banking crisis that began with the collapse of London and County Securities in November 1973. In spite of the rescue attempt launched by National Westminster Bank and Keyser Ullman, London and County's crash triggered off a 'domino effect'. Large depositors began to withdraw their funds from other U.K. fringe banks. Depositors realized that many of the fringe banks were basically in the same situation as London and County: with an insufficient capital base to sustain large losses and most of their loans secured against property or shares that were rapidly shrinking in value. The response of the Bank of England was to launch what was known as the 'lifeboat' under the direction of the Deputy Governor of the Bank of England, Sir Jasper Hollom. The Bank of England, together with the leading clearing banks (Barclays, Lloyds, Midland, National Westminster, etc.), agreed to put £1.2 billion (the figure actually reached £1.3 billion at its peak) into twenty-six secondary banking companies. According to the Governor of the Bank of England, the objective was:

...not to save share and loan stockholders but to secure depositors and by so doing avoid a widening circle of collapse from the contagion of fear . . . It is fatally easy to destroy confidence and desperately difficult to restore it . . . Had the rapidly escalating crisis of confidence passed into the banking system proper . . . had a major established bank defaulted, I do not know where we would have stopped in the course of collapse.[2]

If the fringe banks had been allowed to go under, property values would have declined even further as vast amounts of property came on the market with no prospective buyers in sight. Such property is the security for most of the nation's lending. The clearing banks would probably have been forced to foreclose on many of their loans that were no longer covered or looked financially very weak. The downward spiral towards total financial collapse would have started. As it was, the confidence crisis spread faster and lasted longer than the Bank of England had expected. Share prices plummeted throughout 1974, reaching their low at year end.

The second example in which the Bank of England was involved was the crisis that hit Burmah Oil at the end of 1974. The decline and recovery of Burmah is discussed in greater detail in Chapter 16, but the situation is inextricably linked to the issue of confidence. Burmah's collapse was triggered off principally by the loss in market value of its 21.6% shareholding in British Petroleum, which meant that the large dollar loans secured against the value of these shares automatically became due. If Burmah had been allowed to go into receivership, it would have been the largest international default in U.K. financial history; it would also have meant a further loss of international confidence that was already at a low ebb after the three-day week and the decline in the stock market (reminiscent to some of the Wall Street Crash of 1929 that heralded the start of the Great Depression).

1.2 Large Uncompetitive Firms

Size, whether measured in sales revenues, capital employed or number of people employed, appears to be a factor that determines whether or not the state becomes involved in corporate recovery. With the exception of the property companies that collapsed in the 1974/75 recession, the state has played a key role, either directly or indirectly, in all the big turnaround situations during the past decade. This should not come as a surprise, since large companies whose core businesses are in decline are inherently more difficult to turn around than smaller ones (see Chapter 5), and banks are less willing and less able to take the financial risks necessary to keep an ailing giant afloat. The problem is not peculiar to the U.K., as witness the U.S. government's involvement in rescuing Chrysler during 1980/81.

The best-known example of the state attempting to rescue a large firm is that of British Leyland, although there are many other well-known examples, such as Chrysler (U.K.), Alfred Herbert (the machine-tool company) and Massey-Ferguson, the Canadian farm-equipment manufacturer.

In the case of British Leyland, the government had taken a special interest in the company's welfare since the 1960s, due to its size and its position as the U.K.'s largest exporter. In 1974, British Leyland's sales were £1.6 billion, 38% of which was derived from exports; it employed 170,000 workers in fifty-five plants throughout Britain, and its suppliers employed a further 800,000.

1.3 Smaller Uncompetitive Firms

The state has provided financial assistance in various forms to a large number of smaller firms over the last decade but, unlike the larger firms discussed above, government has rarely taken a majority equity stake in these businesses. The economic logic behind the decision to help in the rescue of smaller firms is usually weaker than that put forward to support the rescue of large firms like B.L., although all the same arguments about employment, balance of payments, national pride, etc., may be used by the proponents of government rescue operations, even though the overall economic impact may be small. More often, it is closures that would mean high local unemployment that are more important factors in determining whether or not small companies are to be rescued. Thus we saw ongoing attempts by, first, the Department of Industry and, later, by the Welsh Development Agency to keep the Triang-Pedigree factory in South Wales open.[3] In 1979, the firm's sales were £4 million and it employed 380 people. Another example of a small firm obtaining partial government aid was Wolverhampton Industrial Engines, who purchased Villiers Engines, the sole U.K. supplier of small-horsepower motors, from the Norton-Villiers-Triumph receiver.[4]

1.4 Defence Contractors

Major defence contractors are always virtually assured of government rescue, as was the case with Rolls-Royce and Ferranti in the U.K. and Lockheed in the U.S. Defence contractors are regarded as strategic industries and the government, as the major customer, is in a position to ensure the viability of at least the most efficient firms. Another factor – an economic one – that also encourages government assistance is the fact that most U.K. defence contractors are also large export earners.

The problems of Ferranti and Rolls-Royce were quite different in nature. Ferranti was a much more straightforward situation, since the cause of decline was in a peripheral business activity. It is discussed in greater detail in Chapter 16. Rolls-Royce, on the other hand, had all the problems of the high-technology industries discussed in the next section; it would probably have been rescued by the government even if it had not been a major defence contractor. Rolls-Royce is a leader in world technology in a growth industry, it is a large earner of foreign exchange, and it also directly employs 57,000 people. Rolls-Royce has consumed almost £600 million of public money since the firm went into receivership in 1971. Most of this money has been invested in the development of the RB-211 jet-engine.

1.5 High-Technology Industries

The government has been involved in a number of rescue attempts, which have had as their objective the creation of jobs rather than the maintenance of jobs. These efforts have been primarily in high-technology industries where the costs of developing new technology have been too high for the firms concerned. Firms falling into this category include: Rolls-Royce – aerospace; Sinclair Radionics – electronics; I.C.L. – computers; Kearney Trecker Marwin – numerically controlled machine tools; Cambridge Instruments – electronic microscopes and microfabricators, etc.

International Computers (I.C.L.) was orginally formed out of a government-sponsored merger of several computer companies in the late 1960s. Then, in 1972, I.C.L. suffered financial difficulties, mainly owing to the heavy cost of developing a new range of big computers. The government stepped in with a loan of £40 million on easy terms, which was repaid by 1976. I.C.L. was profitable for most of the 1970s, capturing 35% of the U.K. computer market.[5] It was helped by a preferential government procurement policy (until year end 1980), which virtually guaranteed that it would win all large central government computer contracts.

Sinclair Radionics is a classic example of an entrepreneurial company being a technological leader but having neither the cash nor management to commercialize its inventions. When Sinclair found itself in a cash crisis in 1976, the N.E.B. stepped in with financial assistance.

Cambridge Instruments, a manufacturer of electronic microscopes, electronic beam microfabricators, image analysers and other high-technology instruments, has been the subject of government attention since 1968, when the I.R.C. backed its acquisition. In 1979, a further attempt was made to rescue the company after it had used up £9 million of public money in five years.[6] Why? The answer lies in the fact that Cambridge Instruments is a world leader in instrument technology and is the only British company of any size capable of supplying the semi-conductor industry, which the government is keen to develop via its investment in INMOS, with the microfabricator, a key production tool.

Kearney Trecker Marwin (K.T.M.) is a machine-tool manufacturer, in which government involvement goes back to the days of the I.R.C. In 1970 the government lent £1.5 million to Marwin Machine Tools to encourage the development of sophisticated, numerically controlled machine tools. In 1973, it helped finance the merger with Kearney Trecker, which, in the event, was disastrous – a loss of £2.1 million on sales of £5.2 million in the first year of combined operations. In 1974, the government stepped in again and increased its equity stake to 50%. K.T.M.'s rescue appears to stem from both the high-technology aspect of its business and the long-standing government attitude that Britain has to have a machine-tool industry as a foundation for its engineering industry.

2. State Intervention: Economics or Politics?

The rescue of large firms has been motivated historically by both economic and political considerations. The two are difficult to disentangle, since large firms are typically not only large employers but are also highly visible, due to the media attention they attract when they are in trouble.

When the banks refused to lend British Leyland any more money in December 1974, there was a major parliamentary and public debate on the merits of rescuing ailing, non-competitive industrial companies. While economic arguments about loss of jobs and balance-of-payments effects were made, the Labour Government's interventionist policy was clearly political in nature; in the House of Commons debate on the government's proposal to acquire a majority stake in B.L., Mr Anthony Wedgwood Benn, then Secretary of State for Industry, said:

I want to see this problem against the background of the spiral of decline of British manufacturing industry which has been in progress, under all governments, over the last thirty years and has accelerated in recent years – namely that we have been losing workers capable of manufacturing cars, ships, motorcycles and many other products, and as a result we have lost export markets and seen greater import penetrations. Quite apart from the slump which now affects the world, if this spiral is not reversed by investment and a new spirit and a new opportunity for industry, it will de-industrialize the United Kingdom . . . There must be a big role for the Government in this.

This view was supported by Michael Meacher, then Under-Secretary of State for Industry, who stated that the Labour Government did not intend to preside over the descent towards a tourist economy when he supported the passage in the Ryder Report which said: 'If the U.K.

were to opt out of vehicle production it is not easy to see where the process of opting out would end.'[7]

The politicians' views are reflected in the tone of the Ryder Report, which, in spite of its terms of reference, appears to have started from the premise that recovery, through a massive injection of government aid, was the right thing to do with B.L. The Report's unsupported assertion that 'vehicle production is the kind of industry which ought to remain an essential part of the United Kingdom's economic base' was a political assertion about prestige and national pride rather than an economic assertion.

In arguing against the infusion of public money into B.L., Mr Enoch Powell talked about how political pressures affect decision-making in these situations:

I do not suppose that one can have a context in which misjudgement upon the prospects of future profitability is more likely than that in which public money is being injected into industrial activities. The whole tendency will not be to put money where it is likely to produce a profit but to put it where it will be politically profitable, where it will answer the immediate anxieties which press upon us as politicians from our constituencies, where it will earn the sort of harvest which, as politicians, it is our business to garner, if possible – the harvest of votes.

As governments change, so does the extent of interventionist policies. However, it seems that no government – even one advocating *laissez-faire* non-interventionist policies – will allow a large industrial firm that is a major employer, particularly in a sensitive location, to go into liquidation. Some form of intervention will take place, either before or after receivership. The decision as to the point at which intervention takes place is again a political decision.

When Rolls-Royce became insolvent in 1971 and Fairey became insolvent in 1977, the government allowed the firms to go into receivership before rescuing them. With most other situations (such as Ferranti, Burmah Oil, British Leyland, Chrysler and Alfred Herbert), the firms have received state assistance to avoid receivership. Is one approach preferable to the other? Receivership is undoubtedly the preferred route for those who favour a free market economy, since it enables the receiver to sell off the profitable parts of the business, make other parts efficient, and close down the rest. Resources are freed for use elsewhere in the economy. The problem with this approach is that it takes no account of the problem of unemployment; this may not be a problem in a healthy economy, but in a country like the U.K., where there is a long-term trend towards increasing structural unemployment, there may be strong arguments put forward to protect what have become known as 'lame ducks'. Receivership does not, of course, mean liquidation, as we saw in Chapter 1: the profitable core of the business remains, but some unemployment is usually inevitable. The extent of the unemployment likely to be caused by receivership and the government's attitude towards it is what appears to be the deciding issue.

In 1971, when Rolls-Royce went into receivership, national unemployment was only 700,000 (compared to 3 million at the end of 1981), but Rolls-Royce was different from B.L. in one very important respect: Rolls-Royce was a principal defence contractor and had competitive products in the world market; on the other hand, British Leyland's mass car division, Austin Morris, which provided a significant portion of B.L. employment, would be most likely to be closed down by a receiver as a non-viable business entity for which no purchaser could be found. The debate over Alfred Herbert's rescue in 1974/75 provides a similar example to that at B.L. The Industrial Development Advisory Board, the group of businessmen who advise the Minister on aid applications under the Industry Act, recommended receivership; but the Secretary of State disagreed.

3. State Approaches to Intervention

State intervention in industrial rescue operations is most commonly made through the Department of Industry, although the Bank of England has been involved directly in some rescues (c.g. the secondary banks and Burmah Oil), while other public bodies such as the Welsh Development Agency have also been involved (e.g. in Triang-Pedigree). Intervention may be either at the initiative of the state or, more commonly, as a desperate, last-minute survival attempt by the failing firm.

State intervention usually takes the form of providing additional finance, directly through equity or loan financing, or indirectly by providing guarantees for commercial bank lending. Sometimes intervention goes no further than 'persuading' banks not to put a firm into receivership or 'persuading' other firms to take over a failing competitor. At the time of writing, there is a considerable amount of 'persuasion' of this kind being undertaken by the Bank of England. The principal methods of intervention are as follows.

3.1 The Provision of Bank of England Loans and Guarantees

In the secondary banking crisis that hit at the end of December 1973, the Bank of England (together with the major clearing banks) provided funds to prop up the secondary (or fringe) banks, as has already been discussed above. The Bank of England is, of course, responsible for 'regulating' the banks, and so it is quite natural that it would become involved in banking turnarounds. Rather different was the Bank's involvement in Burmah Oil, where it not only provided a guarantee for the $280 million loan on which Burmah had defaulted, it also dictated the terms of the subsequent turnaround. Burmah survived, albeit in a radically different shape from what it had been before its cash crisis; but the Bank's actions came under severe criticism and were clearly more interventionist without an equity holding than many rescue situations in which the government acquired a majority equity position.

In return for loan guarantees from the Bank of England, Burmah accepted the principle of selling a 51% stake in the Thistle and Ninian oil-fields of the North Sea to the government, and also agreed to hand over its 21.6% shareholding in B.P. as security, with the understanding that Burmah would share in any profit on the resale of the shares by the Bank if realization of the shares were found to be necessary. On 22 January 1974 – less than a month after the initial rescue package had been agreed – Burmah's management was told that the shares were to be bought by the Bank, on the instructions of the government, at a price of 230p per share, and there was to be no profit-sharing formula. One day later, B.P.'s shares were selling at 268p, and within six weeks the Bank of England had made a profit of £144 million (about 80%) on its purchase of the shares. Burmah subsequently sued the Bank of England, claiming that the 'transfer of shares was unconscionable, inequitable and unreasonable and that the Bank obtained an improper advantage through its role as mortgagee',[8] but failed when their case reached court in 1981. By this time, the value of the B.P. shares was £1.2 billion – over five times greater than the 1981 market capitalization of Burmah!

3.2 Use of the 1972 Industry Act

When Edward Heath's Conservative Government came to power in 1970, it wound up the Industrial Reorganization Corporation, but in 1972 the same government introduced a new interventionist policy under the title of the 1972 Industrial Act. An Industrial Development Unit was established within the Department of Industry to administer the new Act and to do some of the same work as had been done by the old I.R.C. The new Act encompassed a number of different types of aid for industry, including Automatic Regional Development Grants and regional job-creation schemes (under section 7 of the Act), both of which have been indirectly responsible for assisting firms to survive in situations where they might not otherwise have done so. However, it was section 8 of the 1972 Act which provided funds for rescuing failing companies. There are two types of section 8 aid that we have to concern ourselves with: general section 8 aid, that was allocated in the form of grants, guarantees, loans and equity to individual companies; and various sectoral schemes, designed to give aid to individual sections of industry.

Under general section 8 aid, £395 million was paid out between 1972 and the fall of the Labour Government in February 1979. Of this amount, £180 million went to B.L., £82 million to Chrysler U.K., now renamed Talbot and owned by the French group, P.S.A. Peugeot-Citroen. Many small firms also benefited, as, for example, did Wolverhampton Industrial Engines, already referred to earlier in this chapter. The Department of Industry had a fairly high degree of flexibility in structuring this aid. Rarely did it acquire majority equity control, and with its rescue of Chrysler, it showed that it was ready to rescue the subsidiaries of foreign-owned firms as well as U.K.-owned firms. The rescue of Chrysler U.K. in 1975 involved the U.S. parent company and the government in a joint loss-sharing and investment operation. The government agreed to pay operating losses up to £40 million in 1976 and to split all further operating losses fifty-fifty with the car company until the end of 1979. In addition, the government gave a joint guarantee with Chrysler on a £35 million working capital loan and agreed to provide the balance of a £55 million investment programme, providing Chrysler invested £28 million first.[9] The government agreed to continue with these arrangements when Peugeot bought Chrysler U.K. for a nominal $1 in January 1979.

The section 8 sectoral schemes (many of which have now been ended) were open to all companies within a specific industry sector. Some of the special schemes, particularly those still in existence, are aimed at high-technology sectors;* however, during the 1970s

* Many high-technology firms are financed in whole or in part under the Science and Technology Act 1965.

declining industry sectors (such as textiles, ferrous and non-ferrous foundries and machine tools) received aid. Thus, for example, there was a loan scheme that paid out £6.6 million to finance the inventories of machine-tool companies, £5.7 million of which went to Alfred Herbert, and about £500,000 to Hartle Machinery International. Both firms eventually failed.

The major recipients of government rescue money are shown in Table 11.1.

Table 11.1: *Government Investments of over £5 Million in Turnaround Situations in 1979*

Company	Main activity	Percentage voting equity	Investment 1979 (£ million)
British Leyland	Motor Industry	99.1	930
Rolls-Royce	Aero-engines	100	265
Alfred Herbert	Machine Tools	100	44
Fairey	Engineering	100	18
I.C.L.	Computers	25	13
Wholesale Vehicle Finance	Motor Finance	77	10
Cambridge Instruments	Scientific Instruments	25	9
Sinclair Radionics	Micro-electronics	73	8
Ferranti	Electronics	50	7

Source: *Financial Times*, 22 November 1979.

3.3 Act of Parliament

Act of Parliament has not been the route favoured to save failing firms. Although whole industries in trouble have been nationalized, as occurred in shipbuilding, for example, only British Leyland falls into this category as far as individual firms are concerned. When B.L. requested government help in December 1974, the then Secretary of State for Industry, Anthony Wedgwood Benn, requested Parliament to guarantee a bank loan of £50 million to keep the company afloat. At the same time he announced the appointment of a team led by Sir Don Ryder (formerly Chairman of the diversified paper and printing group, Reed International) to advise him as to what should be done about B.L.'s future.

In May 1975 the Ryder Report was ready. It recommended the

modernization and reorganization of B.L. at a cost of £2.8 billion (in 1975 prices) between 1975 and 1982. The plan called for half of the new investment to be provided internally by a new and more profitable B.L.; the remainder was to be generated externally, most – if not all – coming from the government. The Report proposed that the government offer £65 million to B.L.'s existing shareholders and subscribe to £200 million of new shares. The offer to existing shareholders valued B.L.'s shares at 10p, 3¾p above the level at which trading on the stock market had been stopped when B.L. asked for government assistance. A bill was laid before Parliament to enact the Ryder proposals and was passed on 21 May 1975. Funds over and above the £265 million did not require parliamentary approval as there was sufficient statutory power under the 1973 Industry Act (sections 7 and 8) and under the 1975 Industry Act establishing the National Enterprise Board.

3.4 State Pressure on the Private Sector

While some form of direct financial assistance is the most tangible evidence of state involvement in turnaround situations, there is a considerable amount of 'behind the scenes' pressure and persuasion in many other situations. Sometimes the pressure works, as it did when the City rescued Foden's (see Chapter 19), at other times it fails. It has been reported, for example, that the Department of Industry approached both British Petroleum and Shell in late 1980 about assisting I.C.L. to achieve a turnaround, but both declined.[10] Similarly, the Bank of England has been known to participate in discussions to save firms from receivership, as it did, for example, with toy manufacturers Dunbee-Combex-Marx in 1980. The Bank believed (persuaded by whom, it is not clear) that drastic surgery in D.C.M.'s loss-making U.S. operation and the sale of the Hornby train-set business would permit D.C.M. to remain solvent. The Midland Bank would not take the risk and appointed a receiver.[11]

Another, more recent example occurred in January 1981 during the rescue of the multinational agricultural equipment firm, Massey-Ferguson. A Canadian-based company, Massey-Ferguson's U.K. operations, which include Perkins Engines, are nevertheless the largest in the group and account for about 16,000 jobs. It is reported that the Bank of England 'encouraged' Britain's banks to help out, while at the same time talking to central banks in several other countries during the rescue talks.[12]

3.5 Guarantees from the Exports Credit Guarantee Department (E.C.G.D.)

At the time of the Massey-Ferguson crisis, the E.C.G.D. had a loan of £87 million outstanding to the company. The banks and insurance companies involved in Massey's financial rescue converted debt into convertible preferred shares and took equity in lieu of interest. The E.C.G.D. was unable to do this, but played an important role in the recapitalization of the group by guaranteeing an issue of C$90 million convertible preferred shares in Canada. This novel departure is evidence of the lengths to which government will go to save a large firm.

From time to time, substantial government pressure is brought to bear on whole industries with the aim of rationalizing the industry to help it compete more successfully in the world market. Such intervention is related to turnarounds only indirectly, but it can be regarded as an action to avoid the need for future rescue. The best example of this in recent years is the power plant industry, which was studied by the Cabinet Office's Central Policy Review Staff (the 'think-tank') in 1976. The report recommended a series of mergers that would create one boiler-making group (Babcock & Wilcox and Clarke Chapman) and one turbine-generator manufacturer (G.E.C. and Reyrolle Parsons). The mergers did not take place thanks to the determination of both management and unions at Reyrolle Parsons, which subsequently merged with Clarke Chapman to form Northern Engineering Industries (N.E.I.). But, as Duncan McDonald, now Managing Director of N.E.I. and formerly head of Reyrolle Parsons, said: 'I was under terrible pressure to give Reyrolle Parsons to Weinstock [at G.E.C.].'[13]

4. How Government Influences Turnaround Strategies

The generic turnaround strategies adopted by firms rescued by government financial assistance are the same as those used when no government funds are available, except for one important difference. The additional financing made available by government intervention often permits firms to invest in new plant and equipment, something which would not otherwise have been possible. In the case of the high-technology turnarounds (Rolls-Royce, Sinclair Radionics, etc.), the adoption of an investment strategy to assist in the development and marketing of new products is clearly a necessary prerequisite if the firm is ever to become profitable. In other situations, such as that of British Leyland, Alfred Herbert or Meriden – the so-called 'lame ducks' that would be regarded as non-recoverable if in the private sector – pursuing an investment strategy makes little sense when viewed at the micro-economic level, which is the main focus of this book. However, when viewed at the macro-level, it can be argued that if by new investment the firm breaks even and jobs are saved, the cost is less than liquidating the business and paying out social welfare benefits to those who become unemployed in the process.

Government influence over turnaround strategies is clearly greatest in the 'lame duck' category. Some of the lame ducks in which the government invested in the 1970s were clearly non-viable businesses (e.g. the Meriden motorcycle co-operative); but others were potentially recoverable if a focused, product-market strategy had been adopted and drastic surgery performed on the loss-making parts of the business. Politically motivated government action determined that a focused strategy was not appropriate. Let us take British Leyland as an example once again. Many of the recommendations made by the Ryder Report were sound – the introduction of new and vigorous management, reorganization into four major business units with maximum delegation of profit responsibility and a reduction in the number of body shells, engines, etc. – but Ryder's choice of product-market strategy was fundamentally political. In the Parliamentary debate on the Report, Anthony Wedgwood Benn stated:

It is always open to a firm, by a ruthless chopping of its uneconomic activities, to restore itself to profitability as might have been done if British Leyland had closed Austin-Morris, for example, and we might have had a small profitable British-owned motor industry, but the vacuum created by so doing would have led to a huge flood of imports of motor cars . . . and it would have affected our exports as well.[14]

Government influence is usually greater at the time it agrees to put together the rescue package. As part of the terms, it is not uncommon for the government or its agent to stipulate certain changes to be made within the firm; the appointment of new management is the most common requirement. We have already seen that new top management is a virtual prerequisite for a turnaround to be successful, and it appears that the government may be more successful in implementing management changes than banks. The government's leverage comes from the fact that it is offering additional finance, whereas when banks decide to stop lending to a firm, they have no 'carrot' to offer. In situations in which the government rescue package has led to effective government control of the firm, the government or the Bank of England has gone so far as actively to recruit new top management (e.g. Sir Alastair Down at Burmah Oil).

Government-rescued firms adopt the full range of generic turn-around strategies discussed in Chapter 4, including asset divestment and plant closures. Burmah Oil was forced to agree to a rapid asset divestment programme in 1975; part of the Chrysler rescue package was an agreement with Chrysler that it would shed 8,000 of its 25,000 employees. There have been situations, however, at Ferranti for example, where agreements were made to keep specific plants open for an agreed period, at the time when the rescue package was negotiated (see the Ferranti case-history in Chapter 16). Another example of government efforts to delay closure was Eric Varley's attempt in early 1979, when he was Industry Secretary, to take Prestcold Holdings away from its parent, British Leyland, so as to delay the closure of its two Scottish factories. Prestcold manufactured compressors for refrigerators and freezers, and was losing money as the result of severe foreign price competition.[15] The plan was dropped when the Conservative Government took over, and the plants were subsequently closed by B.L.

A number of government rescue packages that have involved injecting cash into a firm over a number of years – as at B.L., for example – have threatened to link future financial assistance to improvements in productivity, but as yet there are no published examples of cash being withheld because productivity targets have not been achieved. B.L. was regarded by Sir Keith Joseph, the Industry Secretary, as having done 'just enough' during 1980, in terms of introducing new working practices, reducing overmanning and launching the Metro motorcar on time, to justify another £990 million in government cash during 1981 and 1982.[16] In the mid-1970s, industrial democracy was a fashionable concept and the Labour Government attempted to introduce greater workforce participation in the decision-making process as a means of increasing productivity. The results of these efforts were minimal, and productivity improvements that have been achieved in government-rescued firms, at Rolls-Royce and B.L. for example, have little to do with the introduction of industrial democracy *per se*.

Other government actions to promote recovery have included preferential buying arrangements and the formation of an expert review body to look for diversification opportunities, as has occurred at Harland and Wolff, for example.

With few exceptions, government influence over the management of turnaround situations has tended to be relatively small once the initial rescue package has been implemented. Those situations that have required annual injections of government money, such as at Rolls-Royce and British Leyland, have been subject to marginally greater control but, by and large, management has been autonomous. The exceptions have been high-technology situations in which the position of the ailing firm has been deteriorating and showing no signs of recovery, despite the firm's obvious potential. In these situations, the government has made additional capital contingent upon bringing in new private-sector partners to manage the turnaround. At Kearney Trecker Marwin, the government brought in Vickers on a two-year management contract in June 1974 and gave them an option to buy the company by April 1976. The cost to the government of allowing Vickers to take 86% of the equity was a write-off of £5 million, an additional loan of £1 million and the injection of £800,000 in the form of non-voting shares. K.T.M. was successfully turned around by Vickers from a loss of £1.6 million in 1974 to a profit of £1.5 million in 1978 (which gave a return on capital employed of 18%).

Cambridge Instruments is a more recent example in which the government entered into an agreement with an individual who had a successful track record in turning around and developing an international instrument business. The individual was given voting control of Cambridge; and he, together with the Midland Bank and I.C.F.C., subscribed £1.2 million of new capital. In return, the government injected a further £6.5 million, in the form of non-voting and preferred shares.[17]

Much of the government monitoring of the firms it has rescued was undertaken by the National Enterprise Board (N.E.B.) from 1974 onwards.* Originally, the N.E.B. was created as an interventionist agency, but after Eric Varley took over from Anthony Wedgwood Benn as Secretary of State for Industry in 1975, it became a holding company for all government investments in the non-nationalized industries. The N.E.B. was staffed principally by businessmen and, until 1979, had union representation on the Board; however, the N.E.B. appears to have had little influence over its subsidiaries and associate companies.[18] Clearly the N.E.B. could not be responsible for the day-to-day management of its portfolio of investments. Like any holding company board, all it could do was pick the right management

* The National Enterprise Board is now part of the British Technology Group.

and fire them if they were incompetent. This, however, was not always easy, as was well illustrated by the N.E.B.'s inability to bring about change at Rolls-Royce during 1979. Sir Leslie Murphy, then Chairman of the N.E.B., believed that Rolls-Royce needed new management and tighter cash control; but he was unable to accomplish this because of government pressure.[19] In the end, the problem was resolved by the government removing Rolls-Royce from N.E.B. ownership and control. In justifying this move, Sir Keith Joseph, then Secretary of State for Industry, said:

The friction [between N.E.B. and Rolls-Royce] is not a passing problem of personalities [– which in part it was] or a difference of opinion on the management of the company but is inherent in the relationship and would almost certainly survive a change of management. Rolls-Royce is a company of a scale and importance such that the supervision of its Board by another Board, however eminent and accomplished, is bound to give rise to strain.[20]

When the Conservative Government came to power in 1979, the role of the N.E.B. in managing rescue operations was considerably reduced, and the N.E.B. came under pressure from the government to divest itself of its saleable assets, both for political reasons (the non-intervention, free-market-economy ideology) and to assist in the reduction of the public sector borrowing requirement. How the assets have been sold is the subject of the following section.

5. Government Approaches to Exit

As part of its policy of reducing government intervention, government has pursued a policy of withdrawing from turnaround situations wherever possible. This section describes the major ways in which this has occurred: (i) by sale of shares; (ii) by sale of company; and (iii) by liquidation.

5.1 Sale of Shares

The sale of government shares, either by public offering or by private placement, has tended to take place in those situations where the government has not been a majority shareholder, as in the case of I.C.L. and Ferranti. This is clearly a route which is open to the government only if the company has been successfully turned around. As far as the firms themselves are concerned, this approach appears to be the preferred option, providing the shares are widely placed, since it maintains the firm's independence. Ferranti argued that its survival as an independent business was (a) essential to its ability to maintain high standards of innovation and technological excellence; (b) necessary to prevent a reduction in competition in defence contracts (particularly if it was bought by G.E.C.'s Marconi Division); and (c) that its management and employees had rescued the firm through their own efforts and therefore 'were against being auctioned off to a single buyer'.[21] In the event, the government acceded to Ferranti's wishes and placed its 50% shareholding with City institutions.

In the case of I.C.L., the government placement was at a discount from market price of only about 4%. Where shares are offered for sale, it seems that the government could possibly obtain a premium over market price by selling the whole of its stake to one purchaser as a prelude to a full takeover attempt, but in the limited number of situations where this has been an issue, the government has preferred to maintain the entity's independence.

5.2 Sale of Company

The issue of independence is also one of key importance when the government has full control and the business has been successfully turned around. In the case of the engineering group Fairey Holdings, which the N.E.B. acquired from the receiver for £18 million in 1977, it is quite possible that the government could have maximized its financial return by breaking up the company. Great interest in buying parts of the company was expressed by groups such as N.E.I., Dowty and Trafalgar House.[22] However, management, under the chairmanship of Angus Murray (of Redman Heenan fame, see p. 279), regarded the preservation of the group in its present form as vital to its future success.[23] In the event, Fairey was sold to Doulton (part of the S. Pearson group) for £24 million (later adjusted downwards, to reflect Fairey's worse-than-projected results for 1980). Doulton declared their intention of running Fairey as a separate subsidiary.

The government has also managed to sell companies in situations where it was not successful in promoting a successful turnaround. The Meriden motorcycle co-operative is an example of a situation that was a classic lame-duck rescue attempt, that did nothing but absorb cash, and was eventually sold. By 1980, Meriden owed the government £12 million and was continuing to lose over £300,000 per month.[24] As part of the terms of sale, however, the government had to waive all loans and interest charges due to it directly and indirectly via the Export Credit Guarantee Department.

5.3 Liquidation/Receivership

The obvious way open for government to exit from a non-recoverable turnaround situation is to stop advancing further funds and to place the firm in liquidation. This is what happened to Alfred Herbert, Britain's biggest machine-tool company and once one of the world leaders in that industry. Alfred Herbert had been a declining firm for most of the postwar period, suffering from poor management, an unwillingness to innovate and a general lack of competitiveness against foreign competition. After a disastrous joint venture into computer-controlled machines, Herbert Ingersoll went into receivership in 1972 and, by the end of the 1974 recession, Alfred Herbert itself was no longer viable. However, under the interventionist policy of Anthony Wedgwood Benn, the group was rescued and eventually taken into full public ownership. From 1975 until the end of 1979, £43 million of public money was pumped into Alfred Herbert. In 1979, the N.E.B. made it clear that no more government money would be forthcoming and that future survival plans would have to be self-financing. It was only then that Herbert management started to plan a turnaround strategy that involved Herbert in focusing on advanced-technology machine tools, redundancies, and divesting itself of certain activities – but the timing was wrong. Herbert's financial situation was too weak to withstand a £16 million loss (after allowing for rationalization costs) at a time when there was a dramatic cyclical drop in machine-tool orders as the recession gathered momentum in 1980. Alfred Herbert made one last attempt to obtain a further £5 million from the N.E.B. in April 1980 'to enable its restructuring programme to be carried through', but the N.E.B. refused, as did its bankers, who refused to lend more money without an N.E.B. guarantee. The final cost of the government's rescue attempt on Alfred Herbert was £56 million, since the N.E.B. agreed to pay off the £12.5 million owing to creditors and bankers.[25]

What is interesting, from the point of view of public policy, is the effect of liquidation on employment at Alfred Herbert. From a peak of about 15,000 employees in the mid-1960s, Herbert's workforce was down to 11,300 in 1970 and had dropped to 5,500 in 1978 and to 4,500 by the end of 1979. The liquidation process that involved the sale of individual subsidiaries and plants during 1980 has saved most of these remaining jobs. One wonders whether receivership in 1974, as was recommended by the Industrial Development Advisory Board, would have been more effective than government rescue as a job-saving device.

Conclusion

An analysis of the strategies adopted by firms that the government has tried to rescue indicates that the economic and management factors causing decline and recovery are essentially the same as those in situations where the government is not involved. The big difference with government intervention is that additional financing is made available if the intervention is direct, irrespective of whether or not the firm can be turned around successfully. In contrast, the banks rarely provide additional financing in failed turnaround situations; they prefer to allow the firm to go into receivership.

Many of the situations in which the state has been involved can clearly be classified as successful turnarounds: Ferranti, Burmah Oil, Fairey, etc.; others, such as Alfred Herbert, were clearly failures. In analysing unsuccessful rescue attempts, we need to distinguish between situations that were clearly not recoverable in the first place and those that might have stood a chance of recovery if appropriate turnaround strategies had been used. Alfred Herbert is a case in point: if the firm (with government approval, of course) had adopted a focused strategy and had divested itself of subsidiaries and plants that were not required in 1974/75 (as it started to do in 1979/80), it might have stood a better chance of surviving.

There remain a number of other situations in which the success or failure of state rescue attempts has yet to be determined, although failure to make profits to date probably indicates that the turnaround strategies that have been adopted will not work. British Leyland, Rolls-Royce and Cambridge Instruments are the obvious examples. In each of these companies, initial turnaround strategies have been changed or modified but, in many cases, years have gone by without the basic strategies being implemented. Thus at Rolls-Royce, it is reported that strict cash-flow management was only instituted in 1979,[26] and that at Cambridge Instruments there were lack of adequate financial controls, poor management and poor production systems throughout the 1970s.[27] At British Leyland, the appointment of Michael Edwardes and the subsequent implementation of his plan to rationalize the business has achieved some results, although there is one key question mark concerning the turnaround strategy being adopted: does B.L. have a viable, long-term future at the low-priced end of the car market? The answer is probably no (for the reasons already discussed in Chapter 2), in which case the cutbacks that have already been implemented have not been drastic enough. Out of 170,000 employees, 52,000 lost their jobs in the first three years of Sir Michael Edwardes's management. It seems that the government is doing little more than postponing the inevitable failure of the group as it stands – and, in the process, perhaps jeopardizing the future of those segments of the business that are profitable. Government rescue may save jobs in the very short term and also allow suppliers a chance to develop new products and new markets; however, there is little evidence that many jobs have been saved in the long term.

From the management point of view, state involvement does not change the need for well-conceived and soundly implemented turn-around strategies. The principles are the same as in the private sector. With few exceptions (as, for example, when government has forced diversification or sales expansion to keep a plant open or not allowed a firm to adopt a focused strategy, as at Alfred Herbert and British Leyland), actions by the Bank of England or the government have facilitated the turnaround process.

Notes

1. 'Fairey Board Favours Hambros-Led Offer', *Financial Times*, 24 February 1980.
2. 'To the Brink of Ruin and Back', *Sunday Times*, 22 January 1978.
3. 'A New Boy Put His Skates On To Save Triang Toys', *Financial Times*, 24 December 1979.
4. 'Villiers Revived by its New Owners', *Financial Times*, 23 January 1980.
5. 'ICL Hits Rough Water', *Financial Times*, 8 January 1981.
6. 'Another Attempt at Saving Cambridge Instruments', *Financial Times*, 30 October 1979.
7. *British Leyland: The Next Decade* (the Ryder Report), H.M.S.O., 1975, p. 33.
8. 'A £1 Billion Claim on the Bank', *Financial Times*, 1 June 1981.
9. 'Chrysler, The Rescue Blueprint in Detail', *Sunday Times*, 21 December 1975.
10. 'ICL Hits Rough Water', *Financial Times*, 8 January 1981.
11. 'How Dunbee-Combex Ran Off the Rails', *Sunday Times*, 24 February 1980.

12. 'The Company that Had to Survive', *Financial Times*, 19 January 1981.
13. 'A Growing Power beside the Tyne?', *Financial Times*, 6 November 1979.
14. *Hansard*, 21 May 1975.
15. 'Varley's Strategy to Delay Closure', *Financial Times*, 18 April 1979.
16. 'BL to Get Nearly £1 Billion in New Government Cash', *Financial Times*, 27 January 1981.
17. 'Another Attempt at Saving Cambridge Instruments', *Financial Times*, 30 October 1979.
18. 'The Future of the N.E.B.', *Financial Times*, 22 November 1979.
19. 'The New Challenge Facing Rolls-Royce', *Financial Times*, 16 November 1979.
20. 'The Future of the N.E.B.', op. cit.
21. 'Ferranti Fears for its Independence', *Financial Times*, 24 May 1980.
22. 'Hambros Hoping to Buy Fairey Holdings from N.E.B. for £19.5 Million', *Sunday Times*, 23 February 1980.
23. 'Fairey Chairman Urges End to Uncertainty over Ownership', *Financial Times*, 2 April 1980.
24. 'Meriden Co-op's Debt to Government Nears £12 million', *Financial Times*, 14 July 1980.
25. 'Herbert Costs State £56.5 million', *Financial Times*, 18 October 1980.
26. 'The New Challenge Facing Rolls-Royce', op. cit.
27. 'Another Attempt at Saving Cambridge Instruments', op. cit.

Part Four

Case-Histories

This section of the book consists of twenty case-histories of U.K. companies, showing the major causes of decline and the recovery actions taken by management.

Chapter 12 contains four case-histories of successful recovery situations in the manufacturing sector (Staveley, Redman Heenan, Ultra and R.F.D.) although, as was explained in Chapter 5, classifying what qualifies as successful recovery and what does not is open to dispute. This is followed in Chapter 13 by case-histories of three successful recovery situations in retailing (Burton, M.F.I. and Queensway). Chapter 14 provides case-histories of Muirhead, Pentos and Alpine Holdings, all of which are good examples of how non-crisis situations use the same management approach as is applied in crisis situations.

Property speculation was a major causal factor of corporate crises in the mid-1970s, so case-histories have been included in Chapter 15 on one hotel group (Mount Charlotte Investments) and one banking group (Keyser Ullmann) as illustrative of the managerial approaches used to effect subsequent recovery.

The case-histories of Burmah Oil and Ferranti in Chapter 16 illustrate the part the government and the Bank of England played in two relatively large recovery situations during the 1970s. State involvement obviously acted as a constraint on some management action, but the general approach used was the same as in the successful recovery situations in manufacturing industry described in Chapter 12.

Lastly, three chapters (17, 18 and 19) describe six firms whose recovery strategies have failed or have been unsuccessful to date. The reason for including these case-histories in a book on corporate recovery is simple: the reader should not believe that corporate recovery is easy to achieve – or even possible in most situations. The unsuccessful recovery situations range from some still surviving to some that went insolvent fairly rapidly after recovery actions similar to those prescribed in this book were implemented. They provide the reader with as much insight into the management of crisis situations as do successful recovery situations. The case-histories that have been included as unsuccessful recovery situations are Evered, Barker and Dobson, Inveresk, Bamford, Foden and Dimplex.

12. Successful Recovery Situations in Manufacturing

Staveley Industries and Redman Heenan International are examples of two classic recovery situations. A comparison of the recovery strategies used shows a remarkably similar approach, although the management styles of Angus Murray at Redman Heenan and of Adolf Frankel appear to be quite different.

Ultra was chosen as an example because it was a high-technology growth firm that found itself in a crisis more through a series of misfortunes than because of bad management. It provides one of the few examples in which new management was not necessary to effect a recovery. Another example of a turnaround of a high-technology growth firm is Ferranti but, because of government involvement, the case-history on Ferranti has been deferred until Chapter 16.

The R.F.D. Group is an example of the two-stage turnaround discussed in Chapter 5. The actions taken by new management in 1973 restored profitability, but subsequent management changes in 1975 indicated that an insufficient number of management actions were taken in the first recovery phase, and that those that were taken were not implemented rigorously enough.

Staveley Industries

Staveley Industries is a group of companies that, for most of the 1960s and 1970s, was engaged in four businesses: machine tools, foundry and abrasive products, chemical extraction and electrical services. Staveley's financial performance had been inconsistent for many years, but 1965 saw a change of strategy that resulted in large losses in 1969 and 1970. The strategy was to build up Staveley's machine-tool business by the acquisition and subsequent rationalization of other companies in that industry. The company's stated strategy during its period of decline was: (i) to eliminate businesses not in the main divisions, or those which were not contributing; (ii) to acquire new business that either overlapped or complemented the existing ones;

(iii) to rationalize products and production within the group; (iv) to concentrate, streamline and strengthen management; and (v) to gear the company within a suitable ratio of loan to equity.

Causes of Decline

What went wrong with this strategy? Five factors have been identified:

(*a*) *Acquisition of poor companies at a high price*: From 1965 to 1967, Staveley acquired five companies in the machine-tool industry (Craven Brothers, Asquith, Newdall & Gent, Lapointe and H. W. Keans) at a cost of over £13 million, with the objective of achieving economies of scale in production through industry rationalization. Nearly all these companies were failing or losing money at the time of acquisition; some had poor products and others declining markets. To take one example, Craven Brothers was primarily a producer of large components for steam engines, but there were few steam engines still in existence in the mid-1960s. This clearly reflects inadequate pre-acquisition planning. After rationalization, the acquired companies added about £13 million of sales to the machine tools division. Assuming an optimistic 5% return on sales, this would indicate that Staveley may have paid a price-earnings ratio of about twenty for these companies – more than twice what they were worth.

(*b*) *Top management*: The architect of the expansion strategy appears to have been Aubrey Jones, who retired as chairman in March 1965 before any large acquisitions were made. He brought into the group two former civil servants, Dennis Haviland, who was appointed deputy chairman and managing director, and Reginald Ratcliffe, who was appointed chief executive of the machine-tool division. Aubrey Jones's philosophy was 'to introduce men of quality who do not necessarily have experience in the fields in which they are expected to operate'. Both men clearly lacked industrial experience and, more importantly, knew little about the difficult machine-tool industry, where significant and rapid changes had to be made if an acquisition strategy was to be successful. When Aubrey Jones retired, Haviland became both chairman and chief executive, with the result that there was no effective watchdog over top management's actions.

(*c*) *Poor post-acquisition management*: Staveley management made some attempt to integrate the acquired businesses with their machine-tool operations, but their efforts were inadequate and they failed to achieve their acquisition objectives. The chairman's statement in 1969 referred to this in the following way:

. . . we must now recognize squarely that Staveley Industries did not have sufficient management and manpower resources to ensure the smooth and efficient integration of the newly acquired companies and their products, and to extol the clusive gain of rationalization . . . The result has been that several million pounds were invested in the purchase of machine-tool companies and their subsequent financing, and we have little or no return for the investment.

(*d*) *Cyclical reduction in demand*: The business of machine tools is notoriously cyclical, and domestic demand dropped suddenly after the acquisition programme began in 1965, although export demand remained buoyant. In an endeavour to fill capacity, management undertook substantial orders with little or no profit margin. It is interesting to note that at the time when the strategy of expanding in the machine-tool industry was being developed in 1964/65, the industry was going through one of its cyclical up-swings.

(*e*) *High gearing*: Staveley financed its acquisition programme primarily by raising debt. Total debt as a percentage of shareholders' funds increased from 2% in 1965 to 100% in 1970. This, coupled with the fact that much of the debt was in the form of bank overdraft and that the machine-tools industry is highly cyclical, meant that Staveley adopted an extremely high-risk financial strategy.

The Crisis

The 1967/68 financial year saw the machine-tool division start to lose money, although in the previous year the division's trading profit has been £1.1 million. The situation deteriorated in 1968/69 as trading profits declined further, interest charges continued to increase and there were large extraordinary write-offs (see Table 12.2) as the machine-tool division's workforce and manufacturing facilities were reduced by over 25%. But the division continued to be a substantial cash drain. Haviland resigned from the board in 1969 and two non-executive directors, Michael Spieler and Arthur Main, were made chairman and managing director on a temporary basis.

Recovery Actions

(*a*) *Appointment of new chief executive*: Dr Adolf Frankel was appointed as managing director of Staveley Industries. Frankel was

Polish-born and had come to England in 1946 from Switzerland, where he had spent ten years and gained his doctorate in Mechanical Design Engineering. He joined A.E.I. in 1960, to become chief mechanical engineer and subsequently general manager of the turbine generator division, where Arthur Main was his boss. Under the new Weinstock regime, he survived and prospered to become managing director of the turbine generating division. Frankel learned much from Weinstock, and his methods at Staveley were influenced by those used by Weinstock following the takeover of A.E.I. by G.E.C.

(b) *Steps to improve cash-flow position*: Frankel arrived at Staveley in February 1970; he quickly found that the position was worse than he had been led to believe. Bank borrowing was £8.2 million; an additional £8 million of long-term loans gave the company a gearing ratio of about 50%. Bank credit facilities at £8 million were already more than used up and the company was living from day to day, surviving only by virtue of the delay in clearing cheques that it paid out. It only required one banker to get cold feet for the company to crash.

The immediate short-term problem was therefore the effective management of short-term cash resources. There was already a complicated centralized financial-control system in operation, but the information it contained was useless. Cash control was centralized, but many managers were operating with cash as if it were 'Monopoly money'.

Frankel attacked the short-term cash problem in three ways:

(i) He immediately put each operating company into credit by taking all debts to the centre. He then personally visited each operating company chief executive and negotiated a revised monthly cash-flow forecast, whereby the subsidiary agreed to remit a given amount of money to head office each month. The chief executives were given full responsibility for meeting the forecasts and had to negotiate with Frankel if there was going to be a short-fall. Failure to give such prior warning left the chief executive liable to be dismissed. This policy produced a cash flow to head office of £2 million in the first three months.

(ii) In May 1970, the Craven Swift Machine Tool Division was closed. It was a major drain on cash resources and was considered beyond rescue. It had bad management, bad labour relations and designs that were ten or fifteen years out of date.

(iii) In October 1970, Staveley's 50% share in Warner Swasey Asquith was sold to Warner Swasey for £2.1 million in cash.

After six months or so, Frankel's actions had taken care of the immediate cash-flow problems and he was able to concentrate on the longer-term position, although his action in closing Craven Swift caused an extraordinary charge of £3.5 million in the 1970 profit and loss statement.

(c) *Appointment of new financial controller and introduction of new control system*: Frankel appointed a new financial controller immediately after his arrival, replacing the Financial Director, who left the company. During 1970, the financial controller's main concern was to implement and monitor the new cash-flow policy; but during the period 1970/71 he introduced a new control system. The system required four main reports from each company: a budget summary that was prepared in July and August for the financial year starting in the following October; a month-by-month cash-flow budget produced for one year ahead; monthly operating reports that held only what information head office believes it is essential for the companies to know to run their businesses effectively (the form of internal control system used is left to the individual companies); monthly cash-flow statements which include progress on budgeted capital spending.

The introduction of this system necessitated the strengthening of the financial control functions within the operating companies. The importance of the finance functions had to be 'sold' to the divisions, where previously they had been considered unimportant. At head office, the central financial team was greatly reduced and replaced by the financial controllers appointed for each product group.

(d) *Decentralization and reduction in corporate staff*: Frankel decentralized management responsibility. He believed that each subsidiary chief executive should be completely responsible for running his own company. He kept control, however, by keeping the right to hire and fire senior managers and by maintaining control over investment. Along with the policy of decentralization, head office kept a low profile and head office staff was dramatically reduced. When Arthur Main took over as managing director in 1969, there were twenty-three people in the head office personnel department. By 1974, there was a total of only twenty-three people at head office – and no personnel people at all. Head office charges were not levied on the operating companies.

(e) *Change of product-market strategy*: When Frankel took over, he was faced with a loosely knit conglomerate with heavy machine-tool producing companies accounting for 60% of the assets but producing no profit, while the remaining 40% of the assets were invested in basically sound and profitable businesses – albeit a little inefficient. The previous objective of expanding in the machine-tool industry was dubious. The U.K. industry had shown little growth in real terms, and Frankel decided that its history of poor management made it a bad industry to be in. However, the long lead time for orders, quite apart from social and financial considerations, precluded the possibility of an immediate close-down of all the machine-tool interests; a slow decline in their importance as a proportion of the total company was required.

Frankel's product market strategy had five main points:

(i) to reduce the relative importance of machine tools to the company, preferably by expanding other parts of the business; (ii) to rationalize the machine tool division and close any businesses that could not be made to operate profitably in their own right; (iii) to make a conscious effort to acquire overseas businesses as a step to counteract the cyclical nature of the industry; (iv) to maintain only the capacity that would allow survival at the bottom of the cycles; and (v) to remove the emphasis from production and increase the agency side of the business.

The effect of these criteria on each of the four main divisions was as follows:

- the machine tool group was reorganized into four principal manufacturing units, each of which was required to be profitable in its own right. The product range was slimmed down to enable the group to concentrate on specific segments of the market. The number of employees in the division was reduced from 5,250 to 2,500 by 1972, while capacity was maintained at 70% of what it had been when Frankel joined. There was little new investment within the group, the four units receiving equipment from the closed plants.

- the foundry and abrasives group continued to increase profits. Limited capital expenditure was undertaken in the period 1970–73, but in 1974 large-scale investment was made in increased capacity to allow the group to compete overseas.

- the electrical group was increased to five companies in 1974 from three in 1970, by splitting up one company and acquiring another. Frankel considered that £1–1½ million turnover was the optimal size for an electrical contractor if the managing director was to maintain control and keep the necessary detailed contact with customers. Emphasis was placed on obtaining business overseas.

● in the chemical group, the capacity of the British Salt plant was increased in 1974 to satisfy the expanding market. Staveley Lime Products Ltd invested in new kilns to reduce unit costs and diversified into aggregates for road-building and the supply of black top.

(f) *Replacement of group chief executives*: Each of the four operating groups – machine tools, foundry and abrasives, electrical engineering and chemicals – was run by a chief executive who was a member of the parent board. Two of these left the company after Frankel took over; the managing director of the chemicals group was dismissed a little later, even though he was achieving a better return on investment than the other divisions: Frankel thought he should be doing better and events bore him out. At the operating company level, there were few management changes, since the management required only the right environment to function effectively.

(g) *Frankel's management style*: Frankel was clearly a performance-oriented executive, but his management style is somewhat different from that of many successful turnaround experts. He dislikes the need to fire anybody and believes in giving people enough time to make up their own minds that they are unable to do their job properly, so that they are quite relieved when the time comes for them to go. He uses the same technique for dealing with companies that have to be wound up. By leaving them for six or twelve months longer than may have been good for the rest of the organization, everybody realized the hopelessness of the situation, and the closures were made without problems. One example of the special culture that developed within the organization was the closure in April 1972 of James Archdale, another of Staveley's acquisitions. Essentially, it was in the transfer machine business for car manufacturers that had become dominated by U.S. companies. By late 1971, the company had run out of orders and it was obvious that it would have to close. Frankel held on, however, and in April 1972 the managing director of Archdale came to see him to say that he thought the company should close. The closure took place smoothly and was carried out by the Archdale management. In the same year, Staveley companies Lapointe in the U.S. and Staveley-Lapointe at Bracknell were also closed because of both a decline in the aerospace business and intense competition.

Frankel's strategy of decentralization was based on his belief that the chief executives of operating companies know how to run their companies better than he does.[1] He travelled 30,000 miles a year to visit the operating companies, as he prefers to meet people on their own ground rather than as the 'headmaster summoning an errant schoolboy to his office'. He saw his role as that of a catalyst, speeding up a process of change that would have happened eventually without his intervention.

Results

By 1976, trading margins for all divisions were the highest they had been at any time in the previous twelve years: gearing was down to 28% and interest cover was nine times earnings. The importance of the machine-tool group had declined to 40% of sales, the same as it had

Table 12.1: *Staveley Industries: Sales and Profitability, 1965–81*
(in £ millions)

	Sales £	Profit before Tax £
1965	30	2.0
1966	44	2.6
1967	47	2.0
1968	47	0.4
1969	47	(0.1)
1970	53	(1.1)
1971	48	1.3
1972	45	1.6
1973	48	2.5
1974	57	2.9
1975	81	3.6
1976	104	6.8
1978*	122	10.0
1979	154	11.2
1980	176	7.3
1981	164	7.3

* Figures for 1978, which was an 18-month period, have been annualized.
Source: Annual Reports.

been in 1965. Since 1976, the Group has maintained its recovery and, despite problems in some divisions in the current recession, is no longer a turnaround situation.

Table 12.2: *Staveley Industries: Financial Performance, 1965–81 (in £ million)*[1]

Financial year	Trading profit		Interest	Profit before tax[2]
	Machine tools £	Other divisions £		
1965	0.6	1.4	–	2.0
1966	1.1	1.7	(0.2)	2.6
1967	1.1	1.6	(0.7)	2.0
1968	(0.1)	1.6	(1.1)	0.4
1969	(0.4)	1.6	(1.3)	(0.1)
1970	(0.4)	2.8	(1.3)	(1.1)
1971	(0.3)	2.6	(1.0)	1.3
1972	(0.5)	2.9	(0.8)	1.6
1973	(0.1)	3.4	(0.8)	2.5
1974	0.2	3.7	(1.0)	2.9
1975	0.5	4.3	(1.2)	3.6
1976	1.6	6.0	(0.8)	6.8
1978[3]	1.7	9.2	(0.9)	10.0
1979	2.0	10.7	(1.5)	11.2
1980	1.0	9.3	(3.0)	7.3
1981	0.8	9.0	(2.5)	7.3

NOTES

1. Brackets ( ) indicate loss.
2. Before extraordinary losses/gains.
3. Figures for 1978, which was an 18-month period, have been annualized.
Source: Annual Reports.

Redman Heenan International Group

The Redman Heenan International Group (R.H.I.) designs, manufactures and supplies specialized engineering products and ancillary services. The group developed as a result of a takeover in 1968 of the Heenan Group (1967 sales: £10 million) by the much smaller Redman Group (1967 sales: £2 million).

Prior to 1968, both the Redman and Heenan groups were centred in Worcester and both owned numerous specialized engineering firms.

The Redman side, a family-dominated group, had gone public in 1964 and in the four years following its quotation took over a number of small engineering concerns in the Midlands. Bert Redman was an inventive engineer who had developed a number of products for the motor industry. The Heenan side was a long-established engineering firm with an old factory in Worcester, a hydraulic engineering business in Gloucester and several smaller specialized engineering subsidiaries. As separate companies, both groups had major strategic and operational weaknesses and may in time have become recovery situations, but the 1968 merger and subsequent management actions were direct causes of the crisis situation that occurred in 1971.

Causes of Decline

Four specific causes of decline can be identified after 1968:

(a) *Post-acquisition management problems*: The board attempted to divisionalize the group and established a central service office in Worcester to co-ordinate financial planning, marketing and personnel. However, the Heenan management resented the takeover and the dominance of the Redman side in the newly structured board. This board-level conflict never allowed group management to become effective, with the result that the subsidiaries remained quite autonomous and rationalization of the group's activities was impossible to achieve. Subsidiaries competed with one another, loss-making companies were left untouched and loss-making product-lines were not eliminated.

(b) *Acquisition of unprofitable company*: The post-acquisition problems were exacerbated by the acquisition of Fisherlow Products Ltd (later called Redman Fisher) in August 1969 for £860,000. Fisherlow, previously owned by British Leyland, was heavily committed to the motorcar industry and had incurred losses for the previous two years. A month after its acquisition, Fisherlow recorded a loss for the 1968/69 financial year of £923,000, although it did break even in the following two years.

(c) *Cyclical reduction in demand*: The group entered the 1970s to survive a recession in the capital goods market. *Management Today* referred to R.H.I.'s problems thus: 'Squeezed between rising costs and falling orders from the motor industry, and beset by technical problems, Redman Engineering was one of the first to slip into losses.'[2]

(*d*) *Lack of control*: Centralized financial control was never implemented after the 1968 merger. There was no centralized management information system and, more importantly, there was no cash control. Debtors especially were out of control, averaging about four months of sales. As evidence of the lack of control, an extraordinary charge relating to previous years of over £500,000 was shown in the accounts of one subsidiary in 1970.

The Crisis

By the summer of 1971, R.H.I. was in a severe cash crisis. For the year ended 30 September 1971, the group returned a loss of £2.4 million on a turnover of £19.9 million. The loss was financed almost exclusively by an increase in overdraft, with the result that total borrowings at year end rose to 183% of shareholders' funds. *Management Today* commented on those critical summer months: 'The overdraft had by then [August 1971] reached £7.7 million – easily exceeding shareholders' funds – and the Midland Bank was at last putting up the shutters. Clearly, the loss for the year would be around £2 million. Suppliers were threatening to cut off deliveries and writs were arriving with almost every post.'[3]

In August 1971, Angus Murray and Eric Spencer were appointed managing director and finance director respectively, in a major board reshuffle engineered by Hambros Bank. Murray and Spencer were among the bank's industrial advisers who were appointed to boards of companies whenever Hambros interests were involved. Their appointment came at the nadir of R.H.I.'s fortunes, and what was to follow can only be called a remarkable turnaround. Key financial data for this period are shown in Table 12.3.

Recovery Actions

When Murray and Spencer arrived, the overdraft had reached £7.7 million and the group was headed for a loss in excess of £2 million. What was needed was quick action to get the overdraft lower and to stop the bleeding. Short-term cash problems were tackled by:

(*a*) *Putting pressure on the debtors*: Control in this area had been slack; Murray and Spencer spent a lot of their time establishing the debtor situation, then chasing the debts. After six weeks, the overdraft was reduced by £1 million to £6.7 million, largely as a result of their personal efforts.

(*b*) *Negotiating with the bank*: During October, Murray had what can only be described as a 'tense meeting' with the Midland Bank (at opposite ends of a long table!) at which, after much persuasion and hard talking, he was given three months to get results, otherwise a receiver would be called in.

(*c*) *Locating and eliminating the loss makers within the group*: Murray and Spencer used the services of so-called 'commandos', part-time specialists hired to find the key problem areas in the group. As a result, three subsidiaries were quickly sold. Redman's Worcester factory was closed (involving 600 redundancies) and put up for sale, the bumper-bar-forming machine business was transferred to Gloucester, and several unprofitable product-lines were dropped, involving further redundancies. Not all the product-lines dropped at this early stage were loss makers: some were dropped because they fitted badly with the group, others because they were small and eased pressure on management. The combined result of these actions was to reduce the overdraft by over £1 million, but this involved some substantial write-offs.

(*d*) *Reducing inventory levels*: The new management team began to work on reducing inventory levels, the results of which, although rapid, were not as decisive a factor in R.H.I.'s survival as the immediate reduction in debtor levels. However, the financial impact over twelve months was significant.

By September 1972, £5.2 million had been generated from the following sources:

	£m
Disposal of fixed assets and subsidiaries	1.1
Reduction in debtors	1.9
Reduction in stocks	2.2
	5.2

Overdraft was reduced from £7.7 million to £3 million and creditors were reduced by £0.5 million. The company returned a small profit of £81,000 on a reduced turnover of £16.2 million (1971: £19.9 million).

While pruning the operations in those early months, Murray and Spencer had to build a group that would be viable in the long term. Towards this end, they took the following steps:

(*a*) *R.H.I. divided into four operating divisions*: Initially the group was split into four operating units, each with a chief executive. Two years later the number had increased to six as divisions were reorganized to take account of industrial logic and the skills and personalities of the management team. Part of the industrial logic for Murray related to the length of the production cycle. Companies with a short cycle, say two months between receipt of order and dispatch, were grouped together (e.g. Redman Fisher); those with a long cycle (e.g. Fielding & Platt) were also put together. The divisional heads (together with Murray and Spencer) made up a central executive committee which in the early days met weekly to co-ordinate activities. Head office activities were kept to a minimum: there were only four executives at head office – Murray, Spencer, a financial controller and a company secretary.

(*b*) *Board and management reorganization*: Murray and Spencer dismissed many directors and made a policy of promoting new talent to the board. By 1976, none of the pre-crisis directors remained, and both Murray and Spencer had handed over operational control of the group to those who grew with the group in the post-1972 era, although they remained Chairman and Deputy Chairman respectively. The management reorganization, however, was not without its problems. *Management Today* reported: 'Many appointments made in the early stages of recovery turned out to be quite as temporary as those of the commandos. Some new men, in effect, arrived at the goods inwards door and went straight through to dispatch; and a lot of established executives failed to adjust to the change of pace. Redman Fisher at Tipton, to take an example, had no fewer than six successive bosses in four years.'[4] When Murray left R.H.I. as a full-time executive in October 1974, he brought in a new chief executive, John Watkinson, from the outside; but within eighteen months he had left, and an insider, Brian Gould, was appointed group chief executive. Gould had been brought into Redman Fisher from G.E.C. in 1973.

(*c*) *Strengthening of marketing and product development functions within operating companies*: The marketing and product development functions were strengthened within all subsidiaries. A more positive approach in these areas was reflected by the rapid growth of Heenan Environmental Systems (which makes refuse disposal and incineration plants), Redman Fisher's increased sales of steel flooring (see below), and an increase in export sales, which accounted for 30% of group sales in 1976 as compared to 22% in 1970.

The financial recovery of the group was impressive in the years after the entry of Murray and Spencer (see Table 12.3), but a look at the

Table 12.3: *Redman Heenan International Ltd: Summary of Key Financial Data 1970–81 (in £ millions)*

	1970	1971	1972	1973	1974	1975	1976	1977	1978	1979	1980	1981
Net sales	£ 19.4	19.9	16.2	18.3	22.1	23.8	28.9	31.1	34.2	45.5	42.1	31.8
Net profit after extraordinary items £	(0.5)	(2.4)	–	0.2	0.6	1.0	2.0	2.5	2.8	3.3	2.8	(1.3)
Capital employed £	7.9	5.1	4.9	5.1	5.2	6.0	7.6	N/A	11.2	15.2	17.4	13.7
Return on capital employed	(8%)	(47%)	0.7%	4%	11%	16%	26%	N/A	25%	22%	16%	(9%)
Borrowings as percentage of shareholders' funds	95	183	92	66	75	56	17	N/A	3	7	3	24
Interest cover (times)	1.7	(2.1)	1.1	1.5	2.1	2.7	8.1	13.8	22.2	39.4	11.1	(1.1)
Current ratio	1.1	0.9	1.0	1.0	1.0	1.1	1.2	N/A	1.4	1.3	1.5	1.1
Acid test	0.5	0.4	0.5	0.6	0.5	0.5	0.5	N/A	0.8	0.8	0.9	0.7

Source: Annual Reports.

decisions taken at the corporate or group level fails to identify the key importance of actions taken within the subsidiary companies. Unlike many diversified firms, Redman Heenan's turnaround was not achieved by divesting loss-making subsidiaries but rather by improving the performance of existing businesses. Successful recovery at the subsidiary level was helped by the use of commando executives, the appointment of capable chief executives and the installation of group-wide financial control systems; but even more critical was the importance given to developing sound product-market strategies at the subsidiary company level. To illustrate the importance of this, we will look at the largest R.H.I. subsidiary, Redman Fisher Engineering Ltd, in more detail.

Redman Fisher Engineering Ltd

The company known today as Redman Fisher Engineering Ltd (R.F.E.) has had a long and varied history. Prior to 1969 it was a subsidiary of the British Leyland Motor Corporation under the name of Fisherlow Products Ltd. It was an 'in-house' supplier of materials-handling equipment for British Leyland, producing conveyor systems for manufacturing plants, metal flooring, and metal pallets for general usage. The sale to R.H.I. was part of British Leyland's rationalization programme, intended to concentrate its resources on manufacturing operations directly related to the assembly of motor vehicles, and part of R.H.I.'s expansion programme into related engineering fields. R.H.I. paid £860,000 in cash and loan stock for Fisherlow, which had a net worth at 30 September 1969 of £1.3 million.

When Angus Murray and Eric Spencer moved into R.H.I. in August 1971, R.F.E. was not an immediate cause of concern, except for the level of debtors, over which they personally took control. The company had made substantial losses from 1967 to 1969 (see Table 12.4), but by 1971 was operating at breakeven. Nevertheless, R.F.E. accounted for 17% of group turnover and was a key business in the group.

Recovery actions

(*a*) *Appointment of new management*: In February 1972, Leslie Thomas, one of Angus Murray's 'commandos', joined the board of R.F.E. and Ken Chambers, the managing director, left the company, together with a number of other senior managers. At the same time,

Bill Stagg, who was later to become managing director but was then production control and works manager, was appointed to the board as production director. Leslie Thomas's appointment was very much a stop-gap measure, until a more permanent managing director, Brian Gould, was found. He was recruited from G.E.C. to be finance director but was immediately thrown into a general management role.

(*b*) *Discontinue major product-line*: As part of a strategy to reduce dependence on the motor industry, the old Fisherlow Company had started to invest heavily in the development of an automated warehouse system in conjunction with a U.S. materials-handling manufacturer. A number of sales of such systems had been made, but the system had proved both difficult to commission effectively and very unprofitable. The engineering and automated controls involved were highly complex and needed vast amounts of resources to develop properly – resources that R.H.I. did not have. As a result of the discontinuation of the automated warehousing, sales in the year to 30 September 1972 dropped 24% and the company incurred a loss of £57,000. This was the last loss the company was to make.

(*c*) *Concentration of marketing effort on one product group*: R.F.E. was now left with three product lines – overhead conveyor systems, metal flooring and pallets – all lines which were well known to the company in terms of production techniques and marketing. Brian Gould made a policy decision to stay with these three lines, although he did reduce the range of overhead conveyors. The one section of business he really concentrated on was metal flooring: this flooring is used in a variety of industrial complexes, such as oil refineries and steel mills, for catwalks and gantry flooring. The manufacturing process is extremely simple, basically the welding of parallel strips of metal to cross-members. Profit margins were high, manufacturing was not capital intensive and, most importantly for Brian Gould, flooring 'had a short delivery time, so was the best thing for the cash flow'.

In 1971, the company had one welding machine working less than one shift a day on turning out such flooring. The policy had been to run this activity down and, to this end, marketing had been almost discontinued. However, through an intensive marketing effort, the company was particularly successful in securing flooring orders for North Sea drilling rigs and production platforms. By 1977, twenty-three out of the twenty-nine production platforms and drilling rigs in the North Sea contained R.F.E. metal flooring.

In 1976, R.F.E. began to phase out pallet production; they recognized this business to have low barriers to entry, to be extremely price competitive, to be labour intensive and to require largely unskilled labour. In its place, they hoped to build up fabrication work in those areas where they could utilize a more highly skilled and stable labour force, and add more value to the product.

| | 1973 | | 1974 | | 1975 | | 1976 | |
	£'000	%	£'000	%	£'000	%	£'000	%
Flooring	1,774	45	2,829	52	3,833	60	4,511	71
Mechanical handling	1,158	30	1,393	25	1,321	21	960	15
Pallets	672	17	1,041	19	1,115	18	830	13
Fabricating	60	2	84	2	58	1	66	1
Other	230	6	121	2	–	–	–	–
	3,894	100	5,468	100	6,327	100	6,367	100

(*d*) *Increase exports*: Starting in the 1972/73 financial years, R.F.E. started a major export drive, with the result that export sales increased from 12% of sales in 1972 to 30% of sales by 1975.

(*e*) *Reduction in size of workforce*: The product-line changes inevitably brought about a cut in the size of the workforce. In early 1973, it stood at 700 employees; by 1976 it was down to 480. This reduction was achieved with the full co-operation of the workforce and unions, despite the fact that, immediately after taking over as managing director, Brian Gould had to make nearly 200 employees redundant. The good industrial-relations climate was largely due to the establishment of works and staff committees that met monthly, and to the quarterly meetings held between management and the entire workforce at which the state of the company's order-book was fully disclosed and explained. Both Brian Gould and his successor, Bill Stagg, maintained close touch with the workforce. The good state of industrial relations is all the more impressive when one considers that the company originated from one of the most labour-troubled sections of British Leyland.

The effects of Brian Gould's recovery action can be seen in the summary of key financial data in Table 12.4. The rapid decision to discontinue the automated-warehouse business, identification and exploitation of profitable growth areas, competent management and effective financial control systems (instituted at group level) all contributed to the turnaround. It is interesting to note that R.F.E.'s sales increase was achieved without any significant increase in fixed assets. Fixed-asset turnover increased from 2.5 in 1972 to 5.3 in 1975, indicating a substantial underutilization of fixed assets prior to the recovery. The company was turned around using only internally generated cash flows, and by 1975 had become a net cash generator for the R.H.I. group.

Table 12.4: *Redman Fisher Engineering Ltd: Key Financial Data, 1968–76 (in £ millions)*

Year ending 30 September	Sales	Net profit[1]	Return on capital employed	Current ratio	Acid test
1968[2]	£4.3	£(0.52)	–	1.3	0.8
1969	2.4	(0.92)	–	1.2	1.0
1970	3.0	0.05	3%	1.0	0.7
1971	3.5	–	–	0.9	0.7
1972	2.7	(0.06)	–	0.8	0.6
1973	3.9	0.30	19%	1.1	0.8
1974	5.5	0.51	24%	1.5	1.0
1975	6.3	0.61	27%	2.4	1.8
1976	6.4	0.72	31%	2.4	1.8

NOTES
1. No taxes paid during this period due to tax loss carry forward.
2. Fourteen-month financial year.

Ultra Electronic Holdings

Ultra Electronic Holdings Ltd was originally founded in 1920 as a small privately-owned company making simple radio components. By 1969, Ultra Electronic Holdings Ltd had become the parent company of five trading subsidiaries, including one in the U.S. and another in Sweden. The group employed over 2,000 people and was engaged in the design and manufacture of a wide range of electronic products, extending from precision-built components to complex control systems. The U.K. trading companies and their principal product lines were as follows:

Trading subsidiary	Principal product lines
Ultra Electronics Ltd	Airborne communication systems, Sonabuoys (submarine detection devices), gas turbine engine control instrumentation, radio telephones
Ultra Data (Components) Ltd	Plugs, sockets, connectors
Ultra Data Systems Ltd	Data-processing equipment

In 1969, sales were £7 million and profits before tax were £352,000. Sales had increased by 17% and profits by 40% over the previous year. To quote from the chairman's statement for 1969:

We are now developing electronic controls for gas turbine engines in commercial vehicles for Ford of U.S.A. . . . our engine controls for the Concorde have performed well during test flying . . . our unique position in the Sonabuoy market is maintained and during the year we received additional orders for Sonabuoys, worth nearly £1 million . . . For Ultra Electronics (Components) Limited, the year has been a good one with a 49% increase in turnover and the order-book has been doubled . . . After several years of non-profitable trading Ultra Data Systems is now contributing to the Group's profits.

The only reservations were these:

The acquisition of a new business and premises, together with the resultant reorganization, must slow down the rate of profit expansion. Although our total order-book is at a record level, the production programme has required a slower start to the current year. However, the increased expenditure on research and development and the recent acquisition will place your Company in a strong position to continue to increase its profits in the years that follow.

In the following year, 1970, turnover fell to £5.3 million and the company made a loss of £718,000 against a predicted profit of £650,000. What went wrong?

Causes of Decline

Five factors appear to have contributed to the sudden loss:

(*a*) *Poor financial and management control*: Ultra's financial control was largely non-existent. At that time, the company's culture was engineering- and marketing-oriented, with little attention being given to cost control. Almost nobody below the level of the managing director was held accountable for their actions.

(*b*) *Cost of integrating an acquisition*: In the 1969/70 financial year, Ultra bought another company in the component business to provide an increased product range, but also to provide it with additional production space. Following the acquisition, Ultra moved its component subsidiary to the acquired company's premises, but encountered unexpectedly high relocation costs.

(*c*) *Technical problems*: There were technical problems with the sea battery used in the Sonabuoy equipment, that prevented the company making deliveries to the Ministry of Defence, thereby losing a major order. This resulted in a 37% drop in sales revenues in the electronics division (which accounted for 66% of 1969 sales).

(*d*) *Cost of market entry for a new product*: At this time, it was the company's strategy to reduce its dependence on government contracts. A new line of radio-telephone equipment was being introduced, but the market-entry costs were high. The company completely underestimated the cost of launching the product range. Management estimated that every £1 of sales was adding £1 to losses during 1969/70.

(*e*) *High overheads*: From about 1967 onwards, indirect labour costs were out of control – a bad sign for a company with a high fixed cost structure. As one manager put it: 'The company was riddled with layers of people we just didn't need. For example, we had two or three delivery trucks on the road. The drivers reported to an assistant transport manager who reported to a deputy transport manager who reported to the transport manager.'

The Crisis

Management's response to the 1969/70 trading result was to take immediate remedial action. First, there was a major reappraisal of all overheads and indirect expenses, resulting in the cutting of more than a hundred staff to match the reduced rate of production. Second, the company's marketing and sales effort was intensified.

The company continued to develop engine controls for the Concorde and new facilities for sea-water batteries; it signed an exclusive agreement with the Ricoh organization for the marketing of word-processing and data-preparation equipment and continued to undertake development work on behalf of the government and other sponsors. Lord

Orr-Ewing (the chairman) stated: 'With more than 60% of our turn-over in the defence and aeronautical field . . . our efforts to become less dependent on these two areas and to develop a range of commercial products will begin to pay off in the coming year . . . we expect to be trading profitably by the end of 1970.'

The effect of the increased selling efforts was to increase sales revenues in 1970/71 by 42%, but the company was still losing money, due to the high costs of reorganization, with the result that the company became desperately short of working capital. It just could not finance the rapid explosion in sales volume, and bank borrowing limits were reached and creditors extended. On top of this, Rolls-Royce, one of Ultra's major customers, crashed, owing Ultra approximately £300,000. However, Ultra did not stop supplying Rolls-Royce as did major companies like Lucas, Plessey and G.E.C. At the time, the decision to continue supplying Rolls-Royce had severe cash-flow implications for Ultra, although in later years 'the loyalty was rewarded'. The company was already under severe pressure from its own creditors and, with the Rolls-Royce crash, creditors immediately began demanding payment and would only supply against advance cash payments.

The company was one of many adversely affected in 1971 by the Rolls-Royce crash; fortunately, the situation occurred at a time when the probability of related companies going under was lower than would be the case at the bottom of a deep recession. Furthermore, there was some hope, because of the importance of Ultra as a supplier to the Ministry of Defence, that the government would come to their assistance as a last resort.

Recovery Actions

The worsening financial crisis forced Ultra into a far more critical analysis of the firm's strategy and organization. The following steps were taken:

(a) *Negotiation of additional borrowing facilities*: In January 1972, Ultra negotiated an increase in their bank overdraft facility with the National Westminister Bank and got the bank to guarantee a Euro-dollar loan of £300,000. The bank was offered a seat on the Ultra board which they declined, but they did assign an accountant to the company in this critical period.

(b) *Sale and lease-back of factory*: This was the turning point in the cash crisis. Ultra sold their Western Avenue factory for £1.2 million in May 1972, and leased back 20% of the site.

(c) *Reappraisal of product-market strategy*: The crisis led to a critical appraisal of the product range, the principal outcomes of which were as follows:
(i) The divestiture of the radio-telephone operation on which the company had pinned its product diversification hopes. The market was dominated by Pye, Ultra's market share was less than 10%, and they could not afford a service network. The operation was sold in July 1972 to a subsidiary of Ever-Ready for £341,000 in cash, considerably below the book value of £600,000.
(ii) The concentration of managerial effort on the electronic equipment and component product ranges.
(iii) The continued support of the data systems division. To the outside observer, this was a surprising and high-risk strategy, in view of the strength of competition in this sector and the fact that the company was still making losses and sales volume was declining. However, the chairman continued to maintain his faith in this division, having stated in 1973, 'It is believed that "word processing" will be the fastest growth market for business machines in the 1970s.' In 1976, despite a setback in the word-processing market in the U.K., a loss of £107,000 (1975) was turned into a profit of £56,000.
Table 12.5 shows divisional sales and profits for the period 1969–76.

(d) *Cost-reduction programme*: During 1971, Ultra had instituted a policy of natural wastage but, in January 1972, one-third of the workforce was made redundant. Ed Birch, the managing director, is reported to have been tough but fair. His resolve to cut costs is illustrated by his recollection of a budget meeting: 'We had all these budget plans lying on the table, but I knew that none was trimmed enough. So I got an axe which I had installed in my office and I thumped it down on top of the papers on the desk and said, "That is what I want done with your expenses." '

(e) *Reorganization into product divisions*: The company was restructured to form four product-based divisions, each separately managed at a different location. The initial decision to restructure the divisions as independent operating units was taken as a defensive posture that would have enabled any failing section to be closed or divested if recovery was impossible. However, the restructuring emerged as a competitive strength. By dividing the group into production units of 300–500 people, management structure was kept simple, personnel relationships became easier, and the reaction time to meet customer needs became shorter. Management believes that the increased flexibility had a substantial effect in improving the long-run market performance of the company after 1972.

(f) *Improved financial control systems*: These were introduced only as a result of the 1971/72 crisis. The post-1972 financial discipline within the group was largely the work of one man who had joined the company in 1969 *before* the crisis; he later became financial director. The financial data in Table 12.6 show how tighter financial control reduced debtor levels, increased stock turnover and improved asset turnover generally.

Results

The recovery actions taken in 1972 had a dramatic effect on both profitability and cash flow. Ultra's basic electronics businesses were sound and continued to grow, and successful new products were intro-

Table 12.5: *Ultra Electronic Holdings Ltd: Divisional Sales and Profit Analysis (in £ millions)*

	1969	1970	1971	1972	1973	1974	1975	1976
Electronic								
Sales	4.5	2.8	4.5	3.8	3.6	3.9	5.0	7.2
Profit before tax	0.2	(0.5)	(0.1)	(0.2)	0.2	0.5	0.4	0.6
Components								
Sales	1.4	1.7	2.0	1.7	1.7	2.0	3.1	3.2
Profit before tax	0.1	–	0.1	–	0.1	–	0.3	0.3
Business systems								
Sales	0.8	0.7	1.0	0.8	0.8	0.9	0.9	0.9
Profit before tax	–	–	–	(0.2)	(0.1)	(0.1)	(0.1)	0.1

Source: Annual Reports.

Table 12.6: Ultra Electronic Holdings Ltd: Key Financial Data, 1969–76 (in £ millions)

		1969	1970	1971	1972	1973	1974	1975	1976
Sales	(£)	6.8	5.3	7.5	6.3	6.2	6.8	9.0	11.3
Profit/(loss) after tax	(£)	0.2	(0.5)	(0.2)	(1.0)	0.3	0.5	0.4	0.5
Profit after tax as percentage of sales	(%)	3	(10)	(3)	(16)	4	8	6	8
Profit after tax as percentage of shareholders' funds	(%)	6	(18)	(7)	(60)	10	16	5	4
Gearing	(%)	48	54	64	72	57	50	56	60
Current Ratio		1.9	1.5	1.3	1.5	2.1	2.4	2.0	2.0
Acid Test		0.8	0.6	0.6	0.8	1.4	1.0	1.1	1.0
Net asset turnover		1.7	1.4	2.2	1.8	2.3	2.2	2.4	2.3

Source: Annual Reports.

duced. Thus, by 1973/74 Ultra had been turned around. What is particularly interesting about the recovery is that no new top management was brought into the company. The chairman, Lord Orr-Ewing, and the managing director, Ed Birch, remained in their positions. It is reported that the board was united in the turnaround strategy and its implementation. The chairman was active in using his experience and contacts for the company's benefit, particularly in chasing up payments on government contracts during the cash crisis. Ultra was purchased by the Dowty Group in 1977.

R.F.D. Group Ltd

In the early 1970s, R.F.D. was established as one of the world's leading designers and manufacturers of life-saving equipment: life jackets, inflatable dinghies and parachutes. The company also manufactured and sold military webbing, gunnery-training simulators and specialist textiles. A considerable amount of backward integration had taken place with the acquisition of two specialist fabric manufacturers.

Between 1969 and 1973, sales revenues increased slightly faster than the rate of inflation, while pre-tax profits stagnated at between £300,000 and £400,000, but in 1974 the group incurred a loss of £350,000.

Causes of Decline

There were four main reasons for R.F.D.'s declining performance in this period.

(*a*) *Lack of control*: This was the critical factor in causing R.F.D.'s problems. The company's financial position was calculated only every six months, and then there was a three-month time-lag before profit and loss statements and balance sheets were produced. There was a lack of budgetary control and the lack of an adequate costing system meant that pricing was wrong. The overhead percentage added to labour and raw material costs, for example, was later found to be substantially inaccurate. In 1971, management decided that control would be improved (and cost savings would result) by grouping four separate activities, that accounted for 60% of group sales, together into one company. The new company was to be known as R.F.D.-

G.Q. Ltd, but its formation had the opposite effect to what management intended: the control problem became worse, because no control *systems* were introduced. Management believed the control problems were greatest in the production area. In an attempt to remedy the situation, they installed a computer and recruited an experienced production manager. The new computer systems were not a success, in part because the employees were unaccustomed to any procedural and administrative disciplines.

(*b*) *Poor management*: The management team operated as a committee to the extent of opening the mail together each morning. Both the quality of decision-making and the team's ability to implement decisions appear to have been poor.

(*c*) *Inefficient manufacturing operations*: There was a lack of adequate production planning and scheduling and, by 1974, there was a thirty-month order back-log.

(*d*) *New factory investment*: R.F.D. built a new manufacturing facility in Newcastle to shift production out of Belfast but, having built the factory, were unable to convince skilled employees to leave Ulster. The factory remained two-thirds empty.

The Crisis

By March 1973, the directors had become sufficiently concerned about the inadequacies of financial reporting and control in R.F.D.-G.Q. Ltd to ask their auditors to assist them in drawing up a suitable system. In doing this, a certain number of accounting anomalies were unearthed. Inventories had been overvalued to the extent that pre-tax profits for the previous financial year had been overstated by £181,000. The reliability of the accounts of R.F.D.-G.Q. Ltd were cast in doubt, and R.F.D. shares were suspended pending clarification. The full gravity of the situation was found out only much later when year-end results of R.F.D.-G.Q. Ltd showed a loss of £756,000 while the other group companies made a profit of only £406,000. The large loss in R.F.D.-G.Q. Ltd was clearly a crisis situation, but the group's financial situation was satisfactory and there was no cash crisis in the sense that a receiver was about to be appointed (see Table 12.8 for a summary of key financial data).

Recovery Actions

R.F.D.'s recovery took place in two phases: from December 1973 to July 1975, and from July 1975 onwards. The two phases correspond to a change of management.

(*a*) *New top management*: After the departure of the R.F.D.-G.Q. managing director in September 1973, a new managing director, Mr G. Boxall, was recruited and appointed in December 1973. Subsequently the group managing director left and was not replaced.

(*b*) *Divisionalization of R.F.D.-G.Q. Ltd*: This loss-making company was split into four operating divisions, each headed by a general manager responsible for the profitability of his own division and put in charge of all functions except finance. About seventy people were made redundant in the process. The group now consisted of six U.K. operating companies and two overseas subsidiaries. Management's rationale for this was simply that 'big problems become more manageable if broken down into smaller ones'.

(*c*) *Introduction of financial control systems*: The company started to work on developing management accounting systems, albeit rather more slowly than many companies in its position would have done. Management, however, was unable to wait for these systems to become operational. Urgent action had to be taken to stop the losses; management therefore approached the problem by making cost estimates in the following way:

- materials: calculated on the basis of the four major materials in the finished item, plus 10%
- labour: known reasonably well already (when reported), plus allowance for downtime and inefficiency
- overheads: previous year's financial statements showed overheads at 450% of direct costs; this percentage was accepted as still valid and applied
- a profit margin was then added.

Rough and ready though this was, it showed that in some cases price increases in the order of 40% were required just to break even.

(*d*) *Immediate price increases*: Price increases were introduced on all products; all major customers were visited personally to inform them of this. All fixed-price contracts, except those with the Ministry of Defence, were renegotiated. A hard line was adopted, as damages for breach of contract were less than the negative margin currently being earned. The Ministry of Defence accounted for a substantial portion of turnover, and an effort was made to understand the M.o.D. pricing formulae, to design products to them, and to have the necessary costings and data available so that R.F.D. could negotiate prices knowing as much as the M.o.D. buyers. One director was appointed to negotiate with the Ministry of Defence; vigorous renegotiation of all unfixed prices, allowable overheads and profit rates took place.

(*e*) *Reduction in sales effort*: Little effort was made to obtain new orders until the back-log of outstanding orders was reduced to six months.

(*f*) *Open communications*: When Mr Boxall took over, he found a company with antiquated procedures. Many of the employees had been with the company for twenty years and were related to one another. There was a huge 'gulf' between management and the workforce, and morale was low. However, Mr Boxall was able to obtain the support of unionized employees by starting a policy of open communications. He kept employees informed via regular speeches and weekly factory meetings during the depth of the crisis; and slowly, as profits improved, so did morale.

By the end of 1974, the recovery strategy had proved successful in terms of short-term financial results. However, in August 1974 the board called in a small consulting firm to review the group's operations; they found that the financial control systems were still inadequate, insufficient attention had been paid to costs, and assets were being under-utilized. One of the consultants, Mr Craig, became a director of the group, and in July 1975 was appointed group managing director. Mr Boxall, who had engineered the 1973/74 recovery, left the company the following month.

Craig undertook the following steps to consolidate the recovery:

(*a*) *Further decentralization*: The operating divisions of R.F.D.-G.Q. Ltd were turned into subsidiary companies, each operating as a profit centre with its own managing director and functional managers (finance, production and marketing). The old divisional general managers were appointed managing directors. Most other senior appointments were also filled from within the group, with the exception of the financial managers, who were recruited from outside. The subsidiary managing directors were made autonomous, except in matters relating to capital investment, transfer pricing and use of financial resources – decisions about which were made by the group managing director, the group finance director and the board. Top management claimed three main benefits from this organization structure: each subsidiary was sufficiently small for its managing director to know what was going on; areas of responsibility were clearly defined; and decisions were made quickly.

(*b*) *Full implementation of financial control system*: By mid-1975 the financial control system was fully installed with the help of Craig and his associates. As group managing director, he implemented it. The system was fairly standard (see Table 12.7).

- budgeting was carried out in the last quarter of the financial year by the subsidiaries and presented to Craig and the group financial director. If it was reasonable and sufficiently ambitious, it was accepted; if not, it was returned for modification
- monthly reports containing the information in Table 12.7 were reviewed by the subsidiary managing directors with Craig and the group finance director.

Table 12.7: *R.F.D. Group Ltd: Monthly Reporting Requirements from Subsidiary Companies*

Accounting information:	Profit and loss statement
	Cash-flow forecast
	Variance analysis (materials, labour, overheads)
	Capital expenditure
	Balance sheet
Reporting information:	Inquiries
	New orders
	Order-book
	Inventories (materials, work-in-progress, finished goods)
	Production output
	Dispatches
	Invoiced sales
	Goods awaiting dispatch
	Payroll

Actual Information Reported Against Budget and Previous Accounting Period

(*c*) *Sale of surplus assets*: The Newcastle factory was sold. The Australian factory was also sold as it was too large for the scale of operations in that country; inflatable manufacturing was moved to

smaller premises and demand for parachutes was met by exports from
the U.K.

(d) *Improvements in manufacturing efficiency*: Various steps were
taken within the subsidiaries to improve productivity.
(i) At R.F.D. Inflatables, for example, manufacturing was reorganized so that all special one-off orders were carried out at Godalming
and all standard orders at Belfast. This allowed longer production runs
in the Belfast factory, resulting in lower unit costs and simplified
control. Special orders are generally more difficult to control and
require more customer liaison than standard items. Thus, by concentrating manufacture of specials at the Godalming factory, management
efforts could be focused more readily on this operation.
(ii) At G.Q. Parachutes, a new managing director entirely rethought
the production organization and closed a packing factory.

(e) *Product-market strategy modified*: Most of the subsidiaries had
some form of competitive advantage throughout this period, usually
in the form of superior product design and, in some cases, in the form
of dominant market positions. Under Craig, however, the subsidiaries
were encouraged to think strategically. One of the principal objectives
was to diversify the customer base to reduce reliance on the Ministry
of Defence. New products, such as oil booms, were manufactured by
R.F.D. Inflatables and another subsidiary moved into the industrial
market for safety netting.

(f) *Management style*: Mr Craig continued the open style of management started by Mr Boxall and made a considerable effort at 'internal'
public relations, convincing the employees that their products were
world-beaters. Considerable publicity was given to the order for life-
saving equipment for Concorde, for example, and one employee was
given a seat on the inaugural flight. Craig changed the company's style
of management from a hierarchical to a more participative one, from
a 'traditional', antiquated approach to business to a results-oriented
approach. He built an organization in which emphasis on tight financial
control did not inhibit initiative and communications.

(g) *Public relations to improve R.F.D.'s image*: The efforts of new
management to improve morale and raise operating standards became
apparent to customers, suppliers and bankers. In all external contacts,
an image of product quality was portrayed.

Results

Five years after the crisis, R.F.D.'s sales had climbed to £21.4 million and profit before tax had climbed to £2.3 million (see Table 12.8). R.F.D.'s recovery had been successful. But in the following year, profits declined sharply as a result of severe price competition, particularly in the specialist textile division. The nature of the problem in 1980 was totally different from that of the early 1970s. Whereas previously the problem had been largely operational, more recent problems are largely strategic in nature.

Table 12.8: *R.F.D. Group Ltd: Key Financial Data, 1972–81 (in £ millions)*

Financial year ending 31 March	Sales	Profit (loss) before tax	P.B.I.T.[1] as percentage of capital employed
1972	6.6	0.4	9.5
1973	7.5	0.3	7.6
1974	7.9	(0.3)	(2.2)
1975	11.6	1.4	23.4
1976	14.7	2.1	31.0
1977	16.0	3.2	35.7
1978	18.7	3.5	34.3
1979	21.4	2.3	18.6
1980	26.4	(0.4)	8.3[2]
1981	27.3	0.8	9.6

NOTES
1. Profit before interest and tax.
2. Before charging £1.2 million for 'rationalization and reorganization'.
Source: Annual Reports.

Notes

1. 'How Staveley Stuck Together', *Management Today*, May 1979.
2. 'Redman Heenan's Second Phase', *Management Today*, June 1976.
3. Ibid.
4. Ibid.

13. Successful Recovery Situations in Retailing

Recovery strategies in retailing are illustrated through case-histories of Burton, M.F.I. and Queensway. The principal causes of decline in each situation were quite different, and yet there are certain similarities in the recovery approaches because of the unique characteristics of the retailing sector.

With the exception of Burton's, the case-histories are of furniture retailers. Consequently, it is not surprising that the business cycle should play an apparently important role in both decline and recovery, since the furniture industry itself is notoriously more cyclical than the economy as a whole. M.F.I. is peculiar in that the cause of its crisis was not retailing but mail order. In that case, expansion of retail outlets was the appropriate recovery strategy; whereas in most other retail crises, closure of retail outlets is necessary. M.F.I. is also peculiar in that new top management was able to work side by side with the entrepreneurial founders of the company during the recovery phase.

Burton's case is unique as a retailing turnaround in that the firm had substantial manufacturing capacity and substantial product-market change was necessary to effect recovery. Queensway was another two-stage turnaround; it illustrates, once again, the need for vigorous implementation of a recovery strategy. Thus, although John Murphy had introduced new control systems when he took over as managing director, Phil Harris subsequently tightened control after his carpet company had acquired Queensway.

The Burton Group Ltd

The Burton Group is a holding company consisting of retailing chains including menswear, womenswear and office supplies, a manufacturing resource that supports its menswear chain, and a property division that contains a valuable portfolio of high-street freehold sites. Started in 1901 by Montague Burton as a single shop, Burton's grew to become the largest multiple tailoring business in the U.K., with 616 retail branches by the time of Montague Burton's death in 1952. The firm grew by specializing in men's made-to-measure suits at the lower-price end of the market.

In 1969 the firm found itself with a management succession problem; the Burton family, who still controlled the voting shares, called in Ladislaw Rice, forty-three-year-old management consultant from Urwick Orr, with no retailing or clothing industry experience, to become group chief executive. At this time, Burton's was a typical stagnant company: still profitable, but its assets were under-utilized, and it was unresponsive to the trends in its environment. Rice recruited fifty new executives within twelve months and created a small executive group, consisting of a commercial director, financial director and personnel adviser who were responsible for planning and implementing group strategies. The new management team was faced with the following problems:

(i) a rapidly declining market for made-to-measure suits and an increase in consumer demand for ready-to-wear suits
(ii) growing competition from foreign ready-to-wear manufacturers and from new retail outlets (e.g. boutiques), and from large multiple stores (e.g. Marks and Spencer)
(iii) 40% of the demand for suits was in the under-thirty age-group, where Bourton's image and representation were poor
(iv) old-fashioned shops with insufficient floor space for the display of ready-to-wear merchandise
(v) an internal failure to perceive that merchandising of ready-to-wear clothes differed from that of made-to-measure
(vi) a large manufacturing operation, consisting of eleven factories, geared exclusively to providing made-to-measure suits for the firm's retail outlets
(vii) inefficient manufacturing methods, due to failure to introduce modern production techniques which resulted in above-average labour costs for the industry
(viii) under-utilized property assets which gave a pre-tax return on capital employed of only 9.5% (with property valued at 1961 prices).
(ix) inadequate inventory control systems
(x) a large, inflexible organization.

Although Burton's was not in a 'classic' turnaround situation at this time, the strategy adopted by Rice and his team nevertheless contained many of the generic turnaround strategies identified in Chapter 4. However, as we shall see, the combined effect of these strategies, together with the continuing trends in the clothing industry away from made-to-measure suits, was to put Burton's into a 'classic' turnaround situation (i.e. a loss-making position) by 1975/76. In discussing the causes of decline, our emphasis will therefore be on why management's actions did not work.

Causes of Decline

(*a*) *Inappropriate product-market strategy for menswear*: Burton decided to expand in ready-to-wear clothing in response to the rapid decline in demand for made-to-measure suits. The percentage of suits made to measure declined from 62% in 1969 to 41% in 1973. One factory was turned exclusively into a ready-to-wear plant and other factories filled their seasonal troughs with ready-to-wear clothing. Within each Burton shop, three different product ranges were offered in suits: the 'director suit' (executive, high-priced), the 'town and country suit' and the 'Mr Burton' line (younger, trendy styling); in addition to stocking their own ready-to-wear lines, shops were stocked with some imported product-lines. The objective was to broaden Burton's image to attract new customer segments. The new strategy was unsuccessful because:

(i) Burton's shops were unsuitable for the type of merchandising required by the new strategy.
(ii) Burton's were unable to attract new customers, because of its firmly established image as a retailer for conservative, middle-aged, lower socio-economic consumers.
(iii) As Burton's placed more emphasis on its ready-to-wear range, established customers became confused and alienated.
(iv) Pressure to fill up manufacturing capacity with Burton's own line of ready-to-wear products resulted in retail management having less purchasing flexibility than boutiques and other ready-to-wear competitors that did not have their own manufacturing facilities.
(v) Burton's lost market share in the declining made-to-measure business, thanks to the execution of more focused strategies by competitors such as Hepworth (more design-oriented for the more affluent consumer) and John Collier (good design at lower price than Burton's for the more price-sensitive consumer).

Burton's fundamental problem lay in its failure to segment the menswear market. It attempted to be all things to all men, and as a result failed to develop a strong market position with any one product group for any one group of customers.

It is interesting to contrast Burton's failure to adopt an appropriate strategy for its menswear division with its success in turning around the unprofitable Peter Robinson chain, using the 'Top Shop' concept. Top Shop was introduced as a young-fashion, shop-within-a-shop concept in the Peter Robinson chain. It was young and dramatic in appearance and its keynote was adaptability, with movable racks and temporary graphics. The crucial factor in the success of the Top Shops, that spread throughout the Peter Robinson chain in 1970 and 1971, was this: for the first time Burton was using market segmentation to create a niche, aiming at the thirteen- to thirty-five-year-olds, with a combination of high fashion and competitive prices. Unlike the menswear division, Top Shop was not held down by a huge, inefficient and outdated manufacturing capacity. It had complete buying freedom, it was small and adaptable and it was controlled by retailers who knew how to apply the basic principles of retail marketing. Of course, it was easier for Burton to pick up market share in the large womenswear market, where it had not had much previous representation, than to retrieve market share in the menswear market, where it was the market leader under attack by competitors with more focused strategies.

(*b*) *Excess manufacturing capacity*: Management tried (although rather belatedly) to reduce manufacturing costs through greater mechanization and the use of new cutting methods; but the real problem was excess capacity as demand for made-to-measure suits declined. Two factories were closed, but this still left nine other plants, including the largest clothing factory in Europe, which employed 10,000 people. The existence of manufacturing capacity was a distinct disadvantage in the retail market for ready-to-wear clothing, where success was increasingly dependent on purchasing flexibility. There were two main difficulties in closing plants: first, most of the plants were located in the Leeds area, and unions (and local plant management?) fought hard against closures; second, the plants were unsaleable, and closure would mean huge write-offs – something top management wanted to avoid, if at all possible. As a result, plant closures and rationalization of the manufacturing facilities did not proceed as fast as the economics of the situation demanded. Exit barriers were high.

(*c*) *Confused organization philosophy*: Rice reorganized Burton into eight operating divisions, each of which was considered a separate profit centre; the manufacturing division was separated from retailing, and became a separate profit centre. The factories would have to become more marketing-oriented: no longer would they be asked to dictate fabric choices and styles. While in theory this was fine, in practice the top management team was not unified in its approach to running the business. The difference was fundamentally one of differing perceptions of the business and management philosophy. In particular the finance director, Jim Power (who was already in the company before Rice arrived) was reluctant to allow the retail division complete freedom of action in the ready-to-wear market, because of the heavy overhead burden of the manufacturing facilities. After the economic downturn in 1974 Power's arguments gained precedence, and he took over the menswear division and for a while in late 1976 was in effective control of the group. He dismantled the profit centres, unified manufacturing with retailing, moved the London buying operation (and his office) back to Leeds to be located with the factories, and attempted to maintain manufacturing volume through price reductions.

(*d*) *Diversification*: Rice believed that because the suit market was flat, assets should be released to be used in more exciting areas. He wanted to move away from Burton's dependence on one product and diversify the group's activities. It was felt that 'any well-managed business capable of expansion, but in need of Burton's expertise in property and finance', would be suitable for acquisition.[1] The new management team identified Burton's main asset as its shops, which were in prime sites in most high streets in the country; they felt that they could apply clothing retailing techniques to other retailing industries. This led to huge acquisitions of many unrelated companies in industries where Burton had had no prior experience.

Burton made five acquisitions and started up one new retail venture ('Orange Hand', a chain of boys' fashion shops) between 1970 and 1973, increasing the number of stores under its control from 645 to 920 (see Table 13.1). The acquisitions were: Evans' Outsizes (a chain of 74 stores selling ready-made clothing for women with 'fuller' figures); Ryman's Office Supplies (the leading operator in a growth market which could use Burton's retail properties); the St Rémy retail chain (a chain of thirty-five retail outlets in France that would provide an outlet for Burton's factory in Boulogne); Green's Cameras (a camera and hi-fi chain that was seen as an entry into the growing leisure market); and

Trumps Employment Agency. With the exception of Evans, not one of these new ventures was successful. Evans was the exception because it had a dominant position in its specialized market segment and the firm was efficiently run by Cyril Spencer at the time of acquisition. Profitability declined, however, for the two years following acquisition as Spencer was promoted to other jobs within the Burton group. With both Ryman and Green, Burton found that retailing experience in one sector (clothing) does not guarantee retailing success in other areas. The products were different, and hence the recipes for success were different. In France there were considerable costs of integrating the existing Burton stores with the St Rémy chain; and the situation was a microcosm of that facing the menswear division in the U.K.

(*e*) *Slow implementation of new control systems*: Rice recognized the need for a complete set of management controls. When he arrived at Burton, there were only two qualified accountants in the whole group, and no capability to produce monthly consolidated accounts. Furthermore, there was no branch control system linking sales, purchasing and inventories. One of the benefits of purchasing Evans (Outsizes) was that Evans already had a computerized branch-control system that worked effectively and could, in theory, be transferred throughout the Burton group. According to a *Management Today* article:

. . . Views differ about the value of the early work which Rice's team gave to developing the Evans' system for the whole group; Halpern [the current chief executive] claims there was no stock control or ordering system working when he took over the menswear division in 1977.[2]

Further evidence of the slow implementation of new control systems is that, as late as 1974, Burton still did not have adequate cash-flow management. When Brian North, recruited from B.S.R. in 1973, took over as director of finance from Jim Power in 1974, the practice of divisional directors 'writing their own cheques from one big bank account was stopped'. North instituted a system under which each division was given its own bank account and strictly defined limits, and the bank was instructed to stop cheques outside those limits. 'We only did it once and, boy, was it effective!' says North.

The Crisis

The overall result of Burton's strategies was declining profitability, with the exception of 1973 when results were improved by the tremendous consumer spending boom of that year. The recession of 1974/75 reduced demand and operating margins fell sharply as Burton tried to maintain volume in a declining market by lowering prices. Burton went into a trading loss in the second half of the 1976 financial year, and the year-end pre-tax loss was £2.4 million. The results for the period are shown in Table 13.2.

During 1976, Rice recognized that most of his diversification efforts had failed; he started to divest its peripheral retailing activities: Orange Hand was closed in January, the Brown's of Chester department stores group was sold in May, and by the end of the year the Ryman branches located in the North and Midlands and Green's Leisure Centres had also been sold.

Recovery Actions

(a) *New top management*: At the end of 1976 – two weeks before the disastrous 1976 results were announced – Ladislaw Rice assumed the position of chairman and gave up his position as chief executive.

One may ask why the Board of Directors had not taken action sooner after it became apparent that Burton's strategy was not working. The answer would appear to be an ineffective board of directors. A *Sunday Times* article described the situation as follows:

[Rice] has, in effect, been ever so nicely pushed upstairs – because the Burtons could not for the life of them bring themselves to kick anybody upstairs. This is why the agony has been for so long drawn out. 'As far as the business was concerned the sons were very kind, very indecisive,' says one former employee. On top of that they'd had 16 years of being made to feel small by Sidney Jacobson when he and his brother Lennie were brought in from Jackson The Tailor to ensure management succession after the company's founder, Sir Montague Burton, died [in 1952]. The sons put up with 16 years of this before another recharge was necessary.'[3]

Cyril Spencer (originally from Evans) became the new chief executive, and Ralph Halpern (from Top Shop) became deputy managing director. Both had proven track records in retailing and had been responsible for the only successful retailing divisions in Burton's. They faced many of the same problems faced by Rice and his team seven years earlier. They returned to Rice's original philosophy of operating profit centres and moved buying back to London away from the production units. Jim Power left the company.

(b) *New product-market strategy for menswear*: The menswear division's previous retail strategy was scrapped and two separate chains of retail shops were established, each with a distinct image. Following the success of the Top Shop chain, that recognized the benefits of market segmentation within womenswear, a similar strategy was adopted in the form of the 'Top Man' shops. These shops catered to the fifteen-to-twenty-four age-group, and Top Man aimed to become the market leader in this segment, since the young men's market was fragmented, with no dominant chain. Management also recognized that 40% of purchases in menswear shops were made by men and women together. Therefore, following Lady At Lord John's lead in having two divisions in one location, Top Man was often located at the same site as Top Shop. The second chain was a new kind of Burton with modernized shops, new buyers to improve merchandise and style, and catered to the twenty-five-to-thirty-five age-group. Abandoning the traditional market for older men, the new Burton distinguished itself from the jazzy Top Man environment by more conservative lighting, interiors and clothing styles. The made-to-measure section received new attention; management decided it was an important aspect of the Burton Group and would figure in both the Top Man and Burton chains.

(c) *Increased emphasis on womenswear retailing*: Spencer and Halpern's group strategy was to increase the share of profits coming from womenswear retailing by increasing Burton's share of this market. They continued to open up Top Shop outlets, and in 1979 purchased the Dorothy Perkins chain (240 outlets) from British Land (69% of the £15.2 million purchase price being paid by transferring some of Burton's large property portfolio). Thus, by year end 1980, Burton's sales of womenswear were on par with those of menswear, although profitability was not yet as high, due to the need to undertake a 'turnaround' on the Dorothy Perkins chain.

(d) *Branch modernization*: Burton entered into a heavy investment programme to modernize and enlarge retail shops. Over 300 branches were refitted at an investment cost which amounted to a peak in one year of £18 million. The combination of new ready-to-wear merchandise and shop refitting increased branch turnover significantly – by 80–100% in many cases.

(e) *Store closure*: During 1977 and 1978, Halpern and North, to whom Spencer had delegated responsibility for menswear, closed 232 Burton Menswear and Jackson The Tailor shops (while opening 44 Top Man shops). The decline in the number of retail shops under Spencer as compared to the growth under Rice is shown in Table 13.1. At the same time, the Jackson head office in Newcastle was closed down and other overheads pruned.

(f) *Plant closure*: The manufacturing division was losing well over £3 million annually at the beginning of 1977 when Halpern and North decided to tackle the problem that Rice's team had failed to resolve. They reduced the large Hudson Road factory in Leeds to cloth cutting and warehousing only, reducing manufacturing capacity by one-third in the process. However, losses continued at almost the same level as before, so in August 1978 they closed a further four plants, leaving the group with only four of the eleven plants with which it had started the decade. The 1979 loss from manufacturing was reduced to £600,000, but in 1980 this increased again to £2.8 million, and further steps were taken to halve manufacturing capacity again – to only two plants.

Table 13.1: *Burton Group Ltd: Number of Retail Shops at Financial Year End, 1970–78*
(excludes employment agencies)

	1970	1972	1974	1976	1978
Menswear outlets					
Burton's Menswear	512	510	481	444	279
Jackson The Tailor	84	88	100	93	26
Top Man	–	–	–	–	44
Womenswear outlets					
Peter Robinson/Top Shop	37	39	–	–	–
Peter Robinson	–	–	13	1	1
Top Shop	–	–	38	61	65
Evans (Outsizes)	–	77	90	91	83
Other retail outlets					
Burton's of London (France)	11	50	49	45	40
Ryman	–	64	86	63	47
Brown's of Chester	1	1	4	–	–
Orange Hand	–	6	14	–	–
Green's Leisure Centres	–	–	33	43	–
TOTAL	645	835	908	841	585

(g) *Close mail-order operation*: The mail-order business lost over £1.2 million in 1980 and a decision was made to close the business down.

(h) *Tighter branch control systems*: The group now has a highly detailed computerized control system operating throughout the group. The system differs very little from that started by Rice, but the difference is that it has now been *implemented*.

Results

The actions instituted by Spencer and his team have reduced employment from 21,400 to 11,000 by the end of 1979. Burton's profitability has been increased substantially, although there have been big 'below-the-line' write-offs (see Table 13.2). There is still some way to go, however, before recovery is complete. The French operation has lost money in six out of the last seven years and mirrors the problem faced by the U.K. menswear division in the 1970s. More retail branches still need to be closed down. In the longer term, it is still unclear whether Burton's segmentation of the menswear market will prove correct. Fashion and hence segmentation change rapidly. However, Burton is

Table 13.2: *Burton Group Ltd: Sales and Profitability, 1972–81* (*in £ millions*)

Year (ending 31 August)	Sales	Profit/(Loss) before tax and extraordinary charges	Profit before tax as percentage of sales	Extraordinary charges (provisions and write-offs)
1972	100.2	8.0	8.0	–
1973	109.8	8.3	7.6	0.4
1974	114.9	3.3	2.9	–
1975	134.4	2.5	(1.9)	0.7
1976	133.2	(2.4)	(1.8)	2.1
1977	139.1	(5.1)	(3.7)	9.5
1978	141.1	6.8	4.8	3.8
1979	150.5	16.9	11.2	3.4 Cr.
1980	196.4	12.6	6.4	10.3
1981	189.6	16.4	8.6	2.0 Cr.*

* Profit on disposal of properties (£10.6 million) less costs of rationalization (£8.6 million).
Source: Company Accounts.

now run by clothing retailers who have a successful track-record and can adapt to changing market conditions.

Management's attempt at turnaround was unsuccessful because it failed to take the drastic action needed in the key problem area: the menswear division and its associated manufacturing capacity. Rice was not a hatchet man by nature and therefore, when up against a family-controlled board (and a finance director) who were emotionally attached to manufacturing and the traditional made-to-measure business, he failed to take the strong action needed for recovery. The required action was clearly much more drastic than even Spencer's team first realized, since they have gone through a succession of plant and branch closures which, at the time of writing, are not yet finished.

M.F.I. Furniture Group Ltd

M.F.I. was founded in 1964 by two entrepreneurs, Noel Lister and the late Donald Searle, to sell a limited range of low-price furniture by mail order, using national advertising. Most of the products were for home assembly, and advertising took place in the national press and in a variety of weekly and monthly magazines. The majority of goods sold were manufactured exclusively for M.F.I., and Noel Lister worked closely with manufacturers to obtain specially designed goods at competitive prices. The stores had lower overheads than their high-street competitors. The retail-warehouse concept was based on high volume, low margins, low overheads and media advertising to attract the customers. Substantial stocks were held to ensure immediate availability.

Generous credit terms, internally financed by M.F.I., were available to both mail-order and retail customers. By 1971, nine retail warehouses had been opened, after-tax profits reached £542,000 on sales of £7.0 million, and M.F.I. went public. M.F.I. was a success story! In the next two years – during the now infamous 'Barber' boom – sales increased by 121% and after-tax profits by 134%; but in mid-1973, M.F.I.'s profitability started to deteriorate rapidly. At this time mail order accounted for 54% of sales. What went wrong?

Causes of Decline

(*a*) *A decline in market demand for mail order*: There was a general downturn in all mail-order business in the second half of 1973 as consumers' disposable income declined, due to the government's income policy, rising inflation and the imposition of tighter hire-purchase controls. The result of changing market conditions meant not only lower sales for M.F.I. but also a rapid switch from cash to credit sales and a threefold increase in bad debts during 1973.

(b) *Increased mail-order operating costs*: M.F.I.'s mail-order business became increasingly uncompetitive in price as compared to retail outlets. The rising cost of sending goods by post, high damage in transit rates and rising labour costs meant that the price advantage of buying via mail order was eroded. Management's response was to *reduce* prices in an attempt to increase volume.

The Crisis

At least six months before market demand started to decline, M.F.I.'s group profit margin had started to decline, even though sales were continuing to increase rapidly. If we could isolate gross profit margins in the mail-order business during this period, we would probably see the tell-tale combination of increasing sales at decreasing margins at an even earlier stage. This is a very common sympton of failure in growth firms (see page 52). By the time management realized that their situation was not just a short-term market hiccup, M.F.I.'s profit for the six months to 30 November 1973 was down from £653,000 (for the previous six months) to £247,000 on a decreased volume.

Recovery Actions

(a) *Board decision to expand retail operations*: The board had already taken a decision in early 1973 to expand retail operations. By the end of 1973, the board realized that action was needed to stop the sharply declining performance and that it was the mail-order business that was causing the problem. They decided that the only solution was to expand the retail side of the business – this was still relatively healthy – and steps were taken to open new stores in the first half of 1974.

(b) *Appointment of consultants*: The board realized that the change of corporate strategy towards greater emphasis on retailing would require an essentially new M.F.I. with a new marketing strategy, a changed organizational structure and new management control systems. A firm of management consultants was appointed in early 1974 to make recommendations.

(c) *Appointment of new management*: The consultants' report argued that M.F.I. needed a new management structure and should appoint new line managers with retailing experience and a new managing director with 'big company' experience. The board subsequently appointed Mr Jack Seabright as joint managing director on 1 August 1974. Noel Lister became joint managing director and Donald Searle was appointed deputy chairman, although both founders had greatly reduced executive powers.

(d) *Adoption of a new management structure*: The new management structure that was adopted was unique; it had as its primary objective the blending of Jack Seabright's professional management skills with the entrepreneurial skills that had characterized M.F.I. in its early stages of growth. Policy decisions were split from day-to-day operating decisions, as is shown in Figure 13.1. Each policy group consisted of three members of senior management with the relevant experience and skills in that area, together with Jack Seabright. A major feature of the new structure was the way in which Searle and Lister were able to concentrate solely on those aspects of the business where their expertise and flair could be most effectively utilized, Searle on advertising and Lister on buying and property.

(e) *Financial credit stopped and financial controls improved*: M.F.I.'s profit decline continued throughout 1974 and a loss was recorded for the half-year ending 30 November 1974; however, more importantly, the company was now in a cash-flow crisis as a result of a sharp increase in bad debts and a switch by customers from cash to credit sales. At the same time, M.F.I.'s suppliers were demanding quicker payment as they feared for M.F.I.'s demise, following that of two other mail-order operators, New Dimension and Headquarters and General. Seabright's reaction was to drop M.F.I.-financed credit and to increase the provision for bad debts from about £650,000 to about £900,000.

(f) *Closure of mail order*: Before Seabright's arrival at M.F.I., the possibility of running down or phasing out the mail-order business never occurred to management. Seabright set about persuading the board that the mail-order business should be run down. The phasing-out of mail order, however, was planned as a gradual process, since management feared that a rapid exit would cause bad debts to increase sharply. Consequently advertising was continued, albeit at a reduced level. Seven months after deciding to phase out mail order, in March

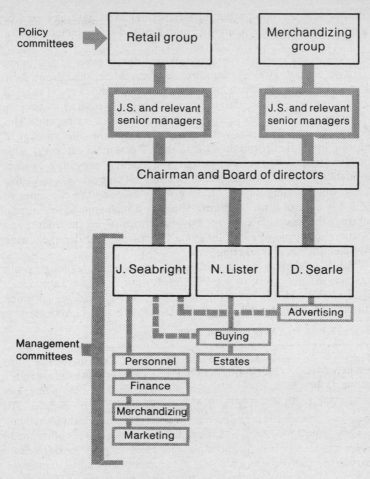

Figure 13.1: *Organizational Structure of M.F.I.*

1975 the decision was taken to close down the operation completely because unit overhead costs were rising fast as mail-order sales declined. The mail-order business was finally closed down in September 1975.

(*g*) *Raise additional finance*: A five-year bank loan of £500,000 was negotiated to solve the immediate short-term cash problem and to provide cash for retail expansion. A further £180,000 was raised by issuing one million new shares to Philip Lait and Co., a major supplier.

(*h*) *New retail marketing strategy*: Within three years of the board decision to concentrate on furniture retailing, M.F.I. had grown from 17 retail branches to 39, and was now operating nationwide. The rapid expansion was possible due to the small capital required in opening new stores and the short pay-back period of about six months. This policy of rapid expansion was accomplished by a product strategy of moving up-market (from the D/E to the C2 consumer category). This involved improving product design and quality, providing product availability by holding high inventories and keeping prices competitive while still spending money on advertising to bring the consumer to M.F.I.'s edge-of-town locations. The was a high-volume/low-margin strategy that necessitated astute buying policies (along the 'Marks and Spencer' principle of controlling one's suppliers) and the application of 'scientific' retail marketing skills.

M.F.I.'s recovery strategy of expansion worked, although profit margins did not return to pre-1973 levels until 1978 (see Table 13.3). By mid-1980, M.F.I. had a total of 140 branches, including 66 which it obtained when it purchased Status Discount Stores in May 1980.

Table 13.3: *M.F.I.: Sales and Profitability, 1971–81*

Year (Financial year ending 31 May)	Sales (£ m)	Profit after tax (£ m)	Profit after tax as percentage of sales
1971	£6.1	£0.5	8.2
1972	10.5	0.9	8.6
1973	15.5	1.3	8.4
1974	16.6	0.8	4.8
1975	15.2	–	–
1976	21.1	0.9	4.3
1977	33.7	1.5	4.4
1978	55.0	5.2	9.4
1979	87.5	10.6	12.1
1980	127.3	12.6	9.9
1981	190.8[1]	10.1	5.3

NOTE

1. Reflects acquisition of Status Discount.

Queensway Discount Warehouses Ltd

Queensway is a chain of discount warehouses established in the late 1960s and early 1970s to sell furniture and carpets at edge-of-town locations. Queensway is somewhat different from the other turnarounds discussed in this book in that the turnaround effort actually began at the moment in time when the firm's profit were at an all-time high in 1975.

Causes of Decline

(*a*) *Boardroom dispute*: Throughout the early 1970s, there were a series of interpersonal conflicts between Queensway's founder, Mr Gerry Parish, and his fellow board-members, that were destructive of the organization. By 1974, Gerry Parish had left to live in France (reportedly as a condition of a proposed but subsequently postponed public flotation of the company) and a new twenty-seven-year-old managing director, Terry Wells, was appointed. The situation did not improve as Wells was reported 'to spend a considerable time in the company's Rolls-Royce and helicopter', rather than running the business. In late 1974, Parish returned from France in an effort to curb Wells's activities and an open split developed in the board. By the spring of 1975, four Queensway directors had resigned to establish a rival firm, and Wells disappeared without warning.

(*b*) *Cyclical decline in demand*: The high-volume, low-margin discount warehouse business is highly susceptible to changes in consumer demand. From 1975 to 1977, demand dropped sharply, and so did profits.

(*c*) *Salary increase*: A few months after the appointment of a new managing director, John Murphy, in September 1975 (see below) the firm's personnel director convinced Parish (unbeknown to Murphy) to index-link salaries to inflation. By the time Murphy had discovered this, employees had been informed that there would be a 36% per annum wage increase; this meant that it was then impossible to develop a meaningful incentive scheme for sales representatives. The personnel director was fired, but Murphy was stuck with a drastic reduction in both gross margins and salesman motivation, just as market demand was falling.

(*d*) *Lack of financial controls*: Queensway control systems had not developed as the firm grew; they were ill equipped to cope with a fall in demand. Budgeting and cash-flow controls were very weak: there was no way of knowing which branches were profitable since only branch sales data were available but these were inaccurate; buying decisions were taken on inventory figures that were two weeks out of date; the branch managers had complete freedom, with no controls from head office, and all branches (twenty-four in 1975) reported verbally to one man, the sales director.

Queensway's financial performance deteriorated through 1976 and 1977, but the firm never reached the cash crisis point. The appointment of John Murphy as managing director in September 1975, two years before the firm found itself in a loss-making position, was in many respects the start of the turnaround period, although – as we shall see – the turnaround took place in two stages.

First-Stage Recovery Actions

(*a*) *Appointment of new managing director*: Murphy's appointment was unusual, to say the least. He had originally been hired by Parish as a consultant in the spring of 1975 to develop a corporate plan. When Wells disappeared, Murphy was asked by a deputation of the staff to run the company and Parish agreed. Murphy took a number of immediate actions, that are described below.

(*b*) *Increase overdraft*: Murphy increased the firm's overdraft from £1.25 million to £1.75 million and gave the bank assurances that recovery was under way.

(*c*) *Stop board meetings*: Murphy preferred to run the company via management meetings which he chaired rather than through board meetings at which Parish would be present.

(*d*) *Changes in distribution and maintenance systems*: All distribution and maintenance had been undertaken out of Norwich (the company's head office); but this meant that maintenance was expensive (a van once went from Norwich to Dundee to change some electric-light bulbs!) and furniture was damaged due to excessive handling.

(*e*) *Appointment of new managers*: Murphy appointed a new finance director and a new marketing director. Marketing was a key function, since advertising expenses accounted for half the gross margin of 30%.

(*f*) *Improve control systems*: Murphy instituted new financial and purchasing control procedure. To facilitate control over the branches, four regional managers were appointed, reporting to the sales director.

(*g*) *Close six branches*: Throughout this period, new branches were continuing to be opened, so that there were twenty-seven branches by 1976. Not all were profitable – particularly the smaller ones – but, due to the lack of control systems, the unprofitable branches were not easy to identify. However, Murphy closed six branches, at the same time improving general branch appearance, which he found helped sales in the long term.

Murphy's actions improved staff motivation and control at Queensway, but the problem of ownership – and in particular Parish's relationship with key managers – remained. Parish was under pressure to sell and he himself approached forty-four potential buyers in an eighteen-month period. To help the problem, Murphy approached I.C.F.C. and National Westminster Bank, who took a combined 30% interest in Queensway. Early in 1977, Murphy approached Harris Carpets; they saw Queensway as an ideal purchase to expand their carpet retailing business that already consisted of ninety-three shops.

Second-Stage Recovery Actions

In July 1977 – by which time Queensway was making trading losses – Harris acquired Queensway and the second stage of the turnaround began. Harris took the following actions:

(i) He fired Murphy and all but one of the other board members and replaced them with his own team.

(ii) He closed seven branches, particularly those not in the mainstream T.V. regions.

(iii) He closed the Queensway headquarters in Norwich and managed the company from the Harris office in Kent.

(iv) He centralized all control systems on himself. Store managers telephoned his office with trading figures four times a week, including weekends.

Harris's turnaround strategy was no different from that followed by Murphy except in two important respects: timing and quality of implementation. There was a cyclical up-swing in demand in the first half of 1978, which obviously helped Harris, but more important were the more vigorous implementation procedures adopted by Harris.

Notes

1. J. Stopford, D. Channon and D. Norburn, *British Business Policy: A Casebook*, Macmillan 1975, p. 167.
2. 'The Retailoring of Burton', *Management Today*, February 1980.
3. 'Gone for a Burton', *Sunday Times*, 28 November 1976.

14. Non-crisis Recovery Situations

Non-crisis recovery situations appear to fall into two groups: those where turnaround strategies are used prior to a serious crisis developing (as at Muirhead in 1970), and those where an entrepreneurial management takes over a stagnant company with the aim of building on and expanding its operations. Typical of such situations is Pentos, built up by Terry Maher, and Alpine Holdings, in which a controlling interest was purchased by Jimmy Gulliver and his associates.

The reader will observe from the case-histories that many of the same management actions used in crisis situations are adopted in non-crisis situations.

Muirhead Ltd

Today the Muirhead group of companies is involved in the design, production and sale of high-technology electronic and electro-mechanical components and systems. The major U.K. subsidiaries of Muirhead Ltd are Muirhead Data Communication (M.D.C.) Ltd and Muirhead Vactric Components Ltd (M.V.C.). M.D.C. manufactures and markets the Muirhead range of fascimile transmission systems, while M.V.C. produces and markets a wide range of electro-mechanical and electronic components from aircraft engine control systems to D.C. motors. Muirhead's other U.K. subsidiaries include Integrated Photomatrix Ltd, which handles opto-electronic components and systems, and Muirhead Leasings Ltd, which provides leasing and rental facilities to customers for Muirhead products. Muirhead has several manufacturing and sales subsidiaries overseas.

Muirhead went public in 1960, and for the first few years both sales and profitability increased at a fast rate. But after 1964, when return on capital employed reached 30%, sales stagnated and profit margins declined so that, by 1970, profit (before interest and tax) was only 3% of sales, and return on capital employed was also 3% (see Table 14.1). The major causes of declining performance and the actions taken to effect a turnaround in the 1970s are discussed below.

Causes of Decline

(*a*) *Poor top management*: The management of the 1960s was oriented towards the technical side of the business rather than to the planning and control side. There was no shortage of new management. As one executive said: 'As the number of Indians rose so did the number of Chiefs . . . so much so that an extension of the executive dining room had to be built.'

(*b*) *Failure of new product range*: The company launched a new range of fascimile transmission equipment for offices in 1965, in addition to its larger models. For this purpose, a special salesforce had been recruited from other office equipment suppliers and an advertising campaign mounted in the appropriate trade journals. Although the office equipment range never accounted for more than 10% of Muirhead's turnover, its adverse effect on costs was disproportionately great. The range suffered from severe problems of unreliability that were never solved, and the project was finally written off in 1969. In retrospect, management believes that the market for this range had been inadequately researched and that the launch had gone ahead before the machinery had been properly developed.

(*c*) *Increased competition*: In about 1964, Muirhead began to exhibit the classic symptoms of the growth company in trouble: sales still increasing but profit margins starting to decline. The principal reason for declining profit margins in the mid-1960s was increased competition from Muirhead's competitors (Xerox, Plessey, Siemens, etc.) in a market sector where technology was maturing and the growth rate of the market was slowing down. Competitors with larger financial and technical resources than Muirhead and lower unit costs were all fighting for market share. In an attempt to compete, Muirhead held or reduced its selling price in the face of rising variable costs.

(*c*) *Lack of management control*: Although high precision was (and is) required in the products made by Muirhead, the company began to make the mistake of pursuing technical excellence as an end in itself. Little control was exercised over the growth of the R. & D. department, which was free to develop products with little consideration for their commercial viability. Equally, the production departments often produced unnecessarily high quality. Apart from the cost penalty of this, there were difficulties in attracting the numbers of skilled craftsmen required from the local employment catchment area.

Purchasing control was inadequate in a number of ways. No part commonality studies were done, with the result that functionally identical parts were often bought from several different suppliers. Purchase orders were issued immediately a manufacturing programme was initiated, with the result that fast-delivery items could sit in the stores for most of the six months that the complex products took to manufacture. With bought-in parts and raw materials representing about 30% of total costs, this was an expensive practice.

As the company's profitability fell, the laxity of its control over creditors and debtors became more obvious. Muirhead had always made a practice of paying creditors within thirty days of the invoice and, even in the adverse conditions of the late 1960s, was still turning creditors over about every seven weeks. Debtors, however, were cleared much more slowly – the debtor turnover being ten weeks in the early 1960s, rising to nineteen weeks by 1970. Some idea of the cost of this lack of control may be obtained by comparing these figures with those that have been achieved since. Using the 1976 figures as an example of what is possible (fourteen weeks debtor turnover, thirteen weeks creditor turnover), the debtors could have been reduced from an average of about £1.5 million to about £1.1 million and the creditors stretched from £0.7 million to £1.3 million.

Recovery Actions

Muirhead's recovery took place in two stages. The first stage (1970–72) was characterized by actions taken to return Muirhead to its formei level of profitability; and the second stage was one of growth by acquisition.

(*a*) *Appointment of new top management*: In February 1970, Sir Raymond Brown was appointed managed director of Muirhead. The company was not in a financial crisis, although the debt/equity ratio had increased and the interest cover declined. Sir Raymond's management style has been described as courteous and informal, yet one that is questioning and control-oriented. Ten members of the former senior management team were made redundant in the first twelve months, and a new finance director was appointed.

(*b*) *Reorganization*: A divisional reorganization structure was adopted. Each divisional managing director was given full responsibility, but tight financial control was maintained at the centre (see below).

(*c*) *Improved management control systems*: The job of the new finance director (appointed in 1971) was primarily to reduce costs throughout the company. He also introduced new cash-flow controls, paying particular attention to working capital. It was, however, Sir Raymond's use of the budgeting system above all else which led to better control and lower costs.

Sir Raymond's approach was informal: managers were asked to scrutinize their own budgets for the coming year and to inform him of any savings that could be made. If none were forthcoming, they would be invited to re-examine their figures to make absolutely certain that this was the case. Once the set of cost budgets had been revised, they were compared against the projected sales figures for that period and the required profit margins for those sales. If a shortfall still existed, the whole process would be repeated until budgeted and required margins were comparable.

Sir Raymond took a very detailed interest in divisional operations to satisfy himself that further savings were not possible. If he decided that the opposite was the case, the usual consequence was that the manager either ceased to work for the company or was moved. The final version of the budgets was considered totally binding, although any deviations from budget during the year would be assessed individually before recriminatory action against the manager concerned was considered.

(*d*) *Product-market changes*: The marketing emphasis for facsimile equipment was moved away from the private to the public sector. Government, local-authority and nationalized-industry contracts were sought, rather than one-off private companies. Product quality was also changed. Muirhead had a reputation for producing a 'Rolls-Royce product for the price of a Ford'. The decision was taken actually to *reduce* the quality to a standard level which would still be acceptable but, at the same time, required less manufacturing skill and time. Part of the reason for this decision was that skilled labour was increasingly difficult to find, and it would enable the company to use less skilled operators.

(*e*) *Reduction in manufacturing costs*: For the first time, purchasing requirements were analysed for such details as parts commonality and lead time. Consequently, materials required for a single batch or production cycle could be phased according to the quoted lead times. The trend of rising inventory levels was halted. Lower prices were also negotiated with suppliers, in return for longer and larger contracts.

Muirhead's workforce was reduced from nearly 2,000 in early 1970 to 1,650 by the end of 1972. This reduction was accomplished by scaling down departments, natural wastage and *investing* in more mechanized production facilities. Wages as a percentage of total costs declined from 41% to 35%.

Many of the cost savings in the manufacturing area are reported to have arisen as the result of factory walkabouts by Sir Raymond Brown during which he would ask questions of the shopfloor workers. The purpose of this exercise was to discover whether any increased efficiency or reduction in raw materials usage were possible. It was often found that the combination of Sir Raymond's apparent naïveté and workforce familiarity with the manufacturing process brought to light resource-wasting habits that had developed over time. The relevant manager would then be informed as to the extra saving that was to be expected from this department and was asked to state a case against this. There were usually few disagreements. Apart from the one-off savings produced by the walkabouts, great emphasis was placed on the role of value engineering. This technique was introduced as a result of the over-quality situation which existed with nearly all of Muirhead's product range.

(*f*) *Reduction in overheads*: Besides a reduction in the number of personnel, a number of other overhead costs were cut back:

(i) As Muirhead expanded in the early 1960s departments had grown,and the company found itself in 1970 with several rented properties whilst the main works at Beckenham were still not fully utilized. All these properties were vacated and the whole company relocated at Beckenham.

(ii) Research and development expenditure, which had been increased by 20% in 1968/69, was carefully scrutinized in 1970/71 so that only expenditure 'necessary to maintain the company's position in world markets' was incurred. Work was carried out only on those projects for which there was good market potential.

(iii) Marketing expenses for the office equipment range were curtailed in 1970, although an increase in these costs had been sanctioned by the previous board in 1969. There was an advertising saving of at least £100,000 per annum.

(iv) The number of company cars was reduced. It became the policy of the company to give cars only to directors and salesmen.

(g) *Reduction in assets*: Two actions were taken to reduce capital employed: first, working capital requirements were reduced by reducing debtors and increasing creditor days (inventory turnover was also improved by the adoption of better purchasing policies); second, the company's freehold sports ground was sold in October 1972 to inject cash into the company for the second phase. The price received for the ground was £600,000, compared to a book value of £40,000.

(h) *Growth by acquisition*: Once Muirhead had been jolted out of its declining position, top management began to spend an increasing proportion of their time on developing growth opportunities. A market study at the time indicated that facsimile transmission might become the most widely used new telecommunication service by the end of the century. Management decided to adopt a selective acquisition policy; they made seven acquisitions in the U.K., U.S.A., France and Germany between 1973 and 1976. The principal acquisition was Integrated Photomatrix, a manufacturer of opto-electronic-based process control systems, an area thought to have considerable long-term growth potential.

(i) *Increased emphasis on research and development*: Muirhead's strategy for growth was to meet most of the future requirements of the fascimile market and, in 1974, the board committed an increased percentage of the company's resources towards research and development, from 7% of the 1973 turnover to 9% of the 1974 turnover.

Results

The actions taken by Muirhead's new management, headed by Sir Raymond Brown, constituted a classic turnaround, as can be seen from the summary of the key financial data in Table 14.1. The firm showed a steady growth in profits from 1970 until 1978, but by 1980 it was back once again in a turnaround situation. The recession, high interest rates and the high value of sterling affected profitability, but Muirhead's latest problem appears to be more fundamental. Muirhead has an upmarket range of facsimile transmission equipment at a time when the volume market is just taking off under strong Japanese leadership. Muirhead have already started importing and distributing Japanese

machines, and it is hard not to draw a parallel with the history of the
U.K. motorcycle industry.

Table 14.1: *Muirhead Ltd: Key Financial Data, 1964–80*

Year (ending 30 September)	Sales	(in £ millions) Profit before tax	Profit as Percentage of sales	Profit as percentage of capital employed
1964	£4.4	£1.0	22	30
1965	4.4	0.7	16	18
1966	5.2	0.8	15	17
1967	5.3	0.5	10	11
1968	5.8	0.7	12	12
1969	5.8	0.5	9	9
1970	5.6	–	1	1
1971	6.1	0.2	4	4
1972	6.2	0.6	10	9
1973	8.5	0.8	9	11
1974	9.5	0.8	9	11
1975	13.1	1.1	9	13
1976	16.5	1.4	9	15
1977	17.6	1.6	9	14
1978	21.2	2.0	10	13
1979	22.5	0.8	4	7
1980	25.1	(2.2)[1]	–	–

NOTE
1. After provision of £977,000.
Source: Annual Reports.

Pentos Ltd

Pentos is a diversified holding company which started as a £100
company established by the present chairman, Terry Maher, in 1971.
Maher is an accountant by training and, in the eight years to 1969,
worked his way up to become the financial controller for the U.K. and
Europe at Carborundum Ltd. From this position he was recruited by
Pat Mathews to become First National Finance Corporation's financial
controller and to take control of F.N.F.C.'s stakes in industrial
companies. Two of the companies which he invested in at F.N.F.C.
were Austin Hall and Marshall, Morgan and Scott. F.N.F.C. had

stakes in both companies and it was generally recognized that the two firms required management assistance. Mr Maher became chairman of both groups. In April 1972, he left F.N.F.C. to set up Pentos as a holding company for his own personal stakes in Austin Hall, where he held 2% of the equity, and in Marshall, Morgan and Scott (8% of the equity). Maher states: 'It wasn't really a decision to do my own thing, although in retrospect it seems so. I just wanted more financial experience and independence.'[1]

Between 1972 and 1975, Maher built Pentos into a successful diversified company through a series of acquisitions and subsequent turnarounds. The acquisitions were financed by issuing new equity and raising debt. We shall next discuss two of these acquisitions and summarize Maher's successful managerial philosophy.

1. Reverse Takeover of Cape Town Gas

Maher started off in 1972 by the reverse takeover of a 'shell' company that was being traded in the U.K. stock exchange. The shell company was the Cape Town & District Gas Light & Coke Co. Ltd. The balance sheet was straightforward, the company had just entered its first year of losses, and no hidden problems appeared during the preliminary search. In 1971, the company had pre-tax profits of £32,000 on sales of £360,000 and net assets of £910,000. The situation had changed very little over the previous five years. No detailed assessment of the turnaround potential was undertaken – it was just assumed that good management would do a much better job. The initial intention was to turn the company around and develop the fuel interests, but there was no definite plan to resell the company, although Maher did not like what he considered to be the political, economic and currency risks associated with South Africa. Maher approached a regional officer of Barclays Bank and, within two days, had obtained a loan of £200,000 to purchase shares worth £250,000. The loan was subject to a personal guarantee from Terry Maher. This loan, together with the loans of associates, was used to purchase 44% of the Cape Town company on the market at approximately 100p per share. The subsequent bid of 125p per share for the outstanding shares had a cash alternative underwritten by Barclays Bank. Prior to the bid, the directors had agreed to accept Maher's offer in respect of their own 14% holdings. The directors needed relatively little persuasion to sell: a major influence on them was that Maher and his associates were in a position to maintain the Cape Town company's dividend. The original directors had a sense of responsibility to their shareholders and were very concerned that they would have to recommend a dividend cut.

Further to the acquisition of Cape Town Gas by Maher, the Cape Town company acquired Pentos Holdings Ltd. A legal reorganization together with name changes took place, resulting in the structure shown in Figure 14.1.

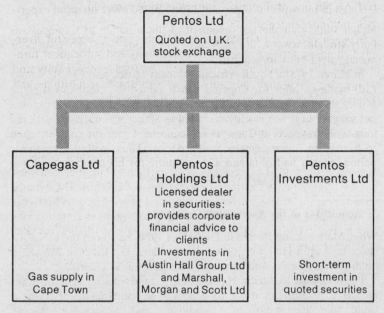

Figure 14.1: *Structure of Pentos Ltd (1972)*

2. Turnaround at Cape Gas Ltd

The poor profit record of Cape Gas prior to 1972 was explained in the company's annual report as being due to 'aggressive competition', 'the difficult economic situation' and 'increasing costs'. In 1972, the dividend would be reduced to conserve cash flow, while a major programme of repair and modernization was long overdue; the company was starting to run at a loss. After the acquisition, one of Pentos's directors spent six months in Cape Town and several changes were made:

(i) A marketing function was established. A campaign was introduced to persuade potential and existing customers that gas was not dangerous, and in fact was making a comeback in 'advanced' countries, such as the U.K. The trade name 'Capegas' was promoted.

(ii) Accounting procedures and the budgetary and management reporting systems were improved substantially.

(iii) A full review of the company's assets was undertaken and considerable wastage identified.

(iv) All but one of the former directors were removed.

Maher states that the improvement of the situation at Capegas was fairly straightforward, the main problem having been generally poor management prior to acquisition.

In March 1973, a South African company (Brick and Clay Holdings Ltd) made an offer for Capegas which valued the company at some £660,000 (a level well above the original purchase price). The bid was not sought but it was readily accepted as Maher was unhappy with the long-term prospects at Capegas and concerned over the risks attached to having an investment in South Africa. Thus, within a one-year period, Maher had obtained a share quote for his company and had made a large capital gain on the vehicle used.

3. Acquisition of the Austin Hall Group Ltd

When Maher set up Pentos in December 1971, he placed the F.N.F.C. stake in Austin Hall with other shareholders, put his own 2% share holding into Pentos, and formalized his position as chairman.

The approach to Austin Hall became a standard approach for other industrial investments made by Maher. The combination of taking a small minority stake in a company and persuading existing directors/shareholders that he should become chairman enabled Maher to gain a good insight into a company's potential at relatively little risk. If the situation turned out to be unattractive, he was able to resign and either sell in the market or place his stake with a company interested in making a bid. The disadvantage of this approach was: as the trading position of a 'suitable' company improved as a result of Maher's efforts, most of the capital gain accrued to other shareholders. However, this latter consideration was less important in 1973/74 because the U.K. stock market was very weak.

The Pentos stake in Austin Hall increased as follows:

Date	Shareholding
early 1972	2%
18 April 1974	12%
19 May 1974	29%
12 June 1974	55%
31 December 1974	100%

The crucial date was 17 May 1974: at that time, Pentos bid for the outstanding shares; Maher considers this the single most important event in the history of Pentos. Pentos was only half the size of Austin Hall, as measured by market capitalization, and the bid was hotly contested. The two factors that swung events in favour of Pentos were a cash bid in a falling market and backing from a venture capital arm of the Bank of America.

4. Turnaround of Austin Hall

Improvement in the fortunes of the Austin Hall Group was pursued from the time Maher had become chairman around 1970 and was not directly affected by the size of the Pentos shareholding. A brief financial summary of the period 1970–75 is given in Table 14.2. The most striking feature of the table is the rapid increase in turnover and profits during 1970/73 and the relatively dull performance thereafter. The industrial background was particularly difficult in the mid-1970s and was directly responsible for the severe squeeze on margins in 1975.

The main decision taken by Maher was to focus product-market strategy on two divisions: garden/leisure products (greenhouses, garden sheds, sun chalets, home chalets, home extensions, etc.); and industrial products based on system building (a whole range of products for permanent or temporary use – classrooms, airport terminals, etc.). At the time, Maher stated that 'this is a logical development which streamlines sales, production and distribution. More significantly, it enables us to make a real reduction in overheads without affecting the existing very profitable business.'

The success of the garden/leisure division appears to have been based on a number of marketing decisions. First, Austin Hall decided to manufacture aluminium products in house since a substantial increase in the price of cedar was making the traditional raw material uncompetitive. Second, a new modular shed system was developed that enabled the product range to be prepackaged; this gave access to a new range of retail outlets, such as leading high-street multiples, and also made the products more suitable for exporting. Third, the number of company-owned show centres was increased to forty-eight by 1974, thus improving representation in the retail market. The net effect of these changes was to increase substantially the market share held by Austin Hall.

Changes in the industrial division were concentrated on both marketing and production. The marketing emphasis was to move into up-market areas that required more sophisticated buildings and where price competition from small manufacturers was less severe. In the areas where Austin Hall competed, it was also the intention to produce a complete product range available for purchase, lease or hire, a service that was thought to be unique in the construction industry. The production changes included closing down one of the three factories and introducing a new production incentive scheme.

5. Maher's Management Philosophy

Maher's early strategy can only be described as 'opportunistic', but nowadays 'a great deal of research is done before an acquisition is seriously considered'. Like many other entrepreneurs with experience in secondary banking, Maher has a liking for industrial companies rather than for property where he can see no definable product. Maher's criteria for selecting businesses and his method of acquisition developed from his early experiences with companies such as Austin Hall. His approach appears to be as follows:

(i) To assess the potential companies or parts of companies but not to try and evaluate abstract concepts. Thus, Maher does not seek a good idea (e.g. D.I.Y.) and then enter the market. He starts with a company and 'throws away' the part he does not want.

(ii) To enter fragmented markets, because this fits with his policy of 'developing businesses with a recognizable product, a reputation for quality and the potential to become leaders in their field'.

(iii) To compete in those sectors of industry where risks are low and where there is a reasonable possibility of achieving a 40% return before interest and tax on funds employed.

(iv) To minimize the risk when entering a new, 'unknown' company by taking a small equity stake and seeking election as chairman. From this position Maher can make a good assessment of a company's potential and, depending on his conclusions, either launch a full bid or sell his small stake and resign.

(v) To develop a balanced portfolio of businesses split between consumer and non-consumer activities, but 'not so diverse that the control is lost'.

Besides an aggressive acquisitions policy, the other key features of Maher's management philosophy relate to the fixation on financial control and his method of managing a diversified group:

(i) Once a company has been acquired, Maher's first priority is to *tighten* financial controls. Maher is still predominantly a financially oriented manager. He has been described by his colleagues as 'pedantic and even nit-picking over finance', but claims that he wants to operate on the principle of 'no surprises'. Divisional budgets are reviewed formally each month, but Maher keeps a constant informal check.

(ii) Three organizational features characterize Pentos: a simple organizational structure, a small head office staff consisting almost solely of finance staff, and payment by results. There is a chief executive in charge of each operating group who, according to Maher, has 'a high degree of authority and is encouraged to develop the business as if it were his own. This works as long as we have very tight financial control exercised from the centre.'[2]

Results

Today, Pentos has six groups of operating companies. They are involved in retail book selling, publishing, garden and leisure products, engineering and office furniture. Pentos sales and profit performance is summarized in Table 14.3. The group's financial position has deteriorated in recent years, causing losses in 1980 and 1981 and an

Table 14.2: *Austin Hall Group: Financial Performance, 1970–75*

| | | | *(in £ millions)* | | |
Year	Sales	PBIT*	Net assets	PBIT/Sales	PBIT/New assets
1970	3.0	0.4	–	14.1	–
1971	5.9	0.9	–	14.6	–
1972	8.6	1.1	–	12.5	–
1973	11.2	1.5	5.9	13.8	26.2
1974	12.9	1.7	6.5	13.4	26.4
1975	13.1	0.9	6.0	7.2	15.8

* Profit before interest and tax.
Source: Annual Reports.

increase in gearing from about 50% in 1977/78 to 90% by year end 1980. Maher is now using crisis turnaround strategies involving cash generation and cost reduction to put the group back on a sound financial basis.

Table 14.3: *Pentos Ltd: Sales and Profit Summary, 1971–80*

| | *(in £ millions)* | | |
	Sales	Profit/(loss) before tax	Profit before tax as percentage of sales
1971	£0.4	£0.04	10
1972	0.8	0.06	7
1973	1.8	0.3	17
1974	14.7	1.8	12
1975	30.4	2.2	7
1976	36.4	3.0	8
1977	41.8	3.3	8
1978	54.8	4.0	7
1979	71.0	4.1	6
1980	74.4	(2.2)	(3)

Alpine Holdings Ltd

Alpine is best known as manufacturer and installer of double glazing. After achieving a record profit level of £950,000 in 1973, profits (before tax) fluctuated between £450,000 and £740,000 (see Table 14.4) until 1977, when James Gulliver Associates purchased a minority stake in the group. For the first time since the group went public in January 1973, the share price rose to exceed the initial offer price.

Causes of Decline

Alpine was a typical stagnant company with poor management and lack of control but its main problem lay in the peripheral business areas into which the company had diversified; its core business in double glazing was sound, being based on a quality product and a relatively high market share.

During 1974 and 1975, the major problem was Alpine's subsidiary, Everest Refrigerators. Everest had been started in 1968 to sell freezers and frozen food direct to the public and, in addition, had retail outlets selling frozen food. The major problems were as follows:

(i) the repeat buying pattern of the frozen food business did not lend itself to direct selling; increasing competition from high-street retailers, such as Bejam, caused severe pressure on margins.

(ii) the volume of sales was insufficient to obtain the necessary economies of scale in distribution. Rising transport costs, especially the oil-price hike in 1974, added to costs considerably.

(iii) losses were caused by food spoilage, which suggests poor purchasing and inventory control.

(iv) approximately 90% of sales were credit sales financed through United Dominion Trust. The credit squeeze of 1974 and the introduction of V.A.T. caused a cutback in spending, and sales declined dramatically. Everest suffered significantly more than its competitors, due to its reliance on credit sales.

(v) complete lack of control: the auditors stated in 1975 that they were unable to determine whether the accounts 'fairly reflect the losses of the company for the period'.

This combination of factors resulted in Everest losing £400,000 in the year ending January 1975. Management responded rapidly to the problem. In September 1974, direct sales and home delivery were stopped; in August 1975 the freezer depot was sold (thereby eliminating all Alpine's debts); and in June 1976, the five rental shops were sold to J.H. Dewhurst.

Just as management was solving the Everest problem, the new industrial-window division started to develop losses. There were three reasons for this:

(i) The recession in the building industry in 1975 and 1976 resulted in a sharp drop in market size and fierce price competition as competitors cut margins to stay in business.

(ii) The failure by management to realize that the skills necessary in the industrial-window market, particularly the selling and installation skills, are not the same as those in domestic double glazing.

(iii) The market was much more price competitive than the domestic market, with most windows sold on a competitive tendering basis. Alpine had no competitive advantage.

Recovery Actions

In May 1977, when Alpine's stock market price had fallen to 15p, Gulliver and his associates purchased 15% of the shares from the three founders of the business, together with an option to purchase an additional 14.9% at a later date. Gulliver had had a successful track-record as chief executive of the Fine Fare supermarket chain in the early 1970s. He then built up Oriel Foods, which he subsequently sold to R.C.A. (only to buy it back again in 1980).

The actions he took to revive the company were as follows.

(*a*) *Change of management*: The acquisition of 15% of the shares gave Gulliver management control, and the three founders took on non-executive roles. Gulliver became chairman; he installed his own team who had worked with him at Oriel Foods. Alistair Grant, who was marketing director at Oriel and at Fine Fare before that, became managing director.

(*b*) *Closure of industrial-window division*: Two months after the change of shareholding, it was announced that the industrial-window division would stop production in September and be wound up.

(*c*) *Divestiture of associate companies*: Alpine's associate companies had not had a big impact on profitability, although Century Aluminium Ltd, an aluminium extruder and an Alpine supplier in which Alpine had a 38% stake, lost money in 1976. The investment was sold in August 1977; the following year, investments in an air-conditioning company and a Northern Ireland window company were also sold. Gulliver's policy was to concentrate on wholly owned subsidiaries as far as possible.

(*d*) *Strengthened financial controls*: A new finance director was appointed and there was a general tightening-up of all control procedures.

(*e*) *Aggressive marketing*: New management concentrated its efforts on marketing domestic double glazing and increased promotional expenditure. Although Alpine was a market leader, it had only a 20% share of the replacement-window market and 14% of the double glazing market. There was a conscious move to depend less on the South-East and the Midlands, and a considerable amount of market development took place in other geographical areas. Sales via Debenham's stores, which had begun in September 1976, were increased and accounted for 20% of window sales by September 1978.

(*f*) *Related diversification*: Immediately after acquiring his stake in Alpine, Gulliver started searching for acquisitions that would fit in with

Alpine. In April 1978, Alpine purchased Dolphin Showers for £1.3 million, half of which was paid at the time of acquisition and the balance paid over a three-year period. Dolphin decreased Alpine's reliance on double glazing from virtually 100% in the financial year ending January 1978 to about 60% in the 1980 financial year. There are many similarities between Dolphin and the traditional Alpine business: they are both in the home improvement market, they are both market leaders and both depend on direct selling and installation of equipment in the home. After the acquisition, Alpine was able to improve Dolphin's profitability substantially, although at least part of the volume increase was due to strong consumer demand throughout 1978 and 1979. In one year, sales revenues increased by 41% and before-tax profits by 137% (see Table 14.4).

Table 14.4: *Alpine Holdings Ltd: Key Financial Data, 1973–81*

Year (financial year ending 31 January)	Sales (in £ millions)	Profit before tax (in £ millions)	P.B.I.T./sales (%)	P.B.I.T./net assets (%)
1973	8.4	0.96	11	53
1974	10.1	0.75	7	31
1975	9.0	0.45	3	18
1976	11.0	0.74	8	52
1977	12.0	0.46	4	32
1978	14.5	0.93	6	50
1979	25.2	1.91	8	60
1980	33.2	2.75	8	51[2]
1981	34.0	1.28	4	31

NOTES
1. Includes goodwill from 1979 onwards.
2. Reflects investment in new fixed assets.
Source: Annual Reports.

Conclusions

Although the credit must obviously go to James Gulliver and his team for injecting a new lease of life into Alpine, the situation might have been considerably worse in 1977 had the previous management not taken action as quickly as they did at Everest. Perhaps they could have acted sooner, but the fact is, if they had let the situation deteriorate and then experienced losses in industrial windows on top of Everest,

Alpine could have found itself in a loss-making situation very quickly. The acquisition of Dolphin Showers was clearly the critical step in Alpine's turnaround. Not only was the acquisition of Dolphin offensive but, most importantly, defensive. During the 1980 recession, profit from the window business disappeared and group profitability was due solely to shower sales (see Table 14.5). Volume declined and marketing expenditure was increased in an effort to maintain market share. This appears to have pushed management, which was largely marketing oriented, into paying more attention to its cost structure.

Table 14.5: *Alpine Holdings Ltd: Sales and Profitability by Division, 1973–81*[1]

| | *(in £ millions)* Double glazing and windows | | Other principal divisions[2,3,4,5] | |
Year	Sales	Profit	Sales	Profit
(Year ending 31 January)				
1973	£3.3	£0.6	£5.0[2]	£0.3
1974	4.4	0.5	5.7[2]	0.2
1975	7.5	0.7	1.5[2]	(0.3)
1976	8.2	1.2	1.4[3]	–
1977	9.0	1.0	1.6[3]	(0.4)
1978	12.0	1.3	1.8[3]	(0.2)
1979	16.3	1.7	7.6[4]	0.5
1980	20.8	1.8	10.7[4]	1.2
1981	20.3	0.1	11.6	1.5

NOTES
1. Excludes some minor activities, and therefore does not agree with Table 14.4
2. Freezers and frozen foods, 1973–5.
3. Industrial windows, 1976–8.
4. Dolphin Showers, 1979–81.
5. Excludes Dreamline Furniture.
Source: Annual Reports.

Notes

1. 'A Fixation on Financial Control', *International Management*, November 1979.
2. Ibid.

15. Property-related Recovery Situations

This chapter describes the case-histories of a small hotel group and a bank that found themselves in recovery situations, due almost solely to the twin problems of high gearing and falling property prices. In the case of the hotel group (Mount Charlotte Investments), property speculation was peripheral to the main business and so recovery was relatively straightforward, even though the crisis occurred at the same time as a cyclical downturn in demand. However, the situation with the bank was more fundamental since Keyser Ullmann had a high percentage of its assets lent to the property sector. The bank was not allowed to become insolvent but, like other financial institutions hit by the property crisis (U.D.T., for example), it did not manage to achieve sustainable recovery as an independent entity.

Mount Charlotte Investments

The principal activity of the group was and still is hotel management and catering. Mount Charlotte Investment's loss-making position in 1974 and 1975 arose solely from the company's involvement in two areas outside its traditional business: property speculation and entry into the brewing business. The hotel business remained profitable throughout the period, although the decline in market demand reduced hotel profit margins in 1974 and 1975, and profitability was undoubtedly affected by management's preoccupation with the property and brewing deals.

Causes of Decline

(a) *Failed property deal*: Mount Charlotte acquired the freehold of the Park Royal Hotel, Cardiff, in July 1972 for £1.25 million. This was a speculative property deal, since Mount Charlotte already owned the leasehold interest and the finance costs (even at 1973 interest rates) exceeded the rent reduction by over £35,000 per annum. In December 1973, Mount Charlotte entered into an agreement to sell the property for redevelopment for £1.8 million plus an option to run a new hotel to be built on the site before the existing premises were demolished. Unfortunately for Mount Charlotte, the deal was subject to planning permission being obtained – which in the event was never forthcoming.

(b) *Diversification via acquisition*: The rationale for diversification into breweries was as follows:

(i) Mount Charlotte would bid for two Cumberland breweries that could then be streamlined into one brewing venture.
(ii) Mount Charlotte would provide new outlets for these products through its hotels and restaurants.
(iii) Mount Charlotte would have a presence in the North-West that would facilitate extending its mainline hotel and catering interests in that area.
(iv) The deal would allow Maxwell Joseph (the principal shareholder in Mount Charlotte at that time) to extend his brewery interests (other than through Grand Metropolitan Hotels), without raising any problems with the Monopolies Commission.

The original offer was an alternative cash or share offer that valued Workington Brewery at £1,170,000 and Jennings at £702,000. Both the potential takeover companies were public (unquoted), but the shareholding was limited and localized. The Jennings shareholders in particular resented what they foresaw as a long-term integration into Grand Metropolitan's brewing arm and feared that an M.C.I. takeover would result in unemployment. Jennings's shareholders feared M.C.I. would close down their brewery and concentrate production in the under-used and somewhat larger Workington facility. Mount Charlotte were concerned to stress their lack of involvement in the brewing industry but, clearly, few of the shareholders were taken in. All the press comments stressed the Maxwell Joseph/Grand Metropolitan connection, and this resulted in Jennings even refusing to negotiate over the price.

The final result was the worst of all possible outcomes:

• Workington was finally acquired in March 1973 at a cost of £1.3 million
• Jennings successfully beat off the bid, despite the fact that the offer was eventually increased to £1.1 million (May 1973)

- M.C.I. had no suitable outlets for Workington's products. It clearly made no sense for a Cumberland brewery to supply beer in any sizeable quantities to a hotel chain primarily based in the South-West
- Workington was not only left with its local rival still in existence, relationships between the two companies were soured by the take-over battle
- Workington shareholders had almost entirely opted for the cash alternatives rather than for Mount Charlotte shares. Mount Charlotte had to find £1.1 million in cash to pay out Workington's shareholders.

Workington's turnover and profits had remained relatively constant between 1969 and 1973. Turnover increased from £1.5 million to £2 million and profit from £85,000 to £104,000. Without the prospect of a merger with Jennings and with no knowledge of brewing, Mount Charlotte had little chance of improving Workington's profitability.

(c) *Financial policy*: Mount Charlotte's financial policy was to grow through the use of debt financing. Total debt/shareholders' funds increased from 10% at year end 1971 to 79% by year end 1973. In early 1974, management was still confident of receiving the sales proceeds from the Park Royal, Cardiff, and acquired a further four hotels and a wines and spirits business. It was just at this time – when Mount Charlotte's gearing was in excess of 100% – that interest rates rose sharply.

(d) *Cyclical decline in hotel and catering markets*: The total demand for hotel accommodation in the U.K. fell by 10% in 1974 over 1973 and remained at a low level until 1976.

Number of Tourist Nights (millions)

	1973	1974	1975	1976
U.K. customers	132	114	117	121
Overseas customers	44	45	49	59
	176	159	166	180

Source: International Passenger Survey.

The provincial hotels (like those belonging to Mount Charlotte) were hit harder than the London hotels by the drop in demand because they were less dependent on overseas tourists. The hotel industry situation was made worse by the large number of new hotels and extensions that were completed over the period 1971–73 as the result of government tax incentives. Prior to 1970, about 2,000 new bedrooms were built annually, but in the peak year 1973, nearly 12,000 were completed, resulting in intense competition and lower margins during 1974 and 1975. Throughout this period, Mount Charlotte's profit margin was below the average for provincial hotels (which in turn was about half of that of the London hotels). The two principal reasons for this were:

(i) The largest concentration of Mount Charlotte's hotel business was in Bristol and Cardiff, where a lot of new hotel growth resulted in intense competition. In contrast to the newer hotels, Mount Charlotte's hotels were old and in need of renovation.

(ii) Management's attention was partly diverted from the hotel business towards acquisitions, with the result that the hotels were poorly controlled and no money was spent on renovation. As evidence of poor control, Mount Charlotte's purchasing costs in its catering business were considerably higher than those of its major competitors at this time.

Purchasing Cost as Percentage of Sales

	1973	1974	1975	1976
Provincial* average	58%	61%	60%	61%
Mount Charlotte	59%	67%	69%	66%

* Based on sample of six provincial hotel chains.

The Crisis

All the firm's trading activities remained profitable, but the high interest charges resulted in losses in 1974 and 1975. Table 15.1 summarizes key financial data for the period 1970 to 1979. With the failure to obtain planning permission for the Park Royal Hotel site at Cardiff, immediate steps were taken to reduce gearing. Neither the Park Royal nor the Workington venture could generate sufficient cash flow to offset the interest charges incurred.

Recovery Actions

(*a*) *Divestment*: Property worth £900,000 was sold prior to the end of 1974, thereby leaving year-end gearing similar to that at year end 1973. In the following year, property worth a further £500,000 was sold and the Workington Brewery was sold for £870,000. Mount Charlotte is estimated to have lost £612,000 over two years by acquiring the brewery:

Loss on sale of brewery	£430,000
Interest charge*	£390,000
Less management charges and dividends received	£(208,000)
Total estimated loss (before tax):	£612,000

* £1.3 million at 15% for two years.

(b) *Change of ownership/board composition*: Slater Walker held a 21% stake in Mount Charlotte until October 1976. The sale of these shares and the removal of the Slater Walker director from the board permitted the introduction of an experienced hotel executive to take charge of the neglected hotel and catering business.

(c) *Introduced cost control systems*: New cost control systems were introduced that had a direct effect on profitability.

(d) *Adopted an aggressive marketing policy*: Mount Charlotte began to think in terms of market segmentation. Mount Charlotte had two hotels in both Bristol and Cardiff; one hotel was upgraded and one slightly downgraded to reduce direct competition. Having decided on the target customers for each hotel, direct marketing efforts were made to attract new customers.

(e) *Investment to modernize hotels*: New management embarked on a major renovation programme as part of its strategy for revitalizing the hotel and catering side of the business.

Results

Mount Charlotte would never have found itself in a turnaround situation had it not been for trying to diversify using a financial policy of high gearing. The strategy of diversification was undoubtedly influenced by the capital-gain objectives of the major shareholders at the time, who were Slater Walker and Sir Maxwell Joseph. The core business (hotels and catering) alone would have weathered the industry decline in 1974 and 1975, with reduced profits but no crisis. Although gearing became very high, a severe cash-flow crisis was avoided by the very quick implementation of a divestment strategy as soon as problems arose in 1974.

Table 15.1: *Mount Charlotte Investments: Key Financial Date, 1971–80*

Year	Sales (in £ millions)	Net profit before tax (in £ thousands)	Profit[1] margin %	Interest cover	Gearing[2]
1971	4.7	295	8	5.3	10
1972	5.0	235	9	4.1	64
1973	6.4	22	6	1.1	79
1974	8.9	(155)	5	0.8	79
1975	8.4	(232)	3	0.5	61
1976	7.1	70	5	1.1	
1977	8.1	522	10	2.9	51
1978	9.4	855	12	4.4	28
1979	10.0	1,045	10	4.6	18
1980	11.6	660	6	2.0	36

NOTES
1. Profit before interest and tax as percentage of sales.
2. Total debt as percentage of shareholders' funds (less goodwill).
Source: Annual Reports.

Keyser Ullmann Holdings Ltd

Keyser Ullmann grew from being a very small merchant bank with a net asset value of only £5 million in 1971 to being the largest British merchant bank in terms of shareholders' funds, with a net asset value of £84 million in 1973. This growth was entirely due to dealings in the booming property market of the early 1970s. Keyser Ullmann's heyday came with the acquisition of Central and District Properties in April 1972 for £68 million in shares, and the subsequent sale of the group for £97 million in cash just fifteen months later. When the property market collapsed and the highly geared property developers to whom

Keyser Ullmann had lent (e.g. Stern, Lyon, Grendon and Guardian) became insolvent, Keyser Ullmann found itself in a severe crisis situation.

Causes of Decline

Four principal causes of decline can be identified.

(a) *Acquisition of a property financing company*: In August 1972, Keyser Ullmann purchased for £58 million (again, mainly in shares) Dalton Barton Securities Ltd, a property financing group run by Jack Dellal and Stanley van Gelder. Dellal and van Gelder joined Keyser Ullmann. It was not clear, however, until after new management took over in March 1975 just what was happening in the property finance company. It had been generally believed that Dellal and van Gelder had been making fantastic profits for first Dalton Barton, and then Keyser Ullmann, during the property boom. However, if borrowers got into difficulties over the repayment of their loans, Dellal and van Gelder would allow 'rollover' of their interest payments by increasing the principal of the loan. In periods when property prices are rising fast, the security of the loan is assured, providing the annual increase in prices is greater than the interest rate. However, not only does this practice cause problems if property prices plateau, let alone fall; but, because the interest payments are declared as profits and tax has to be paid on those profits, it actually acts as a cash drain. The profits which Dellal and van Gelder had been 'making', first for Dalton Barton and then for Keyser Ullmann, had only been paper profits. Keyser Ullmann had bought a cash drain!

(b) *Collapse of the property market*: The latter half of the year 1973 saw anxiety about the property market, and rumours abounded that Keyser Ullmann had made substantial loans to the troubled property sector. In fact, Keyser Ullmann continued making loans to the property sector after others had realized the dangers. In the six months between September 1973 and March 1974, Keyser Ullmann's outstanding loans in its banking subsidiary increased from £216 million to £254 million. Nearly all the new advances were to the property sector. Although net assets were around £140 million (some 270p per share), the share price plummeted from 200p in January 1974 to 120p in March 1974. Throughout this period, Du Cann and the managing directors of Keyser Ullmann, Roland Franklin and Ian Stoutzker, continued to express their bewilderment as to why the share price was so low, and to state how strong Keyser Ullmann really was. In March 1974, Du Cann was quoted as saying, 'We are stronger than any other merchant bank and it wouldn't matter much if some deposits were taken away.'

However, in July 1974 Keyser Ullmann declared a provision for bad debts of over £30 million, due to the demise of four property empires to which the bank had advanced loans, namely, Stern, Lyon, Guardian and C.S.T. Investments. After a valuation on a conservative basis, net assets of £100 million, or 200p per share, were declared. The share price stood at 115p.

(c) *Unbalanced lending portfolio*: Keyser Ullmann's chairman, Mr Edward Du Cann, had written in his 1973 Chairman's Statement that he felt the sale of Central and District Properties 'would restore the balance of the group between banking and property and further facilitate the expansion of the banking company' (for which additional equity funds had been raised during 1972). At this time, about 64 per cent of Keyser's lending portfolio was in property. However, under the influence of Dellal and van Gelder, who were continuing to make property investment under the Keyser Ullmann umbrella, those in the banking subsidiary continued to lend on property, increasing the property portfolio to approximately 80 per cent by mid-1974.

This contrasts sharply with the chairman's statement in July 1974, when Du Cann said 'it has been our policy to reduce our involvement in the property sector, as evidenced by the sale of Central and District. In present conditions, we have been reducing the extent of banking facilities for property transactions.'

(d) *Top management*: Du Cann was clearly not suited to be chairman. As a politician, he was probably more of a figurehead chairman, and left the joint managing directors, Franklin and Stoutzker, who appear to have been neither good bankers nor good managers, to run the company as they wanted.

The Crisis

By September 1974, Keyser Ullmann's share price had dropped to 63p (compared to a peak of over 350p in 1972), but Ian Stoutzker was quoted as saying that the shares were backed by assets of 200p, and he made a firm assertion that the provision for bad debts was fully adequate in present conditions.

By December 1974, it was apparent that a further deterioration in values had taken place and that more provisions for the year ending March 1975 would be necessary. It was at this time that Keyser Ullmann went to the Bank of England to seek a loan of £65 million under their 'lifeboat support' scheme.

Recovery Actions

When Keyser Ullmann made arrangements with the Bank of England under the 'lifeboat scheme' in late 1974, the Bank of England began to search for a new chairman who would retain people's confidence in Keyser Ullmann, and thus maintain the deposits that were essential to its survival. The Bank of England approached Derek Wilde, a vice-chairman of Barclays Bank, and he was appointed chairman in March 1975 to replace Edward Du Cann. Wilde's actions were designed to restore confidence and repay the Bank of England support loan as soon as possible. He thought that only then would ordinary depositors believe the bank had a viable future and return their deposits. His major actions were as follows:

(a) *Dismiss the joint managing directors*: Wilde asked for the resignation of Franklin and Stoutzker soon after his arrival. He could not see anyone having confidence in the organization while they were associated with it. Dellal and van Gelder had left in July 1974.

(b) *Reduce loans outstanding*: According to Wilde, 'a flying squad of top staff, including directors, went into the debt recovery business'. Wilde set up a realization committee of lawyers, accountants, chartered surveyors, etc., whose brief was to establish the identity of the assets which had come into the control of the bank under the charges given by defaulting borrowers, and to plan the best way of finding a buyer. Often, the realization committee had no alternative but to pour good money after bad, as in the case of the Lyons empire, where the bank found itself owning a half-finished yacht and half-finished housing projects. The yacht, worth £5½ million, which could not be sold as it was, had to be fitted out and sailed from Holland to the Mediterranean in order to get it to a suitable 'showroom' to attract a buyer! With housing, the problem was one of maintaining the confidence of the workforce building houses for part of the Lyons empire which passed into the bank's hands. The houses had to be completed on a hand-to-hand basis, with someone from the bank having to turn up on Thursday to pay the wages on more than one occasion!

(c) *Divestment*: Wilde established a second team to look into the possibility of selling off subsidiary loss-making companies. There were nine industrial subsidiary companies at the time of Wilde's arrival. Seven had been disposed of by the end of 1978, since Wilde's vision for Keyser Ullmann was as a bank and not an industrial holding company.

(d) *Repayment of 'lifeboat' finance*: A high priority was given to repayment of borrowing made available by the Support Group established by the Bank of England and the clearing banks. This was achieved in 1976 and replaced in part by stand-by facilities from the clearing banks. The change was important since it indicated increased confidence in Keyser Ullmann on the part of the larger banks.

(e) *Large accounting provisions to generate confidence*: On 15 July 1975, Keyser Ullmann announced results for the year ended 31 March 1975. The provision for bad debts was £64 million. Wilde stated that he had tried to make full provision, and declared a hidden reserve which Keyser Ullmann had not included before under special rules applying to banks and accepting houses. Wilde did this in the following ways: he wrote down all property and other assets to their market value; interest on loans due but not paid was excluded from income, although this had always been included under previous management, and amounted to £18 million. Wilde also included an additional provision, the cost of financing assets which had been acquired as a result of the demise of property groups, until those assets could be sold at their written-down value.

Keyser Ullmann's accounts were qualified by their accountants, who stated that they did not know whether the provisions made were too large or not. By this time, most people knew that the Bank of England was not going to let Keyser Ullmann go under and, indeed, knew that they were continuing to stagger along. Wilde's strategy was, therefore, to 'wipe the slate clean'. He was quoted as saying that the provisions were made on highly pessimistic assumptions in an attempt to generate the confidence lost when the property business collapsed. As will be seen, these provisions were not pessimistic enough, as further provisions were made in each of the next two years. At the time, Wilde hoped he had overestimated the losses which were incurred, and stated that he would be happy to be proved pessimistic. In fact, he had to make further write-offs in 1976 (£7.2 million), and 1977 (£6.5 million), as the property market failed to recover, but Wilde produced very detailed interim statements with the objective of showing the underlying profitability of the banking company despite the property write-offs (see Table 15.2 for a split of banking and non-banking profits).

(*f*) *Develop a balanced lending portfolio*: When Wilde took over as chairman he made a statement to the Press, saying: 'Keyser is heavily involved in property and I hope to see a run-down in our lending in property and an increase in the amount of money going into industrial activities. I shall be very concerned to see that we get a better balance in our lending.' His strategy remained essentially the same throughout – to increase deposits and to build up a balanced commercial lending portfolio.

(*g*) *Reduce overheads*: Wilde's strategy was to cut back Keyser Ullmann to its small, but profitable, core. At its peak in 1974/75, there were 2,900 employees, but by 1979 there were only 676, and some of these were in the remaining manufacturing subsidiary, an electrical refrigeration company.

Results

Under Wilde's leadership, Keyser Ullmann's profitability (see Table 15.2) and balance sheet recovered; but, as Derek Wilde admitted in 1980, 'it has never been able to shake off the bad publicity which it attracted during that period. It has just not been able to attract new business in the volume which its assets could support.' On the basis of its 1979/80 balance sheet, it was estimated that Keyser Ullmann could take on a further £40 million to £50 million of lending. In addition, there were £60 million of unused tax losses which Keyser Ullmann had not been able to exploit. In May 1980, the Charterhouse Group acquired Keyser Ullmann for £43 million, one million below net asset value, in a friendly takeover.

Table 15.2: *Keyser Ullmann Holdings Ltd: Key Financial Data, 1971–80 (in £ millions)*

Year	Profits before tax: Banking	Non-banking	Provisions	Total net profit before tax
1971	n.a.	0.6	–	n.a.
1972	n.a.	0.5	–	n.a.
1973	n.a.	5.1	–	n.a.
1974	12.9	4.9	(30.6)	(12.8)
1975	–	4.7	(64.0)	(59.3)
1976	3.3	(1.3)	(7.2)	(5.2)
1977	2.2	(1.0)	(6.5)	(5.3)
1978	1.2	(0.4)	3.5 CR[1]	4.3
1979	2.2	(0.1)	1.0 CR	3.1
1980	3.4	–	1.0 CR	4.4

NOTE

1. Credits represent overprovision for bad debts in earlier years.
Source: Annual Reports.

16. Successful State Involvement in Recovery Situations

Several different examples of state involvement in recovery situations were mentioned in Chapter 11. Two of these, Burmah Oil and Ferranti, are now discussed in greater detail, so that the reader can better grasp the influence of state involvement as it was in the 1970s.

Burmah Oil Company

The sudden decline of Burmah Oil in 1974 and its subsequent rescue by the Bank of England is a unique example of a turnaround situation. Burmah Oil was the twenty-fifth largest company in Britain and in 1973 showed record sales and profitability of £496 million and £49 million respectively. Within twelve months, the firm was totally insolvent, its total indebtedness to shareholders' funds having increased from 43% to 190%.

Burmah's unique turnaround situation is closely related to its historical ties with British Petroleum (B.P.). In 1914, the British government, on the recommendation of a Royal Commission, acquired a majority interest in Anglo-Persian Oil, a company that had been formed by Burmah Oil to exploit Iranian oil concessions. The name Anglo-Persian was changed to B.P. in 1932. The percentage shareholdings of Burmah and the British government in B.P. declined over the years, so that in 1974 the government held just under 50% of B.P.'s shares and Burmah Oil held 21.6%. The B.P. holdings have been a critical factor in the development of Burmah Oil. At year end 1973, B.P. shares accounted for 49% of Burmah's net assets; but even more important than this was the fact that Burmah's dividend income was directly passed on to Burmah's shareholders and not available (as retained earnings) for investment purposes. Until the 1960s, Burmah's assets, besides the B.P. shares (and a 3% shareholding in Shell), consisted primarily of oil interests in the Indian subcontinent, where there were dwindling oil reserves, low rates of economic growth and foreign exchange problems. During the 1960s, Burmah formulated a new strategy that was designed to reduce the proportion of Burmah's earnings derived from B.P. dividends and to spread risk by concentrating new investment in geographical areas expected to enjoy political and monetary stability. With these objectives in mind, Burmah started to acquire and exploit new oil sources (because, unlike the major oil companies, it lacked significant crude-oil reserves) and to diversify into non-oil businesses. Burmah lacked internally generated cash flow to finance its expansion plans, but planned to borrow against its B.P. and Shell shareholdings although it had no profit to offset the interest for tax purposes.

In the early 1960s the emphasis was on exploration activities in Australia, Canada and the U.S., and in 1962 the Lobitos oilfields in Peru and Ecuador were acquired. From 1966 onwards, however, a major diversification effort began with the acquisition of Castrol Oil. By 1973, Burmah had acquired Rawlplug (a manufacturer of masonry fixtures), Halford (a chain of motor and cycle accessory shops), Quinton Hazell (a motor components supplier), Tabbet (a German caravan producer), Veedol Europe (an oil marketing operation), and J. H. Carruther (a heavy cranes business).

Causes of Decline

Compared with most turnaround situations, Burmah Oil was not a poorly managed company, although there were four principal causes of decline.

(a) *Financing of the Signal Oil acquisition*: It was Burmah's strategy to increase its oil production by acquisition in the U.S., and after failing to acquire Conoco in 1971 and Ladd Petroleum in early 1973, it finally made a successful bid for Signal Oil and Gas. The acquisition of Signal nearly doubled Burmah's crude-oil supplies and gave Burmah a 19% stake in the North Sea 'Thistle' field. The acquisition was financed by a long-term loan of U.S. $420 million from Chase Manhattan Bank and their Orion affiliate. The loan was secured against Burmah's holding of B.P. shares, that were valued at £443 million at year end 1973. However, almost as soon as the financing had been arranged, the U.K. stock market started to fall precipitously. The value of B.P. shares held by Burmah declined to £183 million by year end 1974, thereby contravening a covenant of the loan stock agreement with Chase Manhattan that required that net assets should not fall below a certain multiple of the amounts borrowed.

(*b*) *Sharp drop in tanker rates due to O.P.E.C. oil crisis*: Starting in 1971, Burmah embarked on a massive expansion of its tanker operation. In 1970, the company's fleet consisted of only one owned 16,000 deadweight ton vessel and a few spot charters. This tonnage supplied less than 10% of Burmah's total shipping requirements, since it was Burmah's policy to buy all its crude oil at its market or refining centres. The change in shipping policy came about when management decided to balance its own oil knowledge with the shipping expertise of Mr Elias Kulukundis, a former subordinate of the legendary Aristotle Onassis. Burmah's new policy was not only to supply all its own requirements but also to capture a large share of the then fast-growing cross-Atlantic oil trade (which was based on projections that the U.S. would need to triple its oil imports by 1980). As part of this scheme,

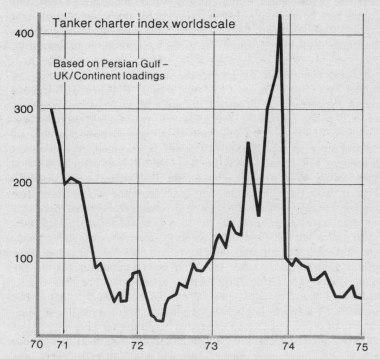

Figure 16.1: *Index of Tanker Charter Rates, 1971–4*

Source: *Economist*, January 1975. Reprinted by permission.

Burmah entered into an agreement to manage a crude-oil trans-shipment terminal in the Bahamas, operating it with its own very large crude carriers (V.L.C.Cs – tankers with capacity exceeding 175,000 dwt). On a rising market for tanker rates in 1972/73, Kulukundis chartered a total of thirty-six ships, considerably more than were required by Burmah, and rechartered out the balance at a higher charter cost. Tanker profits, that were expected to amount to only £2 million in 1973, reached £16 million. However, with the five-fold increase in crude-oil prices at the end of 1973, the tanker market collapsed dramatically (see Figure 16.1) and Burmah was left with relatively high-priced charters for which there was no demand.

Tanker chartering is a highly cyclical and speculative business, and Kulukundis had already made and lost a shipping fortune in the 1950s, when he overexpanded and rates dropped. In 1973 and 1974 there was a repeat performance! Kulukundis, however, has gone on record as saying that he was not solely responsible for the shipping deals that brought Burmah down, but that instructions from Burmah's Swindon headquarters to charter three V.L.C.Cs had caused the problem.[1]

(c) *Lack of control*: It is clear that the shipping business, that was run out of New York, was out of control during 1974. Few of Burmah's senior managers were aware of the scale of its activities. When oil analysts visited Burmah in early 1974, it is reported that nobody knew how large the fleet was![2] The most damning evidence about lack of control is provided by Burmah's attempt to renegotiate its dollar loan agreement with Chase Manhattan and Orion in November 1974, once they saw the value of their security (the B.P. shares) being seriously eroded. The Burmah negotiating team accepted a restrictive new covenant, under which group interest charges could not exceed a certain percentage of operating profit. A year had already passed since tanker rates had collapsed and it seems inconceivable that senior financial managers had not made an estimate of the likely impact on 1974 profits of lower tanker rates. It was only when the preliminary results of an investigation into the shipping operations were prepared in December that Burmah's financial management realized that 1974's profits were going to fall below the point at which Burmah would be in default on its dollar loan. A projection undertaken at the end of 1974 indicated that Burmah's net cash outflow, after deducting lay-out savings and charter-in revenues and assuming no corrective action was taken, would vary between £62 million and £128 million per year for the eight years between 1975 and 1982.

(*d*) *Capital projects*: There were other factors contributing to Burmah's cash-flow problems, notably delays and a large investment cash overrun at the Ellesmere Port refining expansion and the increasing sums of money required to develop Burmah's North Sea oil interests. The latter was an especial problem because in November 1974 the banks announced their refusal to finance the development of the Thistle field against the security of the oil in the ground. Burmah estimated that it needed £450 million to exploit its North Sea oil interests in the Thistle and Ninian fields. Nevertheless, the tanker operations and the breach of the dollar loan agreement were the root causes of Burmah's crisis.

The Crisis

The financial effect of these events was to reduce Burmah's shareholders' funds by 50% in the year ending 31 December 1974. The loss on tankers for 1974 was £31.4 million, which reduced profit before interest and tax to £51.2 million. The key financial data is summarized in Tables 16.1 and 16.2. On 23 December 1973, one year after the date on which Burmah made its bid for Signal Oil, Burmah's merchant bankers went to the Bank of England to explain that Chase Manhattan was calling in its U.S. $420 million loan. If Burmah was allowed to fail, it would be the largest international debt deficit in U.K. financial history. Burmah's proposal to the Bank of England and the govern-

Table 16.1: *Burmah Group Ltd: Sales and Profitability Data, 1972–80 (in £ millions)*

Year	Sales	Trading profits	Investment income	Profit before interest and tax	Interest	Profit before tax
1972	£349	£26	£26	£52	£10	£42
1973	496	49	24	73	16	57
1974	872	29	22	51	41	10
1975	915	11	9	20	33	(13)
1976	846	(6)	7	1	9	(8)
1977	857	7	5	12	8	4
1978	985	29	5	34	17	17
1979	1087	83	5	88	20	68
1980	1231	84	3	87	25	62

Source: Annual Reports.

Table 16.2: *Burmah Group Ltd: Summary of Group Balance Sheets, 1972–8 (in £ millions)*

	1972	1973	1974	1975	1976	1977	1978
Fixed assets	218	304	535	623	180	236	290
B.P. shares	494	443	183	29	16	–	–
Other investments[1]	123	97	99	163	278	151	136
Working capital[2]	6	61	53	81	155	222	204
Net assets	841	905	870	896	629	609	630
Shareholders' funds	667	624	312	333	364	319	316
Loans capital	119	186	487	492[4]	226	244	263
Other[3]	55	95	71	71	39	46	51
Capital employed	841	905	870	896	629	609	630
B.P. shares as percentage of net assets	59	49	21	3	2	–	–
Long-term debt as percentage of shareholders' funds	18	30	156	148	62	76	83
Total debt as percentage of shareholders' funds	27	43	190	216	69	86	92

NOTES
1. Trade investments, investment in associate companies and tanker projects.
2. After deducting short-term borrowings.
3. Minority interest and deferred liabilities.
4. Borrowings increase due to falling exchange rate of sterling.

ment was aimed at securing additional long-term capital without either the sale or pledge of its B.P. shares. This was unacceptable both to the Bank and to the government. The Bank's initial response was to attempt to mount a rescue operation via B.P., either through a complete takeover or by B.P. accepting responsibility for Burmah's management. This solution was unacceptable to B.P. and to the Labour Government of the day. Denis Healey, then Chancellor of the Exchequer, and Eric Varley, then Minister of Energy, wanted to avoid adding Burmah's 22% holding of B.P. to its own 48% as this would have meant nationalization of the industry. (If the Minister for

Industry, Anthony Wedgwood-Benn, had been involved rather than Eric Varley it is quite possible that the 'nationalization' solution would have been preferred.)

Recovery Actions

(*a*) *Refinancing*: Within less than a week – and over the Christmas period at that – the Bank of England and Burmah found a banker's solution to the problem, as opposed to a government interventionist solution. The agreed policy was to provide interim support with appropriate security. The Bank's terms completely dictated the subsequent financial strategy adopted by the company. The main features of the rescue package were as follows:

(i) A Bank of England guarantee to cover £280 million of Burmah's debts for twelve months ending 31 December 1975.
(ii) Burmah would remove Nicholas Williams, its managing director, and Elias Kulukundis, the two men held to be most responsible for Burmah's troubles.
(iii) As security for the guarantees: Burmah pledged its B.P. and Shell shares on the basis that the Bank of England would be entitled to sell the holding if the Bank considered it necessary to protect its own position.
(iv) Burmah would engage in a major divestment programme to pay off its loans.
(v) Burmah would sell to the government 51% of its North Sea oil interests in the future.

In January 1975, Sir Alastair Down, then deputy chairman and a managing director of B.P., was invited to become chairman and chief executive of Burmah Oil, to implement the Bank's divestment strategy. In the same month, the Bank forced Burmah to sell 7.8 million of its B.P. shares at 230p per share as a means of solving its short-term cash-flow problems. This left Burmah with only 5 million B.P. shares. The sale price created much controversy (see page 254), since eighteen months later Burmah was able to sell 3 million of its remaining shares at 595p per share.

(*b*) *The divestment programme*: Sir Alastair Down was faced with three problems, all of which required the use of substantial cash flows. The U.S. debt had to be repaid, the various tanker projects funded, and significant capital expenditure was required to continue to develop the North Sea oilfields. It was estimated that the cost of funding Burmah's share of the Ninian field alone was two-and-a-half times the cash flow generated by the entire group in its peak year, 1973.

During 1975, Burmah sold assets worth £277 million (see Table 16.3), but £178 million of this was accounted for by the B.P. shares

Table 16.3: *Burmah Oil Company: Divestment Programme, 1975–6*
1975

Date	Asset sold	Cash flow generated (£ million)
January	Great Plains Development of Canada	46.3
	77.8 million B.P. shares	177.7
July	Edwin Cooper	22.5
November	4.6 million Shell shares	16.8
	6.5 million Woodhouse-Burmah shares (Australia)	3.1
December	Burmah-Shell interest to Indian Government	10.6
	TOTAL	277.0

1976

Date	Assets sold	Cash flow generated (£ million)
January	U.S. assets	292.1
	51.2% of interest in Anglo-Ecuadorian Oilfields	3.4
March	Woodside Burmah rights	3.0
	Interest in Ninian oilfields	83.0
June	3 million B.P. shares	17.8
August	41.8% holding in Woodside Burmah	47.6
	65% of Thistle oilfield interest	87.0
	95% of other North Sea interests	7.0
	TOTAL	540.9
	TOTAL VALUE OF DIVESTMENTS DURING 1975 AND 1976	817.9

sold in January 1975. By year end, however, the only debt that had been repaid was a Canadian loan of C$55 million. The balance of the funds generated had been eaten up by oilfield exploration and development costs and payment for new tankers to which Burmah was already committed. The loan repayments were far lower than had been envisaged by the Bank of England, and in December 1975 Burmah negotiated with the Bank of England to extend their loan guarantee until September 1976. Burmah divested itself of a further £540 million of assets during 1976. The main activities divested were the American assets that had been purchased two years earlier and the majority of Burmah's North Sea oil interest, that were bought by the new government-owned British National Oil Corporation.

The hardest problem management had to tackle was the shipping operation. The projected net cash outflow had to be stopped by cutting back the fleet and obtaining new charter contracts. By 1977, the fleet had been reduced from forty-two tankers to thirty, and the four super-tankers on order (totalling 1.7 million tons) had been sold while retaining the right to hire them against specific charters. Burmah was paid £90 million for the progress payments already made on the ships and was relieved of future financial commitments for the ships. However, of the thirty tankers in the fleet, nineteen were laid up in 1977. It was only at the end of 1979, when the fleet had been reduced to twenty vessels and only one was laid up, that the shipping operations reached breakeven.

Conclusion

The rescue of Burmah Oil, albeit via the Bank of England, took place without government ownership, although Burmah Oil had to pay a high price for the help it received, in that it was forced to sell its prime assets (B.P. shares and its North Sea oil interests) to the Bank of England and B.N.O.C. In obtaining these assets, the government was able to obtain the 'benefits' of nationalization without taking on Burmah's diversified industrial assets and the shipping fleet. The 'benefits' referred to here relate to a strategic stake in the two major North Sea oilfields and profit from the later resale of B.P. shares.

Ferranti Ltd

The Ferranti Group is engaged in the development, manufacture and sale of mechanical, electrical and electronic engineering products.

Founded in 1882, Ferranti has always had a reputation for technical excellence. The company pioneered many of the early advances in the use of electricity, and in the 1950s Ferranti was a leader in computers and semiconductor devices. Unfortunately, the firm's preoccupation with finding 'elegant engineering solutions' meant that it often failed to turn its knowledge into profitable products.

Causes of Decline

The cash crisis that hit Ferranti in 1974 and necessitated government rescue was caused by the following factors.

(*a*) *Top management*: Ferranti's management had been under the control of Sebastian de Ferranti since 1958; only two other directors (including his brother Basil) had central executive responsibility. Management was not financially oriented and there was no group finance director. Top management were technically oriented, both Ferranti brothers having impressive technical qualifications. Their attitude towards research and development is seen clearly in this quote from Sebastian de Ferranti: 'We have always accepted the risk inherent in developing the new technology on which so much of Britain's future depends. We will continue to invest men and money to work on the frontiers of scientific knowledge even though we have not always prospered in our efforts.'

A strategy of technological leadership is laudable, but the problem at Ferranti was that it was an end in itself. Financial matters always took second place.

(*b*) *Organizational structure*: Ferranti was organized into four divisions, yet the group was not run as though it were a diversified group. With the exception of the Scottish division, there was no divisional management whose responsibility was to integrate the activities of the different factories within the division. Each factory or group of factories would report directly to the chairman, with the result that fifteen different businesses (or factories) were reporting direct to the chairman.

(*c*) *Lack of control*: Controls were poor or non-existent. There was no consistent observation of the group's financial position, no central cash control and poor budgeting control. One manager was quoted as saying: 'We didn't know where we were half the time . . . the relationships in our business can be quite complicated, involving invoices from hundreds of suppliers, progress payments, export bills and so on. You just can't dump all this on a bunch of clerks.'[3] The lack of control was not only financial. In Sebastian de Ferranti's own words: 'We are in such a variety of businesses it is impossible to exercise central control over research and development, management or marketing.'

(d) *The transformer division*: Losses in this division were the major cause of Ferranti's problems in 1974. The division's problems were not new; they had been apparent to industry observers for many years. Since the late 1960s, the industry had been characterized by excess manufacturing capacity – and hence declining profit margins – as the result of the Central Electricity Generating Board having overestimated the future demand for electricity. This had forced Ferranti to seek orders overseas, but the world market was dominated by the Japanese, who were able to dictate worldwide price levels. The onset of rapid inflation in these market conditions meant that costs increased sharply at a time when Ferranti was unable to pass on price increases to its customers. In 1973/74, the division showed sales of approximately £10 million and a net loss of about £1.5 million. Management had been aware of the problem in the transformer division long before the 1973/74 crisis; on one occasion it had even tried to sell the business, although there were high barriers of a psychological nature: the Ferranti family was reluctant to sell or shut the transformer division because it was the business on which the whole Ferranti empire had been built.

(e) *Financial policy*: Ferranti was undercapitalized and depended far too heavily on expensive short-term debt to finance its business. One reason for this was that Ferranti was still controlled by the Ferranti brothers; they held 56% of the voting shares prior to 1975.

(f) *Other contributing factors*: There were a number of other events that, taken together, contributed to Ferranti's downfall: the existence of fixed-price defence contracts with no escalation clauses, just at a time when inflation soared; the three-day week; a five-month-long industrial dispute; and three fires.

The Crisis

In the year ending 31 March 1974, Ferranti's overdraft reached £9.8 million as the cash flow from operations (profit after tax plus depreciation) of £2 million was only half that required to finance increased working capital requirements. During 1974, the overdraft continued to increase sharply as sales revenues increased by 23% (due only partly to inflation) and investments increased at an even faster rate.

In the autumn of 1974, the National Westminster Bank refused to extend Ferranti's borrowing facility any further. Table 16.4 contains key financial data covering this period. Ferranti turned to the Labour Government for emergency support. As a short-term measure, the government guaranteed a loan of £5 million to keep the company afloat until after the general election of November 1974. Ultimately Ferranti had to turn to the government for a reconstruction package soon after the election, as the position had not improved and the existing management seemed unable to solve the problem. Months of negotiations followed; eventually the government injected £15 million of equity capital into the group, taking 62.5% of the equity and 50% of the votes. In addition, £6.3 million was advanced as loans and the government required that a new chief executive and, for the first time, a finance director be appointed.

Recovery Actions

(a) *Appointment of new management*: It was not until August 1975 – a year after the initial cash crisis – that the government appointed a new managing director. The new managing director was Derek Alun-Jones, who had previously been managing director of Burmah Oil's industrial products division. The Ferranti brothers stayed on the board as non-executive directors (and still held 20% of the equity). Besides Alun-Jones and a new financial director, no other managers were brought in from outside the company. Alun-Jones made few personnel changes of his own, relying solely on senior management already in the firm. It has been said that Alun-Jones 'had the management background and his personality . . . allowed him to organize the company without clashing with the scientists who represented its future'.[4] Government involvement brought some major board changes, but this had little effect on management.

(b) *Organizational changes*: Alun-Jones decentralized the company, forcing the decision-making down to the divisional level, and reorganized the divisions into rational groups. An executive committee was established, consisting of Alun-Jones, the new financial controller, plus the general managers of the five U.K. divisions. This committee evaluated each of the divisional budgets and plans, and reviewed all investment decisions. Each divisional head knew exactly what all the other divisions were doing. Competition as to which division was the most profitable was encouraged. The divisions were now profit centres, rather than cost centres as before. Each was responsible for setting and achieving its own profit goals, and knew what share of head office overheads it had to recover.

(c) *Centralized financial control*: Strict financial reporting requirements were introduced. Cash flow in particular was regulated at the centre and reviewed weekly. Operating groups produced two draft plans each year – the annual budget and a rolling five-year financial forecast.

(d) *Diversification within the transformer division*: Even before the cash crisis hit fully, the first recovery steps had been taken to deal with the ailing transformer division. An executive, Bruce Calverley, was taken from the Computer Systems Division and given responsibility for stopping the losses. He took three short-term actions: the division stopped manufacturing high-voltage test equipment; overheads were drastically cut with the loss of 120 white-collar jobs; increased efforts were made to finish the large back-log of orders that were losing money because they had been taken on a fixed-price contract basis.

The longer-term options were to close the transformer plant completely or to fill up the plant by diversifying into other product-lines. The decision was made for Ferranti by the government. The rescue deal with the government involved keeping the Hollinwood factory open and maintaining employment until at least 1977/78. Bruce Calverley therefore set about developing his product line. He established a small team to identify suitable engineering products that would fit the division's skills. The result of their study was a series of acquisitions in the container-handling and agricultural-equipment industries. In December 1976, with the help of a special £1.5 million government loan Ferranti purchased the van-carrier division of Clark Equipment and the following year acquired Alpha-Accord, a small agricultural-equipment business, and another container company. Transformer production was moved into half the space it had formerly required. The results of the diversification were less than satisfactory, and in September 1979 the board decided to phase out the transformer business altogether and accept a total write-off of £6 million. The sales and profit (before extraordinary items) from 1978 to 1980 for the division were as follows:

	1978	1979	1980
Sales (in £ million)	13.3	15.9	11.5
Profit/(loss) (in £ million)	0.6	(1.1)	0.5

By the time the manufacture of power transformers finished, in the summer of 1980, the workforce at the Hollinwood site had been reduced from 1,400 (in 1974) to only 550. Calverley has been described as 'a man who is far from lacking in confidence'.[5] It may be that he kept Ferranti Engineering alive longer than would otherwise have been possible, and that without him the division would have died an earlier death.[6]

(*e*) *Refocusing of electronic components division*: In 1974, Ferranti's components division, which manufactures conductor and discrete semi-conductor components, was only breaking even. The division has since adopted a focused strategy by manufacturing a semi-customized chip. Alan Shepherd, the group's managing director, states: 'We decided we couldn't compete with the giant U.S. micro-electronic firms churning out standard, high-volume chips, and that the best thing we could do was find a slot in the market where we could exploit our geographical proximity to the British and European customer.'[7] The division is now regarded as one of Ferranti's major growth opportunities for the 1980s, although there are clearly considerable technological and marketing risks involved.

(*f*) *Divestment*: In early 1979, Ferranti sold its Canadian transformer subsidiary, Ferranti-Packard, for £7.6 million. Profitability had declined to about £500,000 on sales of £23 million. Other peripheral businesses not fitting in with Ferranti's mainstream operations have also been sold (e.g. a helicopter operating business).

One exception to complete divestment has been the electricity meter business, in which Ferranti, faced with intense foreign competition, has entered into a joint venture with the German electronics group, Siemens. Ferranti contributed the assets and Siemens the cash and technology, to form a new company known as Ferranti Measurements.

(*g*) *Refinancing*: By 1978, three years after the government's cash injection, Ferranti was able to obtain a £25 million loan from a consortium of banks that allowed them to pay off the N.E.B. and reduce short-term borrowings. Under the terms of the 1975 agreement between the government and Ferranti, the N.E.B. then reduced its equity stake from 62.5% to 50%, thereby permitting Ferranti to regain its stock market quotation.

Conclusions

Ferranti was able to make a rapid financial recovery from its 1975 crisis. Part of the reason for this is that neither of Ferranti's two core businesses (the Scottish Division and the Computer Systems Division), which accounted for two-thirds of sales and an even greater percentage of profit, required significant changes to their product-market strategy. Both are heavily dependent on defence contracts and have been helped by increasing defence expenditure. Furthermore, Ferranti's short-term profit position was helped considerably by a £4.1 million profit from the now divested Canadian subsidiary in 1976. This must count as 'luck', although it did not help Ferranti's cash-flow position very much, owing to Canadian restrictions on profit repatriation.

Ferranti's recovery strategy was not purely survival-oriented. The injection of cash in 1975, together with sound management practices since that time, has permitted Ferranti to take a longer-term view of their business and invest in the future. Capital expenditure, which was very low in the early 1970s, has increased sharply.

Table 16.4: *Ferranti Ltd: Key Financial Data, 1973–81*
(in £ millions)

Year (ending 31 March)	Sales	Profit before tax	PBIT as percentage of Sales	PBIT as percentage of capital employed
1973	65.1	£2.4	3.7	10.4
1974	70.2	–	–	–
1975	86.3	(0.5)	–	–
1976	108.5	(4.1)	3.8	8.8
1977	125.4	6.1	4.9	11.8
1978	156.9	9.1	5.8	12.6
1979	192.1	9.9	5.8	12.8
1980	214.6	11.2	5.2	14.2
1981	271.5	18.1	6.6	18.1

Source: Annual Reports.

The effect of government involvement at Ferranti has been minimal, apart from the initial injection of cash and the appointment of Derek Alun-Jones. Perhaps the most noteworthy effect was its influence in keeping the Hollinwood site open and hence the indirect influence on the transformer division's strategy of diversification. Filling up plants in an attempt to recover fixed costs rarely works as a turnaround strategy. Ferranti has proved no exception to that 'rule'.

Notes

1. 'Burmah Oil: The Rocky Road from Mandalay', *Sunday Times*, 5 January 1975.
2. *'How Burmah was Hauled Back from the Brink of Disaster'*, *Financial Times*, 10 December 1979.
3. 'How Ferranti Fought Back', *Management Today*, January 1980.
4. 'Ferranti Transforms Lame Ducks Image', *Sunday Times*, 12 February 1978.
5. 'How Ferranti Fought Back', op. cit.
6. See H. Redwood, 'How to Stop People Spoiling Your Plans', *The Director*, April 1976, for a discussion of how divisional managing directors keep ailing divisions alive longer than they should.
7. 'How Ferranti Fought Back', ibid.

17. Unsuccessful Recovery Situations: The Mere Survivors

There are many crisis situations in which management breaks even on a cash-flow basis and therefore survives, but is never able to develop an acceptable return on capital employed. These are businesses that I call 'mere survivors'. Their best hope is to be acquired, if they are independent businesses, or to be divested, if they are subsidiaries of larger companies. Two case-histories of firms falling into this category are described in this chapter: Evered and Barker & Dobson.

Evered and Company Holdings Ltd

Evered is a typical Midlands light-engineering company. It was founded in 1809 and, although it went public in 1937, it remained a family-controlled company. Until 1968, the company's profit record had been reasonable, if somewhat erratic; but it is that year which can be seen (in retrospect) to have been the start of Evered's declining performance. Apart from a brief reversal in profitability in 1973 and again in 1977 and 1978, profits have been declining or non-existent. Table 17.1 summarizes key financial data.

Causes of Decline

Evered has encountered so many problems it is difficult to isolate the principal reasons for decline. However, six reasons stand out.

(a) *Failure of competitive strategy in two principal subsidiaries*: Two of Evered's principal subsidiaries – those manufacturing gas controls and hardware – appear to have housed the bulk of the group's problems. Historically, the companies had shown some degree of innovation. They were among the first companies to develop plastic hose-pipes and to advocate the use of electronics in the gas industry; but by the early 1970s their products were obsolete and no new products were being developed. The industries themselves began to change rapidly in the 1970s – changes for which Evered's management were unprepared.

The gas industry, already suffering from overcapacity, converted to natural gas; and the hardware industry was severely affected by a recession in the building industry and significant changes in the channels of distribution for building supplies.

(b) *High-cost, antiquated production facilities*: Evered operated from four sites around Birmingham. The largest – and most antiquated – was a thirteen-acre site at Smethwick that housed the head office, the chromium plating, rolling and tube mills and hardware operations. The atmosphere at the site was one of death and decay. The buildings were very old, some were decrepit and unusable, and nearly all the machinery was very old. The production processes tended to be labour intensive. With such production facilities, it is hardly surprising that Evered found it increasingly difficult to compete on price in many areas of its business during the 1970s.

(c) *Financial policy*: Evered's financial policy had traditionally been one of high dividends and little or no reinvestment of earnings. Couple this with a conservative attitude towards debt financing (total debt to equity only reached a maximum of 18% in 1975) and declining profits, and it is not surprising that the company found itself with uncompetitive plant and equipment. Such a financial policy is not unusual in a family-controlled company.

(d) *Management instability*: There was a tremendous amount of management instability during the period of declining profits. From 1970 to 1976, Evered had three different chairmen and four different managing directors, but management turnover was not confined to top management. There were changes in management at all levels due to death, retirement and resignation. The apparent cause of so much management turnover was the trauma of changing from family management to professional management, an event triggered by the death of the last member of the Wilson family.

(e) *Commodity market dealings*: Evered experienced a loss of £386,000 in 1974 by buying forward pure metals to cover its future purchase requirements.

(f) *Inventory write-off*: In the same year, there was an almost equally large write-off of inventory (£324,000), most of it due to the hardware operation, that produced a range of fittings with a poor brass finish.

The Crisis

In 1974, Evered experienced its first loss, largely as a result of inventory write-offs and losses on metal trading, but the company was still making a small trading profit at this time (£68,000 on sales of £10.4 million). In 1975, however, there was a marked deterioration in trading profitability and the group posted a trading loss of over £400,000. Nevertheless, Evered's overall financial position remained relatively strong – gearing (at 18% of shareholders' funds) was only the same as in 1968, and liquidity measures were acceptable. There is some evidence that reasonable financial control was maintained, particularly in the crucial years, 1974 and 1975. A reduction in debtors was the company's principal source of funds in both years, and in 1975 inventory levels were also cut down. This is extremely rare in a declining company.

Recovery Actions

Various attempts to resuscitate Evered have been going on since the early 1970s, even before the company incurred losses. The major actions taken were as follows:

(*a*) *Restructuring of operating subsidiaries*: By 1973, management had recognized the existence of a problem with the gas controls and hardware subsidiaries, and decided to merge the two operations into an industrial products division. This solved none of the basic problems and caused confusion.

(*b*) *Product-line rationalization*: Evered ceased the manufacture of metal hardware in 1975 in an attempt to reduce losses from the hardware subsidiary. The plan was to concentrate on those products in which Evered had a stronger market position, but there is little evidence that this has had a major impact on the subsidiary's profitability.

(*c*) *Divestiture*: Unlike some family-run businesses, Evered has never shown a complete dislike for divestment, which undoubtedly was an asset when recovery became a key management issue. Thus in 1973, Evered Diecasting Ltd (formerly Lloyd and Rider Ltd) was sold to the Delta Metal Group, and Heathrod Ardwyn, a company engaged in plastic moulding, was sold to its management. At the end of 1976, the major part of the troublesome gas controls business was sold to Concentric Controls Ltd.

(*d*) *Rationalization of production facilities*: Product-line rationalization efforts, coupled with the sale of subsidiaries, resulted in substantial redundancies. The workforce at the end of 1976 was less than half what it had been at the start of the decade. However, some of the closures were at the main Smethwick site, with the result that, each time an activity was removed from the site, the site overheads of that activity were reallocated over the remaining activities. This caused already high unit production costs to increase further, forcing management to raise prices to uncompetitive levels.

(*e*) *Expansion of selected activities*: Management believed that its British Casters subsidiary would be one of the areas on which future recovery would be based. Consequently, when the diecasting operation was sold, the factory (which was built only in 1968) was kept for use as a second casting factory. Other noticeable activity during the mid-1970s was a series of investments in small non-ferrous stockholders.

(*f*) *Merger attempts*: . Management spent a considerable amount of time negotiating with potential acquirers as a way out of its problems. A deal that came closest to fruition was a merger with Charles Clifford Industries and a parallel sale of assets to Francis Industries Ltd. It fell through ultimately because of the collapse of Metal Products Company (Wildenhall) Ltd, whose chief executive was the instigator of a plan to merge a number of Midland-based non-ferrous-metal companies into a group. Evered's serious difficulties must have deterred potential purchasers.

(*g*) *New management*: After the period of instability of the early 1970s, a new managing director, Mr Larry Vyse, was appointed in 1976. Vyse's management style was autocratic. He believed that strong leadership was necessary for Evered to thrive.

Results

The combined effect of the above actions was to return Evered to profit in 1977 and 1978, largely as a result of divesting the problematic gas controls business at the end of 1976, but also aided by the up-swing in economic activity. But by the second half of 1979, Evered was once again in a loss-making situation, due to a substantial loss in its tube mill operations (located at the Smethwick site) and losses caused by the engineering strike (estimated at about £250,000). By now, Evered's non-ferrous business (strip, tube and extrusion) accounted for about two-thirds of its turnover since new activities had had little impact.

At the end of July 1979, Larry Vyse departed from Evered and the board took renewed measures to restore profitability.[1] Two of Evered's seven operating subsidiaries were closed (Evered & Co. (Hardware) and British Chromium Plating) and their assets sold.

The latest attempts at recovery are being made, as was the case in the mid-1970s, with the benefit of a reasonable – though deteriorating – balance-sheet situation. At year end 1979, gearing was at about 32%; at year end 1980, it had risen to 54%. An indication of the view taken by Evered's bankers, the National Westminster Bank, can be gleaned from the fact that the overdraft of over £1 million is secured by a legal mortgage on the freehold property, a specific charge on all debts, and a floating charge on other assets. However, whereas after 1976 the company was faced with an improved economic environment, the end of 1979 was only the beginning of the very deep 1980/81 recession. Given the depth of the latest recession and the fact that no successful effort appears to have been made to develop a viable product-market strategy for Evered, the outlook for the future seems extremely bleak. Indeed, it would now appear that Evered's current resources and competitive position would make the development of a viable strategy – and hence a sustainable recovery – an impossibility as long as it remains an independent company.

Table 17.1: *Evered & Co. Holdings Ltd: Sales and Profitability, 1970–80 (in £ millions)*

	Sales	Profit before tax
1970	6.8	0.3
1971	6.5	0.3
1972	7.1	0.2
1973	8.3	0.3
1974	10.4	(0.4)
1975	7.6	(0.5)
1976	9.5	(0.2)
1977	10.2	0.1
1978	11.7	0.3
1979	13.6	(0.1)
1980	11.8	(0.7)

In early 1980, Mr D.M. 'Sandy' Saunders, chairman of Francis Industries, the company to whom Evered was attempting to sell its assets in the mid 1970s. became chairman of Evered. In December 1980, Francis Industries made a takeover bid for the group but this was rejected by the shareholders.

Barker and Dobson Group Ltd

The Barker and Dobson Group (hereafter referred to as B. & D.) competes in the sugar-based segment of the confectionery market and has a chain of confectionery, tobacconist and newsagent (C.T.N.) outlets trading under the name of Lewis Meeson. In 1970, the company's range of activities was much wider and included wholesale grocery and confectionery, retail grocery, the manufacture of shop equipment and wine importing. Previous biscuit and bakery interests had been sold during the 1960s.

B. & D.'s profit history (shown in Table 17.2) indicates that the company made record profits from 1972 to 1974, and that this was in fact a turnaround from a loss in 1970. However, analysis of the causes of the enormous losses that followed in 1975 and 1976 indicates that the recovery from 1972 to 1974 was largely a 'book improvement' only and was itself the principal cause of the subsequent decline.

Causes of Decline

Six principal reasons have been identified as causing the crisis of the mid-1970s.

(a) *A bad acquisition*: In October 1972, B. & D. bought Waller and Hartley, a confectionery manufacturer, for £4.5 million by issuing new shares and loan stock. For this sum of money, B. & D. bought a company with fixed assets (at book value) of £1 million and working capital of £200,000. Waller and Hartley's sales were declining and it produced a trading profit of only £160,000 in the year after its acquisition. For this B. & D. had paid a sum of £3.3 million in excess of book value!

(b) *Problems in the confectionery manufacturing division*: After B. & D. had acquired Waller and Hartley in October 1972, the group owned nine confectionery subsidiaries in Britain and Ireland. The product range consisted largely of 'commodity type' sugar confectionery (boiled sweets, jellies, pastilles, etc.), although there were a few higher-margin products such as Hacks, a medicated confectionery product. In the 1973/74 financial year, a number of problems began to emerge. First, mistakes were made in buying sugar in the commodity market. Large stocks of sugar were bought at the end of 1973 'to hedge against expected shortages', increasing inventory levels by £1.8 million at the end of March 1974. In his annual report, the chairman indicated that 'these higher than usual stocks were well bought'. Unfortunately, the price of sugar dropped dramatically in 1974. Having reached a peak of £650 per ton in November 1973, the wholesale price index for sugar declined from 630 in 1973 to 166 in 1974 (1970 = 100). Second, B. & D. was beginning to meet severe price competition. Its main customers, chains like Marks and Spencer and Woolworths, were demanding lower and lower prices. There is little product differentiation in the boiled sweets segment of the confectionery market where most of B. & D.'s volume was sold, and competition was increasing from unbranded products. B. & D. lost some major customers on price. Third, market demand for sugar confectionery, and boiled sweets in particular, dropped by about 15% between 1973 and 1975. Fourth, there was a total lack of marketing skills (no analysis of discounts, no repackaging, poor advertising and promotion, etc.); and finally, fixed assets were old and in need of replacement.

The combined result of these factors was a volume decline in 1974/75 in excess of 20% and a divisional trading loss in the first six months of the year of £425,000. B. & D.'s managing director, Mr W. D. McPhail, brought in P.A. Management Consultants to investigate; they recommended that two of the eight production plants be closed and that various production and inventory control measures be instituted. Finished goods stock levels were reduced and the division broke even in the second half of the year (excluding the extraordinary expenses of plant closure of almost £500,000).

(c) *Expansion of grocery wholesaling operation*: From about 1970 onwards, McPhail had been investing large amounts of cash in the grocery wholesaling business. By 1972/73, B. & D. operated twenty-eight cash-and-carry warehouses, seventeen grocery wholesalers and one frozen-food warehouse, most trading under the 'Budgetts' name. However, in 1972/73 the trading profit margin was only £300,000 on sales of £40 million (0.7% of sales) at a time when it was B. & D.'s accounting practice to include gains on property sales in trading profit. In the following year, 1973/74, sales volume was down by about 10% in real terms, and the division probably made a loss. No separate profit figure was reported for the division that year, although the annual report referred to 'substantial pressure on margins' – a euphemism for a 'loss' situation. The loss situation continued throughout 1974/75, with the result that the major part of the division was sold in February 1975 for £4.8 million, showing a profit on book value of £740,000. The main reasons for the division's lack of profitability appear to have been mismanagement, lack of adequate controls on margins and possibly a misguided strategy in the cash-and-carry business.

(*d*) *Expansion of Oakshott grocery chain*: McPhail built up the Oakshott grocery chain by the acquisition of small grocery stores at a time when such stores were becoming increasingly uncompetitive and were declining in number. In his 1972/73 annual report, McPhail wrote, 'The neighbourhood unit grocery shops are increasing their influence on their localities and arrangements have been made to open new shops in this sector because we feel it is the direction in which growth lies.' Detailed profit figures are not available for the Oakshott chain, but we can reasonably assume that the major part, if not all, the retail trading profit of £370,000 on sales of £26 million was from the C.T.N. chain, and not Oakshott. This is confirmed by subsequent action during 1973/74 and 1974/75, when 255 out of a total of 379 stores were closed because they were uneconomic. Profitability of the Oakshott chain deteriorated rapidly during this period as margins narrowed continually, and acute cash shortages within the B. & D. group meant that Oakshott was frequently forced to run out of stock. The Oakshott chain lost £1.3 million on sales of £17 million in 1974/75. The main causes of the Oakshott problems were similar to those in the wholesaling divisions: poor management, a misguided strategy and lack of control.

(*e*) *Divestment of profitable cash-generating business*: Almost half of the 1972/73 group profits of £3 million was generated by the disposal of profitable parts of the business. Between 1970 and March 1974, about 300 of the original 540 C.T.N. outlets owned by the group were sold. Other assets sold included the Grayson bottling plant, the only profitable part of their wine importing and distributorship business. The main reason for this policy appears to have been the need to generate cash for the expansion policies referred to above – yet it involved selling off the only cash-generating business in the group.

(*f*) *Management*: From 1970 until 1975, B. & D. was run largely by one man, Mr McPhail. At B. & D., McPhail appeared to sacrifice long-term profits for short-term gains while expanding fast into areas new to the company. Central financial control was weak. McPhail finally resigned in 1975 as losses mounted and bank borrowings reached record levels. He was replaced by one of the non-executive directors, Professor Clarkson, then a professor at Manchester Business School, but little or nothing was done to rectify the deteriorating situation.

The Crisis

The divestitute and closures implemented by McPhail during the previous two years had postponed the ultimate crisis but, as one division after another encountered problems, in 1974/75 the group reported a record trading loss of £2.4 million, and revenue reserves disappeared. Towards the end of 1975, the group's bankers, National Westminister Bank, decided to take action but, rather than appointing a receiver, they called in Ronnie Aitken, a senior partner in the firm of accountants, Binder and Hamlyn.

At this time, the group consisted of the confectionery division with five factories, 160 Oakshott shops, 178 Lewis Meeson shops, and the wine business of Roger Grayson. The situation was as follows:

(i) Oakshott was losing £50,000 per week and increasingly running out of stock as cash was short; it was £800,000 over its borrowing limit.

(ii) The Roger Grayson wine business was losing money.

(iii) The Lewis Meeson chain was marginally profitable, but £250,000 over its borrowing limit.

(iv) The confectionery division was making a small profit, but continuing to lose market share.

Recovery Actions

(*a*) *New management*: Ronnie Aitken was no stranger to acute problems, as he had done a lot of receivership and liquidation work at Binder and Hamlyn, including Headquarters and General Stores. He found management to be poor and dispirited throughout the group. He dismissed all the directors (except the one in charge of property) as soon as replacements could be found. His most important appointment was that of Bill Kenyon, who had previously had big-company experience in the chemical industry, to run the confectionery division.

He was promoted to chief executive in 1978. His other main appointment, a director in charge of the retail division, was less successful and left in 1978 after a disagreement with Aitken.

(b) *Divestiture of Oakshott*: Ronnie Aitken's first problem was to stop the cash drain that Oakshott was imposing on the company, and to get cash flowing in from other sources to cover this period of contraction. The Oakshott chain was reduced almost immediately to forty shops, which was considered at that time to be about the break-even level. The reason given for not getting rid of all the shops immediately was that terminal payments were too high and property values were low at that time. It was hoped that these forty shops would at least break even with better management, but it was at this time that the Sainsbury/Tesco high-street price war started and the Oakshott situation started to slump even more; by September 1978, all the remaining shops had been sold. The cash to fund this period was coming from the Lewis Meeson chain, a cash business with rapid inventory turnover.

(c) *Marketing changes in the confectionery division*: Aitken decided that the confectionery division was to be the basis of future growth, and he set about revamping the marketing operation. Price increases of up to 40–45% were implemented almost immediately, unprofitable customers were dropped, products were repackaged and reformulated, and a new advertising campaign was begun. Aitken was basically optimistic about the potential of the confectionery division; although he cut out unprofitable business in the short term, he decided to keep all five factories, although some were very old.

(d) *Attempt to reorganize Lewis Meeson chain*: Although profitable and generating cash, the C.T.N. business was not producing a reasonable return on capital. The better performers in the C.T.N. industry, like N.S.S., had consistently produced a return on capital in excess of 20%. Aitken experienced difficulty in finding the right management for the chain and thus was unable to capitalize on what he believed to be the chain's profit potential.

Results

These actions resulted in a return to profitability in 1979, but not for long. Losses of £0.5 million and £1.0 million were incurred again, in

1979/80 and 1980/81 respectively. A sustained recovery had not been achieved. The basic strategic weaknesses in B. & D.'s two main areas of business showed through. In the confectionery business, market demand continued to decline, resulting in B. & D.'s sales volume being about 10% lower in 1978/79 than in the previous year. Management's response to the declining demand for sugar confectionery was to increase production of chocolate-based products where they 'believed prospects to be better', but this would appear optimistic, bearing in mind that the company would now be competing against the chocolate giants (Cadbury, Rowntree Mackintosh and Mars). What management has not done is to reduce capacity by rationalizing its manufacturing operations. The reason for the large Irish loss in 1979 would also appear to be basically strategic, although details are not available. In the C.T.N. business, Lewis Meeson's profits still failed to rise above 1% of turnover. Part of the reason for this may be the unsolved management problem; but analysis of the C.T.N. industry also tends to indicate strategic problems. The stores are generally small, poorly located, and lack the local 'monopoly' position enjoyed by their more successful competitors.

Table 17.2: *Barker and Dobson Group Ltd: Sales and Profitability, 1972–81*

	Sales (in £ millions)	Profit before tax
1972	77.0	2.0
1973	81.2	1.8
1974	81.4	1.0
1975	77.4	(2.4)
1976	44.9	(2.4)
1977	41.1	(0.8)
1978	42.9	0.2
1979	33.5	(0.5)
1980	31.2	(1.0)
1981	35.0	0.1

Source: Extel Card.

Notes

1. 'Another Recovery Attempt', *The Times*, 20 May 1980.

18. Unsuccessful Recovery Situations: Short-term Survival but Eventual Failure

One of the four types of recovery situation described in Chapter 5 is that of firms that exhibit all the *symptoms* of successful recovery after the implementation of a recovery strategy, but eventually fail. Many years may go by between initial crisis and eventual insolvency; in the intervening years, profitability may recover substantially beyond that required for 'mere survival'. Both management and outside observers will believe that the firm has been successfully turned around. The two case-histories outlined in this chapter – Inveresk and Bamford's – are firms that fall into this category. In Inveresk's case eleven years passed between cash crisis and failure, while in Bamford's case eight years passed; in both situations the *underlying* competitive position of the firms remained weak.

Inveresk Group Ltd

If a case-history on Inveresk had been written in early 1975 instead of early 1981, it would probably have been included in one of the either chapters on successful turnarounds. From 1968 to 1971, the company went through a period of crisis, but from 1972 to 1974 there were three years of sharply increasing profits. However, starting in 1975, Inveresk's profit position began to deteriorate once again, so that 1980 saw a record loss of £3.5 million (see Table 18.1) and the company's acquisition by the U.S. paper giant, Georgia Pacific. An analysis of what happened at Inveresk over the last twenty years has some important implications for British industry generally and for our analysis of recovery strategies.

Incorporated in 1922, Inveresk grew to become the U.K.'s third largest paper-maker behind the Bowater Corporation and Reed International. However, in the years following the Second World War, the gap between Inveresk and its two main competitors widened, so that by the early 1960s, Inveresk's capital employed was only about 12% of Bowater's and 20% of Reed's. Although much smaller, Inveresk managed to achieve a return on capital employed superior to that of Bowater and Reed throughout the early 1960s.

During 1965, however, two important investment decisions were taken that were to be principal factors causing Inveresk's decline in the late 1960s. Both these investment decisions were strategic responses to changes that were taking place in the paper and pulp industry, changes that were already beginning to affect Inveresk's competitive position in the marketplace. We need to understand these changes if we are to understand the problems of Inveresk.

Table 18.1: *Inveresk Group: Sales and Profitability, 1965–80*
(in £ millions)

	Sales	Profit before tax	Profit before tax as percentage of sales	Profit before tax as percentage of capital employed at year end
1965	27.0	2.03	7.5	9.0
1966	26.0	1.17	4.5	5.5
1967	27.7	0.07	0.3	0.3
1968	23.4	(0.50)	(2.1)	(2.4)
1969	24.7	0.43	1.7	2.5
1970	24.7	0.10[1]	0.4	0.7
1971	18.9	(0.85)[2]	(4.5)	(7.5)
1972	18.2	0.60	3.3	5.2
1973	24.8	2.51	10.1	19.2
1974	37.9	4.66	12.3	25.6
1975	34.6	1.26	3.7	6.8
1976	51.7	1.56	3.0	7.0
1977	70.8	2.23	3.2	8.5
1978	75.4	0.51	0.7	1.7
1979	84.9	0.53	0.6	1.8
1980	63.0	(3.46)	(5.5)	(25.0)

NOTES

1. *Before* extraordinary charge of £3.0 million.
2. *Before* extraordinary charge of £1.5 million.
Source: Annual Reports.

Until 1960, the paper and pulp industry in the U.K. was protected from world markets by a tariff barrier that was set up in the inter-war years. Thus, whereas wood pulp entered the U.K. free of duty, foreign paper and board manufacturers faced import tariffs of up to 20%. As the raw material represented about 60% of total costs, this protection was an essential feature of the U.K. industry. This tariff barrier was initially of little consequence in international terms, since competition throughout the world was between relatively small .companies operating on a regional basis. The international giants did not exist on the scale that we know them today; for example, thirty years ago Canada was an importer of paper and Sweden an importer of both wood and pulp.

However, as the world demand for paper and board began to grow rapidly in the affluent postwar years, two significant changes took place. First, the wood-producing countries began to look for an increase in the added value of their exports, with the result that the main environmental force in the postwar years has been the forward integration of wood producers into pulp production and then into paper and board production. The competitive advantages to integration can be large: for example, integration enables the paper producer to have a guaranteed supply of pulp and hence fewer stocking problems. The cost of the pulp used is not subject to the vagaries of the international pulp market, so the cost of the finished product is usually both lower and more stable than it would otherwise be. In addition,

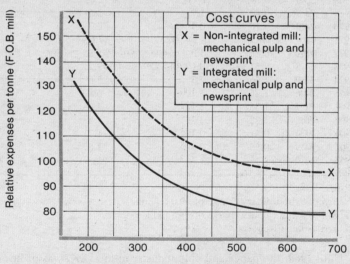

Figure 18.1: *Relative Savings from Integration in the Manufacture of Newsprint as a Function of Mill Size*

Source: Consultants Jaakko Poyry (1973).

certain stages of the production line are eliminated; cost savings here have been estimated as 15% on the capital investment and 12–15% on operating costs.[1] Along with this trend towards forward integration, firms began to increase the size of their production units in order to achieve economies of scale. For illustrative purpose, Figure 18.1 shows the cost savings associated with increases in production unit size, and the additional savings associated with integrated production, in the manufacture of newsprint.

Largely isolated from these changes in world markets by the tariff barrier, the U.K. paper and board industry generally failed to adapt. Although some big groups, like Bowater and Reed, managed to grow in this protected environment, the U.K. industry as a whole avoided keeping up with the main international producers. In spite of the closure of the smallest U.K. mills, U.K. mill sizes became small by international standards and production methods became comparatively less efficient. Furthermore, the U.K. paper and board industry was at a competitive disadvantage in terms of its ability to integrate

Table 18.2: *Official Government Price Indices for the U.K. Paper and Board Industry – Broad Input-output Series*

Year	Input Cost of pulp (Index: 1963 = 100)	Output Selling price of the output of the U.K. paper and board-making industry (Index: 1963 = 100)
1963	100	100
1964	105	102
1965	108	105
1966	105	105
1967	105	105
1968	117	113
1969	126	117
1970	143	128
1971	150	136
1972	147	142
1973	177	161
1974	195	165
1975	276	212
1976	329	238
1977	323	278
1978	254	279
1979	288	311

Source: Department of Trade and Industry.

backwards. The U.K. has only about 1% of Western Europe's coniferous forests, as compared to 61% in Scandinavia. This resulted in the integrated Scandinavian companies being able to sell pulp at increasingly higher prices to the non-integrated British (and E.E.C.) paper mills. Table 18.2 compares the cost of pulp to U.K. paper and board manufacturers with the selling prices obtained for their output, from 1963 to 1979.

Integration, however, cannot be achieved with all grades of paper and board as, for example, where small tonnages do not make a complex investment viable, or in circumstances where a range of diversified products are produced in small quantities such as household and sanitary papers, industrial and special papers. Thus small mills making to order continued to survive by filling gaps in the market. Many of these product-market gaps were characterized by a high value-added content.

By 1960, import penetration of the U.K. market had achieved some 27% despite the tariff barrier, and in certain sectors (as in the commodity type newsprint sector, for example) import penetration was as high as 47%. Worse was to come. As the tariffs protecting the U.K. industry were phased away during the 1960s (following the establishment of E.F.T.A.), U.K. producers became increasingly vulnerable to Scandinavian competition, especially in the bulk, standardized grades of paper. As a result, import penetration of the U.K. market began rising rapidly, reaching 29% by 1962, 35% by 1970, and 48% by 1978 (see Table 18.3).

Since joining the Common Market in 1973, U.K. firms have received some measure of tariff protection against the Scandinavian producers, but along with E.E.C. membership came low-price imports from continental Europe, particularly from the inefficient and subsidized French and German mills. Thus imports of printing and writing paper, that had accounted for 29% of the market in 1973, accounted for 49% by 1979.

It is the U.S. pulp and paper producers, however, who have increased their share of the European market most in recent years (from 44% in 1973 to 60% in 1977), at the expense of the Scandinavians. The Scandinavians preferred to maintain price rather than market-share in face of the U.S. producers with lower cost positions. It is estimated that U.S. mills obtain wood for about 20–25% less than their Scandinavian competitors. Moreover, in looking to the future, the U.S. companies are planning relatively far greater increases in pulp capacity than any other country. In theory, these cheaper pulp supplies should help the independent European paper makers like Inveresk to compete on better terms with the large integrated pulp and paper mills in Scandinavia, as tariff barriers between the E.E.C. and E.F.T.A. are dismantled by 1984. However, if this were so, great pressure would be put on Scandinavian companies to integrate forward more rapidly into those very markets where Inveresk itself has been integrating forward.

Table 18.3: *Imports as Percentage of U.K. Consumption*

	1960	1965	1970	1975	1979
Newsprint	47	43	51	75	77
Kraft wrappings	44	57	72	83	76
Food wrappings	33	28	33	36	41
Printing and writing	1	10	22	40	49
Packing board	24	22	25	22	28
Other paper	16	17	20	18	40
Other board	19	14	24	28	40
Total	27	28	35	44	50

Source: H.M.S.O. Business Monitor Statistics.

Following this outline of the major structural changes that took place in the pulp and paper industry during the 1960s, the reader should be in a better position to appreciate the causes of Inveresk's decline.

Causes of Decline

(*a*) *Increasingly uncompetitive cost position*: With the removal of tariff protection and the trend towards larger, integrated, lower-cost production facilities among overseas competitors, Inveresk found itself increasingly at a cost disadvantage. Inveresk's competitive disadvantage was twofold: first, their paper mills were small and relatively inefficient, putting them at a relative cost disadvantage against the larger Scandinavian producers; and second, Inveresk was at an absolute cost disadvantage in that it was forced to buy its raw material from its competitors. Gross profit margins declined as pulp prices increased and Inveresk was unable to pass on price increases to its customers due to lower-priced foreign competition. As imports increased their market penetration, overcapacity developed in the U.K. industry, further fuelling price competition.

(*b*) *Technical difficulties in implementing mill expansion programme*: In 1965, Inveresk initiated a project to install a high-speed, large-blade coating machine at their Donside Paper Company subsidiary, in response to the industry trend towards larger mills. One of the paper mills was to be rebuilt completely and a new power plant installed. The development was estimated to be completed by 1968 at a cost of £3.5 million. However, by 1967 Inveresk was experiencing 'an exceptional number of mechanical and technical difficulties in starting up the sophisticated and complex plant'. Output was below the planned level, product quality was below par and heavy operating losses were incurred. Similar (but financially less serious) delays were incurred when expanding the Northfleet Mills.

(*c*) *Backwards integration*: Also in 1965, management decided to take steps to ensure at least part of its long-term supplies of wood pulp in response to the development of integrated pulp and paper mills by the Scandinavians. Accordingly, Inveresk entered into negotiations with the Riegel Corporation of the U.S. to build a bleached-craft pulp mill in Louisiana. The cost of the mill was to have been $40 million, and it was planned to come on stream in 1968, although it was not expected to break even until 1973. There was a substantial cost overrun, and by 1968 the cost estimate had reached $50 million.

But two problems, even more important than the higher-than-anticipated capital costs, emerged by the time the plant came on stream in October 1968: first, Inveresk's agreement with Riegel was to purchase pulp from the mill at 'announced' U.S. prices, but in late 1968 U.S. and world 'market' prices were lower than the announced prices; second, by the end of 1968 Inveresk had already closed or sold four paper mills, owing to its increasingly uncompetitive cost position. Consequently Inveresk was unable to absorb within its own plants more than one-third of its share of the pulp mill's output.

(*d*) *New venture start-up costs*: During 1967, Inveresk took a 24.7% share in a new company, British Tissues – a company designed to compete with the U.S. tissue and paper-towel companies, Scott Paper Company and Kimberley Clark. The company suffered large start-up expenses in 1970 and severe trading losses in 1971. The market was a growth market, but it was inevitable that there would be high costs in gaining market share from the entrenched competition, who were (and still are) large multinational companies.

(*e*) *Poor management*: Until at least 1968, Inveresk suffered from a rather 'feudal' management style. Officially, power was centralized in the board but, in effect, the management style was highly decentralized because the divisions were not held accountable for anything. Incredibly, Inveresk's own mills were often competing with one another for the same business, and customers would often play one off against the other for lower prices.

(*f*) *Lack of control*: There was a lack of adequate financial control, as might be expected from what has been said of the management, but this *per se* does not appear to have been a major cause of Inveresk's decline. It was rather a question of poor management. For example, many products in the range were known to be unprofitable in the mid-1960s, but no one was willing to act upon this information.

The financial implications of Inveresk's capital investments became apparent to the board as early as 1966, with the result that they appointed Tom Corrigan, then aged thirty-four, as finance director with the task of introducing centralized financial control procedures; he had joined the company the previous year as company secretary. From 1965 to 1968, borrowings and interest payments increased sharply. Gearing (total debt/shareholders' funds) increased from 4% to 42%, and net interest payments increased from almost nil to £425,000 per annum, at a time when profits totally disappeared. By 1968, Inveresk was financially very weak and, largely under the influence of its finance director, Tom Corrigan, a rescue operation was mounted.

Recovery Actions

There were two distinct phases in Inveresk's recovery: from 1968 to 1972, the company's cash flow was improved, largely by divestments; and from 1973 onwards, when the company's corporate strategy was redirected towards forward integration by acquisition. The major actions taken were as follows:

(*a*) *Divestiture*: In 1968, the board concluded that 'the Group's resources were inadequate to bring the Donside project to a profitable level in an acceptable time'.[2] Consequently, the Donside Mill was sold to Bowater and Reed for £2 million in cash. The board also decided to sell the company's 50% share in the Louisiana pulp mill to a U.S. corporation, Georgia Pacific, for shares and interest-bearing notes, which were cashed as soon as possible. As a result of these (and other small divestitures), Inveresk's financial situation was dramatically improved.

(*b*) *Closure of inefficient mills*: Management had already started to close inefficient mills prior to the sale of Donside, and this policy was continued. The chairman's statement for 1970 reported:

Your Board decided that it was necessary to concentrate the production of certain grades of plain paper in fewer mills and discontinue the manufacture of grades which had become unprofitable. Negotiations were also commenced for the sale of the goodwill of the vegetable parchment manufacturing business. In consequence it was announced that Northfleet and Musselburgh Mills were to be closed. Economies in head office and central service departments have also been implemented. As a result some 1,200 staff and workpeople have been declared redundant.

The two mill closures agreed in 1970 and implemented in early 1971 removed nearly 40% of the company's paper and board production capacity. From a position of having twenty-two mills and about 6,000 employees in the late 1940s, the company had now contracted to eight mills and about half the number of employees. In 1971, however, came a year of recession that necessitated even further cutbacks in production capacity. Thus, the chairman's statement for 1971 reported:

The year proved to be the worst for the British papermaking industry for a very considerable time. [Action taken during the year included] . . . the withdrawal of some less efficient papermaking machinery at certain mills and the concentration of production on fewer and more efficient machines. The manufacture of certain products which had become uneconomic was discontinued. Stringent economies were made in overhead costs at production facilities and in selling and corporate administrative expenses.

(*c*) *Reduction of central overheads*: Head office and central service departments were cut back as the company shrank in size during 1970 and 1971.

(*d*) *Management changes*: In 1971, Tom Corrigan was appointed managing director, two other directors resigned and a third retired. Corrigan has since been described by *Management Today* as a 'rather shy and stiff-mannered accountant with merchant bank experience . . . who as the sole executive member of a tiny, four-strong and otherwise part-time board, including the chairman, enjoyed unusual freedom of action'.[3]

(*e*) *Organization changes*: Corrigan introduced a divisionalized organization structure under which each division became a profit centre within a framework of centralized financial control. Divisions were organized by end use and customers, rather than in the haphazard way they had been previously.

(f) *Property development*: After closure of the Northfleet mill, Inveresk sold 7.5 acres of land but kept 25 acres, and began developing a mixed industrial estate.

(g) *Sale of investment in British Tissues*: During 1973, Inveresk sold its investment in this company for £1.8 million in cash. Management finally realized that 'the prospective capital requirements and the nature of the market it operates in made British Tissues more properly suited to significantly larger owners'.

(h) *Expansion via forward integration*: Corrigan's strategy for Inveresk was to become less dependent on the highly competitive and cyclical paper and board business but not to diversify into totally unrelated businesses. Consequently, he started to integrate forward (to buy businesses which had traditionally been his customers), where he believed Inveresk's resources were adequate to compete effectively. Thus, from 1972 onwards, Inveresk bought a stationery manufacturer and distributor, a packaging company (Vernon Packaging) and a paper merchandising company (Lepard & Smith). These strategic moves meant that, by 1977, papermaking accounted for only 47% of group sales, whereas in 1971 it had been 90%.

Results

The result of these actions, and the cyclical up-swing in market demand during 1972 and 1973, was sharply increasing profitability until the end of the 1974 financial year. Acquisitions played a major role in the recovery; but perhaps more noteworthy is the fact that, despite a bad economic recession in 1975, the group did not make a loss. Several U.K. mills closed down during the recession, but none belonged to Inveresk; their earlier mill-rationalization programme had been successful. Pre-tax profit margins (about 3% of sales) and return on capital employed (about 6–8%) remained relatively low after the 1975 recession, and borrowing increased sharply from 6% (of shareholders' funds) in 1973 to 43% in 1978. In 1977, Inveresk lost about £900,000 when they found their inventories devalued as the result of falling pulp prices. In 1978, one of the newly acquired businesses in the paper merchanting division started to lose money and this, together with the already low profit margins and the advent of another recession (far worse than any other since the 1930s), combined to put Inveresk back in a recovery situation. In an attempt to stem the losses of its paper merchanting business, at the beginning of 1980 a subsidiary was sold. This had the effect of sharply reducing Inveresk's gearing. However, as the recession began to gather momentum during 1980, demand for Inveresk's products dropped sharply and the company went into a heavy loss-making situation. The 1980 loss was £3.5 million. In January 1981, Georgia Pacific made a takeover bid for the company, but Inveresk went into voluntary liquidation before the deal was completed. Georgia Pacific then acquired the assets of Inveresk.

Why would Georgia Pacific want to buy Inveresk? The answer would appear to be a combination of cheap assets and the use of Inveresk as a vehicle for penetrating the U.K. (and European) markets even further with cheap U.S. imports.

What went wrong in the late 1970s? Certainly, Lepard & Smith may have been a poor acquisition in 1976, but this was only a single contributing factor since, after it was sold, Inveresk proceeded to make a record loss. More important were two other factors, both of which were common to the whole of the British paper and board industry. These were, first, a higher unit-cost position than that of foreign competitors, thereby permitting substantial import penetration, and, second, the 1980/81 recession. Whereas in the 1960s the British paper industry found itself at a cost disadvantage against the Scandinavians, it now found itself hit by low-price imports, largely from the E.E.C.countries. The main cost advantages of the E.E.C. paper mills were (and continue to be) cheaper energy prices, large government subsidies and, more recently, higher investment in plant and equipment. In 1979, the high value of sterling also helped. Even more serious in the short term was the drop in market demand resulting from the world recession in 1980; U.K. demand for paper and board products dropped by 11% in twelve months. In one important respect, Inveresk's problems in the late 1970s were the same as in the mid-1960s: they were at a cost disadvantage in the face of foreign competition. But on top of this add a dramatic drop in demand, and the company was bound to find itself in a weak position.

Bamford Limited

Bamford was a medium-sized manufacturer and importer of a wide range of agricultural equipment. Founded in 1871, it built its reputation as a haymaking machinery specialist, serving both home and export markets. The company went public in 1958 and two brothers, Mr Vincent Bamford (the managing director) and Mr Richard Bamford (the engineering director), retained 10–15% of the equity. In the early 1960s, the company added the 'Klaies' imported combine-harvester to its product range, sales of which were substantial and provided a good contribution to profit. However, starting in 1967, Bamford's experienced a sharp decline in profitability, although many of the causes of eventual decline had been present for a number of years.

Causes of Decline

Five reasons can be identified for the decline.

(*a*) *Loss of import agency*: Bamford's lost the 'Klaies' combine agency in 1967 when the foreign manufacturer was acquired. The profit from this product-line had masked inefficiencies elsewhere in the company. Bamford's managed to pick up the Volvo combine as a replacement, but it was a poor substitute for the Klaies product.

(*b*) *Poor management*: The company was a classic example of one-man rule. Vincent Bamford as managing director had absolute authority.

(*c*) *Lack of financial control*: There was virtually no control. There were no sales forecasts, no budgets, no monthly or even quarterly management accounts. Management simply sent all bills and invoices to the auditors at year end and waited to see if they had made a profit! There was a so-called standard costing system that had been intro-duced by the firm's auditors, but it was virtually useless, since part lists did not exist for individual products.

(*d*) *Production inefficiency*: The plant had been allowed to run down, the foundry was antiquated, spare parts were just left lying around, and overstaffing was evident. The plant tended to operate as a highly inefficient job-shop operation. There was inadequate production scheduling to take account of the seasonal sales peak (60% of sales occurred during the March–June period).

(*e*) *Product-market strategy*: By the end of 1960s, many of the firm's products were becoming obsolete. There was little thought given to questions of product-market strategy. When the recession hit the agricultural-machinery industry in 1970 (it is a highly cyclical industry), Bamford's appears to have been hurt more deeply than the equipment industry in general. Bamford's 1970/71 sales revenues dropped by 16%, indicating a volume drop of just over 20%, whereas U.K. sales of agricultural equipment dropped by only about 10%.

Trigger for Change

The combined result of these actions was declining profits after 1968, but the financial situation was not serious. Both gearing and liquidity were acceptable and there was no cash-flow crisis. Unlike many of the other companies we have looked at, the trigger for change was not a financial crisis, but shareholder pressure. In 1967, Bamford's faced an unwanted takeover bid from J. C. Bamford Excavators, a company that had been set up by Mr Joseph Bamford, who had left the family company in 1945 to make trailer and (subsequently) excavation equipment. In order to stop the acquisition, management turned to Fred Burgess, the owner of the largest chain of agricultural dealerships in the U.K. Burgess has a close relationship with Bamford's, both personally and as a major customer. He bought a 22% interest in Bamford's and, as the largest single shareholder, assumed the chairmanship, although the Bamford brothers retained day-to-day control of operations. Fred Burgess was to be the catalyst for change – although not immediately.

From the beginning, Burgess was aware that Bamford's was poorly managed, and so in 1969 he recruited John Varley, who had had twenty-one years' experience with Massey-Ferguson. Varley joined Bamford's in the commercial department, but his brief was to look over the entire operation. By July 1970 it was clear to Burgess that Bamford's management was unable to deal with the pressure of an industry-wide recession. There was a boardroom dispute, and Fred Burgess initiated the necessary recovery actions.

Recovery Actions

(*a*) *Appointment of new chief executive*: Vincent Bamford was persuaded to retire as managing director and Richard Bamford was shuffled into engineering development. John Varley was appointed joint managing director and chief executive. As a public relations move, John Bamford, another family member but one who had not been part of the previous management group, became joint managing director with Varley. Varley's advantage over many chief executives in recovery situations was that he had already spent eighteen months gathering data about Bamford's, and he knew what he wanted to do.

(*b*) *Reduction in costs*: Varley's first action was to cut costs, both direct labour and overheads. Of the firm's 955 employees, 250 were made redundant. Unprofitable operations were eliminated.

(*c*) *Internal reorganization*: Varley set up an executive committee of five directors and five managers to plan, co-ordinate and control operational activities. He reorganized the marketing department, adding new sales management where appropriate.

(*d*) *Management reporting systems*: Simple control systems were instituted to allow Varley and the executive committee to monitor operations. Orders were monitored weekly, and daily and weekly production reports were introduced. The job of developing an accurate costing system was begun, and annual budgeting was started.

(*e*) *Introduction of production planning*: The introduction of sales forecasts as part of the budgeting exercise (based on feedback from dealers) permitted Bamford's to start production planning.

(*f*) *Increase in market demand*: In 1972, the agricultural-machinery industry went from recession to boom. Sales revenues of agricultural-equipment manufacturers increased by 43% over the previous year and, within the U.K., sales rose by a staggering 65%. Against this background, Bamford's sales revenues increased by 77%.

(*g*) *Addition of new product-lines*: Bamford's increased sales were not due solely to the demand cycle. Varley had started adding new products during 1971. In 1972, he dropped the Volvo combine and replaced it with a better Italian product, the Laverda combine. New additions to the product-line were made throughout the mid-1970s. But the most important – and probably the largest single factor in Bamford's recovery at this time – was an acquisition.

(*h*) *Acquisitions*: Jones Balers had been the U.K. operation of Allis-Chalmers. In October 1971, corporate headquarters decided to divest themselves of this operation and they contacted Varley to see whether

Bamford's would be interested in buying. They were. The acquisition added £1.6 million of turnover to Bamford's in 1972 and accounted for a quarter of group sales in that year. Bamford's paid £179,000 in cash; for this, they received (a) a plant in Wales valued shortly afterwards at £350,000; (b) Jones Balers' and Allis-Chalmers' product range; and (c) additional export coverage. During the same year, Bamford's also acquired control of their French distributor.

(*i*) *Salesforce incentives*: Salesforce remuneration was changed from salary alone to a mixture of salary and commission, but with a top limit of 20% of total earnings on commission. We have insufficient information to judge the impact of this change, but Varley considered it to have been an important factor.

(*j*) *Diversification*: A subsidiary, Bamford Structure Ltd, was established to sell a patented steel roof joist and fencing to the building industry. The aim was to become less dependent on the agricultural-demand cycle. This venture failed: the building industry went through a very deep recession in 1974/75 and, furthermore, Bamford's lacked any knowledge of the industry.

(*k*) *Investment*: Starting in 1972, Bamford's invested heavily (for a company of its size) in new machine tools and moulds, partly as an adjunct to its new product development programme, but also in an effort to modernize its old plant and equipment.

Results

The actions taken by management during the early and mid-1970s increased profits (see Table 18.4), so that by 1976 profit before tax reached 18.3% of shareholders' funds. Bamford's appeared to the outside world to be firmly back on its feet; in the following year, new equity capital was raised so that investment in new plant and equipment could be increased further. The company was not overgeared: total debt to shareholders' funds stood at 38% at year end 1978. However, the 1978 results were the last to be published. Excerpts from the chairman's statement that year give a clue to the problems that lay ahead:

Europe has experienced a decline in demand. Excess manufacturing capacity has intensified competitive activity and resulted in reduced margins. Increased costs . . . arising from the strength of sterling . . . high interest rates . . . and inflation rates higher than in France and Germany make it difficult to maintain competitive pricing. In order to remain competitive with balers being produced in Japan . . .

Thus Bamford's is another example of a failed turnaround, due to price competition from lower-cost competitors. There was clearly insufficient attention given to costs in Bamford's recovery phase; but, even if more attention had been given, could they have survived?

Table 18.4: *Bamford Ltd: Key Financial Data*, 1969–78

	Sales (in £ millions)	Profit before tax (in £ millions)	Profit before tax as percentage of sales (in £ thousands)
1969	3.8	241	6.3
1970	4.1	116	2.8
1971	3.5	78	2.2
1972	6.2	377	6.1
1973	7.8	147	1.9
1974	10.5	453	4.5
1975	11.0	576	5.2
1976	12.4	735	5.9
1977	19.7	954	4.8

Source: Extel Card.

Notes

1. P. Berard, 'The Changing Structure of the Paper Industry', unpublished Ph.D. thesis, 1976.
2. Inveresk Annual Report 1968.
3. 'Inveresk's Climb', *Management Today*, May 1978.

19. Unsuccessful Recovery Situations: The No-Hopers

Firms that become insolvent despite management actions to effect recovery were described in Chapter 5 as 'irrecoverable' or 'no-hopers'. Two examples of such firms are given here. Foden provides the classic example of a situation characterized by severe p.'ce competition, a situation common to many of the sectors of the U.K. economy discussed in Chapter 1. Foden as a single-product, single-plant firm with a high fixed cost structure had little or no chance of recovery. Dimplex also suffered price competition, but here the problem was largely one of a massive drop in market demand for the firm's products. Despite management actions to effect recovery, neither firm had any real hope of recovery.

Foden

Foden was a company that produced high-quality commercial vehicles for the haulage, building contracting, local-authority and military markets. A large portion of Foden's truck turnover came from sales of dumper trucks to the construction industry. The market demand for this equipment is traditionally linked to the level of activity in the construction industry itself. In the U.K., the construction industry accounts for about 10% of gross domestic product, and a high proportion of this is in the public sector (75% civil engineering and 50% house building). The high proportion of G.D.P. which is under the direct control of the government makes the industry a tool that successive administrations have used in an attempt to control the U.K. economy. These attempts at control have been characterized by wild fluctuations in construction activity as the government has first increased and then decreased expenditure, with the result that demand for construction equipment has been extremely cyclical. In an effort to ensure some stability of demand for output, Foden, in common with other manufacturers, was forced to look for export markets to counterbalance the U.K. cyclicality. Thus, in the early 1970s, Foden substantially increased its exports to expanding markets like the

Middle East. This strategy, however, brought Foden into competition with the giants of the industry in areas where they did not have the advantage of being the home producer.

Causes of Decline

(*a*) *Product-market strategy*: At the start of the 1970s, the truck and dumper manufacturing industry that constituted the majority of Foden's turnover had polarized into two segments. There were a few giant multinational manufacturers (Fiat, Volvo, Caterpillar and International Harvester) who offered their customers a full product-line and who manufactured most components of those machines themselves; and there were many small manufacturers like Foden, who offered specialized equipment assembled from other manufacturers' components. Foden, however, were following a strategy of producing most of the components (except engines) that were needed for their vehicles in house so as to decrease strategic reliance on suppliers, to keep control of the quality of their product, and to increase value added. The disadvantages, however, were high overheads and a lack of flexibility in adjusting to varying levels of demand.

It was against this background that, in 1972, Foden faced a major strategic decision. Turnover had increased by 48% in two years (primarily from export growth), but there was increasing penetration of the U.K. market by lower-priced foreign competitors. There seemed to be a continuing demand for Foden's higher-quality trucks, but in the long term Foden's management realized that it was not internationally competitive at its current size. The company needed to concentrate its efforts in the smaller, specialist segment of the commercial vehicle market, or to expand and compete with the giants. It decided that, in an expanding world market, now was the time to expand. It therefore started a two-year investment programme, to expand output from 2,000 to 6,000 trucks per year by installing continuous flow, rather than job-shop production methods. The total cost of the expansion was to be £15 million, financed initially from operations and short-term borrowing, and eventually by a rights issue. So as to gain market share to fill the new production line, a policy of reduced profit margins was adopted for the heavy truck market.

(*b*) *Reduction in demand*: The expansion programme was completed by late 1974, but by that time a number of factors had changed and the outlook for Foden was bleak. The entire commercial vehicle industry was hit by a slump in demand affecting the very high-volume vehicles that Foden had spent so much time and money gearing up to produce. Foden's management made an attempt to counter this problem by concentrating production on its more specialized products. Foden had at that time, for example, a contract for some 1,200 low-mobility army trucks. Still, output was less than 60 trucks a week, compared with a plant capacity of 120 per week. Throughout this period, the one bright spot was a strong order-book in the Middle East.

(c) *Strikes*: Foden was also the victim of strikes at original equipment supplier level. Foden was consequently unable to provide engines for its trucks, thereby losing sales and incurring heavy costs as its stock of work-in-progress vehicles mounted.

The Crisis

At this time, inflation was running at about 25% per year and costs were rising faster than prices, partly as a result of government price controls. Meanwhile, interest levels were high and the company found that its trading profit was substantially reduced by interest charges. The result of these cost increases was to escalate break-even production levels from thirty-six to forty-four trucks per week – dangerously near the actual level of production. The addition overheads incurred as a result of expansion, coupled with the factors outlined above, strained Foden's cash resources to the limit. The negative cash flow was £2.6 million in the year ending March 1974 and £2.7 million in the fiscal year 1975; however, whereas in 1974 Foden was able to generate about half its cash flow by extending creditors (the remainder coming from bank borrowings), the 1975 cash deficit was financed almost entirely by an increase in bank borrowings. During fiscal year 1974, Foden's overdraft with the National Westminster Bank increased from £791,000 to £2.3 million, and by January 1975 had reached about £4 million. At this point, the National Westminster called a halt to the borrowing.

Recovery Actions

(a) *Refinancing*: Following the refusal by National Westminster to allow further increases in their overdraft, Foden was forced to look elsewhere for cash. In January 1975 it became the latest in a long line of industrial casualties to ask for government assistance. The Department of Industry, using powers granted to it by Parliament under the Industry Act and on the advice of the Industrial Development Advisory Board, decided to guarantee an increase in the company's overdraft while a long-term solution was being worked out. Talks between the company and the Department were scheduled for April, and Price Waterhouse were asked to undertake an assessment of Foden's financial position and possible cash requirements. In return for their assistance, the government was expected to take a substantial share of equity (approximately 30%), and a long-term merger with British Leyland was expected.

The Price Waterhouse report, commissioned jointly by Foden and the Department of Industry, was presented at the beginning of April and concluded that the company was viable, subject to its being able to fund its working capital requirements. Discussions then started among all interested parties, including the unions, with a view to reaching a decision in a few weeks. It was felt that the Department of Industry was particularly keen to offer assistance because of the 3,000 jobs which were at stake and because of Foden's role as a major supplier of vehicles to the armed forces. The decision facing the Department of Industry was whether or not to inject cash into the company as well as guaranteeing the overdraft, and what form the continuation of the company's business should take.

It was while these discussions were proceeding that the City decided to launch its own rescue of Foden. The background to this decision, a novel departure for the City, was implied criticism (that was accepted in many quarters) by the chairman of Foden that National Westminster had been premature in refusing to extend further credit. The chairman argued in public and at a House of Commons subcommittee that the company was basically a sound operation, caught in a series of unforeseeable events. When this view was supported by Price Waterhouse, the City decided to help out. Various institutions visited the company and, under the leadership of County Bank, the merchant-banking subsidiary of National Westminster, twenty-five investment institutions took over responsibility for the financial rescue from the government.

The scheme devised was that existing Foden shareholders were offered £3,170,000 of 10% convertible redeemable cumulative preference shares, on the basis of two convertible shares for every five ordinary shares held. However, while it was considered that existing shareholders should be given the right to participate in the rescue plan, Foden's chairman warned them that 'conditions would be difficult until demand for vehicles picked up'. On full conversion, the preference shares would account for about 61% of the equity. Shareholders were asked to approve the plan on 18 August 1975, and the company's stock market quote was restored on 20 August. The rights issue was under-written by the group of twenty-five institutions who, in the event, had to pick up the 96% of the issue which was left on the table.

The institutions involved claimed that the rescue was based on sound financial motives. 10% net after tax from the preference stock and 60% of the company after conversions looks very attractive if the company is assumed to be able to regain profitability. However, there is no doubt that pressure was applied by the Bank of England when two large investors pulled out of the deal, and several more were needed to replace them. The major factor that made the deal feasible was the improvement in the capital market that rendered it possible to make a rights issue again; but the interesting aspect of the case is that the Department of Industry was willing to hand the company over to private enterprise rather than to take a substantial part of its equity. This may be explained by the complications Foden would possibly have added to the problems of British Leyland, the main item occupying the Department of Industry at that time.

(*b*) *Management changes*: The institutions were naturally unwilling to see their £3 million disappear into Foden without some management changes being made. A new non-executive chairman and a finance director were all they received. The day-to-day running of the company remained in the same hands – those of Mr Bill Foden – who had controlled it during the period of its downturn. However, the new chairman, Mr Leslie Tolley, who was put in by the institutions though not a company doctor or turnaround expert, had a very successful track-record with Renold, the power transmission group. Clearly the insti-tutions hoped that a man with his experience would succeed in opening up what had previously been a remarkably closed group of directors at Foden and help the firm to recover. His profit record at Renold (1962–75 profit increased more than sixfold) was certainly impressive enough to allow people to hope for good results from Foden.

(*c*) *Increase sales and reduce inventories*: Within the company, management saw two priorities: a need to reduce the high stock levels that had almost driven Foden into liquidation, and a need to increase sales. However, management action had no impact on the 1976 profit and loss statement. Sales declined by about 20% in real terms during the year, and the company reported a loss of £1 million. Stock levels remained virtually unchanged, although Foden had attempted to reduce stock levels by obtaining progress payments on non-speculative truck building. In this respect the army and local authorities were both asked to be much more flexible than they had previously been.

However, in the year ending March 1977 the level of sales improved dramatically – from £28 million to £47 million – and the same level of output was achieved again in the following year. This was due to a resurgence in demand from the Middle East and from Africa, as well as the fact that U.K. demand was more buoyant. Other U.K. truck manufacturers did not experience this boom in demand. E.R.F., the closest competitor, increased sales only from £21 million to £26 million. Foden's sales increase must be explained in part by a revitalization of their salesforce.

Causes of Insolvency

The large increase in volume in the 1976/77 and 1977/78 financial years put Foden back in profit (see Table 19.1) and improved gearing and

Table 19.1: *Foden Ltd: Summary of Sales and Profitability, 1973–80 (in £ millions)*

Financial year	Sales	Profit before tax	Profit as percentage of sales	Profit as percentage of capital employed
1973	17.3	0.9	5.2	10.5
1974	22.6	0.2	0.9	2.3
1975	28.3	0.9	3.2	9.4
1976	28.6	(1.0)	(3.5)	(8.8)
1977	47.1	1.7	3.6	14.2
1978	52.8	2.8	5.3	15.1
1979	N/A	N/A	N/A	N/A
1980 (6 months only)	28.5	(1.7)	(6.0)	N/A

liquidity ratios (see Table 19.2). Management was optimistic enough about prospects to invest in tooling up for a new range of trucks to be launched in 1979. However, many of the problems that caused the 1975 crisis were still there; the most important of these was Foden's cost structure and the lack of adequate financial control. Foden's final decline can be attributed to the following factors.

(a) The cost of component manufacturing: Apart from the fact that Foden had a high overhead structure, resulting from its 1972 decision to triple plant capacity, Foden's cost structure was high, due to its uneconomic component manufacturing facilities. Management did make some attempt to tackle this problem, but it was a case of too little, too late. The gearbox components facility and the aluminium foundry that served it were closed in October 1979, and at the beginning of 1980 management had only just started to collect the data necessary to review the in-house production of axle gears.

Table 19.2: *Foden Ltd: Key Ratios, 1973–8*

Financial year (ending 3 March)	Gearing	Interest	Current ratio	Acid test	Inventory turnover	Debtor days
1973	50	4.3	1.6	0.39	2.3	44
1974	69	1.4	1.3	0.34	2.5	40
1975	110	1.9	1.2	0.28	2.1	46
1976	80	0.3	1.4	0.36	2.0	63
1977	61	2.2	1.4	0.34	2.9	39
1978	69	3.9	2.0	0.40	2.6	34

A secondary but important consequence of manufacturing components in-house was the effect it had on service at the distributor level. Parts were not interchangeable with those of other manufacturers, and the low sales throughout meant that holding stocks of spares was extremely expensive for dealers.

(b) Lack of financial control: Foden's cost accounting and management-control systems were clearly inadequate throughout the 1970s. This is evidenced by the fact that in early 1980, Bill Foden, the chief executive, was quoted as saying: 'The accounting system doesn't tell us the individual and correct cost of a component.'

(c) Decline in demand: By mid 1978, market conditions in the export markets of Africa and the Middle East had become much tougher, while at the same time important government contracts came to an end. Unit sales volume dropped by about 15% for the year ending 31 March 1979. Foden's response was to establish a marketing department for the first time.

(*d*) *Strikes*: Just as Foden's new range of trucks was ready for production in 1979, the engineering strike occurred; on top of the 1978/79 loss, this proved to be a severe cash drain on the company, increasing borrowings to over 100% of shareholders' funds. The resulting lack of working capital meant that Foden could not produce more than fifty-five trucks per week, barely above the break-even level of about fifty trucks per week. The steel strike of early 1980 forced production down to the break-even level.

(*e*) *Recession*: Even before the U.K. recession started to gather momentum in early 1980, Foden's financial situation was continuing to deteriorate. By the financial year end (31 March) 1980, borrowings were an estimated 140% of shareholders' funds. It therefore took only a 10% drop in market demand for Foden to fall into receivership. Ironically, up until the end of May 1980, they were the only British heavy-truck manufacturer to increase sales in the U.K. over 1979 levels but, by the end of June, Foden's truck registrations were down 10% on the previous year.

A number of last-minute 'desperate' actions were taken to try to rescue Foden, but they were too late. In February 1980, a new executive chairman took over with the intention of reducing overheads and inventory. At the end of June, a 25% cut in the workforce was announced, involving 630 redundancies by October, and the plant was put on a three-day working week; but these actions were too late. On 14 July 1980, the receiver was called in. There was nothing left for the shareholders, and unsecured creditors received only about 50% of what was owed them. The receiver sold the assets to the U.S. premium trucks group, Paccar, who have now relaunched Foden as Sandbach Engineering Company.

Dimplex

Dimplex Ltd was a small group of companies engaged in the manufacture and sale of electric heating appliances, controls and elements. It was best known for its oil-filled thermostatically controlled radiators. Both sales and profits increased in the late 1960s and early 1970s. Sales grew from £4.6 million in the year ending March 1968 to £13.4 million in 1973, while after-tax profits increased in the same period from £171,000 to £836,000.

Dimplex's major problems started towards the end of the 1974 fiscal year, with the O.P.E.C. oil crisis and the three-day working week, although careful analysis of the company would have pointed to operational weaknesses before that time.

Causes of Decline

(*a*) *Decline in U.K. market demand*: Dimplex competed primarily in the electrical central-heating segment of the heating-equipment market. Its main products – storage heaters and oil-filled radiators – were not 'true' central-heating systems, although there was clearly a degree of product substitution with both non-electrical central-heating systems and with space heaters (e.g. electric fires).

The O.P.E.C. oil crisis caused some dramatic changes in the market. First of all, growth in the overall heating market declined in real terms and did not recover its 1973 level. More important from Dimplex's point of view, however, were the changes that took place within the market. There was a pronounced swing away from electrical heating equipment, because of the higher cost of electricity as compared to other heating fuels. Table 19.3 compares the fuel price index for electricity with that of other fuels for 1974 and 1976.

Table 19.3: *Fuel Price Index*

	1974	1976
Gas	100	145
Coal and coke	100	175
Electricity	100	219

Source: *Digest of Statistics*, H.M.S.O., December 1976.

The relatively higher price of electricity was stressed by organizations such as *Which?* magazine and the Department of Energy. *Which?* said: '. . . if you've got a choice of fuels . . . electricity is the most expensive', and the Department of Energy produced a consumer heating booklet showing that, whatever the heating use, electricity was consistently the most expensive.[1] The effect of the higher price of electricity and the publicity it received was to reduce the market demand for Dimplex's products by a substantial amount. We can only estimate how much by reference to data for the electrical space-heating market. That market declined by 66% in volume terms from 1973 to 1976:

Table 19.4: *Electrical Space-heating Market, 1973–6*

(in £ millions)			
	1973	1974	1975	1976
---	---	---	---	---
Market size (current prices)	£49.9	£42.0	£34.2	£26.0
Market size (in 1973 prices)*	£49.9	£37.8	£25.0	£16.9
Volume index	100	76	50	34

* Calculated by using the electrical-heating equipment price index for electric fires from *Business Monitor*.

If we make the assumption that demand in the electric central-heating segment declined by a similar volume, we can obtain a rough comparison of Dimplex's sales performance in the U.K. against the market. We see in Table 19.5 that Dimplex volume declined by about 70% over three years as compared to a market decline of about 66%:

Table 19.5: *Dimplex U.K. Market Performance*
(in £ millions; Dimplex financial year ends 31 March)

	1972/73	1973/74	1974/75	1975/76	1976/77[1]
Dimplex sales (current prices)	£10.5	£13.4	£9.8	£8.7	£6.6
Dimplex sales (in 1972/73 prices)	£10.5	£12.6	£7.9	£5.7	£3.8
Volume index (1973 = 100)[2]	83	100	63	45	30

NOTES
1. Half-year figures annualized.
2. Based on electrical-heating equipment price index for storage and other heaters, applying 1972 index to Dimplex 1972/73 figures.

The analysis is very approximate since we are making assumptions about market performance and comparing calendar-year market data against financial-year sales data (e.g. 1973 market data have been compared to 1973/74 sales). However, we may draw the conclusion that the decline in Dimplex sales reflected a decline in market demand.

(b) *Competitive position*: While the above analysis would tend to indicate that Dimplex maintained its market share of the electrical segment of the central-heating equipment market (estimated at 30%), there was evidence that Dimplex was extremely vulnerable to price competition by 1976. Dimplex had always attempted to develop a quality image for its products, permitting them to be charged at a higher price than those of competitors, but by 1976 the price differentials were far too high to be competitive. Dimplex's 1-kilowatt, oil-filled radiator was nearly double the price of the London Electricity Board (L.E.B.) model (manufactured by Dunlop-Westayre), and 50% higher than the Belling model. Its storage-heater prices were, on average, 22% more than the L.E.B.'s and 38% more than Belling's. These relative price differences probably reflect a higher cost structure at Dimplex than was to be found with competitors. We cannot be sure that Dimplex had a relative cost disadvantage prior to the O.P.E.C. oil crisis, but when sales volume declined, Dimplex found unit costs increasing sharply as overheads were spread over declining volumes. Its position was clearly aggravated by the rising cost of raw materials, primarily steel, cost increases which it found increasingly difficult to pass on in the form of higher prices in a declining market.

(c) *Marketing operations*: Market research in late 1976 indicated that Dimplex's marketing effort was somewhat less than dynamic. The principal marketing thrust was one of sales push to dealers, mostly builders' merchants and central-heating specialists, but the products were difficult to find in stock, and few dealers appeared interested in taking orders for Dimplex products. Promotional literature was in short supply, and little or no promotional effort was put into launching new products. A new extractor fan launched in 1976 was a typical example. Dealers had received one (dull) leaflet through the mail, but had no idea of the price, availability, colour or other product features.

(d) *Production planning and control*: The production process was quite simple, entailing no more than cutting, pressing and welding the radiator panels, adding legs and a simple control unit. However, production planning and control systems appear to have been poor or non-existent. We know that, during the year ending 31 March 1974, the company was unable to meet demand due to 'shortages of materials' and 'lack of production capacity'; yet at the same time, inventory levels were increasing rapidly. At 31 March 1974, inventories were 100% above the level of the previous year, while sales revenues were only 10% up. Even allowing for the disruptions caused by the three-day week and management's desire to have an adequate supply of raw materials, this is a clear indicator of lack of control. Management's objective at this time was to maintain historical production levels. The chairman's 1974 statement talked of an effort to maintain both employment and production at an economic level. In mid 1974, six months after the beginning of the fuel crisis, when Dimplex sales had already dropped sharply, Dimplex management was still talking about 'lack of production capacity'. Not surprisingly, therefore, inventory levels continued to rise, during the 1974/75 fiscal year, by a further 12%, while sales revenues declined by 17%.

(*e*) *Lack of financial control*: We have little direct information about Dimplex's financial control systems, except that provided by the financial statements themselves. We have already seen how inventories went out of control. Debtors also went out of control during the 1974/75 financial year, increasing from 55 days to 78 days in twelve months. This could also reflect a loose credit policy to gain sales, or an increasing proportion of export customers in the customer mix.

(*f*) *Management*: Our discussion of the company's marketing operations and production control tends to indicate that management lacked marketing expertise and, if anything, was production-oriented. Careful reading of press articles and annual reports from 1974 to 1976 tends to show management with their heads 'stuck in the sand'.

In the 1974 annual report, the chairman stated that he was 'optimistic that storage radiator sales would recover . . . and . . . a return to the pattern of increased profit was planned'. A year later, he wrote: 'With hindsight it is clear that the adverse publicity last year concerning electricity tariff increases . . . confused the consumer and had a disastrous effect on home market sales', but he went on to reiterate, 'there is no doubt . . . electricity will become the main source of energy within the home'. After a record loss in the first half of the 1976/77 financial year, management's attitude had not changed. They attributed lower sales in the home market to the 'continued deterioration in the economy . . . the prolonged spell of hot weather . . . and difficulty still being experienced in making consumers aware that domestic heating by electricity has many advantages over heating by other fuels'![2]

Recovery Actions

There is no doubt that management took what they considered at the time to be adequate steps to keep Dimplex afloat, although it was only from September 1974 onwards – nine months after the beginning of the fuel crisis – that the seriousness of the situation became apparent to management. Initially, management set itself two priorities: even greater concentration on exports, and broadening the base of the group by entry into the insulation market. Altogether, six recovery steps may be identified:

(a) *Increased emphasis on export markets*: During 1972 and 1973, Dimplex's export sales had accounted for about 19% of Dimplex sales volume. At the beginning of 1974, the company embarked on a major export drive with the aim of increasing exports by 40% (during the fiscal year ending 31 March, 1975) in order to offset the loss of sales in the domestic market. The actual increase achieved was 33%, but because of a substantial drop in home sales from £13.4 million to £9.8 million during this period, export sales increased to 31% of the company total. A substantial amount of the increase in 1975 came from Middle Eastern markets, but in the following year (fiscal 1976) export sales revenues did not increase further.

(b) *Product-line expansion*: In July 1974, Dimplex acquired a small company called Warmawall Ltd, so that it could compete in the rapidly expanding insulation market (a market that grew as fuel prices increased). Dimplex developed a scheme called 'Tri-Plan', in which storage radiators provided the warmth, a sophisticated multi-zone controller organized the system, and Warmawall provided cavity-wall insulation. This plan was not a success. Warmawall's turnover declined from £327,000 in 1974/75 to £245,000 in 1975/76, and the company incurred a loss. Dimplex blamed this on public reaction to adverse publicity on cavity insulation. However, Dimplex knew little about the home building business; there was a great deal of competition in this sector; and the case for cavity insulation was not technically or economically proven. Furthermore, additional overhead was incurred by establishing four regional depots around the country. Management's eternal optimism continued: they predicted a resurgence in market demand and thought that future prospects looked bright.

(c) *Reduction in scale of operations*: Only in September 1974 did management start to cut production and reduce overheads in response to a rapidly deteriorating cash-flow situation. Out of a total of 1,500 employees, 450 were made redundant. The press release stated that this action would 'permit a return to profitability in 1975–6 on a reduced turnover'.

(*d*) *Reduction in inventories*: Although management was aware of an imbalance in inventories as early as the spring of 1974, effective action to reduce inventories did not occur until well into 1975. Only in the 1975/76 financial year did inventory levels decline, but inventory turnover still remained at less than two:

Dimplex Inventories, 1973–6

	1973	1974	1975	1976
Inventory as percentage of sales*	24	44	60	51

* Cost of goods data not publicly available.

(*e*) *Changes in top management*: Just prior to the advent of the fuel crisis, some organizational changes took place among the top management group, following the elevation of the chairman to the non-executive, honorary post of president. A new chairman (Mr J. D. Lake) and managing director (Mr H. R. Heath) were appointed from within the company. In April 1974, the post of deputy managing director was created for Terry Goddard, the finance director, and a new finance director was recruited from outside (he subsequently left eighteen months later). In August 1974, however, just as Dimplex's cash problems were mounting, Heath became group chief executive, and Goddard was appointed managing director; it was the latter who was obliged to implement the redundancy programme. While some of these changes were part of a prearranged succession plan, it would be interesting to know what influence, if any, Dimplex's bankers (Midland Bank) had in promoting Goddard at a critical stage in the company's decline. Was he the only senior executive able and willing to carry out surgery in what appears to have been a rather sleepy organization?

(*f*) *Introduction of new products*: Almost as a final, dying effort, Dimplex introduced a new range of small electrical appliances in the summer of 1976, hoping the Dimplex brand-name would help them. Unfortunately, these were all essentially 'me too' products that were attempting to compete against large established competitors with lower unit costs than Dimplex.

Table 19.6: *Dimplex: Financial Results, 1973–6*
(in £ millions; financial year ends 31 March)

	1972/73	1973/74	1974/75	1975/76	1976/77 (6 months)
U.K. sales	£10.9	£11.9	£8.4	£7.7	£N/A
Exports	2.5	2.8	3.8	3.7	N/A
Total sales	13.4	14.7	12.2	11.4	5.1[1]
Profit (loss) Before tax	1.4	1.0	(0.7)	(0.5)	(0.6)
Capital Employed	4.4	4.8	5.6	5.1	N/A
PERFORMANCE:					
Profit as percentage of sales	10.4	6.8	(5.7)	(4.4)	(11.8)
Profit as percentage of capital employed	31.8	20.8	(12.5)	(9.8)	N/A
Asset turnover	3.1	3.1	2.2	2.2	N/A
Inventory (days outstanding)[2]	88	160	218	185	N/A
Debtor days outstanding	60	55	78	82	N/A
FINANCIAL STATUS:					
Long-term debt/Shareholders' funds	–	–	22%	24%	N/A
Total debt/Shareholders' funds	21%	79%	149%	136%	N/A
Interest cover	14.6×	4.0×	0.25×	0.4×	nil
Current ratio	1.47	1.25	1.26	1.27	N/A
Acid test	0.6	0.3	0.3	0.4	N/A

NOTES
1. Sales for 28 weeks to 15 October 1976; sales revenues identical to those of previous year at this time.
2. Cost of goods sold unavailable; therefore calculated using gross sales revenues. Consequently, days understated.

Source: Annual Reports.

Results

The recovery actions attempted by management had some small impact on the company's financial position, but the actions were insufficient to prevent management asking for a receiver to be appointed in May 1977. The actions had delayed the final demise of Dimplex for a longer period than would have been possible if the company had not been in a strong financial position when the initial crisis occurred.

By reducing inventories by £1.5 million in the year ending 31 March 1976, Dimplex was able to reduce bank borrowings by an equivalent amount. However, sales volume continued to decline, due to both the declining market and Dimplex's increasingly inferior cost position *vis-à-vis* competitors, with the result that operating losses could not be funded. The financial results for the period 1973–6 are summarized in Table 19.6.

The receiver was unable to find a buyer for the company and he scaled down the operations further while negotiating a sale of the main trading assets to Dimplex's competitor, Glen Electric Ltd. Realization of the company's assets failed to repay the debenture holders in full, with the result that unsecured creditors and shareholders lost in excess of £5 million.

Notes

1. 'Compare Your Home Heating Costs', Department of Energy, January 1977.
2. 'Dimplex Deficit Grows but Chairman Still Confident', *The Times*, 14 December 1976.

Index

MORE ABOUT PENGUINS, PELICANS AND PUFFINS

For further information about books available from Penguins please write to Dept EP, Penguin Books Ltd, Harmondsworth, Middlesex UB7 ODA.

In the U.S.A.: For a complete list of books available from Penguins in the United States write to Dept DG, Penguin Books, 299 Murray Hill Parkway, East Rutherford, New Jersey 07073.

In Canada: For a complete list of books available from Penguins in Canada write to Penguin Books Canada Ltd, 2801 John Street, Markham, Ontario L3R IB4.

In Australia: For a complete list of books available from Penguins in Australia write to the Marketing Department, Penguin Books Australia Ltd, P.O. Box 257, Ringwood, Victoria 3134.

In New Zealand: For a complete list of books available from Penguins in New Zealand write to the Marketing Department, Penguin Books (N.Z.) Ltd, P.O. Box 4019, Auckland 10.

In India: For a complete list of books available from Penguins in India write to Penguin Overseas Ltd, 706 Eros Apartments, 56 Nehru Place, New Delhi 110019.

AN INSIGHT INTO MANAGEMENT ACCOUNTING
John Sizer

During the last decade managements have had to learn to live with high rates of inflation, low levels of profitability, and serious liquidity problems. The more sophisticated techniques developed by management accountants in response to these conditions are described in the second edition of Professor Sizer's best-selling work. It has been extensively revised and extended by almost two hundred pages.

'For managers and management students rather than professional accountants. The author explains the elements of financial and cost accounting and goes on to consider financial planning, investment appraisal, budgetary control and decision making. This is no easy popularisation but a substantial contribution an important subject' – *The Times Educational Supplement*

MANAGEMENT THINKERS
Edited by A. Tillett, T. Kempner and G. Wills

'British management was backward by the end of the nineteenth century and, with notable exceptions, has never caught up.'

'The Ford Co. from October 1912 to October 1913 hired 54,000 men to maintain an average working force of 13,000. This was a labour turnover of 416 per cent for the year.'

With observations like these this book vividly recalls and presents the problems of industry from the industrial revolution to the present day.

Management Thinkers contains readings from the pioneers of management thought – Frederick Taylor, Henri Fayol, Seebohm Rowntree, Mary Parker Follett, Elton Mayo and C. I. Barnard.

OPPORTUNITIES
A HANDBOOK OF BUSINESS
OPPORTUNITY SEARCH

Edward de Bono

'An opportunity is as real an ingredient in business as raw material, labour or finance – but it only exists when you can see it.'

Everybody assumes that he or she is opportunity-conscious – but is frequently only conscious of the *need* to be opportunity-conscious. For often what looks like an opportunity isn't one after all.

Opportunities is a handbook which offers a total, systematic approach to opportunity-seeking at both corporate and executive levels. It is Edward de Bono's most significant contribution to business since he developed lateral thinking – and it should have just as much impact. Remember: 'Just before it comes into existence every business is an opportunity that someone has seen.'

ALMOST EVERYONE'S GUIDE
TO ECONOMICS

J. K. Galbraith and Nicole Salinger

'Economics preempts the headlines. It bears on everyone's life, anxieties and, if more rarely, satisfactions.'

Believing that 'the state of economics in general, and the reasons for its present failure in particular, might be put in simple accurate language that almost everyone could understand and that a perverse few might conceivably enjoy', Professor Galbraith has collaborated with Nicole Salinger in an entertaining dialogue.

She leads him through a step-by-step explanation of economic ideas with such clarity that all can understand the basic nature of classical, neo-classical and Marxian economics, the role of money and banking, the modus operandi of fiscal monetary policy, the part played by multinationals, the reasons for simultaneous inflation and unemployment and the causes of the present crisis in international economic and monetary affairs.